Sport in the Global Society

General Editor: J.A. Mangan

THE TOUR DE FRANCE
1903–2003

SPORT IN THE GLOBAL SOCIETY

General Editor: J.A. Mangan

The interest in sports studies around the world is growing and will continue to do so. This unique series combines aspects of the expanding study of *sport in the global society*, providing comprehensiveness and comparison under one editorial umbrella. It is particularly timely, with studies in the cultural, economic, ethnographic, geographical, political, social, anthropological, sociological and aesthetic elements of sport proliferating in institutions of higher education.

Eric Hobsbawm once called sport one of the most significant practices of the late nineteenth century. Its significance was even more marked in the late twentieth century and will continue to grow in importance into the new millennium as the world develops into a 'global village' sharing the English language, technology and sport.

Other Titles in the Series

THE
TOUR
DE
FRANCE
1903–2003

A Century of Sporting Structures,
Meanings and Values

Editors

HUGH DAUNCEY
GEOFF HARE
University of Newcastle

FRANK CASS
LONDON • PORTLAND, OR

First published in 2003 in Great Britain by
FRANK CASS PUBLISHERS
Crown House, 47 Chase Side, Southgate,
London, N14 5BP

and in the United States of America by
FRANK CASS PUBLISHERS
c/o ISBS, 920 NE 58th Avenue Suite 300
Portland, Oregon 97213-3786

Copyright © 2003 Frank Cass & Co. Ltd.

Website: www.frankcass.com

British Library Cataloguing in Publication Data

Tour de France 1903–2003 : a century of sporting structures,
meanings and values. – (Sport in the global society)
1. Tour de France (Bicycle race) – History 2. Bicycle racing
– France – Social aspects
I. Dauncey, Hugh, 1961– II. Hare, Geoffrey
796.6′2′0944

ISBN 0-7146-5362-4 (cloth)
ISBN 0-7146-8297-7 (paper)
ISSN 1368-9789

Library of Congress Cataloging-in-Publication Data

The Tour de France, 1903–2003 : a century of sporting structures,
meanings, and values / editors, Hugh Dauncey, Geoff Hare.
p. cm.
Includes bibliographical references and index.
ISBN 0-7146-5362-4 (cloth) – ISBN 0-7146-8297-7 (pbk.)
1. Tour de France (Bicycle race)–History. 2. Bicycle racing–Social
aspects–France–History. 3. Nationalism and sports–France–History.
I. Dauncey, Hugh, 1961– II. Hare, Geoff, 1945– III. Title.
GV1049.2.T68T68 2003
796.6′2′0944–dc21
2003011128

This group of studies first appeared as a special issue of
The International Journal of the History of Sport (ISSN 0952-3367),
Vol.20, No.2, June 2003, published by Frank Cass

Printed in Great Britain by MPG Books Ltd., Bodmin, Cornwall

Contents

Illustrations

Acknowledgements

Thanks to:

Frank Cass, Jonathan Manley and Tony Mangan for believing in the project.

The contributors for getting the work in (relatively) on time.

INSEP for documentation, library facilities and other help.

Alister Cox, Phil Dine, Andy Gaskell, Robert Gadiollet and the Amicale philatélique bressane, Hugues Journès, Philippe Le Guern, Dominique Marchetti, Andrew Ritchie, Philippe Sévy and staff of the Bourg-en-Bresse office of *Le Progrès*, Eugen Weber, for other help.

Andrew Ritchie for supplying illustrations from his collection.

And Jean-Marie Leblanc for his readiness to be interviewed.

Foreword

EUGEN WEBER

A hundred summers ago, the Tour de France was born out of political conflict, and from a circulation war between competing sports journals. Before he and Gustave-Thadée Bouton pioneered a stream of Dion-Bouton automobiles, Marquis Albert de Dion had spent his life constructing sports machines: a quadricycle in 1883, followed by a steam tricycle in 1887 and a one-cycle petrol trike in 1895. He also financed the daily *Vélo* that catered to thousands of cycling amateurs, to the rivalries and publicity of cycle manufacturers, and to the crowds attending track meetings or cheering road race riders on.

In 1899, however, at the height of the Dreyfus Affair, Dion and his anti-Dreyfusard friends were involved in an absurd political shindig at the fashionable Auteuil horse races, where a royalist baron's cane dented the top hat of the Republic's president. A government – one more – fell in the wake of the brawl but, more important to our story, the Marquis was sentenced to 15 days in jail and a 100-franc fine for his part in it. Tailor-made for the sporting press, the incident evoked critical comment from the *Vélo*, which had already revealed regrettable Dreyfusard sympathies. Incensed, Dion and other anti-Dreyfusard friends like Edouard Michelin set up a rival daily, *L'Auto-Vélo* – soon shortened to L'Auto to reflect the latest fashion in the world of sports.

L'Auto's editor, Henri Desgrange, himself an enthusiastic cyclist and cycle racer, needed a sensational publicity venture to attract new readers. Particularly since the introduction of stopwatches in 1870, indoor and outdoor races had provided spills, thrills, exploits, champions, prizes and a paying public for sports promoters and the sporting press. Intercity bicycle races – Paris–Rouen, Paris–Roubaix, Bordeaux–Paris – had been popular for decades. So Desgrange began his campaign by reviving the Paris–Brest road race, which had last been run in 1891. But although the 1901 winner knocked nearly two hours off the previous record and vast crowds gathered to follow the progress of the race on the immense map that hung on the façade of *L'Auto*'s editorial offices, a limited contest provoked only limited excitement and sales. Something more grandiose would be found in the unheard-of notion of a bicycle race around the whole of France, from Paris to the Mediterranean and back, that partly reproduced the circuit followed by the schoolboy heroes of *Le Tour de la France par deux enfants*, 'the best-loved schoolbook' of the *fin de siècle* which had sold more than six million copies since its publication in 1877.

The distances that the new race involved strained belief and, possibly, the capacity of human beings: a good gambit to keep the public panting, even though 21 of the first 60 competitors actually managed to finish the 'monstrous' trial. The first Tour, in 1903 – 2,400 kilometres in 19 days – was a great success: *L'Auto*'s print run doubled, *Le Vélo* foundered. The winner, Maurice Garin, had all the makings of a popular favourite: born in the Val d'Aosta, brought to France as a boy, his father had sold him to a chimney sweep for a wheel of cheese. Road racing had offered escape from a constricting trade, and made him famous in cycling circles as *le petit ramoneur* (the little chimney sweep). Now, the first prize of 6,125 gold francs made him rich.

The next year's Tour turned out a disaster for him and for the race. Garin was disqualified (along with several other riders) for a variety of infractions; Desgrange doubted that the race would be run again. But the reported threats from gamblers and supporters of rival racers, the gangs of toughs blocking the roads along the course, the roadside pistol shots, the cyclists being attacked and wounded, provided all the ingredients of drama. Sales soared. Night courses were eliminated, and the Tour rolled on.

By 1906, the distance covered had almost doubled to 4,600km and the starters were more numerous by one-third. In 1914, 145 contenders started out to cover 5,400km and 54 finished: as much a tribute to training and improved performance as to Desgrange's success in persuading riders that they could rise to ever stiffer challenges, and persuading the public that the runners' solitary struggle against natural obstacles, accidents and weariness had an epic quality deserving special attention. As Geoffrey Nicholson has put it, he 'turned his riders into champions and his champions into heroes'. Not a bad thing, when other kinds of hero were thin on the ground.

During the Tour of 1913, the popular Eugène Christophe broke his front wheel while tooling down a Pyrenean pass, shouldered his bike, ran seven miles to the closest blacksmith's shop, repaired it with his own hands as the rules required, and rode on two hours late. Unfortunately, while welding back his broken stem, he had allowed a little boy to work the bellows at the blacksmith's forge. For this, Christophe was penalized three minutes, and with this penalty he entered racing history: the stuff of legend. Like the French genius for improvisation, the French revulsion against officious officialdom and its rules had found a new domain, and the human yearning for something to admire could focus on new objects: the self-made man and press-made Giants of the Road, no less admirable than the men of sword or state that the establishment set up for public acclaim.

The Tour contributed more to France than new-model heroes. It put flesh on the dry bones of values taught in school but seldom internalized: effort, courage, determination, stoic endurance of pain, and even fair play. It familiarized the nation with its geography. It brought life, activity, excitement into small towns where very little happened; it introduced a festive atmosphere wherever it passed; and it acquainted provincial backwaters with spectacular displays previously available only in big cities. At Cosne-sur-Loire, 174km from Paris, the Cosnois rejoiced to view at last 'the spectacle of a great highway drama'. At Nevers (227km), 'the town, normally calm, is extremely animated' – cycling clubs riding in en masse from surrounding centres. At Moulins (281km), 'great liveliness … this is a new spectacle'. At Lyon, a major staging point where the start took place at 2.00 am, all the regional cycling clubs first rode past carrying lanterns, while the crowd went wild.

Many towns, like Montauban, had never seen a bicycle race: 'enormous enthusiasm, indescribable animation, noisy crowds'. Others, however small, turned out to see the local champion pass. At Grisolles, a village halfway between Toulouse and Montauban, 'everyone is on the road to see Dargassié … At 4.00 am the highway is black with people'. Even the shambles of 1904 testified to engagement of the public, its partisanship going as far as violence and rioting, an identification as novel in its object as it was in degree.

By 1905 and 1906 the Tour had acquired many aspects familiar to us today; first and foremost as a parenthesis amidst current everyday doings. The curious streamed in by train or bicycle, horse-carriage or car; the roads were lined with sightseers; shops, offices and factories let employees out to watch. Where the Tour stopped for the night, or even at a halt or checkpoint, impromptu fairs sprang up: illuminations, marching bands, local cycle races, boxing matches, public dances. Mayor and municipal council came out to greet the racers, to toast them and make speeches. Soon, roads began to be cleared and closed to traffic, public transport halted, children were let out of school. As the sports writer Géo Lefèvre wrote in 1906: 'the Tour is henceforth the mighty annual tam-tam which for a whole month wakes an entire nation to cycling ... the prodigious vulgarising cavalcade of sport.'

He might have added 'and of business'. The colourful publicity caravan advertising drinks, smokes, foods, whatever, appeared officially only in 1930, but its forerunners were there before the First World War; and the Tour was already being criticized for crass commercialism. Crass or not, it was and has remained a commercial enterprise designed to sell more papers, then more bikes, then any number of products that subsidized riders or advertised in *L'Auto*, not counting the wine and beer drunk on its passage, the booths that sprang up, the entertainment offered to fans and to the merely curious. Without the commercial impulse there would have been no Tour, nor the excitement that went with it. There would have been no incentive to buy more bicycles, hence the mass manufacture that made them accessible to consumers at ever more modest prices; or the aspiration to imitate champions, to become rich and famous and perhaps save enough to buy a farm or open one's own café or store when one reached middle age. The Tour carried modernity with it and revealed more of France to the French, if only on the maps on which so many followed its progress.

It also reflected the aspirations of its time. Maurice Leblanc, creator of the gentleman-burglar Arsène Lupin, began as a contributor to the sporting press, celebrating first bikes, then cars: their speed, the liberation they allowed, the self-expression they afforded, the excitement, adventure and power that they represented. In 1897 Leblanc published *Voici des ailes!* (Here Are Wings) that gloried in the wingspread velocipedes could lend us. Then he got excited about the *frisson du chauffeur* that new automobiles induced, the intoxication of energy and force one felt behind the wheel. We're jaded about it now, and dubious about the virtues of auto-intoxication. But terms like power, energy, speed, adventure, liberation, were big new words just before and after 1900. An individual sport practised in teams, as in the Tour, incarnated notions that popular fancy found easy to glorify: the personal exploit and the solidarity of teamwork, both tests of character, both essential to winning.

After the Second World War, it was time for the Tour less to reflect than to inflect social trends, when it helped television shift from a marginal position to a central role. When upstart TV first set its sights on the Tour de France in 1948, the high price of sets in a credit-starved country discouraged potential purchasers and kept the number of viewers in the low thousands. Paris intellectuals looked down on a spectacle destined for *des êtres primaires*, but non-intellectuals soon caught on to the stunning coverage it offered. In the late 1940s and the early 1950s, TV news revealed a novel kind of reality-coverage more compelling than that of existing media. Within a decade, the number of television sets in use had surged from a few thousand to over a million; by 1975, more than four in five French households boasted a set. What Keiran Dunn defined as the symbiotic relationship between the three-week race and the new medium that broadcast its most visually-arresting scenes *en direct*, had stimulated sales 'and legitimized the fledgling medium'. It also made clear that sports had become part of the entertainment industry – a dramatic diversion, recreation, festivity, technologically enhanced.

Modern a hundred years ago, the Tour continues supremely contemporary today, and just as much a reflection of its times, which are now our times too. Only the scale has changed. These days, over 26,000 gendarmes and local police are mobilized to keep indulgent eyes on twenty million-odd fans that line the roads. The travelling circus that precedes and follows the Big Loop (*la grande boucle*) of the Tour distributes free samples, flyers, magazines and lashes of advertising lyricism featuring beers, aperitifs, cigarettes, electronics, soaps, toothpastes and detergents, mail order companies, department stores, bike and auto brands. It rallies TV crews, reporters and photographers, team officials, mechanics, masseurs, chauffeurs, salesmen, judges, and a medical personnel that also administers the daily drug tests ('Congratulations, you've passed; and you're pregnant'): over two thousand camp followers, not counting the 200-odd riders. It has its own judiciary, motorcycle police, ambulance service, and travelling bank (the only one in France open on 14 July). And the daily circulation of *L'Equipe*, successor of *L'Auto* and co-sponsor of the race, rises by over one-third in July.

Faster, Higher, Stronger, as Coubertin once put it and, one assumes, more remunerative as well, the great race is more enormously popular than ever. As much a part of the national and international fabric as soccer's World Cup or the Olympic Games, the Centenary Tour deserves its centenary tributes. Hugh Dauncey and Geoff Hare have provided one that is worthy of it.

March 2003

Series Editor's Foreword

A year after the last FIFA World Cup but one, Hugh Dauncey and Geoff Hare published their subsequently applauded *France and the 1998 World Cup: The National Impact of a World Sporting Event* in the Cass Sport in the Global Society series. A measure of the book's appeal was its speedy translation into French. Now in the centenary year of the unique Tour de France – 'the greatest cycle race in the world,'[1] – they have published *The Tour de France 1903–2003: A Century of Sporting Structures, Meanings and Values* in the same series. No doubt, it too will be translated sooner rather than later into the French language.

In his forthcoming *Bicycle Racing: Sport, Technology and Modernity* shortly to be published also in Sport in the Global Society, Andrew Ritchie describes the nineteenth-century background to the Tour's emergence: 'Set in, and centred amid, a rich historical scene of social change and technological development, the sport of bicycle racing has evolved for 130 years and taken its place among the oldest and most celebrated modern international sports. Unofficial "world championships" took place between England and France in the early 1870s. Cycling's first national governing body, the Bicycle Union, was founded in London in 1878, the League of American Wheel Men followed in 1880 and France's Union Vélocipédique in 1881. Official World Championships were first held in 1893, provided by the newly constituted International Cyclists' Association, and cycling was among the sports included in the first modern Olympic Games in 1896.'[2]

Then, of course, came the Tour de France in 1903!

Ritchie, in his authoritative *Bicycle Racing*, also writes of four dimensions to the sport of cycling in its early moments: competitive, non-competitive, recreational and utilitarian. He remarks: '... The relationship between competition, recreation and utility was a complex ... one, but ... competitive sport was the dynamo or engine which pushed innovation, technical change and progress.'[3] He then provides a summary of the nineteenth-century growth of bicycling in its various forms: 'by the late–1890s the bicycle had become an industrial success story and a recreational and utilitarian fact of life all over the developed world, a widespread technological and transportational movement within which competitive sport had become the concern of the minority ... In 1897, the British journal *The Hub* offered the following statistics: In 1885, the United States had six cycle factories producing 11,000 machines. In 1890, 17 factories turned out 40,000 machines. In 1895, 500 factories produced 600,000 cycles and in 1896, over 7000 factories manufactured 1 million bicycles.'[4]

Ritchie also states, interestingly, that the French media world of the time was already well supplied with specialist literature on bicycling. 'Bandry de Saunier's *Le Cyclisme Théorique et Pratique*, published in 1892 in Paris, contained advertisements for fourteen periodicals (weeklies and monthlies) then currently on sale in France which concentrated exclusively on cycling or featured it heavily. They were: *La Revue des Sports, La Revue du Sport Vélocipédique, Le Véloce-Sport, Le Cycle, Le Monde Cycliste, La France Cycliste, Les Sports Athlétiques, L' Industrie Vélocipédique, Le Cycliste, Le Bulletin Officiel de l'Union Vélocipédique de France, Le Cycliste Belge, Le Cyclisme, La Bicyclette* and *L'Écho Des Sports de Paris.*'[5] Ritchie notes in passing that the list did not include the Parisian *daily* cycling newspaper, *Le Vélo*, which first appeared in December 1892.[6]

Ritchie lays legitimate emphasis of the role of technology in the evolution of cycling and concludes with equal legitimity, 'it is precisely this heavy technological quality of the sport that allows us now to define it as "modern" sport. ... "modernity" consists of increased specialization, increasing social division of labour, quantification, and in [Weber's] special sense of the term, rationalization.'[7] Thus, in *Bicycle Racing*, Ritchie sets the scene for *The Tour de France 1903–2003*.

To move then from the general to the particular (from Ritchie to Dauncey and Hare), the Tour is first and foremost a celebration of France – its geography, its history, its culture. As Dauncey and Hare remark, it defines France as it rolls past châteaux, over rivers, up and down mountains, through La Ville and La Campagne. To repeat George Vigarello's marvellous observation – the course of the Tour is as much a symbol of the national heritage as it is the route of a bicycle race.[8]

For Vigarello, Dauncey and Hare note, the route of the Tour 'marked out a territory in which the physical landscape of France became a backdrop to a sporting spectacle and where France's history was constantly evoked through reference to figures of glorious memory such as Joan of Arc, Napoleon and Clemenceau.'[9] And it is most certainly more

– the theatre of sport housed within a larger environment than a building – a unification of geographical place with cultural artefact; what French geographers call an *ensemble* involving the interaction of landscape with activity that contribute jointly to experience.[10]

The Tour, as Ritchie declared, is also modern sport. It defines it – avaricious commercialism, creative technology, competitive obsession, media addiction, doping enhancement: 'a pre-modern context conveying "modern" values in a "post-modern" context'.[11] One aspect of its modernity, driven by a sharp eye to profit, has been its continuous invention and re-invention. It was, and is, to use the Dauncey and Hare term 'confected'[12] by shrewd middle-class manipulators.[13] *Laïcité* may now be a characteristic of contemporary France, but what Mark Twain once suggested is true of religion, is unquestionably true of the Tour: 'He [man] cannot even invent a religion and keep it intact; circumstances are stronger than he ... Circumstances and conditions are always changing, and they always compel him to modify his religion to harmonize with the new situation.'[14] Nothing illustrates this better than the evolution of the race registration of the riders – originally as individual competitors, then sponsored teams, then national and regional teams, then national teams, then from 1962 to the present, commercial teams.

The relationship between nationalism and representation, always present in some form or other, has been complex; 'it is clear', argue Dauncey and Hare, 'that the Tour de France has always been an arena in which national rivalries have confronted each other', however, 'less as feuds between individual riders than as conflicts between national self-perceptions and stereotyping by other nations'.[15] Happily for French *amour-propre* the French are well ahead as a winning nation. France has double the number of victories (36) of its nearest rival, Belgium (18).[16] France has dominated the race for long periods of time and indeed the patriotic importance of this can be measured in the fact that 'during the inter-war period, champions in yellow were very likely to be national heroes as sport served as the continuation of war by other means'.[17] The Tour de France has been, in effect, 'a theatre for the negotiation of [national] sporting identities'.[18]

One aspect, incidentally, of nationalism, both as a historic and a contemporary reality[19] is the fact that the 'Anglo-Saxon sporting culture – essentially a blend of "Le Fair Play" and physical effort as opposed to resourcefulness and French flair',[20] has made little impact on this very Gallic creation. Thus the Tour is most assuredly, but only up to a point however, 'an interesting example of a competition in which French and "Anglo-Saxon" sporting values interact without direct contact, unlike sports like rugby and soccer'.[21] This assertion by Dauncey and Hare, which certainly makes a useful point, must be treated with some caution. It is an argument that frays somewhat at the edges. The Tour in its time has celebrated masculinity, endorsed militarism, embraced commercialism, and capitulated to the media – an evolution not all that far removed from 'Anglo-Saxon' sport.

One of the minor pleasures, amid many major pleasures, of *The Tour de France 1903–2003* is the mild humour with which Barthesian perspicacity is rightly appreciated but its obliqueness is gently ridiculed. Barthes's 'literary reading' of the Tour 'as a competition of heroic deeds and epic narratives fits well, *for all its unnecessary convolutedness*', (emphases added), remark Dauncey and Hare, 'with analyses of much of the journalistic reporting of the Tour in which epic feats and heroic stories are invented as ways of communicating and selling stories'.[22] It is worth quoting Barthes in full to appreciate their delicate humour:

> ... the Tour is the best example we have encountered of a total and thus ambiguous myth; the Tour is both a myth of expression and myth of projection, and therefore realistic and utopian at one and the same time. The Tour expresses and liberates French people through a unique fable in which traditional impostures such as the psychology of essences, the ethics of combat, the magickery of elements and forces or the hierarchies of supermen and servants mix with forms of positive interest, with the utopian image of a world searching obstinately to reconcile itself through the staging of a totally clear portrayal of the relations between man, men and Nature.[23]

As Dauncey and Hare are quick to point out, this exuberant Gallic romanticism leaves out rather a lot, and contributes little to an understanding of the Tour as politics, commerce and culture rather than merely emotion.[24] The provision of this understanding is the greatest virtue of *The Tour de France 1903–2003*.

Of course, epics, myths and legends, heroes and all their associated ritualism have an important part to play in human existence, and inquiry would often be impoverished without them. Without doubt the Tour de France has acquired a ritualistic significance in French culture as a consequence of its scale, its scope and the nature of the mythically heroic exploits of its iconic supermen. To adopt momentarily a Turneresque approach – with their ability to transcend the existence of everyday life, rituals are the antithesis of alienation. Their dramatic metaphors generate meanings that allow experience of 'communitas'. They blend together values, actions, abstractions and realities. The Tour is an annual communal ritual.[25] It is, in essence, the non-religious equivalent of the medieval mystery play[26] defining (and redefining) the nature of masculinity, glory and heroism. It is at once both a secular and sacred experience.

In summary, Dauncey and Hare, following Paul Boudry, make it very clear that *Le Tour* is multifaceted with multiple meaning – sporting, political, economic, cultural and literary. Their sophistication is pleasing.

J. A. MANGAN
International Centre for Sport, Socialization and Society
De Montfort University (Bedford)
May 2003

NOTES

1. Some argue it is more: 'The Tour de France, in terms of speed, stamina, strength, output of a purely cardio-vascular nature, the ability to recover quickly physiologically, is frequently claimed to be, and almost certainly is, the most demanding sporting event in the world' – the judgement of Andrew Ritchie in a letter to the author of 16 March 2003.
2. A. Ritchie, *Bicycle Racing: Sport, Technology and Modernity* (London: Frank Cass, forthcoming), Prologue, p.2.
3. Ibid., Epilogue, p.349.
4. Ibid.
5. Ibid., Epilogue, pp.350–1.
6. Ibid.
7. Ibid., p.361.
8. H. Dauncey and G. Hare (eds), *The Tour de France 1903–2003: A Century of Sporting Structures, Meanings and Values* (London: Frank Cass, 2003), p.20.
9. Ibid.
10. See K.B. Rartz (ed.), *The Theater of Sport* (Baltimore: The Johns Hopkins University Press, 1995), p.ix. See also pp.16–24.
11. Dauncey and Hare, *The Tour*, p.6.
12. Ibid., p.7.
13. To set this late nineteenth-century middle-class movement in its wider European setting, see J.A. Mangan (ed.), *Reformers, Sport, Modernizers: Middle-Class Revolutionaries* (London: Frank Cass, 2002). This is the fourth annual *European Sports History Review*.
14. Quoted in R. J. Higgs, *God in the Stadium: Sports and Religion in America* (Lexington: The University Press of Kentucky, 1995), frontispiece. For a brief but interesting discussion relevant to this point, see W. Safran (ed.), *The Secular and the Sacred: Nation, Religion and Politics* (London: Frank Cass, 2003), Introduction, p.8.
15. Ibid., p.15.
16. Ibid.

17. Ibid., p.16.
18. Ibid., p.17. For a further and fuller discussion of nationalism and sport in Europe, see J.A. Mangan (ed.), *Tribal Identities: Nationalism, Europe, Sport* (London: Frank Cass, 1996).
19. Ibid., p.18.
20. Ibid.
21. Ibid.
22. Ibid.
23. Ibid., p.19.
24. Ibid.
25. For an elaboration of this point, see M.J. Deegan, *American Ritual Dramas: Social Rules and Cultural Meanings* (New York: Greenwood Press, 1989), Introduction.
26. Dauncey and Hare, *The Tour*, p.3.

The Tour de France:
A Pre-Modern Contest in a
Post-Modern Context

HUGH DAUNCEY and GEOFF HARE

THE IMPORTANCE OF THE TOUR

The Tour de France is unarguably an important sporting and cultural event. Both quantitatively and qualitatively this sporting competition attracts a popular attention that every year confirms its status as one of the premier sporting events in the world. Equally, however, the Tour's scale and social and cultural significance demands the academic attention that it has not always received. As France's pre-eminent sports competition enters its second century, the studies brought together in this volume hope to provide some understanding of how and why the Tour is so important.

Quantitatively, the Tour is a huge event in terms of the logistics of its preparation, organization, running and reporting. Every year, the Tour's route has to be re-invented over nearly 4,000 kilometres of French (and neighbouring countries') roads. Every year, a score of teams and some two hundred riders have to be engaged to compete. Every year, a travelling village of some 4,000 people and 1,000 vehicles wends its way through three weeks of French summer. Every year, millions of spectators line the roads near their homes, or make extensive pilgrimages to the key points of the Tour's route to watch the bunch of riders (*peloton*) and its leaders pass by. Every year, the Tour is reported in ever increasing detail and accomplishment by the written press, radio, television and the Internet. Financially and commercially, the Tour involves significant amounts of money, and in terms of rewards for the competitors, total prize money amounts to some $2.5 million.

Qualitatively, the Tour de France remains, after a century, unarguably the greatest cycling race in the world. No other country or sporting organization has been able to invent and stage a cycling competition that matches the Tour. Amongst countries where cycling has traditionally been a sport eliciting mass interest, such as Italy and Spain, the national Tours (the Giro in Italy and the Vuelta in Spain) have, until recently when major riders have opted to concentrate solely on riding the Tour de France in a given season, often been seen as secondary races, to be ridden in preparation for an assault on the Tour de France, rather than competitions of equal standing. Other countries where cycling has a strong popular following, such as Belgium and Holland, have been unable – for obvious geographical reasons – to produce similar races, and in the United States (the traditional home of sporting gigantism, in many ways) the relatively recent upsurge of interest in cycling towards the end of the twentieth century (encouraged by the Tour successes of Greg LeMond and subsequently Lance Armstrong) has only created competitions such as the Coors Classic.

The quantitative and qualitative uniqueness of the Tour goes some considerable way to explaining its special status in France. Above and beyond the fanatical interest shown in the race annually by amateur and recreational cyclists (an interest which focuses as much on the race itself as on individual favourite riders, and very little on the commercially-sponsored teams), the Tour has traditionally captured the imagination of the French people. The imagination of French society is sufficiently engaged every summer by the Tour for it to be said that the Tour de France has acquired a symbolic significance in French culture, based on its scale, its scope and the nature of the exploits ('mythically heroic') of its iconic heroes. To give some indication of the passion aroused by the Tour, the victory of a French rider in 2003 would be welcomed in the same way that an English public would greet England beating Germany at soccer, Australia at cricket, and the All Blacks at rugby (all during the space of a three-week summer of sporting success). Although the US public remains largely indifferent to the Tour (even if Lance Armstrong was voted sportsman of 2002), French fervour approaches that of Americans for USA victories over the USSR or Russia in ice hockey or basketball in the Olympics. The days the stage goes up the Alpe d'Huez or the Tourmalet climbs or down the Champs-Elysées are the equivalent of the British Grand National horse race or the soccer Cup Final in England, or the Super Bowl or World Series finals in the USA.

To use a lyric from The Beatles, the Tour de France has become a 'magical mystery tour' in which sport, culture and politics coalesce. The Tour is mystery and magic through the ways in which it represents and performs (in place of the biblical themes of English and French medieval mystery plays) subjects which describe, define and redefine the nature of sporting exploit, heroism and celebrity within the context of a France (past and present, social, cultural and political) which is also performatively created and recreated. The Tour de France is a kind of 'memory machine' which every year projects a repeated screening of France's epic sporting soap-opera from the dusty roads of summertime France.

The France that is performed and celebrated by the Tour as guardian of French sporting, social, political and cultural memory is a complex composite. The France represented by the symbolism and myth of the Tour is both France as nation and France as Republic, and it is arguably the riders who stand at the centre of the overlapping value-systems. The Tour interprets France as nation and Republic in the ways in which its route annually maps out the traditional physical boundaries of the Frances of both the Ancien Régime and post-Revolutionary Republican eras. The way in which the Tour is presented by its media coverage as an exploration of France's historical, cultural and political heritage leaves those who follow it in little doubt as to the significance of castles, rivers, mountain passes and battlefields. Although it is indeed the 'Republican' boundaries of France which have attracted the greatest attention from the Tour (especially those of Alsace and Lorraine, disputed with Germany during the Third Republic), it is arguably more in terms of its ethos and sporting principles than a geographical itinerary that the Tour interprets French republicanism. As a product – most directly – of late-nineteenth century France, not only was the Tour pre-occupied by the territories lost to Germany after France's defeat in the Franco-Prussian war of 1870, but it also shared – implicitly at least – some of the beliefs and values which France's elites hoped would ultimately allow '*la revanche*' (revenge). At the forefront of such beliefs was the idea that French men should improve their physical fitness in order to perform better in war, and it was during the Third Republic that a vogue for physical fitness (typified by *la gymnastique*) grew up, encouraged by a republican State which believed that it was the responsibility of citizens to keep themselves prepared to help defend the Republic. The fact that 'revanchism' in the late-nineteenth century was shared by both Left and Right, republicans and anti-republicans, indicates one way at least in which the Tour negotiates a space between Republic and nation: French sporting heroes celebrate France in all its guises.[1]

As Georges Vigarello has pointed out – quoting from the description given by *L'Auto* itself of the role of the race – the Tour presented itself from its inception 'a self-consciously modern project in which sport was to become a "gigantic crusade", a herald of progress and discovery'.[2] Cycling and the Tour were instruments for the definition of France and for the improvement of French society through technology (the industrially mass-produced cycling machine) and the athletic prowess of her menfolk. In this way, 'modern' concerns with the instrumental role of sport and technology coalesced with the fundamentally 'pre-modern' gladiatorial contest of riders pitted one against the other and against thousands of kilometres of badly-surfaced roads. Now that sport, society, culture, technology, the politics of the body, international relations (especially Franco-German) and the media have significantly departed from the ways in which they structured the Tour in its early and even more mature years post-1945, the Tour finds itself negotiating not only a space between nation and republic within French society and culture, but also, in a world where even the cleanest of cycling champions are tainted by suspicions of doping, re-inventing the role of sporting hero.

The Tour de France is a complex and at times contradictory sporting event. In its current version, and as it adapts to the changing constraints of sport, business, media and politics in the twenty-first century, it can sometimes appear that rooted as it is in the society and culture of 1903 and 1946/47, it has been, is, and will be increasingly a 'pre-modern' contest conveying 'modern' values in a 'post-modern' context. Self-consciously aware of its own status as a media construction, the Tour de France has always been actor, director, producer, audience and critic for its own heroics.

THE CENTENARY 1903–2003:
LOOKING BACKWARDS AND FORWARDS

During the three weeks between 5 and 27 July 2003, the Tour de France celebrates its centenary. In a prologue and 20 stages, over a total distance of 3,350 kilometres, 22 teams of nine professional riders will produce the latest version of France's annual summer sporting spectacle. In France itself, the Tour will be subject to more than even the usual media frenzy, and the media coverage worldwide of the competition via the written press, radio, television and the Internet is set to break records. 2003 has already seen the launch of a new logo for the Tour de France and the appearance of a commemorative medal produced by the Monnaie de Paris (the Paris Mint) and a postage stamp from La Poste (the French Post Office). The 2003 Tour looks backwards over the twentieth century and forwards to the future.

The Tour 2003 is the ninetieth to have been staged since 1903; only the First and Second World Wars (and the difficulties of France under Occupation, when various kinds of substitute races were organized) prevented the Tour being run. Whatever the problems of the Tour in the past – whether caused by politics and society, such as in the rebuilding of France in the late 1940s, or by the changing organization of the race itself such as the shifts between national and commercial teams – until the late 1990s the Tour seemed to have become an unshakeable sporting institution. However, in 1998, the explosion of doping scandals in professional cycling in general and in the Tour itself led many to doubt whether the competition would ever reach its centenary. But the Tour has survived, and continues into the twenty-first century. As part of its self-conscious and self-referential post-modernity, the Tour is acutely aware of its own history, and the 2003 race will even more than usual engage in a dialogue with the competition's past.

The Symbolism of the 2003 Tour Route

The Tour de France of 2003 is to take a route which follows in the tyre-tracks of the inaugural Tour of 1903, but which, at the same time, takes into account the ways in which sport and society have evolved over the century of the Tour's existence. As the organizers of the race state in their presentation on the Tour website, the contemporary race has to balance its history and its future and to reconcile sporting ethics with the search for racing which will enthuse the spectators:

> We couldn't – the rules being what they are – and didn't want to revolutionize the race [for 2003], and thus disrupt the balance and rationale which contribute to its credibility. So there will be neither more mountain stages than usual, nor fewer time-trials, nor any unnecessarily lengthy stages or excessively demanding ones. Moderation and reasonableness are the spirit of the day, and what is nowadays expected of the Tour de France is that sporting ethics should not be flouted simply in order to produce a spectacularly interesting race.[3]

Such reasonableness in the design of the 2003 route is in many ways the mirror-image of the outrageous physical demands imposed on riders in the early years, which led to the invention of the term 'les forçats de la route' (forced labourers of the road) and culminated in the protests of competitors such as that of the famous Pélissier brothers in 1924.

The 2003 Tour will make its initial departure in the Paris suburbs from the famous Réveil-Matin café in Montgeron from which the original Tour departed on 1 July 1903. However, there will also be a detour to pass in front of France's newest and most prestigious sporting monument: the Stade de France in Saint-Denis, associated with France's famous football World Cup win in 1998 and a central feature of future bids for hosting other international showcases such as the Olympic Games. The major cities which welcomed the Tour in 1903 will also host it in 2003: Lyon, Marseille, Toulouse, Bordeaux, Nantes, no longer as the turn-of-the-nineteenth-century isolated urban, industrial centres representing the future of France's transformation from rural and agricultural backwardness, but as modern, de-industrialized, multi-ethnic conurbations open to European transport axes. The route will include Alpine and Pyrenean mountain stages, which have come to symbolize the superhuman demands placed by the Tour on its riders: le Galibier, l'Alpe d'Huez, l'Izoard, le Tourmalet, Luz-Ardiden.

The 1953 Tour (the fortieth Tour to be run), the anniversary of 50 years of the race was a considerably less self-conscious celebration of the competition, whereas, departing from the 1903 route, the 2003 Tour will make detours to commemorate its founding fathers Géo Lefèvre, Henri Desgrange and Jacques Goddet.

THE TOUR: ORIGINS, NATURE AND COMPLEXITY

'It is the job of the press to magnify. Enthusiasm became its normal tone. It did not seek to persuade its readers but to impose its point of view. The marketing logic was impeccable: *L'Auto* organized a race that only a newspaper could report' (Vigarello).[4] The Tour was an event invented by a newspaper, *L'Auto*, as a marketing tool in its competition for readers with its older rival, *Le Vélo*, published on green paper. *Le Vélo*'s editor, Pierre Giffard, is credited by Vigarello[5] with inventing a new kind of specialist sports paper in 1892. He concentrated on reporting results of sports events, and indeed financed competitions, increasing the number of events, not just cycling but pigeon racing too, for example. In 1900 a rival, published on yellow paper, was founded, *L'Auto-Vélo*, later forced to change its name to *L'Auto* having lost a lawsuit brought by Giffard. *L'Auto-Vélo's* editor, Henri Desgrange, had a dispute with Giffard over the Dreyfus Affair, the political scandal that rocked the Republic at the turn of the century and divided Left and Right, families and colleagues into pro-Republicans and anti-Republicans. The paper's financier Marquis Alphonse de Dion and the paper were anti-Dreyfus and so in a sense against the parliamentary Republic.

As part of this rivalry, the young head of the cycling desk at *L'Auto-Vélo*, one Géo Lefèvre, came up with an idea to outdo Giffard's organization of big road races – such as the Paris-Brest-Paris and the Bordeaux-Paris – with a race that would include France's largest towns and be called the Tour de France. Knowing the demand for road races to pass through provincial towns, Desgrange, a former holder of the world cycling one-hour record, consulted the newspaper's accountant Victor Goddet to see if they could afford to organize such a race and quickly decided they were on to a winner. And indeed during the first Tour in summer 1903 circulation of *L'Auto* rose from 20-30,000 to 65,000 daily. Within a few months of the second Tour they had so eaten into *Le Vélo's* readership that Giffard was bankrupted and *Le Vélo* disappeared.

Desgrange and the 'Confected' Nature of the Tour

The Tour was a 'confected' event, both a media and a commercial event aiming to sell papers and bikes, and the complexities of its organization and management turned its progenitors, initially Desgrange, into iconic figures just as much as its riders.

Many stories, the folklore of the Tour, portray Desgrange imposing tough rules on the racers to protect the difficulty of the event, to ensure that its winners, even those who just managed to finish, were seen as heroes, and the race itself as the stuff of legend, the triumph of will over nature and human frailty. The distances were immense; regulations banning help were draconian; when mountain climbs were included, the conditions could be atrocious – wind, rain, snow; tales of Pyrenean bears stalking the route added a hint of further danger. One quote sums up the image Desgrange wished to portray: 'The ideal Tour would be a Tour where only one rider managed to complete the event.'[6] Gaboriau examines the early Tours below in much greater detail.

In a further essay below, Campos shows how the very idea of a Tour of France appeals to a collective memory of the French about earlier notions of tours of France that historians and novelists, even school textbooks, had used to define and describe the geography and history of the new nation. The Tour appeared designed to appeal to 'memory'. If this was the cultural overlay that gave a symbolic national, indeed nationalistic dimension – going up to and later into the 'occupied' territory of Alsace and Lorraine had strong political overtones – there were two other principles on which the Tour was founded, as Vigarello has pointed out.[7] The first of these principles was that the race brought together in one event three burgeoning social phenomena: modern sport, mass circulation newspapers and modern advertising strategies. The newspaper financed the event and had two client audiences in mind: it sold papers to readers wanting to follow a race they could not otherwise see; and it sold advertising space (especially to the expanding cycle industry) made available only by the existence of the race. Modern techniques speeding up news-gathering and its circulation were of course crucial to this.

The second principle on which the Tour's popularity was built was the use of a form of press reporting, a style of writing, that appealed to the imagination, and created a mythology and a legend of the Tour that turned its exploits into an epic, its protagonists into heroes. Wille, in his chapter, looks at this phenomenon, and how it has been taken into the modern era via television. The organizers knew instinctively that the Tour should not remain static. It transformed itself, changed its route, adapted to the spirit of the times, but in doing so came back regularly to certain key features of previous races, particularly difficult climbs for example, and ending in the capital city or its environs, in the Parc des Princes velodrome or more recently on the Champs-Elysées. The rules of the competition were gradually refined and complicated allowing aficionados to build up a whole Tour culture. It was a classic invention of tradition.

Goddet, L'Equipe *and the Reinvention of a Tradition*

The Second World War, the collaborationist regime of Marshal Pétain and German Occupation were almost the death of the Tour. While a weak and ageing Desgrange insisted on announcing the 1940 route during the Phoney War, the German invasion and the Armistice prevented the Tour from being held. He died in August 1940, in the depths of the 'débâcle'.

Jacques Goddet, son of *L'Auto*'s financial director, succeeded Desgrange as editor of *L'Auto*, having regarded his predecessor as his spiritual father and journalistic mentor. He had taken over the directorship of the Tour in 1936. Goddet was determined for the paper to start appearing again in the autumn of 1940. In 1941 the majority shareholder had sold out to a German consortium. In his autobiography, Goddet described his role in this period as having led his newspaper through the 'minefields of the Occupation' without too much damage. Goddet did not go so far as to try to organize a Tour under the Occupation, when encouraged to do so by the German occupant in the later period. In the atmosphere of collaboration and resistance, attempts to restore 'normality' had political and ideological overtones. A socialist organization staged a smaller race called 'Circuit de France' (1942). *L'Auto*, to mark their territory, organized a 'Grand Prix du Tour de France' (1943 and 1944), not a stage race but a classification based on results in nine classic one-day races.

On the liberation of Paris and the establishment of a provisional government, *L'Auto* fell under the orders coming from de Gaulle that all newspapers appearing during the period of collaboration must cease publication. Studies suggest that while the paper had certainly been Petainist, it had not been ultra-collaborationist.[8] This could easily have been enough to prevent Goddet and his newspaper from seeing the light of day again. However, the tribunal that tried the paper and its director found them not guilty of collaboration. Goddet had taken an active part in the liberation of Paris, as an eleventh-hour resister (earning him the Médaille de la Résistance). More importantly, apparently unknown to him, his print workshop had been a long-term centre of resistance, even printing de Gaulle's posters and tracts. Two of his journalists had been known resistance workers. A factor in his immediate post-war survival seems to have been his bringing Patrice Thominet, another active resister, into *L'Auto* as co-director and administrator. The key to his success in being allowed to build up a new sports paper, to be called *L'Equipe*, to fill the gap left by *L'Auto*, was support from an influential pillar of the resistance, Emilien Amaury, later to become one of the biggest press barons of post-war France.

Marchand recounts how there were three main sports dailies champing at the bit to start publishing in early 1946.[9] *Sports* had the support of the Communist Party, *Elans* was backed by some Socialists in the wine trade, and *L'Equipe* was fronted by all the resisters mentioned above, while Goddet remained in the background. After 100 days *Elans* merged with *L'Equipe*. Just as *L'Auto* had proclaimed its apolitical stance to distinguish itself from its rival *Le Vélo* in 1903–04, so did *L'Equipe* against its communist-backed rival in 1946. What seemed to have been the main factor in *L'Equipe*'s success, however, was its experienced sales and distribution networks inherited from *L'Auto*. A second front in this press war, Marchand tells us, was the organization of major sports events, particularly cycle races. The rights to the Tour de France name were still held in official sequestration along with other property of *L'Auto*. The Tour was the open-sesame to the sport-press-advertising market, the event was so well known.

In 1946 lack of equipment and logistical difficulties led the French cycling governing body to ban races of more than five stages (five days). Both *Sports* and *L'Equipe* organized one such small event. Again, experience from *L'Auto* meant that the Monaco-Paris stage race pitting Vietto against Robic went well, showing that *L'Equipe* was capable of organizing the Tour de France. Géo Lefèvre, now working for *L'Equipe*, was able to re-establish the old commercial links with previous advertisers. Financially, *L'Equipe* was doing well. The final element was when Amaury, by now *patron* of the major Paris daily, *Le Parisien libéré*, called in his moral debt, persuading Goddet to partner him in a joint bid for the Tour to be run by a new company, the Société du Parc des Princes, of which Amaury and Goddet were to be the principal shareholders. Thus, Amaury became 50 per cent owner of the Tour, and Goddet inherited a co-director of the Tour, *Le Parisien*'s Head of Sport, Félix Lévitan.

The Amaury Group, Goddet and Lévitan

The 1947 Tour was not only successfully organized, and an exciting race, but it was won by a Frenchman, Robic, thus increasing popular interest. *Sports*, expressing support for ideas of sport as enjoyment in opposition to the commercialization of professional sport, lost readers and income, and did not last beyond the end of the year. *L'Equipe* had established its monopoly as the French sports daily.

Lévitan and Goddet dominated the Tour for 40 years. From different social backgrounds, they did not apparently get on well personally. Lévitan was always on time, Goddet always late. Somewhat grudgingly they shared the organizing role: Lévitan the administrator, the innovator, Goddet the Tour's conscience, sensitive to its traditions. Lévitan made himself indispensable to the smooth running of the Tour de France machine. Under his trademark colonial helmet, Goddet directed the race from his car that for the three weeks of the Tour was his office.[10]

Two long court cases marked their later careers and rocked the Tour. With the Amaury press empire having gained control of *L'Equipe*, and of the Tour, Emilien Amaury was killed in 1977 in a horse-riding accident. After six years of legal battles over his will, his son Philippe Amaury gained control of the press empire and, in collaboration with Goddet, sacked Lévitan in 1987. The ensuing court case ran until 1995 when the appeals system exhausted itself in a compromise. Goddet had by then left the position of race director in 1989.[11]

La Société du Tour de France, part of Amaury Sport Organizations, is the current organizing body of the Tour; Jean-Marie Leblanc, its managing director, is responsible for the race, its organization and its running. While a modernizer in terms of sport as a television spectacle, Leblanc is from the Goddet-Lévitan stable. He is an ex-media man, but has the advantage of having raced in the Tour. He knows and respects the traditions of the Tour, and can see the point of view of riders, the media and the organizers. In recognition of the crucial influence of Jean-Marie Leblanc, the next chapter of this volume is an extended interview with him, in which he discusses how the Tour has changed as it has increasingly become the object of media coverage.

Understanding the Tour as a Sporting Competition

Most people picking up this book will already have a good idea of what the Tour de France constitutes in terms of cycling competition, but it is nevertheless useful to review a number of its fundamental characteristics.

In terms of competitions and riders, the Tour is an overall competition which includes a variety of competitions for different prizes, the most prestigious of which is that for the overall Tour lead and overall Tour victory at the end of the three weeks of racing. The winner of the Tour is the rider whose overall aggregate time for the total distance (including all stages, whether they be prologue, normal stage, individual or team time trial) is the smallest. A yellow jersey (maillot jaune) to mark the rider with the current shortest aggregate time is given out at the end of each day's riding, to be worn on the following day's stage. The further the race progresses (and the greater the variety of stages encountered) the more the yellow jersey reflects its wearer's overall strength in the different kinds of riding (flat-land riding, mountain-riding, time-trialing). Riders who are more competent in a particular kind of riding – such as mountain climbing, or sprinting for stage finishes – can figure in the King of the Mountains competition (the red polka-dot jersey – maillot à pois – attributed for the leading points tally in hill-climb finishes and various *primes* along the route of each stage) or the sprint competition (the green jersey – maillot vert – rewarding the greatest tally of sprint points). A white jersey competition rewards the best placed young rider under the age of 26, a *prix de la combativité* marks the most aggressive rider, and the aggregated times of the riders in any one team determines their position in the team competition.

The Tour is thus a race in which there are a number of competitions running in parallel. It is also a race in which individuals and teams are pitted against each other, and although individual riders of exceptional abilities in all the skills required may do well in the race overall, success for even such riders often depends on the support of their team. Team strategies in defence of their leader's position in the yellow jersey competition for overall leadership of the Tour, or other competitions, or in defence of the team's specialist sprinter or hill climber, may lead to collaboration with other teams who have shared interests in blocking breaks away from the peloton of various competing racers.

In terms of teams, currently, the Tour peloton is made up of some 20 professional teams, each containing nine riders. The teams allowed to compete in the Tour de France are selected by the Tour organizers in the spring of each year, according to the Tour's own procedures and the overall rankings established by the sport's governing body, the International Cycling Union (UCI). In 2002, the 21 participating teams were AG2R Prévoyance (Fra); Alessio (Ita); Bonjour (Fra); Cofidis Le Credit Par Telephone (Fra); Credit Agricole (Fra); CSC – Tiscali (Den); Domo – Farm Frites (Bel); Euskaltel – Euskadi (Spa); Fassa Bortolo (Ita); Fdjeux.Com (Fra); Ibanesto.Com (Spa); Jean Delatour (Fra); Kelme – Costa Blanca (Spa); Lampre – Daikin (Ita); Lotto – Adecco (Bel); Mapei-Quick Step (Ita); ONCE – Eroski (Spa); Rabobank (Hol); Tacconi Sport (Ita); Team Deutsche Telekom (Ger); US Postal Service (USA). Of these six French, five Italian, four Spanish, two Belgian, one Dutch, one Danish, one US and one German teams, 16 were chosen to participate in the first round of the organizers' choices (the team of the previous year's overall winning rider, the leading teams of the 2001 Tour, Giro d'Italia and Vuelta de Espana, the leading team in the 2001 UCI

World Cup competition, the leading ten teams in the UCI rankings), and the remaining five were invited to enter the Tour in early May 2002.

As can be seen from the team names and the banking, insurance, telecommunications and other businesses they represent, the contemporary Tour is based on a corporate team format. Before 1969, the Tour was run at different periods according to either a national team (and French regional teams to make up the numbers) or corporate team format. The businesses sponsoring the teams have not always been dominated by financial institutions and – generally – industries with no direct connection to either cycling or sport. Originally the Tour itself and teams were associated with bicycle manufacturers and other sports-related companies, but progressively team sponsors have become 'extra-sportifs'. Whereas the official sponsors of the Tour de France tend still to be predominantly French, the teams demonstrate a wider European – and in the case of Lance Armstrong's US Postal Service squad, American – range of financing. Although they are financed by French, Italian, Spanish or other companies, the team squads contain riders of various nationalities, with a predominance nevertheless of members from the sponsor's home country; it was thus that the Spanish ONCE team employed the star French rider Laurent Jalabert for many years in the 1990s. Part of the reason for employing riders of different nationalities is that each team needs a number of specialist competitors – in addition to the team leader (supposed to challenge for the yellow jersey) – in order to figure in the various competitions which run in parallel to the General Classification for overall race leadership, such as the Sprint and King of the Mountains classifications. Each team's star riders are supported by the rest of the team members, who have no ambitions for individual success in the Tour, and are employed to serve as 'domestiques', looking after and protecting the team's challengers for the yellow, green and polka-dot jerseys.

THE TOUR AND IDENTITY

Holt, Mangan and Lanfranchi (in their volume *European Heroes: Myth, Identity, Sport*) identify the Tour de France as 'indisputably heroic' and suggest that 'it has come to define the very idea of the hero in Europe'.[12] They emphasize the particular significance of cycling heroes in Continental Europe, and how in the Tour French, Flemish, Swiss and Italian riders have had (nationally) 'transcendent moments and personalities'. The Tour forms identities both on the level of individual sporting heroes and on the level of nationality and national stereotyping. As the Tour has become increasingly internationalized – particularly with the success of American competitors – these issues have become more complex than traditional rivalries between France and Belgium for mastery of the yellow jersey.

Heroes

The American rider Lance Armstrong, who will be riding as the leader of the US Postal team in 2003, has already won the Tour de France on four successive occasions. Added to his victories in 1999, 2000, 2001 and 2002, a win in 2003 will place him on an equal footing with the Spaniard Miguel Induráin (who took the yellow jersey in 1991, 1992, 1993, 1994 and 1995). Only Jacques Anquetil (France), Eddy Merckx (Belgium) and Bernard Hinault (France) have also won five Tours, but not in succession. Armstrong is both typical and atypical in the extraordinary nature of his cycling success. He is typical of Tour winners in terms of his athletic and racing abilities: he is an excellent climber and time-trialist, has an unflinching determination to win and commands the respect of his team-mates. He is untypical of Tour winners in terms of his nationality (only Greg LeMond has previously been a US winner – 1986, 1989, 1990) and because he has returned to professional cycling after recovering from cancer.

Armstrong is the archetypal figure of a contemporary hero or star of the Tour de France, but he is not a star whose heroic qualities go unquestioned. It is this doubt to which the 'heroism' of Armstrong and other riders are subjected which characterizes their 'modernity' as stars of the Tour in the late 1990s and now at the beginning of the Tour's second century. Armstrong has emerged as the leader of the Tour peloton in the wake of the 1998 'Tour of Shame' marked by doping scandals, the withdrawal of riders and whole teams and the subsequent disgrace for drug-taking of its winner, the Italian Marco Pantani. The more Armstrong declares his aversion to drug-taking amongst the professional riders, the more the (French) media seem to question his honesty, suggesting that his performance is incompatible with someone who once underwent long treatment for cancer.

Two chapters in this volume deal with French and 'foreign' cycling heroes of the Tour de France and what their representations demonstrate about both 'heroism' and 'identity'.

The Tour de France and National Identity

The role played by 'nationality' in the Tour de France has been changing and complicated. At different periods in the history of the Tour, riders have competed as mere individuals, as members of regional teams, as members of national teams, or (as currently) as members of commercial teams. Whatever the principles under which competitors have registered to ride, however, it is clear that the Tour de France has always been an arena in which national rivalries have confronted each other, less as feuds between individual riders than as conflicts between national self-perceptions and stereotyping by other nations. For France – for whom the Tour is a 'national' competition although it is run as an international contest – the success and failure of French riders on French soil seems to be felt even more keenly than the expectation and pride heaped by countries such as Belgium and Holland on the competitors who yearly represent them in France.

It is worthwhile considering in a little more detail the principles which have governed the registration of riders to compete in the Tour. Originally, the competitors were accepted as individual contestants (of varying nationalities, even in the inaugural Tour of 1903). In 1910 teams became sponsored by businesses (Alcyon, Le Globe, etcetera) until in 1930 five national teams of eight competitors each (France, Italy, Spain, Belgium and Germany) were entered as well as 60 other contestants in regional teams (1939 – no participation by Italian, German and Spanish teams). Between 1930–39 and 1947–62 the Tour was run with national teams, with German riders only returning post-war in 1955 in an international team (until 1960 German riders were included in Luxembourg or Swiss teams). From 1962 commercial teams were again introduced, prompting the pithy headline in *Le Miroir du Cyclisme*: 'Tour des Patries, Tour des Patrons?'.

Stephen Wieting in an analysis of the ways in which the drug scandals affecting the 1998 Tour have brought about 'the demise of unambiguous athletic performance' (or as he puts it in the title of his article, the 'twilight of the hero in the Tour de France'), underlines just how 'French' the Tour can appear.[13] Naturally, the Tour is French in terms of origin and location (although there is obvious symbolism in its detours to neighbouring countries), but less predictably, the competition is also predominantly French in terms of the nationalities of victors, since France (36 victories) is well ahead of Belgium (18), Italy (9), Spain

(8), the USA (7) and Luxembourg (4). But, additionally, as the somewhat intimate gathering of former champions at the presentation of the route of the 2003 Tour demonstrated in November 2002, the number of champions (or heroes) is even more restricted and even more French. In effect, over the 89 runnings of the race so far, there have been 55 winners, some of whom have won more than once, such as the multiple champions Anquetil, Merckx, Hinault, Induráin and Armstrong; 21 of these 55 winners have been French. An issue for the French public, however, is that the last French win came in 1985.

Apart from the early years of 1903–09, when there were only French winners of the race, the Tour has exhibited French domination in the 1930s, 1960s and 1980s (five or more 'home' victories in each decade), a strong national showing in the 1950s and 1970s (four victories in each decade), and weakness in the late 1980s, 1990s and 2000s. During this latest barren period for France, her only hopes have been the immensely popular 'nearly-champion' Laurent Jalabert (who never seemed to fulfil his all-round potential) and the 'flawed-favourite' Richard Virenque, the grimpeur tainted by the Festina drugs scandal of the 1998 Tour of Shame. It is difficult to see any French rider challenging credibly for the maillot jaune in 2003.

It is, however, possible that viewing the Tour as a theatre – amongst other things – of national sporting conflict is too simple, or too anachronistic an approach to the analysis of a cycling competition which has evolved considerably since its early years as an example of French society's late-nineteenth century angst. It would seem probable that a sporting spectacle such as the Tour de France would particularly lend itself to national struggles between riders and teams in periods of international tension within Europe. Thus, throughout the early decades of its running, as Europe prepared for the Great War, then suffered an armistice of 20 years (to borrow Marshal Foch's description of the Treaty of Versailles) during the inter-war period, champions in yellow were very likely to be national heroes as sport served as the continuation of war by other means.

However, after the Second World War, as European integration developed momentum (and German riders were absent from the Tour until 1955), and then as growing prosperity and Franco-German amity defused the most geopolitically founded of sporting rivalries within the ranks of Tour teams, it would seem likely that the 'national' element of riders' heroic status would have receded in importance. In fact, German riders returned to the Tour in 1955 only as members of an international team, and until 1960 German riders were included in Luxembourg or Swiss teams rather than making up their own national formation. So as the national selections gave way to commercial teams in 1962, the absence of Germany in the Tour in an official capacity during the post-war years was marked. Such an interpretation of the contemporary Tour at least – as a competition which is less marked by discourses and behaviours of nationalism and national conflict – finds some support in Georges Vigarello's contention – in his analysis of the Tour as one of France's *lieux de mémoire* – that, 'As democratic societies develop, one finds less of a search for federation, less of an impulse to unification'.[14]

The Internationalization of the Tour

In the post-war period, the Tour began – geographically – to extend itself beyond the 'beating of the bounds' of France (to borrow the terminology of Christophe Campos in this volume) by including starts and other stages in neighbouring countries, and as Vigarello again briefly points out, this can be seen as an indication of diminishing 'national concentration', although he emphasizes that such a trend must be considered within the context of a race which is still very much 'rooted in French soil'.[15] As well as the excursions abroad, during the contemporary period the 'national concentration' of the Tour has been diluted by the arrival of competitors from countries not traditionally involved in internal European national rivalries, such as Colombia, Paraguay, Chile and Brazil, Ireland, Australia and the USA. The exotic contribution of South American riders (mostly pure grimpeurs who never figured prominently in the overall competition) has probably been less significant in terms of the development of the Tour as a theatre for the negotiation of national sporting identities than the presence of what the French call the 'Anglo-Saxons'. Pociello has suggested that the fundamental generative principles of 'French' sporting characteristics are to be discovered in the interactions between French and 'Anglo-Saxon' culture.[16]

Anglo-Saxon culture has been represented in the Tour most strongly by American riders such as LeMond and Armstrong (Australians, New Zealanders and the Irish are generally perceived by the public as plucky ex-colonials or Celtic underdogs rather than ambassadors of Anglo-American values). Apart from the tragically famous Tom Simpson, and most recently Chris Boardman, neither of whom was really successful enough to provide a direct embodiment of what the French see as Anglo-Saxon sporting culture (essentially a blend of 'le fair-play' and physical effort as opposed to resourcefulness and 'French flair'), in the Tour itself British riders have been rare. Indeed, the absence of significant British competitors in the Tour has made it an interesting example of a competition in which French and 'Anglo-Saxon' sporting values interact without direct contact, unlike in sports such as rugby and soccer.

ACADEMIC APPROACHES TO THE TOUR

There is a considerable literature on the Tour de France, but this literature is preponderantly journalistic in style and hagiographic in analysis. It would seem, in fact, that the serious material on Europe's greatest annual sporting event – now a truly worldwide competition – is actually severely limited.

Existing Academic Studies

The relatively few properly academic studies that do exist constantly refer to the same exclusive list of works, amongst which the following authors figure most prominently.[17]

It was Roland Barthes whose 1957 volume of essays entitled *Mythologies* arguably first started the intellectual analysis of the Tour de France. In a series of studies of aspects of French popular culture during the 1950s, *Mythologies* provided an approach which unravelled and unpacked the hidden assumptions and meanings of subjects as diverse as the *Guide bleu* restaurant guide, the DS Citroën saloon, wrestling and the Tour de France.[18] In the essay 'Le Tour de France comme épopée' ('The Tour de France as epic') Barthes applied his technique of essentially semiological literary analysis to the organization of the Tour and (although he does not state it explicitly) the media representation of the race. Thus Barthes considers the ways in which riders are represented, and how their images (regional stereotyping) and names (diminutives and nicknames) are created and modified to construct a system of references and relationships which mirrors that of the literary epic (and the ways of thinking that accompany it). Equally, 'The Tour de France as epic' considers how the 'geography' of the race is presented in epic terms through the personification of nature (stages are 'burning', the Mont Ventoux is compared to an evil demon) and the 'naturalisation' of the competitors' struggles (they can become 'bogged down' in some stages and 'refreshed' by others, depending on the geology and climate). Barthes also discusses doping, suggesting that those riders who depend on drugs to provide the 'inspiration' for their moments when they go beyond simple 'physical conditioning' to produce miraculous exploits can be seen as a 'sacrilegious' act, whereas those riders who accomplish their miracles through communion with the gods are blessed: 'an adept of physical conditioning, Bobet is a wholly human hero who owes nothing to the divine, gaining his victories from simply terrestrial qualities enhanced by that most human of qualities: will. Gaul embodies the Arbitrary, the Divine, the Marvellous, Chosen-ness and complicity with the gods.' These examples provide a flavour of the way in which Barthes – predominantly a literary critic – approached the Tour. The conclusion to his essay is what he describes as 'Lexique des coureurs (1955)' which lists a number of the major riders and – as in a presentation of the dramatis personae of a play (or, doubtless, an epic) – presents their fundamental characteristics (or essences), but before this, he provides a typically Barthesian aphorism: 'Le Tour est un conflit incertain d'essences certaines' and a (somewhat) more accessible explanation of what he sees the Tour to mean:

> I think that the Tour is the best example we have encountered of a total and thus ambiguous myth; the Tour is both a myth of expression and a myth of projection, and therefore realistic and utopian at one and the same time. The Tour expresses and liberates French people through a unique fable in which traditional impostures such as the psychology of essences, the ethics of combat, the magickery of elements and forces or the hierarchies of supermen and servants mix with forms of positive interest, with the utopian image of a world searching obstinately to reconcile itself through the staging of a totally clear portrayal of the relations between man, men and Nature.

Such a 'literary' reading of the Tour as a competition of heroic deeds and epic narratives fits well – for all its unnecessary convolutedness – with analyses of much of the journalistic reporting of the Tour, in which epic feat and heroic stories are invented as ways of communicating and selling stories which may be much simpler, but it does little, really, to help us understand the Tour as politics, commerce and culture rather than merely emotion.

Eugen Weber has a dual importance for anyone wishing to take the Tour de France seriously as an object of academic enquiry. Students and researchers of sport in general, and French sport in particular, owe much to seminal articles written in the early 1970s by Weber, drawing attention to the social, cultural and political significance of French sport.[19] The verve and style of Weber's prose, combined with impeccable research and vast knowledge of nineteenth-century France, did much to introduce the topic of sport as a valid subject for historical and cultural investigation by academics. As well as helping legitimize the academic study of sport as a social and cultural phenomenon, Weber has also devoted himself to analyses of cycling, perhaps the most easily accessible of which is the chapter 'La Petite Reine' (an affectionately casual term for a bicycle) in his cultural history of France in the 1880s and 1890s, *France, Fin de Siècle*.[20] Weber's approach is a characteristically wide-ranging and well-informed survey of the social, economic and cultural dimensions of cycling as a leisure pursuit of the moneyed classes (both male and female) and as a sport practised by working-class professionals.

Georges Vigarello's chapter in *Les Lieux de mémoire* (translated as *Realms of Memory*), entitled simply *The Tour de France* quickly became – after its publication in 1992 – the central work of synthetic analysis of the Tour and its cultural importance to France. Vigarello's approach is that of the cultural historian, identifying the ways in which the race functions as a 'memory tour', how it has become a national institution and how it has created its own memory and mythology. As he states in his introductory paragraphs, the histories of France and of the Tour itself coalesce to touch the national consciousness: 'The course of the Tour is as much a symbol of the national heritage as it is the route of a bicycle race. The history of the Tour's setting is as important as the history of the race itself. The memory of the race combines two histories, one long, the other short, and together these two histories define its meaning.'[21] Vigarello shows not only how the Tour was created in the image of other traditional tours of France undertaken by sovereigns and journeymen or by schoolchildren in republican primary schools but also how it proposed a proselytizing mission of progress, health, technology and modernity. He demonstrates how the route of the Tour marked out a territory in which the physical landscape of France became a backdrop to a sporting spectacle and where France's history was constantly evoked through reference to figures of glorious national memory such as Joan of Arc, Napoleon and Clemenceau. Vigarello rapidly traces the developments in the organization of the race from the early days to the era of intense television coverage, asking the question whether in an era of lesser regional disparities and decreased 'national concentration' within an increasingly unified Europe the Tour ultimately become an 'anachronism'. The answer to this is to be found – as Vigarello illustrates – in the Tour's own memory of itself, and its capacity to recreate interest in itself, no longer as a race which marks out a territory of republican France, but which self-referentially engages in a dialogue with its own myths and history.

Philippe Gaboriau (one of the contributors to this current volume) is one of the foremost analysts of the Tour de France and of cycling in France. He has published a number of articles and chapters on the Tour, concentrating especially on the early years of its creation and development. The work that is most referred to is his book *Le Tour de France et le vélo: histoire sociale d'une épopée contemporaine*.[22] Much of Gaboriau's stimulating analysis centres around the changing nature of cycling as a practice throughout the early decades of the Tour, and linking this to the developing technologies of transport, to the social, political and cultural significance of cycling and the Tour. Gaboriau's thinking explains how cycling and the Tour have been dominated by popular (that is, 'working-class') influences by showing the ways in which cycling was initially the preserve of the bourgeois middle classes who alone could afford bicycles (for leisure riding), before progressively becoming accessible to workers (for transport purposes) and then subsequently providing a leisure pursuit to the working classes, as their prosperity and access to free time gradually increased. Much of Gaboriau's argument links the bicycle and the car, in showing how driving replaced cycling as the preferred leisure of the rich and as cycling became a widespread practice of the workers during the first half of the twentieth century, until cars became affordable to them also. Another major aspect of Gaboriau's path-breaking work is his constant reference to the newspaper reports of the Tour itself, thus tracing the invention – in the media coverage of the racing – of the competition as 'epic'.[23]

Paul Boury's *La France du Tour: Le Tour de France – un espace sportif à géométrie variable* is an interesting study which provides a comprehensive overview of the Tour's history, development and functioning, focusing on the role played by the riders in building the Tour as it has become.[24] Boury's wide-ranging and sensitive analysis investigates all kinds of writing on, by and about the Tour, covering literature as well as sociological approaches, and through an attention to the different dimensions of the race – sporting, technical, economic and literary – brings out the multiple meanings of the Tour.

Publications Aimed at a more General Readership

What comes into the more serious category of study are the first-hand accounts by Jacques Marchand, the veteran sports writer who worked closely with Goddet on the Tour and for *L'Equipe* and for rival papers. These include an authoritative biography of *Jacques Goddet* (Anglet: Atlantica, 2002). Another work of interest on the journalistic side of the Tour, dealing with Giffard, Desgrange and Lefèvre among others, is Marchand's *Les Défricheurs de la presse sportive* (Anglet: Atlantica, 1999). Less easy to obtain now is Goddet's autobiography, *L'Equipée belle* (Robert Laffont-Stock, 1991, edited by D. Mermet).

For the uninitiated reader, the following popular introductions give engaging and reliable information and analyses. Serge Laget's *La Saga du Tour de France* (in Gallimard's *Découverte* series, first published in 1990, but since updated) gives a heavily illustrated history of the Tour both in terms of its organization and of course its sporting aspects. *L'ABCdaire du Tour de France* (Flammarion, 2001) by Jean-Paul Ollivier ('Paulo la science'), French television's race consultant, gives a history of the Tour via a thorough run-through of the iconic names and places of the Tour – again well illustrated. Radio-France's veteran Tour reporter, Jean-Paul Brouchon (who has covered 37 Tours), concentrates on the post-war period, and gives a succinct analysis of the racing side of the Tour in *Le Tour de France. Les secrets, les hommes, l'évolution* (Editions Balland/Jacob-Duvernay, 2000).

On the bookshelves in France appear numbers of biographies and ghosted autobiographies of the stars of cycling. Among the autobiographies are *Moi Bernard Hinault, champion des champions* (Calmann-Lévy, 1992). The market for popular biographies in France seems to have been cornered by Jean-Paul Ollivier – among his books are *Tom Simpson: Un champion dans la tourmente* (2002), *Laurent Fignon* (2001), *Louison Bobet* (1998), *Bernard Hinault* (1998), *Fausto Coppi* (1998), *Bernard Thévenet* (1997), *René Vietto* (1997), *Eddy Merckx* (1996), *André Darrigade* (1996), *Jacques Anquetil* (1994), *Raymond Poulidor* (1994) (all in the *La véridique histoire* series of Editions Glénat), plus *Celui qui soufflait contre le vent... Jean Robic* (Editions de l'Aurore,

1992). (It is to be hoped another Frenchman wins the Tour soon.) He has additionally published more general histories: *Le Tour de France: Lieux et Etapes de légende* (2002), *Le Tour de France et les Alpes* (2002), *Maillot jaune* (2001). A popular study of the Anquetil-Poulidor rivalry is *Duel sur le volcan* by Christian Laborde (Albin Michel, 1998).

Large, lavishly illustrated coffee-table books abound. One containing short texts from good writers and important protagonists, plus some fine black and white photographs, is *M. Milenkovitch* (ed.), *Cyclisme, 50 histoires du Tour de France* (Editions du sport, 1997). Ahead of the centenary *L'Equipe* has published the three volume (784 pages, 2,500 photos) *Tour de France 100 ans* (Editions de l'Equipe, 2002), an important source of the iconography of the Tour.

From the British side of the Channel, an important recent study, aimed at the general reader, is William Fotheringham's biography of Simpson, *Put Me Back on My Bike: In Search of Tom Simpson* (Yellow Jersey Press, 2002). Other quality popular writing about the Tour comes from Graeme Fife, *Tour De France: The History, the Legend, the Riders* (Edinburgh: Mainstream Publishing, 2002, and republished updated for the last three years), which gives a feel for the difficulties of racing in the Tour as well as an accurate and lively history; and *Inside the Peloton: Riding, Winning and Losing the Tour de France* (Edinburgh: Mainstream Publishing, 2002), a study of key British and French riders. Other books deserving of mention are: Matthew Rendell, *Kings of the Mountains: How Colombia's Cycling Heroes Shaped Their Nation's History* (Aurum Press, 2002); Richard Yates, *Master Jacques: the Enigma of Jacques Anquetil* (Mousehold Press, 2001); a translation of Philippe Brunel's *An Intimate Portrait of the Tour de France: Masters and Slaves of the Road* (Buonpane Publications, 1996), and Phil Liggett's *Tour de France* (Virgin Books, 1989). The annual *Tour de France 2002: The Official Guide*, by Jacques Augendre, is now published in English (Velo Press, 2002).

ANALYZING THE TOUR

As we have seen in the discussion so far, any consideration of the Tour involves thinking about the relationship of sport and commerce, the relationship between sport and politics, sport and society in its historical development, cultural issues (especially the expression of identity through sport), ethical issues, and constantly and increasingly the relationship between sport and the media. It is thus that this current volume addresses at different points the key role played by the media both in the invention of the Tour and a century later, as the Tour is arguably a media event more than anything else. The modern mass media are central to most of the other issues raised by study of the Tour. For convenience, we have split the volume into two main sections, the first dealing with the organization of the Tour, some historical considerations, the economics of the Tour and its changing relationship through the years with the media. The second half deals with cultural issues and values: issues of national identity, of stars and heroes, of sporting ethics and doping, and of the value of the Tour to protesters and supporters of extra-sporting causes. There is finally a brief chronology of key aspects of the Tour's first one hundred years.

Organizing, Reporting, Watching

The Tour Director Jean-Marie Leblanc, specially interviewed for this volume by Dominique Marchetti, gives a privileged insider's view of how the Tour is organized, for the benefit of the riders and the fans, but especially for the media, and the audiences of press, radio and television. As someone associated with the Tour since he rode in it in 1968, and then reported on it, Leblanc is able to reflect on organizational changes that have come about in the last 35 years. As the third most heavily broadcast sports event worldwide (after the football World Cup and the Olympic Games – both founded, also, by Frenchmen), the Tour illustrates the evolution of television, and has been in the vanguard of the increasingly close symbiotic relationship between sport and commerce. The Tour has always been seen as a vehicle for selling things, initially papers and bicycles, and later extra-sporting goods and services, with riders increasingly appearing like sandwich-board men, as the competing teams need sponsorship to exist, just as the lavish television coverage is driven by the amount of support coming from advertisers and sponsors. What is interesting from a cultural point of view, however, is that French TV coverage has remained in the hands of the public service television channels rather than the private companies. Reviewing these themes, Leblanc addresses the issues of the increasing size of the event (financially, logistically and from the security point of view) and the more recent doping 'affaires' and legal issues. He has particularly interesting insights into the changes in approach of modern-day sports reporters and the relations between the written press and television.

Philippe Gaboriau looks at the origins of the Tour and its founding years, detailing the role of the press and particularly of course of the sports daily, *L'Auto*, and its editor Henri Desgrange and his chief cycling reporter Géo Lefèvre, in their circulation war with the rival *Le Vélo*. He also looks at the early image of the Tour.

Christopher Thompson's look at the history of the Tour in the inter-war years situates the Tour within the ideological debates of the time. He takes the case of the French champion Henri Pélissier, the most celebrated rider of his era, who abandoned the race in 1924 in a protest that became a *cause célèbre*, particularly as it was famously written up by the writer-journalist Albert Londres under the idea of the Tour riders being *forçats de la route* (convict labourers of the road). It was also taken up by the Communist press, who compared the treatment of professional Tour riders by the commercially driven race organizers to the exploitation of workers in general in capitalist society. Thompson examines this debate that was also about views of the modernization of industrial society, Taylorist working patterns and new views of the human body as machine. Thompson finally examines the contradiction posed to the organizers who understood that the widespread appeal of the race was the heroic challenge it presented to competitors, while also making the organizers vulnerable to charges of bourgeois exploitation of working-class athletes. The Tour thus found itself at the centre of the great social and political debates of the inter-war years.

Eric Reed presents a history of the business side of the Tour and the modernization over more recent years of the economic aspects of a competition that was created from the start as a commercial, for-profit event but which had important cultural ramifications: at the intersection of business and culture, the Tour's evolution is an example of how commercial interests have shaped France's mass culture in the twentieth century. Reed looks finally at the transformation of the Tour into an international commercial phenomenon illuminating the French relationship to cultural and commercial globalization.

The important impact of television on the Tour is examined in detail by Fabien Wille. He looks particularly at how the Tour has been an agent of change in media production in France. Part of the chapter is a history of the changing technologies and logistics of reporting and covering the race – which was seen by French television as a test bench for outside broadcasting techniques and innovations in sports reporters' professional practice. The other aspect of this chapter examines how modern audiovisual media adapted their coverage to reflect the major attraction of the Tour – its capacity to create heroes and recount epic struggles. The Tour is after all an itinerant competition that hardly any spectator sees live more than fleetingly and whose very invisibility encouraged sports writing based on imagination and fostering myth and legend. How did television combine realism and imagination into the gripping annual three-week odyssey that it has become?

Meanings, Metaphors and Values

Issues raised by Wille bring us straight into the cultural issues associated with the Tour de France. Christophe Campos shows how the Tour has been an important (ideological) vehicle defining French identity. The five million French citizens who annually turn out in their village or go to a nearby or distant vantage point to watch the peloton pass when they could see the race better on television are well aware that they are participating in a celebration as much as a sporting event. After looking at earlier national 'tours de France' – from Royal tours to craftsmen's tours in the Middle Ages and the famous late-nineteenth century school textbook featuring two French children's tour in a search for their identity, Campos uses the metaphor of an annual 'beating the bounds' to clarify the cultural origins and the contemporary importance of the Tour to ordinary French men and women.

The Tour also produces cultural icons, media stars and heroes who stand for different aspects of French identity. Hugh Dauncey examines the key French sporting heroes to have emerged from the Tour. He looks particularly at the images and careers of four post-Second-World-War cyclists who are still the benchmarks for the mythical future French winner of the Tour: Bobet, Anquetil, Hinault and the eternal second, Poulidor, whose status as French sporting hero is all the more important culturally for his never having worn the famous yellow jersey. Their heroic status is discussed as representative of their eras.

If the media coverage of the Tour helps create icons of French identity, then the reception of foreign stars sheds light on French attitudes to its neighbours, another way of defining identity. John Marks looks at the way the Tour has become internationalized and studies in some detail how the Italian Fausto Coppi and the English rider Tom Simpson were integrated into the Tour and its system of values. He situates their star status within the framework of the French desire to integrate into the democratic and forward-looking 'European' project that the Tour implicitly supports and symbolizes. As the wider internationalization of the Tour gathered pace in the 1980s, Marks studies the difficulty of American riders to fit into this framework, raising the issue of French attitudes to globalisation in general.

Doping, as the French call the taking of banned performance-enhancing substances in sport, to distinguish it from other forms of drug-taking, has been an issue in different eras of the Tour. Simpson's death in 1967 was attributed indirectly to the taking of amphetamines and led the Tour organizers to institute regular testing. The Festina 'affaire', emerging in the 1998 Tour and ending up in the courts in 2000, marked the Tour's lowest point in recent years, as Leblanc says in the interview mentioned above. Patrick Mignon looks at the history of doping in the Tour, at the pressures on riders to resort to the use of performance-enhancing substances, and at the medicalization and organization of doping. He also discusses the difficulties of definition and monitoring in his examination of the politics, ethics and culture of performance enhancement.

The final chapter by Jean-François Polo looks at how the Tour, as media coverage of the competition has grown, has been increasingly 'ambushed' by supporters of political and social causes. He identifies, however, the limits of such disruptions of the race that protesters ignore at their peril, limits governed by the Tour de France's very popularity and iconic status particularly among the French working class. This gives trades union protesters, for example, a fine tightrope to tread in using the Tour as a sounding board for their own causes. Polo shows too the various ways the Tour organizers have attempted to cope with potential disruptions, for example by incorporation of trades union organizations into the Tour caravan.

* * *

The authors of this book on the Tour's centenary have had to complete their work some months in advance of the peloton once again leaving the Réveil-Matin café at Montgeron. Other studies of the Tour, which we would have wished to take into account, will no doubt emerge in the meantime before the book sees the light of day. What seems clear, however, is that the 2003 celebratory circuit will tour a France which is now securely committed to a European future, where questions of identity are more concerned with ethnicity than with regions, and where the idea of the Republic is more in need of renovation than construction. We can only hope that the Centenary Tour will be neither a Tour of Shame nor, too much, a Tour of Suffering, although the pre-modern gladiatorial contest has always been a pre-requisite for the creation of heroes that has made the Tour so popular. New French identities and political aspirations doubtless suggest that the improbability of a French winner will not be too traumatic for French followers who turn out in their thousands along the route. Initially a symbol of industrialised modernity, but always a commercially oriented media creation, the Tour is now firmly set in a post-modern context, and exists more on television than in the two-minute bubble that floats seamlessly along French roads. If – as everyone suspects – Lance Armstrong equals Indurain's record of five successive Tour wins, it will be interesting to see how such a heroic exploit is received by a French audience that has so far appeared as reluctant to accept American domination of a globalised economy as American domination of what – even in the twenty-first century – they still consider *their* race. The opposing stances of France and the USA on the war in Iraq may have a role to play here too.

NOTES

1. Space here precludes a more detailed discussion either of the complexities of nationalism, republicanism and anti-republicanism in late nineteenth-century France or of the ways in which French sporting heroes are perceived. However, the success of the multi-ethnic French national soccer team in the 1998 World Cup gave rise to much debate over the values represented by soccer players of immigrant origin, some of which issues are discussed in H. Dauncey and G. Hare (eds), *France and the 1998 World Cup: The National Impact of a World Sporting Event* (London: Frank Cass, 1999), translated as *Les Français et la coupe du monde* (Paris: Nouveau monde, 2002).
2. G. Vigarello, 'Le Tour de France', in P. Nora (ed.), *Les Lieux de mémoire*, Volume II, *Les Traditions* (Paris: Gallimard, 1992). Translated as *Realms of Memory: Rethinking the French Past* (New York: Columbia University Press, 1997), vol.2, p.271.
3. 'La course, nous ne pouvions pas – les règlements sont ce qu'ils sont – et nous ne voulions pas non plus la révolutionner, briser ses équilibres et sa logique qui participent à sa crédibilité: il n'y aura pas plus de montagne, ni moins de contre la montre; pas de longueurs intempestives ni de difficultés excessives. Les temps sont à la mesure et à la raison. C'est ce qu'on attend du Tour de France aujourd'hui, dans le droit fil de l'éthique sportive, qu'il ne convient pas de provoquer, au profit du seul attrait du spectacle.' See http://www.letour.fr/2003/presentationfr/index.html
4. Vigarello, 'Le Tour de France', vol.2, p.481.
5. G. Vigarello, *Passion sport. Histoire d'une culture* (Paris: Editions textuel, 2000), p.123.
6. G. Fife, *Tour de France* (Edinburgh: Mainstream, 2002, first edition 1999), p.112.
7. Vigarello, *Passion sport*, pp.136–7.
8. See J. Marchand's biography *Jacques Goddet* (Anglet: Atlantica, 2002), and F. Pierre, 'Le journal l'Auto sous l'Occupation (1940–1944)', Maîtrise (MA) thesis, Université de Bourgogne, cited by Marchand pp.53–64.
9. Marchand, *Jacques Goddet*, pp.72–7.

10. Ibid., p.126, and pp.137–56 on the relationship of Goddet and Lévitan.
11. Ibid., p.150.
12. R. Holt, J.A. Mangan and P. Lanfranchi (eds), *European Heroes: Myth, Identity, Sport* (London: Frank Cass, 1996), p.6.
13. S. Wieting, 'Twilight of the Hero in the Tour de France', *International Review for the Sociology of Sport*, 35, 3 (2000), 349.
14. Vigarello, 'Le Tour de France', p.487.
15. Vigarello, 'Le Tour de France', p.489.
16. C. Pociello, *Les cultures sportives: pratiques, représentations et mythes sportifs* (Paris: PUF, 1995), p.118.
17. Most recently, the Tour has become an object of interest to media studies researchers in France. In *Réseaux* (1993, issue no.57) B. Grevisse looked at narrative technique and identity in media coverage of the Tour. Fabien Wille's doctoral thesis in Nanterre University's Info-Com Department took the Tour de France as a case study of the way televised sport drives change within television production. A number of publications have emerged from Wille's work – one, on the evolution of media coverage of the Tour, in P. Gabaston and B. Leconte (eds), *Sports et télévision, regards croisés* (Paris: L'Harmattan, 2000), which also contains articles on television coverage of the doping scandals (A. Arnaud and M. Chandelier), and on the fine detail of TV coverage of a stage of the Tour (B. Leconte).
18. R. Barthes, *Mythologies* (Paris: Seuil, 1957). Translated by Annette Lavers as *Mythologies* (London: Jonathan Cape, 1972), but as a selection without the essay on the Tour de France.
19. See, for example, E. Weber, 'Pierre de Coubertin and the Introduction of organized Sport into France', *Journal of Contemporary History*, 5, 2 (1970), 3–26, and 'Gymnastics and Sports in fin-de-siècle France: opium of the classes', *American Historical Review*, 76 (Feb. 1971), 70–98.
20. E. Weber, *France, Fin de Siècle* (Cambridge, MA: Harvard University Press, 1986), Ch.10, pp.195–212. See also E. Weber, 'La Petite Reine', prologue in P. Arnaud and J. Camy (eds), *La Naissance du mouvement sportif associatif en France: sociabilité et formes de pratiques sportives* (Lyon: Presses Universitaires de Lyon, 1986), pp.11–25.
21. Vigarello, 'Le Tour de France', pp.469–70.
22. P. Gaboriau, *Le Tour de France et le vélo: histoire sociale d'une épopée contemporaine* (Paris: L'Harmattan, 1995).
23. Amongst other studies, interested readers should look at P. Gaboriau, 'Le Vélo: lenteur des riches, vitesse des pauvres', in *Sport et Société* (Saint-Etienne: Université de Saint-Etienne/CIEREC, 1981), pp.153–62; *'L'Auto* et le Tour de France. Regard critique sur l'histoire du cyclisme et l'année 1903', in T. Terret (ed.), *Histoire des sports* (Paris: L'Harmattan, 1996), pp.39–49; and 'Sport et culture populaire: le Tour de France cycliste', *Histoire sociale des pratiques sportives* no.8 (Paris: INSEP, 1985).
24. P. Boury, *La France du Tour: Le Tour de France – un espace sportif à géométrie variable* (Paris: L'Harmattan, 1997).

ORGANIZING, SPECTATING, WATCHING

The Changing Organization of the Tour de France and its Media Coverage – An Interview with Jean-Marie Leblanc

DOMINIQUE MARCHETTI

INTRODUCTORY REMARKS BY D. MARCHETTI

The special nature of Jean-Marie Leblanc's working life – as a Tour rider, as a Tour journalist and now as Tour organizer – gives a particularly well-informed perspective on the Tour de France. Indeed, the current managing director of the *Société du Tour* (born 1944) was initially a rider for the amateur teams of the Northern region of France around his birthplace, and then a professional rider for four years, finishing 65th and 85th in the Tours of 1968 and 1970. During his time with the professional teams, he was also a trainee reporter at the *Voix du Nord*, a major French regional daily newspaper, which he joined as a full-time journalist in 1971 to cover both boxing (he had obtained a training diploma in boxing at the end of the 1960s) and cycling. He followed the Tour for the *Voix du Nord* in 1974 and 1976, and then from 1978 for the French daily sports newspaper *L'Equipe*, as head of cycling coverage. Finally, he started his career in the organization of the Tour by taking the post of *directeur des compétitions* (director of racing) in 1988, and then by becoming *directeur général* (managing director) in 1994. This highly-informed view of the Tour[1] provides us with a better understanding of how the Tour de France – like other 'events' – is co-produced by its organizers with, increasingly, the reporters who follow it; in other words, how this spectacle is nowadays aimed as much at the media audiences (readers, listeners and viewers) as at those who attend the race itself.[2]

   The evolution of television channels in France and across the world in the 1980s and 1990s – as the first part of the interview reveals – strongly contributed towards changes in the overall financial organization of the race through the rise of marketing and corporate hospitality, changes to income streams brought by exclusive television rights and the appearance of ever more numerous sponsors. The exponential growth in media coverage of the Tour – which is more than just the increase in *television* footage – has enormously enhanced the Tour's impact on sponsors and on the general public, requiring Jean-Marie Leblanc and his colleagues to attempt to control the Tour's drift towards economic 'hypertrophy'. The Tour's current *directeur général* thus lists the changes that have occurred in the organization of this part of the entertainment industry whose activities take place at the intersection of rationales which are sporting, financial, media-related, and more recently, legal. Much seems to indicate that Jean-Marie Leblanc's social background – which is very different to that of managers of some other major sporting events – is important in explaining his visible desire to avoid structuring the Tour de France simply according to financial and media imperatives.

The second part of the interview deals more extensively with the effects of television on the increasing media coverage of the Tour de France. After a review of the impact of the different media (successively the written press, radio, television and internet) the interview shows how developments in television broadcasting and the rising visibility of the Tour have contributed to changing the way it is seen by the general public. This has occurred firstly because the television channels no longer simply show a sports competition, but produce a show through the use of the most sophisticated televisual techniques, and secondly because television viewers see the race almost 'better than the journalists'. The television coverage of the Tour has also significantly changed the ways in which the written press reporters work since they have had to reposition themselves relative to their colleagues in television. Thus we see how the Tour can appear as a microcosm revealing a number of changes in the media which have modified the production of news in general, whether these be the dominant influence of the audiovisual media, the intensification of competition and its effects (more numerous drug-taking 'affaires' and the race to obtain exclusives), the increase in 'armchair-reporting', or the increasing pace of work schedules. The Tour is also revealed as an example of the changing relations between sports reporters and their main sources (riders, doctors, race organizers, etcetera) caused by the growing importance of finance and more recently, the doping 'affaires'. As the conclusion to the interview reveals, illicit practices such as these have thrown the work of organizers and sports journalists alike into confusion. The 'affaires' have had a dual effect on the work of the specialist sports reporters, as some have felt betrayed both by their sources (riders, doctors, organizers and so on) and by their editors, who have sometimes asked for such subjects to be covered by journalists in other specialisms.

INTERVIEW WITH JEAN-MARIE LEBLANC, CHIEF EXECUTIVE OF THE TOUR DE FRANCE

I have what some people consider to be an advantage, or at least the characteristic of having been a protagonist in the Tour de France in three different ways. Firstly, I participated in the Tour as a rider (even if only of minor status) since I was a professional rider for five years and did the Tour twice in 1968 and 1970. 1968 was the last year of the national teams and I was in the France B team, and in 1970 I rode in the Bic jersey during the heyday of Eddy Merckx. Then, as I realized that I wasn't going to have a great [he smiles] career as a rider, I moved into journalism, a career that I had been preparing for even as a rider. I was a professional journalist for the *Voix du Nord* daily newspaper from 1971 until 1977, where I did my early years in the profession and covered two Tours.

– *You were already closely involved in the world of cycling?*
– Of course, because before being a professional rider you have to have been an amateur racer as well. I was even the French university champion in 1964, but I started cycling late because of staying in secondary education until I did my *baccalauréat* in Philosophy, and then I did (started but not finished, since cycling was already taking up too much of my time) a degree in Economics at Lille University. In short, there was all that after a short professional career and my early days in provincial journalism at the *Voix du Nord*. After that, I was asked by *L'Equipe* to take responsibility for their cycling columns, which I did from 1978 until 1988. At the end of 1988 I was invited by Jean-Pierre Courcol to take the post of competition manager of the Tour de France, in other words being the Number 2 behind the General Manager Jean-Pierre Carenso. Since then, I've continued with the Tour until now, becoming General Manager of the *Société du Tour de France* in 1994. Since 1994 there has been another modification to the statutes of the Tour de France in that the *Société du Tour* now only exists as a legal shell, now that all the companies that organize races – whether it's the

Société du Tour, the Thierry Sabine organization (Paris-Dakar, the Touquet enduro race) or *Athlétisme Organisation* (the Paris marathon and half-marathon) – have been merged into the *Amaury Sport Organisation* which has been transformed from a holding group into a proper company.

THE DAY-TO-DAY ORGANIZATION OF THE TOUR

– *What is the daily work that you do in organizing the Tour – there are so many parameters to look after, and how have they have developed over the years?*
– My role essentially consists in co-ordinating, on the one hand, work concerning two aspects of the Tour – the work of the sites involved and the work of the competition, because naturally I have oversight of their activities. There are strategic choices to be made concerning the length and difficulty of stages, choosing the teams to take part in the Tour and so on because in one way or another I am responsible for things like this in the eyes of the outside world. So, I have to direct the work of the cycling office and co-ordinate it with that of other departments such as the legal office, the commercial office, the media office and the logistics office. This is an all-year-long office activity with numerous meetings, but also work in the field, as well as a significant role representing the Tour, since, whether I like it or not, I embody the Tour de France as an institution for people in general, fans, supporters and aficionados. I believe in this role and I fulfil it with real pleasure, because on the one hand, it's an honourable duty to represent the Tour, and also because [...] I always say that cycling policy and the policy of the Tour de France in particular should not just be made on the fourth storey of a concrete tower in Issy-les-Moulineaux [...]. And I haven't mentioned – and it takes up a lot of my time – managing relations with the Union Cycliste Internationale, with the sports ministry and with various sports federations.
– *What does the organization of the Tour represent in terms of personnel?*
– [...] I would say that full-time there are somewhere in the order of 70 people employed, to which should be added in the field during the month of the Tour, part-timers numbering about 220, but that of course is only a partial view of the numbers, since there are also the service firms which provide barriers and security in general and so on. [...] I would say that in July, working in a strict sense for the Tour organization

and for the outside service companies there are 400–500 people, closer to 500 in my view, in fact. And that's not including television, sponsors and people who prepare the route.

– *And what takes the most time? What are the most time-consuming tasks, and how have they changed over the years?*

– That has obviously changed quantitatively. [...] I can say that the areas in which we work have became much more varied. For example, there is a field in which ten years ago we hardly did anything – legal issues – and in which we now do everything, or perhaps too much. Nothing is done now without the say-so of our legal office or without legal precautions being taken. I won't say it's a bad thing, but ... this is not specific to the Tour de France, it affects all companies.

– *What aspect does this involve the most? Is it essentially concerning security?*

– Security, contracts, drawing up of regulations, for example, policy on doping. Doping scandals and the problem of doping in general have obviously led us nowadays to be very careful with legal matters. There is another aspect that is very important: the media. Fifteen or 20 years ago, I would say, during the Bernard Hinault period or the era in which more or less I joined *L'Equipe*, the media was essentially just the written press as far as the Tour was concerned on a daily basis. Today we are concerned with the press, I won't say less, but proportionately compared with television it's not very important, and nowadays there is also the Internet.

– *You've cited the legal and media fields...*

– The commercial field also – I don't know of any business which doesn't seek to be profitable, to earn money, thus to be efficient in its marketing, in other words in the designing of the products or services it is selling. And also, another area of activity which didn't exist 15 or 20 years ago, but which is necessary to complete this marketing work, is public relations and corporate hospitality. As an example, nowadays guests are ferried from Paris to the stage town each day – two planes for mountain stages and one for flat stages – and taken back the same evening. We have a Tour village that welcomes 2,000 people every morning, so you can see the scale of the apparatus.

KEEPING CONTROL OF THE INCREASINGLY
GIANT SCALE OF OPERATIONS

– *The machine has expanded...*

– Has expanded a lot quantitatively and qualitatively, because since we are considered to be the Number 1 race in the world, we have our own challenge of keeping this reputation and being the best possible. [...] Our sport has advantages and disadvantages compared with others. Disadvantages such as our 'ground' being the road. So by definition, and even if we protect it the best we can, the road is open and exposed to all kinds of imponderables – meteorological, geographical and so on. There are also unpredictable problems which are linked to the public, because of the enormous concentrations of people in some places – starts, finishes, mountain passes – which produce dangers that we have to try to foresee. There are also problems coming from outside: I recall that we have had troublesome demonstrations on the race route – farmers' strikes, sheep breeders' strikes, shopkeepers' strikes, protests by environmentalists... [...] We are as vigilant as we can be because we are never safe from accidents – I can't but remember the fatal accident we suffered two years ago. Imagine that we are a town of 3,600 people covering 3,500 km during three weeks – going fast because it is a race [smile] and coming into contact with tens of millions of spectators. [...]

Because of the means at the disposal of TV nowadays and thanks to the quality of the work done by those in TV, the Tour de France is now a real social phenomenon. For a whole month, people do tourism, history, sport obviously; they rub shoulders with drama, share moments of joy and the victories of great champions – in short, a wide range of things. And that's how I explain the explosion in popularity and media coverage of the Tour. I also think that the drama of the TV depiction of the Tour encourages people to go to see it in reality, to experience it and touch it. The Tour is a social cement: I know a Breton and a guy in the Alps whose families meet up every year in such-and-such a mountain col – camping-car next to camping-car – to have a few drinks together and then watch the Tour the next day, say at L'Alpe d'Huez. [...] And since we're on the subject – and I'm criticizing no-one, cycling is not a sport where there's one team against another – in comparison with other sports, there's no national chauvinism, no violence, no hooliganism; people on the Alpe d'Huez encourage all the riders. [...]

– *Another feature of the Tour is that it is very popular...*

– Of popular origin. It still has a strong popular streak. [...] Studies have been done on this, of course. But it's important not to lump spectators and TV viewers together. The spectators on the spot are families and thus there are a lot of women – from the statistics, from memory, the public is made up of working-class families. [...] But the TV viewers are preponderantly more male, older and less working-class. [...] And the marketing people are concerned to see that compared with other sports, we are a bit less 'young'... For me, I'm not too troubled, because the spectators are more and more numerous and the people who come out to watch the race were all 20 once and thus I don't despair of the idea that young people of 20 today will still love the Tour and that others will progressively come to join them. [...]

– *To continue on the organization of the Tour, since you have touched on some of the economic aspects, I'd like to ask what have been the major stages in the development of the Tour economically since the war. The set-up was originally much less professional.*

– I identify two main stages. The first was marked by the replacement of the national teams by commercial teams. This was a structural change because until then professional cycling was based – more or less until the 1960s – on bicycle manufacturers, but then, as bicycle sales started to fall, new sources of funding were needed, and thus advertising on jerseys was introduced. [...] That was a necessity for cycling, unlike for football or other sports which brought in income from gate receipts. [...] And moreover, our costs are higher, since we – I reiterate – have to maintain our sports ground by paying the police and gendarmerie and highway maintenance and so on.

The second turning point was brought about by television and television rights. [...] TV for a long time was not a source of income for the race organizers. Moreover, TV has been a source of income for all sports, but for cycling, this has been all the more important because it needed television rights to improve its image and status and so-on. The appearance of TV rights can be put at the end of the 1980s. [...] And this is the reason why my predecessors are to be admired for having kept the Tour alive with the support of two newspapers, *L'Equipe* and *Le Parisien*, at a time when there were no TV rights and sponsorship was very far from what it has become now. We have profited from TV in the form of rights and from media coverage. TV coverage is so good that it is a good deal for the sponsors of the Tour and for the team sponsors – everyone benefits from it.

— *How have income and expenditure evolved over the years?*

— [...] We can say that at the start of the 1990s the income of the Tour came — except for 1 or 2 per cent — first and foremost from sponsoring, secondly from TV rights (which had appeared before the 1990s), and thirdly, from payments from towns hosting the stages. In the ten years since 1990 — more or less — the proportion of funding coming from municipal sources has reduced from 20 per cent to 10 per cent. This is a political decision on our part, since we realize that public money is scarce and also that the explosion of media coverage encouraged and pushed us into being more demanding with our broadcasters and consequently with our sponsors. Nowadays, in approximate terms, the income of the Tour comes from sponsoring (45 per cent), TV rights (45 per cent) and from Town councils (10 per cent). [...] The quantity and quality of TV coverage has refocused the financial resources of the Tour towards TV and those who are keen to appear on it, namely sponsors.

— *As you have just stated, the competition is now on a huge scale. What problems do you have to deal with as a result of this?*

— The development of TV coverage has produced a development in the sport. It's easy to understand since television provides better visibility for sponsors, including team sponsors (as cycling is structured around team sponsors). [...] There are therefore now more teams, who build their team selections for the Tour de France. [...] When we had to choose the teams on 2 May to compete in 2002 we were faced with 35 teams. [...] In 1989, 1990 and 1991, we chose teams to compete and this hardly ever gave rise to any discussion: we would make a five-line press-release stating that we had approved such-and-such a team and that was that. But in the second half of the 1990s we became aware of a growing number of very enthusiastic prospective teams. [...]

The stakes are huge, and the team's participation in the Tour de France can often be the guarantee that the sponsor will stay with you (sometimes the sponsor threatens to leave). That's why there is so much pressure over the selection of teams to take part and I can assure you that in five or ten years' time, it will still be just the same. The poor old Tour organizers are still a long way from being free of criticism [smile] — that's the price of success. [...] So all that makes life a bit more complicated, of course, and makes relationships more strained, since the stakes — sporting, economic and media — are very high.

— *You have other signs of the huge scale of operations. What problems do you nowadays have to deal with which did not arise before?*

– Problems to do with the huge scale of things, and quantitative problems. We could simply accept more and more teams and journalists wanting to cover the Tour, more and more guests and sponsors and more and more TV channels and so on. The Tour provokes much envious interest and my role is to try to resist the effects of this success. It's my duty to say no, or to tell my colleagues to say no, because if we allowed ourselves to be carried away by our own growth, the Tour would suffocate. Firstly, we would no longer be able to go to some small towns or regions of great sporting interest simply because of the size of our competition. Secondly, the Tour must not be drowned in the future by too many guests or cars – we have taken measures to restrict the number of cars on the route of the race. [...] The sporting competition has to remain the priority, and that encourages us to control, to manage and so to limit.

– *Your main function is thus to resist this inexorable economic development of the Tour.*

– Yes, and it's not easy to convince my colleagues in marketing and sales that we should stop selling. We have more and more sponsors, but we have no more room. [...] The Tour is a small town where everyone who works in it has to live together during three weeks of fatigue, heat, thirst, hunger, stress and boredom because you are away from your family. [...] When we don't get on – I won't say happily, but at least comfortably, in good humour – the atmosphere can get awful between the riders, the journalists and so on, and a vicious circle of ill-humour can settle in. Everyone has to feel good in the Tour, most notably the main protagonists, the riders themselves, whom we look after attentively, whether it's a matter of rest, transport, accommodation or food. Do you know – as an anecdotal example – that we invite three Italian chefs each year to the Tour so that they can cook or show local restaurants how to cook pasta *al dente* as the staple diet of our riders [smiles]?

– *To talk about economic aspects again, what kind of advertisers do you have, and how have they changed over the years?*

– That has changed over time, but not perhaps as much as we might have anticipated. That's to say that in comparison with other sports, it's to be noted that our sponsors are not multinationals – I make no value judgment. We have a lot of French firms which are not very European and even less of world scale, both in terms of team sponsors and sponsors of the Tour itself. La Française des Jeux is French, Bonjour is French. For Belgium, we have Lotto; for Germany, Deutsche Telekom.

We could say that Deutsche Telekom is European now perhaps, but we still don't have either Visa, a worldwide car manufacturer or a world airline. What does that say? I don't know. Maybe cycling remains a very national sport in its connotations. [...]

THE DESIGN OF THE TOUR

– *So concerning the sporting aspects of the Tour, what have been the main changes? You've mentioned, for instance, the replacement of national teams by commercial ones.*

– I would say that this is the aspect that has not seen any revolutions. I think revolution should be avoided here, not because I'm an out-and-out conservative, but ... I'll talk first about the design of the race before discussing the rest. In the Tour de France there will always have to be flat stages, mountain stages and time trials. Our mountain stages will always be in the Alps and the Pyrénées, that's unavoidable, and we will always finish in Paris. We have rules that set limits such as not being able to go beyond 3,500 km nowadays and having to have two rest days. In short, there is a framework. [...] These rest days existed in the past, often two, sometimes one, and the restriction on the number of kilometres also, but if we look at what's happened since the war we can see that the length of the race has shortened – that's modernity, but it's also in order to bring more dynamism and speed to the race. All of that was going on already, but 1998 encouraged the sporting authorities to codify it. I can't see any major changes being made in the design of the race route because the Tour has to be able to be won equally by a specialist climber as by a flat stage expert. That's what I've taken with me from what I was taught by Jacques Goddet, and he was right. Next, concerning the structure of the system and the teams, that involves changes which also take place naturally, but which from time to time are codified by the rulings of the UCI when it says for instance: 'there must be x number of riders in teams in the big national competitions' – nine or ten, as it happens, it's nine. [...]

– *How do you go about designing a route for the Tour each year? What are the main criteria you apply?*

– The criteria have been drawn up through experience. When I took charge of the Tour, there were already – and there still are – four, five or six mountain stages, but never more. Twenty or so big cols (second, first and hors catégorie) to climb, but never fewer. There were 100–120km of individual time-trials, and there we have gone down a bit to 100km, but that does not make much difference. The past has given us a balance, which it would be a bad idea to change. Very quickly, if we did, we would see ourselves accused of favouring a climber rather than a rouleur... We are constrained both by the criteria imposed by the rulings and by the parameters inherited from the past. The fashion is now for stages that are a little shorter. It should be noted, however, that in comparison with more distant eras (or at least just before the war) the Tour was more a trial of endurance, health and recuperative powers than a test of simple athletic ability. Nowadays, powers of recovery are still necessary, as are strength and bravery etcetera, but the Tour is more a matter of intrinsic athletic ability ... a bit less to do with strength and robust physicality, that's what we sense nowadays...

– *Yes, so a bit more lively.*

– Yes, being able to go up a climb more quickly is a change, but in my opinion, one that is not restricted to the Tour de France ... it's something that is natural in cycling in general, and doubtless in all sports.

THE EFFECTS OF TELEVISION ON THE MEDIA COVERAGE OF THE TOUR

– *Given your experience as both a rider and a journalist, what are in your opinion the major stages in the changing media coverage of the Tour de France?*

– There's one transformation that I did not experience myself but which I can perceive through hindsight and from what I read, which is the progressive switchover from paper and the written press towards radio coverage, and the change that I have seen more concretely has been the movement towards ... I won't say all-TV but the preponderance of TV coverage. Concerning the first transformation, it's easy to understand. Essentially, one of the factors that created the popularity and the enthusiasm for the Tour de France was the telling of its story on paper, because it was a sports event that spectators couldn't see, unlike a football match where spectators are present, or any other sports event. So people imagined the contest from the summaries – often in epic style – which were sometimes perhaps a little out of proportion, enlivened by the journalists, whom themselves didn't see a lot, or at best saw things incompletely.

– *No-one used to see the Tour as well as we do today.*
– And there wasn't even Radio Tour as there is today. Journalists in the past who reported the Tour had only fleeting perceptions of the race or had reports told to them which were perhaps themselves already exaggerated. [...] I'm sure there was romancing, and exaggeration, but it was pretty. I think this was one of the reasons for the enthusiasm for the Tour de France. You can imagine the epic tales of mountain stages and the probable exaggerations – the snow, the wind, the potholes, the wolves, whatever, the bears [laughs].

And then later, there was photography. Remember that papers like the *Vie au grand air* in the 1920s – a sort of *Paris-Match* devoted to sporting and physical activities – was the first real proper paper to devote photos to sports events. Try to imagine what huge effect photos could have on people who couldn't hear or see what a cycle race was all about! [...] After the war – I saw these papers when I was little – they came out three times a week [...] there were two of them on the market: the *Miroir des Sports* and *Miroir Sprint*. And the memories that I have of them are strong and vivid, because, I repeat, these papers were made up more by pictures than by text. The photos were really beautiful and strong, with wide-angle shots of snow, mountains and landscapes.

I should make clear that these were three golden periods for the Tour de France: the first is the one we've been talking about – text and photos – and the second was the magic of live commentary on the radio with Alex Virot, Georges Briquet and so on, all these great reporters. [...] People would listen live to the stage finishes, the day's results, the mountain climbs. We should remember that at that time there wasn't much of a supply of sports or leisure activity, and therefore the radio reporting of the Tour was a second cornerstone of the popularity of the Tour.

And the third, contemporary element in media coverage is obviously television. [...] Only yesterday I attended a press conference by France Télévisions on this coming year's coverage of the Tour, and Jean-Maurice Ooghe, the producer, reminded us of his thinking on how the Tour should be shown on television by saying that he aims to show not only the Tour de France but also the tour of France as a country. In other words, he includes the landscapes and elements which I might call social, sociological and human rather than simply showing a breakaway, a race leader or the peloton – he widens his field of vision to things that he has seen and researched around the route. Jean-Maurice Ooghe reconnoitres the race route for weeks before the Tour – he follows the road and takes notes on a château to the right, here a bridge, there a cathedral on the left – everything is noted down and given to the cameramen so that they know all the time what they should be showing in addition to the race in order to direct it and put it in its context. We are lucky to live in a country which is extremely diverse, which has a history and a culture, all kinds of attractions, and that, also, for me is another of the keys to the success of the Tour. [...] I often say that television 'magnifies' the Tour. TV places the race within a decor that is varied, changing, attractive and emotive. It can be frightening. When these days we see riders descending from a col at 90 or 100kph on wet roads, that reaches out emotionally to the viewers, and it's the same when it's hot, and we see them splashing themselves with water, sweating and suffering. And in addition to these human, emotional features, there are those aesthetic aspects that I have already mentioned, the landscapes, the climbs, the descents, the bridges, castles, churches...

– *And what has changed in television coverage since your day?*
– The technical facilities available: the helicopter cameras, the cameras on extendable cranes and booms, the camera that lets us see the sprints in close up ... all the qualitative and quantitative technical equipment. And also the talent and professionalism of the people who use these tools. Nowadays there exists a real expertise in France in showing cycling on television. [...]

– *The screening of the final Tour finish came in 1949, and the whole of the race in 1952, but it was essentially at the end of the 1960s that TV really started to expand. What can you say about the TV coverage when you were a rider?*
– I think there was only the coverage. Whereas today they show the final 120km live, when I arrived in the organization of the Tour it was just the last 60 or 90km. [...] But television showed mainly just the race, perhaps because of the equipment – big heavy cameras, no signal relays or helicopters and planes. In my view, the Tour was then seen as a big sporting competition, a huge cycle race which had to be reported and whose outcome had to be given. Nowadays, the Tour de France is – in my view – the foremost great cycle competition in the world, but also a kind of social phenomenon which is therefore to be put in the context of other factors, such as tourism, culture, emotion, history and international issues, since there are now Australian, Scandinavian, American and Colombian riders.

‒ *And that, also, has changed…*

‒ That has considerably widened the scope of the Tour de France. For example in this year's Tour there is going to be – for the first time – a Chinese TV team. I see that as something important. They're going to use the 26-minute summary produced by France Télévisions and the Tour itself and add to it with reports that they will undertake themselves. I find it great that this immense country is going to discover the Tour de France and *France* [he stresses]. So, and I often say it, we are basically – involuntarily and indirectly – great ambassadors for certain aspects of our country, notably tourism.

‒ *You have witnessed the arrival of new international TV coverage, since initially, the Tour coverage was essentially just French.*

‒ Indeed – as was cycling. Subsequently, the Tour coverage became very West-European, based on countries which were founders of cycling and of Eurovision television such as Italy, Belgium, Holland, Switzerland, Germany and Spain. Germany more recently, and Denmark the most recently. I'd say these were the founding cycling nations. And then the range expanded: the LeMond years brought us the United States and Colombia as well, but they have financial problems so some years they're here and others not. Japan has been with us for 15 years or so and more recently some Commonwealth countries such as South Africa, New Zealand and Australia with their own TV group. […] And then more recently still Europe expanded eastwards and former Eastern-bloc countries have given us riders, for example the Russians came about ten years ago. […] It's said that nowadays pictures of the Tour are seen in 160, 170 countries worldwide, either as live transmission or as clips in news programmes. For the first time the Tour can be watched live on a sports pay-channel in the US called OLN (Outdoor Live Network), and that's been going for three or four years, or, in addition to what we already had, in a weekly summary on Sundays on CBS.

‒ *So the Americans arrived in the 1980s. But what were the initial effects of their television coverage – were there effects on the race itself?*

‒ No, we can't say that. […] There was all the less impact on the race because we were determined that there shouldn't be an effect. One year the Americans – at the start of the 1990s – more or less asked us (I can't remember the exact details) that we have a time-trial on day four, and that on Sunday there should be a mountain stage (laughs). They wanted us to design a Tour route that would fit perfectly with their schedules, needs and audiences. Obviously, we sent them politely packing, and they didn't ask again. So we can't really say that television has had an influence, except marginally – and I'm repeating myself – to bring us spectators and US or Australian tour-operators.

– *Has television paradoxically not increased the popularity of the Tour?*

– I remember this debate when I was at *L'Equipe* and we often had arguments over whether television, too much television, better television, more broadcasts wouldn't threaten or even kill off the paper. Jacques Goddet, who used to chair the editorial meetings, was on the side of those – he was more visionary and younger than any of us – who said that we should support television because television would serve our races, by a kind of boomerang effect. He was right. [...] In other words, *L'Equipe* even formed a kind of partnership with television and today this is still the case. Television doesn't stop a spectator who watches the Tour on TV every day and enjoys it for five days from getting in his car the sixth day to go and see the Tour as it passes 150km away from his home. Of that I'm sure; people want to go and see for themselves, to smell and to touch the race. Our sport has another advantage, which is that it is free to watch – no-one pays to go to see the Tour, and when you take your place by the roadside on the Alpe d'Huez, you can see the riders only a metre or two away, and you can smell the sweat and embrocation. There is an incredible closeness [...] which is only found here.

– *There have been other effects of television on the economics of the Tour, which have perhaps been the major effects.*

– I would put at the end of the 1980s and the start of the 1990s the drive towards exclusive TV rights for all sports, not just cycling. Before, television produced and broadcast, but later, it was essentially the privatisation of state-controlled television channels which developed competition and over-bidding. Prices went up, and suddenly, television became a source of income for the Tour organizers, and because television channels had paid a lot for the right to exclusive pictures, they broadcast a lot, and a lot of good material. This is the case of France-Télévisions – what happened was that the Tour sponsors were pleased, and that helped us to obtain sponsors for the teams. The fact that we have 35 applications for 22 teams to take part in the Tour reflects the desire of these 35 sponsors and groups of sponsors to be seen on television for three weeks. So the whole economy of cycling, and not just the Tour organization, was boosted. And the team sponsors have played along with television – I don't know if you've noticed in the last two or three years, but the team sponsor is now shown on the back of the riders' shorts as a direct consequence of the nature of TV coverage ... because most of the time in breakaways and in time-trials, the cameras have to be behind the riders in order not to provide any shelter from wind and therefore film them from behind, so the sponsors have cleverly adapted to this. There has been a closer and cleverer linkage between the supply of TV coverage and the economic interests of the Tour, sponsors and teams.

One result of that has been that television has obliged the written press to work differently, because the spectator in his armchair now sees the Tour better than the journalist. Before television coverage was so complete, the journalists had to follow the race, were in the caravan, listened to Radio Tour, followed the breakaways and talked with the team directors; but nowadays, they are hardly ever in the caravan and stay at the finish watching the race on TV rather than seeing it themselves. [...] They're no longer in a position to tell the story of the race, because the TV viewer has seen everything, so they are obliged to provide a supplement, perhaps in the form of interviews, since we organize a videoconference with the stage winner, the yellow jersey and the longest breakaway. You might say that the TV viewers also see that, so generally, the journalists ought also to produce an analysis of what's said, and to provide some kind of perspective, what might be the strategies for the following day. The journalists should understand cycling, which is not always the case, whereas the generation of cycling journalists that I knew – Parisian and provincial – had the profile I've just mentioned and were not just reporters of stages, but tried, using their experience and interviews, to explain and anticipate the development of the stage. Nowadays, because they are younger and have less experience, the journalists can't really do all that, and because the story of the race is told elsewhere, they're a bit short of material. And for me, that's a reason why they are more tempted by what I would describe not as a slippage of ethics, but as a laziness, this trend towards the spectacular, the emotional and scoops at any cost. In news, and I'm not talking just about sport, there are two things: facts, pictures and narration; and then explanation and the whys and wherefores. We don't get much of the second in journalism in general, nor in sport, and especially in the Tour. This is a disappointment for me because there only remains the desperate search for the emotional story and the scoop. That's the general trend – a soundbite, a killing fact, polemical journalism.

THE TOUR AS INDICATOR OF CHANGING WAYS OF REPORTING INFORMATION

– *Is that valid for just the specialized press, or...*
– For all reporting, all reporting – in the Tour, the trend occurs probably tenfold because we have a population which lives together for 23 days [laughs] in the same way – and I'm just thinking about it now, as I'm talking to you – as the riders. The riders are all together for 23 days, watching each other, seeing who's going better than the others and wondering whether he's got a secret, is taking something, they talk about it and that's how rumours start. It's the same with the journalists. You wouldn't guess the number of false rumours that start in the Tour de France because someone launches a false piece of news that is taken up and exaggerated, although there's no truth to it at all. All that because we live in a bubble. That's just being human, and I don't criticize that, and maybe if I was still a journalist I might go in for it, but however you look at it, that all goes on at the cost of the seriousness of the analysis. What I'm expressing here is the viewpoint of an 'old-timer' – the older one is, the more one wants this kind of news and reflection, whereas when one is younger, what is wanted is facts and exclusives. In other words, there may be old-timers who work for old-timers and youngsters working for youngsters, I don't know [laughs]. [...]
– *Have there also been changes in the way journalists are hired?*
– I don't really know, because I'm a self-made man. I didn't go to a school of journalism, whereas nowadays, the young reporters are mostly the products of such institutions. [...] I'm an atypical example – I was speaking about cycling, having come from a cycling background, and obviously, you can't expect all cycling journalists to have done some cycling. But I do know some youngsters, good ones, who haven't done cycling, but who are good because they take an interest in it, they've worked hard at it and are intelligent. I remember that when I worked for the *Voix du Nord*, for my first job I was parachuted into being their boxing correspondent, and while I already liked boxing, one of the first things I did to gain credibility was to go and do a week's coaching course with boxing trainers, and boxers, learning about rules and training: I

even put on a pair of gloves [smiles]. Jacques Marchand[3] is very keen on that, and is right to be so – *training, training* [stress].

– You were talking about the ways in which written press coverage has changed, and mentioned, for instance, that there are more interviews. How did the press reporters of your days as a rider go about their work and how do they work today? You said that today they sit in front of the TV…

– But it's more difficult these days. I should think that until the 1960s it was easy, but as television coverage became more and more extensive and of better quality, the reporters in the other media had to find other things to say. Today it's difficult, because television shows everything, or almost everything. What more can press reporters give to their readers? Well, firstly, and I say it again, pertinent analysis and putting the race into perspective – and that is, for me, typically the responsibility of a good press journalist. Secondly, news, what people are saying, little interviews, profiles, summaries of careers, work which enriches and feeds the reports … and I've forgotten in this list to mention a good probing interview… We used to do a lot of that at *L'Equipe*. […]

– Isn't it harder also because – it can be seen in other sports – access to riders has become more difficult for press journalists? Maybe this is less true in the Tour?

– It's partly the case. […] It's both easy and difficult to have contact with the riders. Easy because unlike all other sports, where after the event the competitors go off and lock themselves in the changing rooms and there are relatively stereotypical and sanitized press conferences, in the Tour, if you're lucky, wily, brave, you have the opportunity to go and talk to the riders you want to see. Why? Because the finishing line is open, and journalists have the right – although there are rules on where and when – to be there. Firstly, there's a videoconference at the finish, so the hero of the day and the race leader are there – not everyone, obviously – but the journalists can ask questions and talk with them. These questions and answers are relayed to the main press room 300m or a kilometre away, from where journalists who have already started work on their copy can intervene and ask a question. It's two or three riders maximum, of course. Then on the finishing line the Breton reporter who wants to do a piece on the Breton rider can go and find him in his car for reactions on the day's stage. In my day – and this hardly ever happens now unfortunately – we would go off and do the hotels, since we had a book with the names of the hotels where the teams were lodged and we would go off in the car and see them. But that doesn't happen anymore for two reasons: firstly, there's less time to get copy off and secondly, it's not our fault, but the hotels are no longer in the town centres, but outside the town 10 or even 20 or 30km away, so it's complicated, even though there are always mobile phones [laughs]...

– *If you had to compare the relations between riders and journalists when you were a rider or reporter, how would you describe them – excepting the doping affairs that have arisen recently?*

– These relations don't seem to me to have deteriorated. All these nice people seem to me to be more hurried, and that's not something restricted to cycling and sport. Before, reporters used to take the time to talk to the riders, and riders used to talk to the reporters. It was simpler and more relaxed. Nowadays, there are more things to do, timetables are tighter and we're more hurried, I'd say that's the word.

– *And you as organizer?*

– The same [laughs].

– *For example, on a day-to-day level, what are the problems raised by the intense media coverage of the Tour?*

– I have to be very watchful, since it's in the interest of the organizers of the Tour that the media coverage of what goes on in the race is done, and well and quickly. We try to give the media information, because I'm a former journalist and have a fairly good idea of their needs, and also because it's my job as organizer. It's better to give information than to let rumours or untrue news spread. We have a system which is not the best possible, but almost: we produce on paper and on the internet a story of the race in French and English; we do interviews (what we call 'quotes') and give these to the journalists in the press room so that someone who has come in at 2pm and who is starting their report without having seen any of the TV pictures of the interview with the stage winner, they have at least three sentences from the winner that they can put in their piece if they need. We obviously also provide documentation on riders' careers and on the history of the Tour itself in paper form and on the Tour website.

– *And what are the forms of media which cover the Tour? We've mentioned television and the arrival of the Internet... How does the regional daily press cover the Tour nowadays?*

– There are three important things to say: firstly, the press-pack is now heavily internationalized, with 60 per cent from abroad and 40 per cent French; secondly, and this has been very recent, the internet media have arrived, and we've set up ground rules, but even with these rules it's becoming a bit invasive, because they need space in the press room and they need facilities. [...] Internet reporters are often young journalists with no experience, and during the course of the year I often see people coming out with false news items. So we then get false news on a website taken up by a press agency and passed on. And if the news is passed on by an agency, it's then in the public domain and gets into radio, TV and newspapers, which is something that sometimes scares me. The third important thing to say is that the regional newspapers are in retreat: whereas big regional papers such as *Ouest-France*, the *Voix du Nord*, the *Télégramme*, *Sud-Ouest* and the *Dauphiné* used to have two special correspondents – one doing the stage summary and the other doing the news around the stage – some nowadays have only one, or none at all. [...] Some papers still have two reporters, but that's rare now. [...] I'm not happy about that because the Tour de France is above all provincial in character, travelling to meet the regions in turn, and the fact that the regions aren't represented through their press seems to me to be a regrettable step backwards. All that's down to economic factors, of course.

– *About the race motorcycles, how do you choose them?*
– The number of motorcycles is restricted to 14, I think. We have a system which allows for 12 'institutional' motorcycles, one for each of the big press agencies, the big papers, *L'Equipe*, the *Agence France Presse*, one for each foreign country competing, and then two bikes, one put at the disposal of the newspaper of the region we're going through, and the other to be used by any journalist who wants it. In 1996 I realized that the journalists were disconnected from the field because they didn't go out on the road, but just went straight from the start to the finish.

– *Why?*
– I had been criticized in the *Figaro* because the race was running late every day, and the *Figaro* journalists were thinking all kinds of things such as that we had changed the timetable of racing to put back the finish to suit television. It was completely untrue, because we were riding into a headwind – we were leaving from Hertogenbosch in Luxembourg, moving westward into a west wind, every day we had the wind and rain and because of that we were going at two or three kph less than planned and were thus late. The *Figaro* reporters have the earliest deadlines and they were complaining about us, and I said to myself that the reason they didn't understand why we were running late was that

they were doing it all in their car, and didn't know if it was slippery – they couldn't smell the tar, they had lost contact with the roads... So the following year we gave them a couple of motorbikes to use if they wanted, as press reporters to be in touch with the public, the wind and the roads. And we still do so.

– *And are there a lot of takers?*

– I have to say that there's been mixed success. [...] Although it's marvellous to be able to do a stage of the Tour on a motorbike like it used to be done in the 1950s, I don't begrudge their not doing so because they're so rushed... On a motorbike, you have to get dressed up, and it rains, it's hot, it's not always most comfortable. [...] In the old days, you had to be a bit of a fighter and a bit of an adventurer, but now they're not like that at all, not enough in my view. [...]

– *Nowadays reporting is increasingly done sitting down.*

– Ensconced in comfortable surroundings, yes. People need the computer, archives, and all the rest. [...]

– *Because nowadays they can still follow the Tour from cars.*

– Yes, of course. [...] They have access to the race, so if there's a breakaway five minutes ahead they fit in between the break and the peloton. [...] They have Radio Tour in the cars and can even have television, so it seems to me that there's a kind of resignation rather than the willpower needed to go on the bike and the pressure of schedules. However, I've always tried to ensure that the finishes aren't too late and that we never go beyond 5.30pm. There are two reasons for that: firstly concerning the riders, they need rest and recuperation, massage and travel to their hotels; secondly, because of the journalists, their copy schedules and hotels being what they are, sometimes 60–80km away. If the stages finish too late, the reporters have less time to work, will work more quickly and less well. [...] I'm also aware – and here we're back to the 23 days spent together in a bubble – that journalists are human beings, and when they're together all day, get back to the hotel to find the restaurant closed, they're knackered, and get to bed late, and get up early the next day, they get bad-tempered. [...] It's important to take care of the journalists' working conditions.

– *How many journalists are there on the Tour this year, for example?*

– There are 1,000 of them, all media included, counting ones who come and go... The journalists from the Pyrenean regions for instance just do three stages – and there are written, radio, TV and press reporters among them. And they don't all work in the same place – our press rooms for the written press are designed for approximately 400 people. [...]

THE MEDIA COVERAGE OF DOPING

– *To conclude perhaps on these infamous doping scandals and the recent years, what is it that has most perturbed you... perhaps you could give me your conclusions, now that a bit of time has passed?*
– I prefer to talk about all that, indeed with a bit of distance. [...] I'll be very frank, I can, I could today accept relatively easily the suffering we went through in 1998 if we could be sure that it was something we had to go through to get to safety. My own personal suffering in that is of secondary importance, even if it was hard to bear, that's what I'm there for. The Tour de France suffered – it almost stopped, and if it had stopped, I'm not sure it would have got going again. Now, I can accept all that – I can accept the intrusion of the police because at that juncture there were no other effective ways of intervening – if at the end of the tunnel there is salvation.
– *What do you mean by salvation?*
– I won't say the disappearance of doping or its suppression, but its spectacular reduction, which is what I think has happened, although I can't be sure. In any case, 1998 was a painful, brutal but necessary wake-up call [...] because everyone rolled up their sleeves – sports authorities, government, scientists, laboratories – and in the space of two or three years we were able to identify the use of EPO. We've made considerable, *considerable* [stress] progress. But why oh why didn't our scientists wake up to this before? So, in short, today we can see the light at the end of the tunnel because all these efforts – of the sporting authorities, the UCI, the ministry for sport which has drawn up a good law in that it complements the sporting regulations by pursuing the pushers and providers – are beginning to bear fruit.
– *So not just pursuing the consumers of banned substances?*
– Not just the consumers, because the UCI only pursues those who take the drugs and who are subject to drug tests. So we have the help of the sports authorities, government and the collaboration of scientists. Nowadays they are getting together, and additionally we have the AMA (Agence Mondiale Antidopage) – when they first announced it I thought it was going to be another thing that would be useless. However, contrary to my fears, I think it is putting itself in place relatively rapidly and is

developing a worldwide anti-doping code which will complete both the regulations of sports federations and the law, and individual countries will have to subscribe to the code. [...] All that seems rather a good thing and I would say that we cyclists are perhaps ahead of other sports. But of course, drug-taking will always exist...

– *You've stated that view.*

– Obviously, I repeat it. I don't think that we will have any serious scandals in the coming Tour de France. I think that we are safe from a blitz on doping, like there was in the Tour of Italy last year. I think that the riders and their doctors are influenced by some good sense and a lot of fear. I say again: a bit of good sense and a lot of fear. Naturally, we're not going to let our efforts slacken: blood tests are accompanied by urine tests and compared with the long-term blood parameters of riders. [...] That's why I say that the net is closing in. There will be more EPO testing this year than last because the lab has more capacity. [...] And we're investing in research, supporting the CNRS (Centre national de recherche scientifique), supporting young cyclists to help prevent drug-taking in the future, we've drawn up a code of conduct which is worth what it's worth, but at least we're showing that we're keeping an eye on things. [...]

– *And what conclusions about the media do you draw from these 'affaires'?*

– People talk about 1998, because everything blew up in 1998... I was talking just before about the search for the sensational, the emotional, the scoop, the exaggeration, and in 1998 we saw all that; I experienced and suffered all that. [...] It's due, firstly to the trend or the evolution of the profession of reporting which we talked about before and also to the bubble in which we live in the Tour. Secondly, it's due, in my opinion, amongst a lot of journalists to disenchantment or a disappointment that they feel concerning the love they once had for cycling. They're like cuckolded husbands, and I know that for some of them the scars haven't yet healed. So I understand this second reason, at least, but the first, I understand it less.

– *You're talking about the specialist sports journalists?*

– Yes, the specialist journalists.

– *Because the general news reporters, they appeared on the Tour just at certain points.*

– But the specialist journalists were partnered in 1998, and even in the following years, by general news reporters who turned up attracted by the whiff of scandal, and all that created a confusion, exaggerations, a terrible malaise.

– *And then the sports journalists themselves were challenged over the issues.*
– They were criticized: 'You knew, but you didn't say anything'. [...] Yes, it's true they were criticized by outside journalists. The sports journalists felt doubly wounded, since they'd been deceived by the riders, the doctors, the team-managers and made to look stupid by other journalists specialized in everyday reporting. It's very difficult for them, very uncomfortable, and even more so for my friends at *L'Equipe*, since they are considered to be more or less attached to the Tour organization, which isn't the case.

– *What are the relations between the Tour and L'Equipe and how have they developed?*
– In 1998, the reporters of *L'Equipe* wanted to demonstrate that they were not wedded to the Tour organization.

– *Like the public-sector TV channel France 2 for example?*
– By being perhaps more royalist than the King, and saying, 'Hey look, our friends at *Libération* and *Le Monde* – we're criticizing as well. Don't think for a moment we're dependent on the Tour, look at our freedom to write what we want.' They wanted to reject any idea that they belonged to the Tour. Our relationship was a bit spoiled – mine at least since I'm part of the Tour organization – in 1998. But not on a personal level, I was just tired of seeing every day on the front page of *L'Equipe* photos about that problem, and nothing else. But then again, it's not certain that I'm right, maybe I'm a bit paranoid [smile]. It's very difficult. Everything now has gone back to normal. [...] That's my personal view, and in what I tell you, there's both objectivity and subjectivity.

NOTES

1. This interview, by Dominique Marchetti, is an edited version of two 75-minute conversations with Jean-Marie Leblanc on 12 and 13 June 2002, who has read and slightly amended the final text.
2. For a discussion of street demonstrations see P. Champagne, *Faire l'opinion. Le nouveau jeu politique* (Paris: Minuit, 1990), Ch. 4.
3. Former president of the Union syndicale des journalistes sportifs de France (Sports Journalists' Union). Was a journalist at *L'Equipe* and is a friend of Jean-Marie Leblanc.

The Tour de France and Cycling's Belle Epoque

PHILIPPE GABORIAU

The year 1903 is an important date in the history of French sport. The year of the birth of the cycle Tour de France, 1903 must above all be thought of as a time of rupture. The year 1903 marks, in effect, the end – within the confines of France – of an era. The golden age of the bicycle came to a close and the practice of the velocipede, spearhead of upper-class values at the end of the nineteenth century, was losing its fashionableness amongst the moneyed classes, who were now dreaming more of engines, cars and planes. But the creation of the Tour de France was also a sign of a new beginning. The falling price of bicycles was allowing them to be bought by other classes, and the sporting press, bicycle manufacturers and cycle races were giving more and more coverage to cycling activities.

Let us immerse ourselves in the mindset of these initial moments of the Tour. The Tour de France was born just as the great car races on public roads (the grand Paris–Madrid of May 1903) were being banned by the French state. Let us consider the Parisian and bourgeois context of the Belle Epoque in France. The Tour de France was one of those extraordinary events of the start of the twentieth century that produced such admiration and astonishment. Lifestyles were being transformed by the burgeoning of industrialisation, the metamorphoses of means of locomotion, the death throes of aristocratic and rural civilization based around the horse, and the growth of patriotism. As Emile Gauthier wrote in *L'Almanach des sports 1903*: 'Civilization is developing and becoming more refined every day, with bewildering speed. Modern Man is freeing himself from the constraints of the natural world, now domesticated and mastered ... Miracles are to be expected, and what our forefathers would have thought of as utopian dreams, hallucinations or madness is gradually becoming everyday reality.'[1]

Let us try to understand, for example, why the professional racing cyclist Maurice Garin – future winner of the first Tour de France in July 1903 – found himself holding the handlebars of a motorcycle at the start of the Paris–Madrid race car and motorcycle race on 24 May of the same year.

1903 – THE DRAMATIC END OF A GOLDEN AGE

We should start by exploding a myth. The media event of 1903 was *not* the Tour de France cycle race. The great sports contest which was attracting the passionate interest of the public and newspapers was the Paris–Madrid car race organized by the Automobile-Club de France. But the competition was to end in the evening of 24 May, at the finish of its first stage, in drama, blood and death (eight fatalities and more than 20 injured).

With the banning of this event, a grandiose era drew to a close, that in which the bicycle and the car were associated with science and industry in a joint sporting adventure at the forefront of modernism. Velocipede values – as they were called at the time – were then similar to car values. Cycle races (on roads and in velodromes) had an influence on early car races, and inventions aiming to improve velocipedes helped thinking on the new means of mechanical locomotion.[2]

Between the first Bordeaux–Paris cycle race of 1891 and the Paris–Madrid car race of 1903, a whole series of road races can be considered as a single category of competitions linking sports, newspapers and industries to values of endurance, record-breaking and mechanical modernity:

May 1891.   The first Bordeaux–Paris (550km) paced annual cycle race (singles, tandems, triples). From 1897, cars and motorcycles used in pacing.[3]

Sept. 1891.   The first Paris-Brest-Paris (1200km) paced cycle race. A man on a velocipede can 'transcend human strength'. The press – Pierre Giffard's *Le Petit Journal* – presented a sporting event advertizing various cycles, frames, chains and tyres. Cycle races at this time involved pacers, considered necessary to increase speeds, and an aspect of as much interest as the order in which competitors crossed the finishing line.

1894.	The first car race, Paris–Rouen, organized by *Le Petit Journal*.
1895.	The inaugural Paris–Bordeaux-Paris car race.
1896.	The inaugural Paris–Roubaix cycle race (an annual paced race, like Bordeaux–Paris).
1898.	The Paris–Amsterdam car stage-race.
1899.	The Tour de France car race. 2,350km in seven stages. (Winning average speed of 51.3kph.)
1901.	The Paris–Berlin car stage-race.
1902.	The Paris–Vienna car stage-race.
1903.	The Paris–Madrid car stage-race.[4]

So here we are in May 1903 at the start of Paris–Madrid. 'The great sporting and industrial event', 'colossal international trek' grips the crowds and the media. *Le Petit Journal* (18 May 1903, 4) writes: 'There will there be present cars which no-one would have imagined possible a few years ago; cars of 110 or 90 horsepower, real war machines in construction and appearance. The speeds that will be reached with these devices promise to be truly fantastic.' And the newspaper *Le Vélo* (24 May 1903, 1) writes,

> After Amsterdam, after Berlin, it is the turn of Madrid to be the target of the huge annual event, now accepted into European values. Every capital of the Old World covets this honour, and with the progress made by the automobile, it is to be hoped that each will have its day … Every annual car race is a successful demonstration of 'the Idea', which, in this way, in the wake of a succession of triumphal races is spreading to the cardinal points of civilization.

The competitors in the Paris–Madrid race were, according to the newspapers, 'almost all famous in the world of sport; many are celebrities of new industry. Former cycling champions and mere mechanics raised to the rank of drivers because of their skills rub shoulders in the out-of-the-ordinary list of entrants with well-known aristocratic figures and even millionaires'. More than 300 vehicles were entered. Old velodrome stars were numerous amongst the drivers, such as the Farman brothers (winners of the Paris–Vienna car race), Fournier (winner of the Paris–Berlin car race), Charron, Terront and so on. Many still active racing cyclists were also entered and were racing motorcycles, such as number 159 Rivierre, number 309 Garin (future winner of the Tour de France the following month), number 178 Lesna (winner of the Paris–Roubaix cycle race, but who was to be permanently disabled after Paris–Madrid). The motorcycles were ridden by cycle racers because in this era it was necessary to pedal when going uphill in order to go faster.

All the newspapers described the 'extraordinary' enthusiasm around the start of this 1903 Paris–Madrid. More than 200,000 Parisians spent a sleepless night at Versailles 'in an indescribable hubbub' waiting for daybreak and the first departure (vehicles started at one-minute intervals from dawn on 24 May). The hold of the race was enormous, 'so great is the fascination of the crowd for the miracle of speed and bravery produced by this so modern of couplings: fearful mechanical science and human will' (*Le Gil Blas*, 25 May 1903, 1). The newspaper *Le Matin* wrote that, 'The start of the incredible race of 1903 was something extraordinary, unheard of, gigantic. There is no term strong enough to describe this human torrent' (25 May 1903, 2). Many cyclists – seen as the 'ferments of the sport' – came from Paris to attend the start of the race at about 3 am.

> And for hours which passed quickly, so great was the animation, there was a continuous stream between Versailles and Saint-Cyr of bicycles and cars, of multicoloured lamps and dazzling lanterns. Through the clouds of dust thrown up by the tyres, it was like a fantastic army of huge shiny, noisy insects marching or rather racing towards a happy victory, or the emigration of a people of Chinese shadows carried by their enthusiasm towards a promised land … One felt, towards the end, a kind of constant daze, and it became impossible to keep one's eyes on this endless, fiery, smoky, dusty, constantly twisting and ever renewing cortege. (*Le Parisien*, 25 May 1903, 2)

Géo Lefèvre wrote in the newspaper *L'Auto*,

> Nocturnal visions of a crowd which swells, throngs and crushes, of a torrent rushing from Paris to Versailles, carrying everything with it and throwing far out into the countryside visions of break-of-dawn rising blue-grey over a human sea made of eddies and whirlpools from which there rose towards the horizon a huge clamour, visions of pulsating monsters, huge and docile, moving under the control of masked men who hold them still until the

starting signal ... All that still plays before my eyes and will do so for a long time, in a chaotic, infernal and profoundly moving set of images. (25 May 1903, 1)

Two hundred and twenty one competitors depart at one-minute intervals. Henri Desgrange wrote:

> But pale dawn is showing on the horizon: the silhouettes of squat monsters stand out clearly in the confusion of the ending night. Above the eager engine, the man is there, masked like a great bird of prey. The seconds count down. Go! And with a prodigious explosion of power the car literally takes flight. Another takes its place. In a few hours, Versailles will be empty again. And all along the road, the crowds will be saluting the great victory passing by, that of the French automobile industry. (*L'Auto*, 25 May 1903, 1)

Maurice Garin on his moped started at 6.44 am. Two million spectators, so the newspapers estimate, lined the roads from Versailles to Bordeaux. The whole of Bordeaux – in other words 200,000 inhabitants – attended 'the arrival of this sensational race' (Maurice Martin, *La Petite Gironde*, 25 May 1903, 2). The spectators are often foolhardy, 'endlessly invading the road and giving the racers the impression of plunging through the crowd' (noted Georges Prade in *L'Auto*, 25 May 1903, 1). 'A veritable human hedge bordered the road, and this continually moving hedge ceaselessly wavered and seemed to want to close in front of us' (wrote the driver Maurice Farman, in *Le Petit Parisien* of 26 May 1903, 2).

And this fantastic race towards progress (the high point of these hopes) end in drama and chaos. Accidents – terrible ones – became more and more numerous. Marcel Renault's car hit a tree: one dead, one injured; the car of Loraine-Barrow ran over a dog and crashed into a tree: one dead, one injured; a level-crossing: one dead, one injured; a woman was killed crossing the road; a car caught fire: the driver died burned alive, one injured; a car ploughed into the crowd: two dead, one injured, and so on. The high speeds and the naive crowd lining the roads caused numerous accidents and the race was banned. The press covers the events as headline news for three days: 'Latest: Race Banned'... 'This Bloody Race' headlines *Le Matin* (25 May 1903, 1). Foremost accused was 'the folly of speed', which in this Paris–Madrid race seems to have reached its frenzied climax. It was a disaster. 'A pitiful spectacle: cars overturned, broken, shattered, in pieces; lifeless bodies of men killed instantly, of unconscious or moaning wounded lying on the ground in pools of blood and amongst shapeless debris surrounded by panicking groups of shocked helpers who have run to their aid', reported *L'Illustration* (30 May 1903, 371). 'It has to be concluded that despite the good intentions, foresight and hard work of the organizers, it is materially impossible to rid the route of dangers, and in these conditions, road races cannot be permitted, especially at speeds such as those reached between Paris and Bordeaux' (*Le Petit Journal*, 27 May 1903, 1). 'These races of thoughtless speed prove nothing' (*Le Journal*, 26 May 1903, 1). 'The madness of speed has brought too many victims, even in the eyes of car-racing fans' (*Le Journal*, 25 May 1903, 1).

It was the end of an era. 'Like awful monsters, the cars, like a whirlwind, appeared in the distance, and then, like lightning, passed by and disappeared into the dust! The drivers were pressed back in their seats, almost lying on their backs, in order to lessen air resistance, and were scarcely visible. They seemed merged with their cars' (*La Petite Gironde*, 27 May 1903, 2).

1903–1904, THE POPULAR AND CHAOTIC BEGINNINGS OF THE TOUR DE FRANCE CYCLE RACE

It is in this social context, one month after the grandiose and catastrophic competition of the Paris–Madrid car and motorcycle race that the Tour de France makes its debut (it was initially planned to run from 31 May to 5 July, but was postponed at the last minute). The start of the first stage of the Tour de France was much more modest than that of Paris–Madrid. The race started in the Paris suburbs near a simple hostelry named 'Le Réveil-Matin' in the vicinity of Villeneuve-Saint-Georges. Six long stages linked the major French towns of Paris, Lyon, Marseille, Toulouse, Bordeaux, Nantes and Paris again in a journey of more than 2,400km. The shortest stage was 270km between Toulouse and Bordeaux, and the longest, between Nantes and Paris, 470km. The competition took place between 1 and 19 July, and several rest days were planned between each stage.

Surprisingly – maybe to close an era, or perhaps to rekindle a quarrel – it was with a reference to Emile Zola (a writer committed to political values which he did not share – the famous *J'accuse* of the Dreyfus

Affair)[5] that Henri Desgrange, editor-in-chief of *L'Auto*, started his editorial of 1 July:

> With the wide and powerful gesture that Zola lends to his ploughman in *La Terre*, *L'Auto*, a journal of ideas and action, is about to send out over France those tough and uncomplicated sowers of strength, the great professional roadsters. [...] This type of competition, more than all the great velodrome races, catches the public's imagination, since it speaks directly to them. It is on his roads, surrounded by his fields, in front of his cottages, that the peasant is to see the Tour de France competitors battling it out. The little local newspapers will tell him which of these men won, and he will never forget him, because he will have seen him. (*L'Auto*, 1 July 1903, 1)

Like all the road car- and cycle-races of this period, the infant Tour de France was linked to the sporting press (it was the newspaper *L'Auto* which organized the competition) and the sports sector, put in place by the cycle manufacturers (a sector made up of professional riders: Maurice Garin – nicknamed 'the Little Chimney-Sweep' – rode a La Française bike). But the Tour de France differed from the other bicycle races in two essential respects. Firstly, in a major innovation, it was run without pace-riders – the riders competed alone, against nature and themselves in a solo competition. The era of speed records to be broken (through being paced by powered machines) had gone, and time had now only a secondary importance. What was important was the order of the classification of riders, the comparisons between individual competitors, and their physical and moral qualities. Secondly, the Tour de France was a stage race. In this, it copied car road races, which were also organized in stages that fragmented the competition and the reporting of the journalists. As *L'Auto* notes: 'The principle of a battle on equal terms, without pace-riders or soigneurs, last year enabled astonished watching publics to see a blacksmith like Dargassies, a little butcher's boy like Pothier, an unknown Belgian like Samson or a barkeeper like Brange, keep up with kings of the road such as Garin, Aucouturier and Muller' (1 July 1904, 1).

The director of the organizing newspaper *L'Auto* was a charismatic and ambitious young man aged 38. He was flanked by competent collaborators, such as the youthful Géo Lefèvre and Victor Goddet. Desgrange was attempting to distance himself from the (then) iconic

Pierre Giffard, the famous reporter for *Le Petit Journal* and subsequently from 1894, editor-in-chief of the daily sports paper *Le Vélo*. Pierre Giffard's slogan was 'The velocipede is more than a sport; it is a benefit to society'.[6]

In 1900, a new daily sports paper – *L'Auto-Vélo* – was founded, which relied on the political and financial support of the two rapidly growing sectors, the automobile and the bicycle industries. The objective of *L'Auto-Vélo* was to compete with and overtake the newspaper *Le Vélo* (or even put it out of business). Henri Desgrange was appointed director of *L'Auto-Vélo*. He was a former solicitor's clerk with an enthusiasm for cycling, as a former racing-champion of the 1890s, and the first French unpaced hour record-holder. He had written a book on cycling in 1894 entitled *La Tête et les jambes* (*Head and Legs*), in which he wrote, 'The sport of cycling demands of someone who wants to indulge in it two kinds of quite different qualities, which are complementary: head and legs. No-one can become a complete rider unless they possess both these qualities in equal measure.' The creation of the Tour de France was to allow *L'Auto* (newly-named after an unsuccessful court case) to decisively overtake *Le Vélo* in 1904.

The nascent Tour de France represented a new kind of sporting competition focusing on the democratization and popularization of sporting values. The Tour moved away from the old model of contests focused on (technical and social) progress and speed records. Even *L'Auto*'s competing newspapers noted the difference:

> The Tour de France race organized by our colleague *L'Auto* has revolutionized – we can use the term – the whole sporting world, and now that this great competition has finished, it is impossible even for those who are not interested in sport not to admire the heroes of this great sporting tour who have achieved prodigious feats. [...] For nineteen days, these cycling heroes have travelled through most of France, visiting one after the other Lyon, Marseille, Toulouse, Bordeaux, Nantes, crossing regions of all kinds and struggling against wind, rain and heat. Everywhere, thanks to their courage, they have astonished those who lined the roads to applaud these giants, these athletes of exceptional quality who have just finished the most beautiful sporting rally ['raid'] imaginable. (*Le Journal*, 21 July 1903, 6)

The first Tour de France met unarguably with popular success. A free spectacle passing by people's homes, it went out to the small towns and villages of France. The editor-in-chief of *La Petite Gironde*, Maurice Martin, reporting on the stage from Toulouse to Bordeaux in a car too slow to keep pace with the leading group of riders, notes that, 'In each village, there are feast-day crowds. No, cycling is not dead' (*La Petite Gironde*, 13 July 1903, 2).[7]

Hooliganism and the Fragility of the Race

But the race was still fragile, and everything could have ended in 1904. The spreading of sporting ideas to the masses was difficult. 'Popular passion' caused problems and the safety of competitors was 'threatened by hooligans'. Each town wished to support the local champion, and the riders themselves, too used to pedalling behind pacers, had a tendency to cheat. The first four riders to finish the second Tour de France in 1904 were subsequently disqualified by the sport's new governing body, l'Union Vélocipédique de France.

It is thus with bitterness that Henri Desgrange wrote in *L'Auto* on 25 July 1904:

> The Tour de France has ended, and I fear very much that its second staging will have been its last. It will have died from its success, from the blind passions that it has provoked and from the insults and the unhealthy suspicions of the ignorant and the evil that it has attracted. And yet, it seemed to us and it still seems to us that with this great contest we had built the most long-lasting and important monument of cycle sport. We had the hope that every year we would be able – across most of France – to spread a bit of sporting good. The initial results of last year showed us that we were right to think this way, but here we are now at the end of the second Tour, sickened and discouraged to have lived through three weeks of the worst calumnies and insults. (*L'Auto*, 25 July 1904, 1)

The incidents at Saint-Etienne were described, for example, as an act of complete savagery, a veritable assassination attempt made in the col de la République. According to the riders' own statements, it was 3 am and the night was dark, and, 'Suddenly, towards the summit of the climb, Faure accelerates briskly and takes a lead of two or three lengths. We look up and notice about 50m in front a group of about 100 people making a tunnel on either side of the road. They're armed with cudgels and stones. Faure bravely went forwards and passed through, and then the cudgels came down on those following.' Several riders were injured, some seriously, and faced with repeated violent incidents, the much worried competitors 'promise to ride equipped with revolvers' (*L'Auto*, 13 July 1904, 1). Desgrange himself recounts:

> The drama lasted a few seconds. I remember only the sight of a pile of bikes on the ground, of Maurice Garin getting to his feet with a few other riders. I didn't even see poor Gerbi fall. There was a second as the following cars came to a halt, then I saw a horde of savages with long sticks in their hands starting to flee through the fields. One of them – with a haggard face – pointed at Faure and shouted at us, 'See the number 58 Faure of Saint-Etienne – that's who we want to see in the lead'. In the time it took to get up to the riders – now quite a way ahead – we heard a real volley of shots and then the headlong flight of all the criminals across the fields. (*L'Auto*, 14 July 1904, 1)

The cars following the race defended themselves with revolvers, and Desgrange reports that, 'The attack in Saint-Etienne unfortunately proved only too clearly that our sport of cycling finds itself at a real turning point in its history, where its very success can be the cause of its downfall and where the enthusiasm that it arouses can become the cause of the worst outrages' (*L'Auto*, 14 July 1904, 1). 'These stupid and criminal louts thought they could protest by knocking riders senseless' (*L'Auto*, 15 July 1904, 1). Such excesses of violence can be compared with today's football hooligans. Aggression seemed necessary to support the club or local champion against adversaries from elsewhere. The groups of hooligans (called 'apaches' in 1903) were made up of youths (young men rather than women) from the lowest strata of the working classes. They expressed a violent and delinquent sub-culture of aggressive masculinity.[8]

Jacques Miral, who wrote the year's report on cycling in the *Almanach des Sports 1905*, noted that 'cycling seems in 1904 to have turned towards a new model',[9] and suggested that after the sanctions imposed by the Union Vélocipédique de France in disqualifying the first four riders of the 1904 Tour, 'next year we may have honest riders'. According to Miral: 'The major road races have become almost anything except sports events'; 'Some less honest riders [...] not content with tucking in behind cars, don't hesitate to get themselves a lift for kilometres and then get out ten kilometres before a control-point where they sign in fresh and relaxed. [...] They cap their chances of success by strewing kilos of nails behind them for following racers to fall victim to.'

Yes, indeed, the years 1903 and 1904 were the end of a cycling era. Was the Tour de France, like the Paris–Madrid race, heading for an early demise?

FROM 1905 TO 1914:

THE PATRIOTIC REBIRTH OF THE TOUR DE FRANCE

From July 1905 and every July until the First World War the original Tour de France was to go from strength to strength as every summer came round. The cycling competition, which moreover increasingly took the form of a great loop, still began and ended in Paris. It visited the towns at the frontiers of French national territory (including Metz from 1906–10, a town located in German-occupied Alsace-Lorraine) and took in the mountain-pass frontiers of the Alpine and Pyrenean mountain ranges. The stages were more numerous (11 in 1905, 13 in 1906, 14 in 1907, 1908 and 1909, and 15 in 1910–14). The 1913 Tour de France, for example, covered 5,388km in 15 stages (the shortest was 325km and the longest 470km) between 29 June and 27 July, allowing the competitors, after leaving Paris, to confront Normandy, Brittany, Aquitaine, the Pyrenees and their passes, Languedoc, Provence, the Alps and their passes, Lorraine, the Northern region and its cobblestones before its return to Paris.

And Marcel Viollette was able to write in 1912:

> Few races are as popular as the Tour de France. There is no other race which produces such support. Think of the regions that it passes through, some of which never see any other sporting event from one year to the next! [...] You have to have followed the race to properly understand the crowd that masses around the checkpoints or the joyful surprise of the good peasants as they see the bunch of good-humoured young men riding through the streets of their village at 35kph whilst still finding the time for a joke or a kiss blown to a pretty girl. And pretty girls aren't in short supply along the route![10]

In these patriotic pre-war years, the riders were often described as the soldiers of sport. 'Elite troops' or 'sacred battalion', the riders of the Tour de France can give 'a useful lesson in energy' to French youth.

As Victor Breyer noted in *L'Auto* in 1906:

> The huge sporting epic whose last act was concluded yesterday brings back school day memories. It reminds me of those formidable pitched battles whose thunderous clashes fill the pages of our history books and where entire regiments would disappear in the blaze of combat. The tales told by the few remaining survivors perpetuate the legend of these awful confrontations. For all that – thank God – it took place on a more peaceful ground, the long battle which we have just witnessed has also produced victims, who, happily, will feel much better after two or three good nights' rest. Of the impressive rolling squadron of 77 combatants who lined up in the dawn of 4 July, only 14 returned safely home after completing the most terrible athletic task ever asked of men. The others fell by the wayside, beaten by fatigue, floored by the immensity of a never-ending effort. Every kilometre-marker of our French roads has seen the fall of those at the back of the bunch, like those left behind by routed armies. And it's truly a proud selection of old soldiers of the pedal, of tried and tested roadmen that Paris honoured yesterday as it fêtes its heroes, in other words, in a way that makes them forget in an instant all the bitter hours of their ordeal ['calvaire']. (*L'Auto*, 30 July 1906, 1)

Seven years later another commentator reported: 'Our 32 old soldiers don't have a single ounce of fat left to lose. They have the burned faces of soldiers who have fought in all climates, but they also have pride, and also no little good humour' (R. Desmarets, *L'Auto*, 15 July 1913, 3).

Desgrange and the Creation of Obstacles to be Overcome

Each year, the organizers increased the level of difficulties to be overcome. They sought to push back the limits of the impossible and every year imposed more and more draconian rules. One major innovation introduced by Henri Desgrange was the mountain stages. In 1905 the riders climb the Ballon d'Alsace, in 1910 the Pyrenean passes (the Tourmalet, Aubisque and Aspin cols, nicknamed 'the circle of death'), in 1911 the Alpine passes (Galibier and Allos). The difficulties sought out by the organizers highlighted new terrains (the mountains), regions difficult to reach, empty lands far from towns and spectators and frontier areas perceived by reporters as 'divine and pitiless backdrops'.

Lucien Petit-Breton, winner of the race in 1907 and 1908, remarked that, 'What is special in the Tour de France is that every year, its difficulties are increased and that every year, the riders find themselves equal to the new tasks demanded of them. It's not that the men of three or five years ago were inferior to those of today, but the merit of riders of today is that they know how to profit from the lessons provided by their forerunners.'[11]

The Luchon-Bayonne stage became the great Pyrenean stage of the 1910, 1911 and 1912 Tours. Run in the other direction in 1913, from Bayonne to Luchon (with the major Pyrenean cols at its end), this stage became the judge and jury of the Tour de France until 1929.

As *L'Auto* of 20 July 1910 reports: 'Tomorrow night, the riders of the Tour de France will set off with the mission of accomplishing the most fantastic raid ever organized. From Bagnères-de-Luchon they will have to reach Bayonne via the cols of Peyresourde, Aspin, the Tourmalet, Soulon, Tortes and the Aubisque. It's an awful task that we are asking them to undertake.' 326km on mountain roads with six cols of nearly 2,000m in altitude lie in wait for the competitors.

> Tomorrow, in the tenth stage of the Tour de France [...] road champions, riding fragile bicycles, will provide the whole world with the most beautiful demonstration of valour that can be imagined. Let us follow this Homeric battle closely. Let us show compassion in advance for those who will not be able to overcome this awesome test. Let us prepare to acclaim its winners. The Tour de France has arrived at the most dramatic of its phases, the monstrous stage that all sportsmen await with impatience and which will give rise to universal enthusiasm. Pygmies against giants. I have an idea that the pygmies will astonish the world. (*L'Auto*, 20 July 1910, p.3)

Henri Desgrange was the organizer, 'the boss of the Tour'. He was also the director of the newspaper that had the near-monopoly of information on the race. As the founding father of the competition, he was an antithetical character, both organizer and reporter, contradictory positions which made him simultaneously merciless, kind and admiring.

In order to be read, understood and heard, and to celebrate with enthusiasm the exploits of cycling and of the riders, Desgrange and his collaborators (who followed the Tour in cars) recapitulated each day's stage in a lyrical, florid, extravagant, exaggerated style, where the dominant mode was the superlative. Everything tended towards the embellished, the excessive and the spontaneous. The writer, the speaker was at one with the reader. He admired just as much as the other did. In the tone of the writing, a new kind of communication took shape: the live report. Nature becomes personified, cols become giants who are challenged and monsters who are defeated by mythical heroes ('our men'). In grandiloquent narratives, mountains become – for the imaginative reader – a communicative relay between Heaven and Earth, between the Inaccessible and the Real:

> As it seemed to us that we had been climbing this giant for hours, we asked some peasants at the doors of their cottages nested in hollows between rocks, 'Is the top close?' and they answered, 'Less than 12km to go'. And in the countless bends of the road, we made out below us – far below us – and above us – far above – moving ant-like figures: our men working to eat away at the giant with each turn of their pedals. Finally, the summit came into view, just as the snows began to surround us on all sides. One final act of defiance from Nature in the form of some Edelweiss; some heliotropes were held out for us by adorable Savoyard urchins, and then the snow held everything in its silent shroud. Our road scarcely pierced its way through two walls of snow, scorched and potholed from below. Up there, it is bitterly cold, and when Georget goes past after being the first to stamp his victorious foot on the head of the giant, when he passes close to us, dirty, his moustache full of mucus and food from the last checkpoint, his jersey stained with the rubbish of the last stream in which, burning with heat, he has wallowed, he hails us – filthy but in awe: 'It takes your breath away!' (Henri Desgrange, *L'Auto*, 11 July 1911, p.1, after the Alpine Galibier stage)

Racing cyclists were often perceived as hard-working and admirable workers. The contest enabled their new machines to be in the public eye, as machines which shatter distance, machines of play linked to speed. The bicycle fascinated the working classes. Its price was still high, often out of reach for mere workers, but the bicycle was, soon, it was hoped, to become a useful means of locomotion, able to bring white or blue-collar urban workers closer to the countryside and to link peasants or agricultural workers with the city. Indeed, the bicycle would soon offer new horizons to the Sundays and paid holidays of working people.[12]

In order to overcome the difficulties of the Tour de France, the competitors had to demonstrate their expertise and the reliability of their machines. The spectating public saw Tour de France riders as professionals and men who refused to give up when faced with the worst problems, capable of extricating themselves, alone, from the worst predicaments: 'Hoping and fighting to the very last is a duty'.[13] The epic image of the 'forçats de la route' (forced labourers of the road) was beginning to take shape.

The bravery of racing cyclists became legendary. The ill-fortunes of the French rider Eugène Christophe, nicknamed 'the old Gaulois', in particular gave people something to talk about. In 1925, the old race-follower Alphonse Baugé remembered thus:

> In July 1913, after having broken his bike at the top of the Tourmalet, Christophe, carrying the bike on his shoulder and wearing light racing shoes, had to come down the 14km from the giant Pyrenean col to Sainte-Marie-de-Campan in order to repair his now useless bike. Once this harsh ordeal was accomplished, without so much as a minute of rest, he set himself to the forge of this little hamlet at the foot of the mountain and worked for three hours, unaided – as required by the pitiless Race Rules – and without pausing, to repair his bike. He bore the atrocious heat of the forge's brazier, added to the African temperature of mid-summer. This improvised repair completed at the cost of extraordinary labours, Christophe bestrode his bike again and in shadows rendering the night menacing, beneath an oblivious blue sky studded high with shining stars, he climbs the cols of Aspin and Peyresourde, arriving in Luchon at midnight, having demonstrated that human will can vanquish all obstacles and that nothing in the world is more deserving of admiration than a man who can triumph over misfortune with courage.[14]

Professionals and Amateurs, the Stuff of Legend

At this time, competitors in the Tour de France were classed in two categories: professionals and amateurs. The professionals – whose objective was overall victory – were grouped in teams (of bicycle makes) and benefited from technical support. The amateurs approached their participation in the Tour as an adventure and aimed above all to complete the event – having done the Tour gave a man status. The amateurs were themselves divided into two categories: on the one hand a few moneyed dilettantes, and on the other many enthusiasts with great technical ability.

The best riders were professional cyclists, fitted out with equipment by the bicycle firms for whom they raced all year long. Like all competitors in the Tour, they took part as individuals and repaired their bikes alone. Soigneurs and managers were only present at the checkpoints and in the stage-towns. The great majority of these professional riders came from a working-class background, like Maurice Garin, the first winner (a former chimney-sweep), Trousselier, the winner in 1905 (former florist), Pottier, winner in 1906 (former apprentice butcher), Petit-Breton, winner in 1907 and 1908 (former bellboy), Faber, winner in 1909 (former docker), Lapize, winner in 1910 (former office clerk), Garrigou, winner in 1911 (former fruiterer from Pantin). The other riders were what were called *isolés* ('independents'). These competitors were either fanatical enthusiasts of cycling who paid for their own equipment – the last few remnants of the bourgeois fans of the velocipede, who were to fade away after the First World War – or mechanics, masons, peasants, 'king' cyclists of villages, cantons or departments who were able to come to Paris to start the Tour because of a benefit organized for them at home. Such 'independent' riders made up the vast mass of the Tour de France (in 1910, for example, 110 out of 136 riders were 'independents').

Let us re-invent, for example, the ambience of the 1907 Tour de France. Alphonse Baugé, as the young manager of the 'Labor' team, wrote a letter every evening after the completion of the day's stage to his director in Paris. These letters provide us with first-hand documentation.[15]

Baugé organized the daily details of his professional riders' lives, whom he managed masterfully. Feeding and assistance was provided at the checkpoints and rest and massage laid on each evening in the stage-towns. As the stages went by, the team was reduced to a few individuals (only two Labor riders would eventually reach Paris). 'I quickly made them realize that they were not competing in the Tour de France as tourists, but as racers, in other words not as people out for a gentle run, but as men at work.' The Labor riders had to keep to their hotels (they read papers and their mail, or sent postcards) and avoid going out into the towns after each stage (after stages, riders had at least one rest day).

The leader of the Labor brand team, François Faber, was not allowed to go and drink a glass of wine on a café terrace: 'He is rather upset that I should formally ban him from drinking both Saint-Emilion '72 and 1907 plonk, since according to him "There's nothing like a nice drop of red to set a man up again".'[16]

The manager of the Labor team allows us to make the acquaintance of an extreme case, the eccentric and dilettante 'véloceman' ('speedster') Pépin de Gontaud:

> Roubaix, 9 July 1907 ... The aristocrat Pépin de Gontaud [...] is taking part in the Tour as a true 'tourist', but like every self-respecting millionaire, M. Pépin de Gontaud dislikes travelling alone, even on a bicycle. It is thus that – in exchange for some financial incentives *à prix d'or* – he has procured the services of the happy colossus Dargassies and the loyal Gauban, who must not abandon him for even a second. Dargassies calls this doing a pottering Tour, and Gauban, whose southern blood boils in his veins, sometimes wishes that Monsieur Pépin would allow him to run off with the lead bunch. But their boss will have none of that. Monsieur Pépin is taking part in the Tour 'to do some sport' as a bourgeois, or – I would even say – as a *grand seigneur*, and since he pays richly he formally prohibits his assistants from any attempt to drop or jump him.

Right from the start of each stage, Pépin's little group is behind the peloton: 'Lyon, 14 July 1907. [...] As a laugh, you can't beat it. Those riders find life pleasant and the Tour de France a charming dander. Stops in hotels at lunch- and dinner-time. The full works, from the Pernod aperitifs to the sugar in the coffee! (...) copious meals, heady wines, singsongs over dessert... for the watching locals such is the programme of this "modern-style" quartet from Toulouse.' (A quartet, because in mid-race the rider Teycheime from Toulouse also entered the service of Pépin de Gontaud.)

Alphonse Baugé note especially the bravery and misery of the independent riders, particularly the Breton racer Le Bars, whom he occasionally helped out. Day after day and stage after stage, he bears witness:

> Roubaix, 9 July 1907 ... The obstinate Le Bars arrived here yesterday evening on a borrowed machine, after having broken the front wheel of his own in a fall four kilometres from the start of the

stage. The unlucky Breton came to see me at the hotel this morning to tell me his troubles, and I did everything I could to make him understand that in such conditions it was not in his interest to continue […] I met with wild obstinacy. So, making use of the withdrawal of Faure, I agreed to lend him his machine. As the ultimate justification, listen to what Le Bars told me: 'The Tour de France is going through Morlaix, and I have to be there. If I'm not, the people there will think I'm just a phoney.' You couldn't make it up.

Toulouse, 23 July 1907 … Like the Golden Calf, Le Bars is still standing. He is visibly wasting away and comes in every day harassed with exhaustion. On his waxy face all you can see are two huge eyes from which dart shafts of lightning, just as if this infernal Breton had a storm going on inside his skull. 'So, Le Bars,' I asked him, 'Morlaix's not far now, just another 1,000 km or so?' 'That's right, sir' he replied, 'it's getting closer, and there aren't too many climbs left. From now on, it's all downhill.' The Breton is both unbreakable and priceless.

Nantes, 29 July 1907 … Le Bars is still standing. Tomorrow, he feels, always brings a ray of sunshine and a ray of hope. He is literally a walking skeleton, who is painful to look at sometimes. His performance proves once again that the long-distance cycle race as a sport is all about willpower.

Brest, 31 July 1907 … Le Bars is besides himself. It's tomorrow that we go through Morlaix. He came to the hotel to ask for a brand new Labor jersey and I gave in to his wishes. He put it on immediately, and I can still see him standing up to admire himself in the mirror. You could read the joy on his face. He was standing as straight as a guardsman.

Caen, 2 August 1907 … Le Bars has turned out to be unreal! He passed through Morlaix, but do you know how? Two minutes down on the leading group! When I think of the energy he must have spent to keep himself in such a good placing, frankly, my mind boggles. His fellow countrymen gave him a cheer you can't imagine, and alongside the road, luminous banners inscribed with 'Vive Le Bars' shone out into the dark night. At the checkpoint, the crowd shouted with joy while clapping. For Le Bars, it was the deserved reward for dogged work and quietly-borne suffering.

AROUND THE BATTLEMENTS OF FRANCE

In the heartland of the French countryside, 'the racers come from Paris' were awaited and admired. In these pre-war years, the pedalling heroes of the Tour de France, often nameless and remarkable on their modest bicycles stood for the arrival of social and industrial progress, progress on the move which comes up against the sedentary world of the crowds, who were often provincial and rural. In such a world, the bicycle and the motorcar created two opposing and complementary groups. In the roadside dust, the long-expected riders of the small leading group suddenly appear: 'There they are! There they are! They're here, they're here!' The 'auto' (*L'Auto* newspaper, a means of locomotion, and a symbol) follows the bicycle. The novelist Colette writes in 1912:

> I saw going past us, immediately swallowed in heavy dust storms, three slender riders with black and yellow backs with red numbers, three beings apparently with no faces, their backs arched and their heads down towards their knees under white caps ... They disappeared very quickly, amid the tumult they alone were mute, their haste to drive forwards and their silence seemed to separate them from what was going on here. It didn't seem that they were competing with each other, but more that they were fleeing from us as the prey of this escorting mix – in opaque dust – of shouts, bugle blasts, cheers and rumbles of thunder.[17]

The values of a modern industrial France, the dynamism and vibrant health of a courageous, working-class and sporting youth would be acted out thus around the battlements of the French hexagon in an ostentatiously processional circling of the country.[18]

> Ah! This handsome and splendid work shows how truly the human engine must be made up of inexhaustible resources, of violent courage, of stubborn willpower and of unbreakable tenacity to allow men so valiantly to survive this awful and moving ordeal ['calvaire'] to the very end.[19]

Throughout the twentieth century, the Tour de France was to undergo other changes. But right from its origins, it opened a royal road for a better understanding of French 'popular cultures', of which it has remained, up to the present day, both an expression and an echo.[20]

NOTES

1. E. Gautier, 'Le sport et la civilisation', in Maurice Leudet (ed.), *L'Almanach des sports 1903* (Paris: A. La Fare, 1903), p.2.

2. Géo Lefèvre sees this clearly in autumn 1902 when he writes the chapter devoted to 'Cycling' in the 1903 *Almanach des sports*:

   Find what one may, never will the little queen [*la petite reine* – an affectionate slang term for a bicycle] – or should I now say the great queen – be dethroned. She will remain the poor man's horse and the instrument of choice for sporting activity. She was the first to solve the problem of mechanical locomotion by road and, in so doing, she prepared the way for cars. The car, born from the bike has given rise to the lightweight motor, and the lightweight motor has allowed air navigation. Everything is linked and follows on, but the first link in the chain, the first ring to which all the others have successively been attached, is the bicycle. (G. Lefèvre, 'Cyclisme', in Leudet (ed.), *L'Almanach des sports* 1903, p.132).

   This statement is interesting because it was written at the end of 1902, at the very time when Géo Lefèvre was suggesting the idea of the Tour de France to his director Henri Desgrange. See Gérard Ejnès and Serge Laget (eds) with Raoul Dufourcq and Gérard Schaller, *L'Equipe, Tour de France 100 ans, Tome 1: 1903–1939* (Paris: L'Equipe, 2002), which uses reports and photos from *L'Auto*.

3. It should be noted that the first winner of Bordeaux–Paris was an English amateur by the name of Mills, who covered the 577km of the route in 26 hours 34 minutes. 'M. Mills only took the time to swallow a few mouthfuls of raw meat and a few draughts of soup during the race, and never did these pauses go beyond three minutes. Did pacers spelling each other accompany him throughout the route? It was they who were to smooth the difficulties of the road for him, light it during the night and lend him their machine in case of accidents.' (*L'Illustration*, May 1891, p.480). In the course of the 1890s, in her own way, France was to turn English sporting practices into spectacle. G.P. Mills Esq. was a leading rider of the Liverpool-based Anfield Bicycle Club (ABC) founded in 1879, of which the co-editor of this volume H. Dauncey is currently a member.

4. This far-from-exhaustive list numbers only the main events. Numerous Parisian or regional newspapers organized their own endurance races in honour of the speed of new mechanical devices.

5. Emile Zola had only recently died, having suffocated in his flat on 28 September 1902. On 13 January 1898 in the newspaper *L'Aurore* the novelist had published, under the famous title 'J'accuse', a public letter to the President of the Republic demanding a review of the Dreyfus trial. The 'Dreyfus Affair' is to be seen as one of the founding issues producing contemporary France (of the same importance as the 1789 Revolution or Vichy). On this theme, see Pierre Birnbaum (ed.), *La France de l'affaire Dreyfus* (Paris: Gallimard, 1994).

6. The original phrase is: 'Le vélocipède est autre chose qu'un sport; c'est un bienfait social.' Pierre Giffard (1853–1928) created Paris–Brest–Paris in 1891 and some of the first car races. He is a central figure in velocipede circles in the 1890s. As a progressive and a humanist, strongly rooted in Republican and Dreyfusard values, he is too often ignored by *L'Equipe*, when it periodically commemorates the birth of the Tour de France in its mass-audience publications. In 1899, Giffard came into conflict with the owners of French industry who – as anti-Dreyfusards – declared war against him and his newspaper *Le Vélo*.

7. Spectators attended the Tour right from the first race in 1903. Describing the third stage from Marseille to Toulouse for example, *Le Petit Provençal* newspaper notes that at Arles 'nearly 500 people waited all night, only leaving the square after the closure of the checkpoint'. And at Béziers 'from 5 a.m. onwards, thousands of onlookers lined the roads'. (*Le Petit Provençal*, 10 July 1903). Contemporary photos show a male crowd, with few women or children present.

8. See the studies of Eric Dunning on this issue, especially E. Dunning, P. Murphy and J. Williams, 'La violence des spectateurs lors des matchs de football: vers une explication sociologique', in N. Elias and E. Dunning (eds), *Sport et civilisation, la violence maîtrisée* (Paris: Fayard, 1994), pp.335–67. See in English: N. Elias and E. Dunning, *Quest for Excitement: Sport*

and Leisure in the Civilising Process (Oxford: Blackwell, 1986); and E. Dunning, P. Murphy and
J. Williams, *The Roots of Football Hooliganism: an Historical and Sociological Study* (London and
New York: Routledge and Kegan Paul, 1988).

9. See Jacques Miral, 'Le cyclisme', in Maurice Leudet (ed.), *Almanach des sports 1905* (Paris: La
   Fare, 1905) p.222. Miral also points out in this article that track cycling was endangered by
   middle-distance races, which like the 1903 Paris–Madrid were affected by 'the madness of
   speed'. The world record for paced speed had risen to 87kph, and several racing champions had
   died in their attempts, being paced by motorcycles that were too large. The Union Cycliste
   Internationale (the regulatory body created in 1900) had recently stipulated – in late 1904 – the
   use of smaller pace motorcycles that provided less protection from wind resistance. 'The year
   began with unreasonable speeds, but at the end of the season, thanks to the new ruling on
   drafting, speeds have fallen, allowing us to watch races where the individual worth of the riders
   has replaced the skill and technique of the pacers' (p.229).

10. Marcel Viollette, Lucien Petit-Breton, Thornwald Ellegaard, Louis Darragon and others, *Le
    cyclisme, 1912* (Geneva: Ed. Slatkine, 1912; new edition, 1980), p.110.

11. L. Petit-Breton, 'Les courses sur route', in: Viollette *et al.*, *Le cyclisme, 1912*, pp.219–20.

12. On the history of cycling practices in France during the nineteenth and twentieth centuries and
    on the democratization of the bicycle, see the author's previous studies: Ph. Gaboriau, 'Les
    trois âges du vélo en France', *Vingtième siècle*, 29 (Jan.–March 1991), pp.17–34; and Ph.
    Gaboriau, *Le Tour de France et le vélo. Histoire sociale d'une épopée contemporaine* (Paris:
    L'Harmattan, 1995).

13. This maxim is taken from a book by G. Bruno, *Le Tour de la France par deux enfants* (Paris:
    Librairie classique Eugène Belin, new edition, 1976). This famous little book, which sold several
    millions of copies, was used as a reading book in French primary school classes at the start of the
    twentieth century. Two young orphans from Lorraine travel around France on foot, following an
    initiatory and patriotic route through the geography and values of France. Other maxims: 'The
    whole of life could be compared to a journey in which one endlessly meets new difficulties'; 'Is
    life not made up entirely of obstacles to be overcome?'; 'Bravery in defence of the motherland
    makes equal rich and poor, great and small'. See also Chapter 7 below, pp.156 ff.

14. A. Baugé, *Messieurs les coureurs. Vérités, anecdotes et réflexions sur les courses cyclistes et les coureurs*
    (Paris: Librairie Garnier frères, 1925), pp.60–61.

15. Alphonse Baugé is an important figure of the early Tours de France. As a former speed rider
    (véloceman) of track racing, he was a respected pacer and trainer and a master tactician who
    won the Tours of 1909–14 for the leaders of the bicycle-manufacturer teams he managed (the
    Luxemburger Faber in 1909, the Frenchmen Lapize et Garrigou in 1910 and 1911, the Belgian
    Defraye in 1912, and the Belgian Thys in 1913 and 1914). He published an early work as the
    young manager of the Labor team in the 1907 Tour: A. Baugé, *Lettres à mon directeur* (Paris:
    Librairie de l'Auto, 1908); and a second book, prefaced by Henri Desgrange, in 1925 as an old
    and experienced sporting director (*Messieurs les coureurs*, 1925).

16. The best professional riders of these first Tours de France knew how to prepare themselves and
    train. For example, the winner in 1907 and 1908, Petit-Breton, gives some advice to readers in
    1912: 'While riding, I advise you to avoid any solid foods. I always have in my musette two 75cl
    bottles of chocolate, creamed rice, tea or lemonade. At each checkpoint, you swap the empties
    for others of your choice. I drink a lot during the race'. [...] 'Always carry [...] with you what
    you need for repairing your machine – spanners, spare parts, a pedal and its axle are the things
    that break the most – and practise, before the race, how to do the most difficult repairs as
    quickly as possible.' (In Viollette *et al.*, *Le cyclisme, 1912*, p.224.)

17. Colette, *Dans la foule* (Paris: Grès, 1918), p.83 onwards. The author tells of the arrival of the
    Tour in the Paris region on 28 July 1912.

18. The Tour de France firmly established the idea of a France unified by her geography. The
    imagery of almost impassable mountain cols gives a total unity to France, installed and
    protected by seas and mountains. On this point, see G. Vigarello, 'Le Tour de France', in P.
    Nora (ed.), *Les Lieux de mémoire, III, Les France, 2 Traditions* (Paris: Gallimard, 1992),
    pp.886–925.

19. A. Baugé, *Messieurs les coureurs*, p.41.

20. On the analysis of 'popular cultures', see C. Grignon and J-C. Passeron, *Le savant et le populaire. Misérabilisme et populisme en sociologie et en littérature* (Paris: Seuil, 1989). On the Tour de France and 'popular cultures', see Gaboriau, *Le Tour de France et le vélo*, 1995; Ph. Gaboriau, 'Le Tour de France', *Universalia 97* (Paris: Encyclopaedia Universalis, 1997), and Ph. Gaboriau, *Les spectacles sportifs, grandeurs et décadences*, forthcoming 2003.

The Tour in the Inter-War Years: Political Ideology, Athletic Excess and Industrial Modernity

CHRISTOPHER THOMPSON

INTRODUCTION

Early in the 1924 Tour de France, the popular defending champion Henri Pélissier dropped out, complaining of the race's humiliating rules. Couched in the language of worker rights and magnified by the Communist press in particular, his remarks sparked a national debate about the race's abusive nature that lasted through the 1930s. A new representation of the Tour racer was born: the '*forçat de la route*' ('convict labourer of the road'), a sinister counterpoint to the conventional celebration of racers as 'giants of the road' and 'survivors' of the most difficult event in all of sport. To ensure that the Tour lived up to its reputation, its organizers – the sports daily *L'Auto* – had indeed created numerous rules. Some imposed a rigorous self-sufficiency on Tour racers: for example, they had to effect all repairs entirely on their own. Responding to bourgeois spectators outraged at the racers' 'scandalous' conduct, the organizers had also formulated other rules, fining contestants for begging, stealing, cursing, public urination, and acts of aggression against fans, race officials, and each other. Invoking these rules and building on a widespread contemporary understanding of long-distance cycling as harsh physical labour, *L'Auto* portrayed the race as a civilizing process that transformed its uncouth contestants into honourable, disciplined '*ouvriers de la pédale*' – 'pedal workers' – worthy of emulation by their lower-class fans.

The organizers were, however, caught in a fundamental contradiction. On the one hand, they knew that the Tour de France owed its widespread appeal to the extraordinary challenge it represented. The mountains, the weather, and the distances covered day after day made it the toughest sporting event in the world, while the Tour's many

rules only added to its severity. On the other hand, the extreme nature
of the race, when combined with the language of work adopted by both
its advocates and opponents, left *L'Auto* and the Tour's commercial
sponsors vulnerable to charges that they were exploiting exhausted
working-class athletes. This criticism, present from the very first Tours,
intensified in 1924 and lasted for the balance of the inter-war era when
the depiction of Tour racers as slave labourers politicized the race as
never before. Comparing the organizers' treatment of racers to
capitalism's abuse of factory workers, critics used the *forçat de la route*
controversy to insert the Tour into contemporary French debates about
economic and social justice and the nature of modern industrial work.
How this came about is the subject of this chapter.

LEGISLATING AGAINST ATHLETIC EXCESS?
THE CASE AGAINST THE TOUR

The magnitude of the Tour as an athletic challenge had never met with
universal approval. Many late-nineteenth-century physicians were
concerned about immoderate physical exercise and, specifically, the
harmful effects of endurance events in the new sport of cycling.[1]
Politicians and other commentators feared the deleterious impact of
long-distance bicycle races on contestants and public alike and called for
restrictive legislation that would make such events safe for all involved.
Three weeks before the first Tour, the *député-maire* of Sens regretted
'that the necessities of existence reduce men to such excesses; [...] laws
that regulate work prevent human beings from going beyond the limits
of their normal strength except in the event of an urgent obligation; [...]
it is up to the public authorities to bring an end to such a state of affairs
[...]'.[2] His criticisms were echoed by the Tour's opponents through the
inter-war period: the race's primary *raison d'être* was to promote the
French cycle industry; its excessive demands upon contestants led to
exhaustion, injury, sickness, and even death; and it endangered the lives
of roadside spectators to whom it offered a deplorable spectacle. True to
his word, the mayor issued a municipal directive relating to long-
distance bicycle races that limited the racers' speeds to a maximum of
ten kilometres/hour in his town and required them to proceed on foot
when they encountered busy roads or other crowded public spaces. The
departmental prefect, representing the French state, authorized its
immediate implementation.[3]

The mayor's reference to labour legislation, which confirms that even before the inaugural Tour the association between work and long-distance cycling was firmly established, needs to be contextualized. The decades preceding First World War saw a number of legislative initiatives and reforms under the Third Republic designed to address workers' grievances and improve their work experience and quality of life. Such reforms, many Republicans believed, would guarantee social peace and the political allegiance of increasingly organized industrial workers during a period marked by disruptive strikes. The social impact of ideas such as entropy, derived from the new discipline of thermodynamics, also contributed to initiatives to shorten the workday, reduce the risk of accidents, and improve the health of the working classes. Meanwhile, a scientific focus on fatigue and its elimination resulted in studies on work performance, mental fatigue and nutrition; their objective was to calculate and conserve the nation's productive capital.[4] *L'Auto* was thus obliged to defend the rigours of the Tour at a time when considerable attention was being focussed on the quality of the French worker's experience.

For much of the nineteenth century, French governments and employers under a variety of authoritarian regimes resisted attempts by workers to improve work conditions and decrease work hours. Worker organizations had been outlawed during the first French Revolution in 1791 and strikes, illegal until 1864, were vigorously repressed. Early attempts in the 1840s to regulate child labour and limit the hours of adult male workers met with limited success.[5] After the foundation of the Third Republic in 1870, French governments and legislatures proved more sensitive to labour issues. Faced with an expanding working class influenced by socialist and syndicalist ideas, politicians were keenly aware that industrialization and universal male suffrage formed a potentially explosive cocktail that labour reforms might defuse. They addressed a number of worker grievances, particularly from the 1890s, as more progressive Republicans – the Radicals – became a leading political force.[6] Health and safety regulations, obligatory accident insurance and old age pensions were implemented, while collective bargaining became more common in French industry immediately before the war. A significant issue that related directly to long-distance bicycle races and may have motivated the mayor's directive was the length of the workday: 12-hour workdays and seven-day work weeks were the norm for many industrial workers, artisans and low-level service sector employees. By the late nineteenth century, the reduction of work hours had become the leading demand of organized workers, an important objective of syndicalists and socialists, and a frequently expressed grievance in strikes. Governments of the Third Republic responded initially by addressing child, adolescent, and female labour before reducing hours for adult males and creating a weekly day of rest. Work-related issues became so central to French political life that one of Georges Clemenceau's first acts as the head of a new government in 1906 was to create a Ministry of Labour under the independent socialist René Viviani.[7]

Notwithstanding their partial scope, imperfect implementation, inadequate enforcement, and the opposition they faced, labour reforms during this period represented a fundamental shift in how French governments, legislators, employers and workers addressed the work experience and productive process, especially in industry.[8] The issues involved – the length of the workday, the organization of work, authority in the workplace, and the ability of workers to influence work conditions – were also relevant to the experiences of Tour racers. In this context, the charges made by the mayor of Sens, bolstered by his conviction that public officials should prevent long-distance bicycle races, were ones *L'Auto* could not afford to take lightly, particularly as this mayor sat in parliament and could launch a national campaign against such competitions.

In his spirited response, 'A mayor who is ten years behind the times', *L'Auto*'s editor-in-chief Henri Desgrange argued that the spectators, merchants and hotel-owners of Sens would suffer the most from their mayor's edict, as the Tour and other races would bypass their town, eliminating a source of revenue and entertainment for the community. He mocked the mayor's contention that road races had caused racer fatalities. On the contrary, long-distance cycling was part of a sports movement that was improving the moral, physical and intellectual state of French students and soldiers. Races like Marseille–Paris and Bordeaux–Paris required far less energy and were less tiring than a 100-metre foot race or a 200-metre bicycle sprint.[9] That Desgrange made such an argument in one article while extolling the extraordinary physical demands of the Tour in countless others underscores the contradiction in which he was trapped. Criticism of the race as abusive repeatedly forced *L'Auto* to adopt contradictory – even ludicrous – positions in its defence.

Unfortunately for Desgrange, the mayor of Sens was not alone in his concerns or determination to intervene. Belgian critics dismissed the

Tour as 'idiotic', a 'mental depravity', and 'a base speculation on the frailties of human nature' that debased human nature, covered heroism in ridicule, and transformed its injured, bloodied participants into 'madmen', 'degenerates', and 'abnormal' individuals. They decried the poor example such 'stupid and immoral' races set for the general population: 'for a handful of gold, free men play the role of ancient gladiators and, through the sterile labour of the *forçat*, sprinkle 300-kilometre ribbons of road with their sweat and blood. They arrive panting, broken, exhausted, unrecognizable under the mud, dust and bruises.' The Tour's spectators were 'gawking onlookers' filled with 'base passions', while those who lived off the racers' efforts were 'parasites of human stupidity'. A legislative solution was required, founded on an understanding that bicycle-racing was work: 'Parliaments pass laws to limit the workday; they rigorously supervise unhealthy or dangerous industrial establishments. [...] Could they not regulate the maximum effort which the whim of sportsmen would have the right to demand of the human machine?'[10] French commentators dismissed the Tour as a 'ridiculous event' dominated by the thirst, hunger and exhaustion of its participants, as a 'deviation of sport', and a 'degeneration of our time' that 'consisted in making the individual play the role of a motor in which his legs will become pistons'.[11] Contradicting *L'Auto*'s claim that the race civilized its participants and made them models of strength and endurance for a nation insecure about its physical condition, critics portrayed racers as brutalized creatures symbolizing a more general degeneration. They cited as evidence the fact that long-distance races dehumanized racers by transforming them into machines. In so doing they challenged an influential contemporary understanding of the human body that had inspired press coverage of the racers since the very first Tour.

THE HERO DEHUMANIZED:
THE BICYCLE RACER AS MACHINE

L'Auto and other observers frequently depicted racers as tireless automata and machines – particularly locomotives – as if the fact that pedalling resembled the action of a machine implied that like the latter, racers were impervious to pain and, above all, fatigue.[12] This image was buttressed by technical articles in *L'Auto* that explicitly treated the human body as a machine.[13] For example, Charles Faroux, a regular contributor to *L'Auto*, explored the 'acceptable productivity' and calorific output of the 'human machine' or 'human motor'. During the 1936 Tour he wrote a series of articles analyzing the pedalling cadences of various racers with respect to their height, weight, nutrition, gear choice, pedal crank length, wheel size, the power they generated, and the fluidity of their pedalling action under stress.[14] A few weeks later, in an article entitled 'The Human Machine', Jean Gilly argued that the frequent comparison of the human body with a machine was quite accurate with respect to its 'feeding and structure'. Noting the popular practice of describing champions as 'handsome machines' and 'locomotives', he proceeded to examine the 'chassis', 'motor' and 'body' (*carrosserie*) of the human 'machine'.[15] By reducing athletic performance to mathematical relationships between quantifiable variables, such articles suggested that the efforts of Tour racers were best understood in terms of output and productivity rather than courage, endurance and suffering.

Comparisons between man and machine in Tour coverage had their roots in nineteenth-century ideals of efficient work and increased production, and the resulting scientific interest in precisely measuring the physiological and psychological limits of human performance. As they became interested in quantifying muscular energy, doctors and scientists came to understand the human body as a machine. Some actually studied the performances and recuperation of top-flight bicycle racers, particularly in endurance events, because the bicycle provided a unique intersection of high-performance sport and experimental science: it could be ridden both to demonstrate and – when employed as an ergometer – to measure performance. New devices were invented, capable of measuring human physical performance and potential. For example, Jules-Etienne Marey's chronophotographs, which broke down a movement into its component parts, could be employed to teach manual labourers a more efficient way of producing goods, just as they could suggest more energy-efficient techniques to athletes.[16] In the late-nineteenth-century context of European industrial and military competition, and given specific French concerns about demographic stagnation and the debacle of the Franco-Prussian War in 1870, maximizing human energies had clear implications for the international balance of power and French national security.

The metaphor of the human body as a motor, popularized by scientists in the late nineteenth century, resulted from a new conceptualization of energy and labour inspired by recent scientific discoveries. Chief among them were Hermann von Helmholtz's formulation of the universal law of the conservation of energy in 1847 and, a few years later, Rudolf Clausius's discovery of the second law of thermodynamics, which explained the irreversible decline of energy in entropy. The working body was now seen as a productive machine with measurable energy and output that exemplified the universal process by which energy was converted into mechanical work. As a result, the image of labour was dramatically transformed: the expenditure and deployment of energy came to replace older notions of work founded upon human will, technical skill and moral purpose. Only fatigue distinguished human effort from the operation of industrial machines capable in principle of perpetual work. But if the human body was governed by the same dynamic laws as industrial machines, would it not be possible to eliminate fatigue and unleash society's latent energies and the triumph of productivism? A variety of scientists and social reformers committed themselves to seeking a cure and a new science of work was born, inspired by the utopian ideal of a body without fatigue.[17]

Given this conceptual shift, it is hardly surprising that cyclists received particular attention from the scientific community. Desgrange himself defined the Tour as 'the greatest scientific experiment [*épreuve de documentation*] that the sport of cycling has ever given us'.[18] The race reproduced the work conditions of modern factories where precisely measured work pace and output mirrored a racer's gear choice, pedalling cadence and technique, and aerodynamic position. Efficiency in those areas led to a higher 'yield', which would presumably lead to victory.[19] Hence the mathematical analysis of Faroux and others, which provided a scientific foundation for evocations of the racers as locomotives, motors and machines. However, an important disjuncture existed between the scientific or social reformist agenda of engineers and fatigue experts and the press's representations of racers as machines. The former sought to eradicate fatigue through the application of scientific knowledge about the way the human body works and thus fully unleash society's productive potential. For the Tour organizers and most of the media covering the race, there could be no question of eliminating fatigue, for fatigue and its consequences – suffering and attrition, as injured and exhausted racers dropped out – created the drama of the Tour, confirmed that it was the toughest competition in the world, and transformed its contestants into exceptional beings worthy of mass interest. The racers might look like locomotives, even move like locomotives, but theirs was the exquisite suffering of mortal man pushed to his limits and for whom survival *was* victory. This in turn left the organizers open to charges that they were abusing Tour racers.

TOUR RACERS AS '*FORÇATS DE LA ROUTE*': THE PÉLISSIER AFFAIR

In his attempt to impose autonomy and self-reliance upon Tour racers, Desgrange required that they finish each stage with all the equipment and clothing with which they had started. In 1924, this rule sparked a controversy involving the defending champion, Henri Pélissier. As stages often began at night in chilly temperatures, he had taken to wearing several jerseys, gradually peeling them off and tossing them away as the day warmed up. A team manager pointed out to Desgrange that this was a violation of article 48 of the Tour's regulations. Added in 1920, this article was intended to prevent the wasting of sponsor-provided equipment. It was thus part of Desgrange's campaign to instil bourgeois values in the racers, in this instance respect for property, particularly that of others.[20] Desgrange discussed the matter with Pélissier who informed him that the jerseys were his own and had not been provided by his sponsor. The issue was apparently still unresolved when, at the start of the third stage, a race official ran his hand down Pélissier's back to check the number of jerseys he was wearing. Enraged, Pélissier declared that he was dropping out of the race. He reconsidered and started the stage only to withdraw later in the day. His brother Francis, an excellent racer in his own right, and the Pélissiers' *protégé* Maurice Ville also dropped out to express their solidarity with the aggrieved champion.

The brothers' withdrawal was big news as they were two of the most gifted and successful French racers of their day. Henri had begun his racing career in 1911, rapidly accumulating prestigious victories in one-day *classiques* such as the Tour of Lombardy (which he won three times), Paris–Roubaix (twice), Milan–San Remo, Bordeaux–Paris, and Paris–Tours. He also finished in the top three in the French road-racing championship five times between 1919 (when he won) and 1924. Before dominating the 1923 Tour he had finished a close second to the Belgian Philippe Thys in 1914. The younger Francis, meanwhile, although a professional only since 1919, had already won Bordeaux–Paris twice and the French road-racing championship three times.[21]

The incident took on unexpected proportions when the prominent journalist Albert Londres, covering the race for *Le Petit Parisien*, interviewed the three racers. Describing the race as a Calvary, Henri Pélissier evoked the diarrhoea and weight loss experienced by Tour racers and used the English term 'hard labour' to characterize the Pyrénées. He expressed outrage at having to check with Desgrange before throwing away his own clothing and mocked the rules requiring self-sufficiency of Tour racers: 'When we are dying of thirst, before we place our water bottles under the running water, we must make certain that someone fifty yards away isn't pumping it. Otherwise: penalization.' The racers showed Londres the drugs they took simply to survive the race, including cocaine, chloroform, and pills which Francis Pélissier mysteriously referred to as 'dynamite'.[22] No doubt inspired by his recent trip to French Guyana, where he had reported on the penal colony, and moved by the racers' accounts of the Tour, Londres referred to them in his article as '*les forçats de la route*', the convict labourers of the road.[23] Having already reported on the stomach and eye ailments and frequent punctures experienced by Tour participants, he now expanded his critique of the Tour in a series of scathing articles exposing the terrible weather, dangerous roads, chaotic crowds, pain, injuries, fear and harsh regulations confronted by Tour racers. His headlines trumpeted, 'Tour de France, Tour of Suffering!' and stressed the race's terrible attrition rate.[24] For the first time the various charges made against the Tour since 1903 were brought together for a large audience.

In a letter published a few days later in the Communist daily *L'Humanité*, Henri Pélissier accepted 'excessive fatigue, suffering, pain' as part of his profession. However, he asserted that racers wished 'to be treated as men and not as dogs' by 'well-behaved, competent and impartial officials', and demanded 'the right to dispose of our person as we think fit, without having [Desgrange's] permission'. He noted that 'our Directors were very satisfied with the results we have obtained for them and [...] have understood perfectly the kind of harassment against which we have had to revolt. It is not us they blame.' Pélissier acknowledged the legitimacy of a social hierarchy based upon 'great moral worth, knowledge, talent, [and] genius', but refused to submit to 'enriched autocrats' like Desgrange.[25] The racer's views, like Desgrange's, were founded upon the image of the Tour as work, but instead of a civilizing process that transformed racers into respectable members of society, he portrayed the race as a dehumanizing factory where workers toiled long hours in the harshest conditions, their every move controlled by the mean-spirited agents of their capitalist boss.

Desgrange acknowledged that *Le Petit Parisien*'s use of '*forçat*' would not be easy to deflect: 'The word creates an image. It helps to paint a picture. It evokes a contrast and, as the public is not required to think, it immediately enjoys considerable success.'[26] The most obvious reference was to penal colonies, particularly Guyana, which by the inter-war years had, in the words of one historian, become a 'myth'. The press titillated millions of readers with real and imagined accounts of convict revolts and escape attempts. Londres's investigative series in *Le Petit Parisien*, which ran from August to October 1923, was published as a book, inspired a play and a song, and fuelled a media storm that contributed to reforms.[27] Londres would certainly have been aware of the massive public interest in *forçats* as he searched for a compelling image to convey the plight of Tour racers and increase *Le Petit Parisien*'s sales. Meanwhile, the increasingly mechanized, rationalized factories of nineteenth-century France with their numerous rules and fines, had inspired references to industrial 'penal colonies', workers as 'convicts', and foremen as 'guards', which came into general usage between 1860 and 1880. Labour newspapers often included an 'abuse column' or columns about factory conditions entitled 'The Review of Penal Colonies'. Workers' and Socialist papers – *The Convict, The Convict's Cry, The Convict's Revenge, The Convict's Awakening* – self-consciously embraced the term which was also featured in the opening lines of the 'Internationale', the anthem of the international working-class movement and, later, of international Communism.[28] Clearly, by 1924 '*forçat*' was a term that evoked horrific, exploitative labour.

THE COMMUNIST CRITIQUE OF THE TOUR

The impact of the Londres-Pélissier interview on public opinion was considerable due to the popularity of the Tour, the celebrity of both men, and the language they used. The Parisian and regional press of all political hues addressed Pélissier's complaints. Not surprisingly, the most aggressive criticism of the race sparked by the *forçat* controversy came from those who saw the defence of the worker as their fundamental mission. The Communist daily *L'Humanité* immediately seized on the affair with dramatic headlines about the 'rebellion' of the Pélissier brothers who were brandishing 'the banner of revolt'. Like Henri

Pélissier, *L'Humanité* accepted Desgrange's vision of the Tour as work only to turn it on its head. The racers who had dropped out were 'strikers', the Tour a vast commercial operation with 'absurd regulations' organized by sports profiteers who exploited the 'cycling proletariat'. *L'Humanité* contrasted 'the commercial calculations' of morally bankrupt bourgeois spectator sport with the 'severe [...] and disinterested joy' of the pure Communist sporting ideal. It was 'the duty of sporting Communists to exploit the Pélissier incident to denounce forcefully the ploys of the sports profiteers' and 'begin to unveil the hidden side of the Tour de France'.[29] This represented a shift for *L'Humanité*. During the three previous Tours its coverage had generally been uncritical and limited to brief updates and stage results. Although aware of the terrible attrition rate and rigours of the race, *L'Humanité* had echoed *L'Auto*'s most cherished themes, emphasizing the racers' exceptional will, courage, energy, recuperative powers and popularity.[30] *L'Humanité* may have begun to adopt a more critical stance towards the race's commercialism in the early days of the 1924 Tour before the racers dropped out, but the shift to outright opposition and an explicitly political reading of the race was a direct result of the Pélissier incident.[31]

L'Humanité sustained its critique of the Tour for the balance of the inter-war period. Satirizing *L'Auto*'s coverage, it denounced the organizers' 'ferocious and at times criminal exploitation' of 'the "giant" pedal workers'.[32] Racers endured cold, rain, hunger, thirst, fatigue, climbs, lack of rest, sleep deprivation and lengthy stages in order to generate an ever-increasing profit for Desgrange. They were obliged to race at the hottest time of the day to prevent evening papers from scooping *L'Auto* by reporting the day's results: 'Like an exploiter in the factory, he requires ever greater productivity with less security and more fatigue. The result: punctures, accidents, falls, death, men in hospital...'[33] Contrasting the profit-driven immorality of bourgeois sporting events like the Tour with the disinterested purity of races organized by the Communist *Fédération Sportive du Travail*, *L'Humanité* hoped to convince workers to join Communist sports clubs created in the early 1920s rather than the corporate clubs established by the French *patronat* in the inter-war years where they came under bourgeois influence.[34] To further arouse the class-consciousness of French workers, *L'Humanité* promoted its own model Tour 'worker'. In the 1930s, the paper praised the unsponsored racer René Bernard for being a 'class-conscious worker' who belonged to a 'revolutionary co-operative' and a trade union. It claimed that Desgrange had refused to include Bernard in the French national team because he had been a delivery man for *L'Humanité* and penalized him more heavily than the stars of the national team to prevent him from achieving a high place in the overall classification.[35] *L'Humanité* hoped to rally the Tour's working-class fans behind a racer who symbolized class-conscious rebellion and thereby encourage 'the exploited [workers] of commercial cycling to organize themselves for the struggle against their bosses, whose rapaciousness is no longer in need of being demonstrated'.[36]

The implications of *L'Humanité*'s campaign transcended sport. The paper sought to capitalize on Henri Pélissier's popularity, his act of revolt, and public interest in the Tour to launch a Communist campaign against modern industrial capitalism. The race was 'the exact copy of the rationalized work supervised by the warder of galley slaves in the great factories', for like an industrialist, Desgrange punished exhausted racers who did not satisfy the pace requirements laid out in the Tour's regulations.[37] Before the first Tour in 1903 Desgrange had indeed decided that racers averaging under 20 kilometres/hour for a stage would forfeit the daily wage of five francs paid them by the organizers.[38] This minimum pace amounted to imposing productivity standards below which racers would no longer be paid for work deemed unsatisfactory. While he relented at the Tour's conclusion, thereafter, whenever Desgrange believed that racers had failed to meet the minimum required pace due to a lack of effort, he threatened to, and occasionally did, cancel prizes and bonuses.[39] The Tour thus replicated the factory where worker protest often took the form of a slowdown and the boss responded with fines.

TAYLORISM AND THE TOUR

L'Humanité's linking of Desgrange's obsession with maximum productivity to the degrading exploitation of workers under modern industrial capitalism reflected the growing influence in France of recent theories of industrial management, particularly Taylorism. The American Frederick Winslow Taylor's ideology of scientific management, developed at the end of the nineteenth century, sought to increase worker productivity and implement an optimum work pace. Functional foremen, time and motion studies, new work routing systems, bonus payment plans and other incentives were designed to increase efficiency and managerial control, motivate workers, and subdivide the productive process in ways that reduced reliance on skill. Taylor argued that while this appeared to transform him into 'a mere automaton', the factory worker under scientific management was more efficient and productive than the self-employed, autonomous craftsman, precisely because he forfeited his monopoly of technical knowledge to management's planners.[40] The obedience demanded of workers found an obvious counterpart in the discipline that Desgrange sought to impose on Tour racers, which he too justified by claiming it would allow racers to develop their potential to the fullest. And, despite Taylor's disclaimer, scientific management, like competitive long-distance cycling, seemed to transform workers into automata. Taylorism viewed the worker as a machine potentially capable of infinite productivity and resistant to fatigue once his body had been subjected to 'scientifically designed systems of organization'.[41] Like Desgrange, Taylor sought to prevent loafing, which he saw as the greatest obstacle to attaining maximum pace and productivity. This was one of the reasons work processes and paces were to be devised by management's planning departments, rather than by the workers themselves. The benefits of scientific management were then measured mathematically in the form of increased output.[42] The numerous parallels between Tour racers and 'Taylorized' workers were not lost on Communist critics of the modern factory.

Even before the war, when confronted with early attempts to implement scientific management, the French trade union press had argued that Taylorism was simply a way of organizing 'overwork' or 'exhaustion' (*le surmenage*) that de-skilled workers and robbed them of their dignity. *La Guerre sociale* saw Taylorism as 'the insane intensification of work to the point of slavery'; Alphonse Merrheim, the syndicalist leader of the metalworkers' union, described it as 'the most ferocious, the most barbaric system of work devised by capitalists'. *L'Humanité*, until 1920 the major organ of French Socialism, and Merrheim predicted that the new system would transform men into 'thoughtless machines' and 'automat[a] ruled by the automatic movements of the machine'. The language of this critique was identical to that of opponents of long-distance bicycle races who decried the dehumanization involved in the repetitive, unskilled application of human muscle power. Meanwhile, workers at a number of automobile plants struck against attempts to impose a work pace determined by time and motion studies in which they had had no say.[43]

During First World War the need to mass-produce military material of consistent quality with fewer skilled workers provided an impetus for the implementation of Taylorism, while the war's devastating impact on the labour supply generated post-war interest in management theories that promised increased worker productivity. Between the end of the war and 1927, Taylorite innovations and scientific management remained the exception in French industry, but by the late 1920s Taylor's techniques were being received more enthusiastically in France, which emerged as one of Europe's leaders in applying scientific management.[44] As they had earlier, French factory workers seem to have resisted the trend towards greater rationalization, for it rendered even harsher their already difficult working conditions. Their resistance took many forms, including absenteeism, following the pace of the slowest worker (particularly when they were being timed), high turnover rates, and resistance to shop floor discipline.[45] Their behaviour resembled the withdrawals, slowdowns and rules violations of Tour racers seeking to control their work conditions and maintain a degree of autonomy. In 1929 and 1930, *L'Humanité* published Communist trade union reports that condemned the new factories for reducing workers into a 'vast army [...] making the same mechanical movements under the watchful eyes of the company's [...] stooges'.[46] The language of such reports clearly informed its critique of the Tour: *L'Humanité* rejoiced each time racers thwarted 'the boss's regulations' and rebelled against the pace requirements – described as rates of production (of kilometres) – by initiating a 'productivity strike' (slowdown).[47]

Criticism of the Tour as abusive work in the wake of the Pélissier incident was not confined to the Communist Left. Noting that racers were not 'pieceworkers' and their work not 'piecework', *Paris-Soir* criticized the organizers for imposing a minimum pace; one had to accept that fatigue and strategy would occasionally result in uninteresting stages and slower paces.[48] The satirical *Le Canard Enchaîné* took the Tour to task in humorous cartoons that highlighted the dangerous conditions faced by racers and the callousness with which they were treated by race officials.[49] No friend of the Pélissiers in 1924, *L'Intransigeant* nevertheless criticized the organizers in 1937 for subdividing a day's racing into two or three segments to increase profits. Racers facing three mini-stages in a day would naturally choose not to race hard all the time.[50] In Brittany well into the 1930s, newspapers and their readers assailed the Tour's commercialism and Desgrange's cynical exploitation of 'the weaknesses of men' who 'cycle six thousand kilometres in a row for just a few one-hundred-franc bills'. The Tour's rules – including fines for not racing fast enough – reflected Desgrange's 'ingenuity in forcing them to work'. Like *L'Humanité*, Breton critics were appalled that he required racers to cycle during the hottest time of the day.[51] Meanwhile, André Reuze, undoubtedly inspired by the Pélissier incident and possibly even by one of Londres's headlines, dedicated his novel, *Le Tour de Souffrance*, to Tour racers, 'sandwich men of the cycle manufacturers, useless heroes, heroes nevertheless [...] as a testimony of sympathy, admiration and pity'. Noting that his novel was inspired by real incidents, Reuze described all manner of dirty tricks by teams to ensure that their racers won and parodied Desgrange's editorials praising the Tour, which he criticized as the inhumane commercial exploitation of racers who risked their lives for little gain.[52]

Not all commentators took the Pélissiers' side. Although critical of the Tour's regulations, *L'Echo de Paris* suggested that Henri Pélissier's 'ill humour' and poor conditioning had led to his withdrawal. Other critics, particularly right-wing papers like *L'Action Française* and *L'Intransigeant*, rejected characterizations of the Tour as a penal colony and its racers as convict labourers. They claimed that Pélissier's jerseys did in fact belong to his sponsors who had opposed the racers' withdrawal, accused the brothers of attempting to destroy the very event that had brought them fame and fortune, and argued that they were losing the respect of their fans. To support this last point, common folk were interviewed: a gendarmerie lieutenant asserted that the racers were being 'severely criticized' while a peasant assailed their poor work ethic and hypersensitivity. Meanwhile, a Tour racer noted that no one was forced to enter the race, downplayed the Tour's difficulties, and suggested that journalists were overly sensitive about race conditions. He referred to his 'little sporting goods store', a reminder of the economic benefits that motivated Tour racers. The implied question was obvious: could a self-employed shop-owner be an exploited proletarian? By emphasizing the economic gains and free will of Tour racers and discrediting Henri Pélissier as a wealthy racer grown soft, his critics (particularly on the right) hoped perhaps to undermine the potentially explosive example of his rebellion, which the Communists were so determined to exploit.[53]

COMMUNISTS, SOCIALISTS AND THE TOUR AS EXPLOITATIVE CAPITALISM

If *L'Humanité*'s critique of the Tour was shared by some Parisian and regional papers, the Communists did not initially succeed in uniting the French Left against the race. *Le Peuple*, the organ of the Confederation of French Labour, seemed to blame the racers' irritability more than Desgrange's rules, while the Socialist daily, *Le Populaire*, emphatically rejected the image of Tour racers as *forçats*.[54] The latter argued that unlike real workers, racers were free to choose their career, that the Tour was not the 'murderous' event described by 'certain experts in brainwashing' – a reference to *L'Humanité* – and that the racers' 'demands' were 'in no way comparable with those of true workers'. Stars made large sums thanks to the Tour and sponsorship contracts; professional cycling allowed them and their less accomplished team-mates to escape a more humble fate 'on the farm [...] or in the mine'. When *Le Populaire* drew attention to the success of a Socialist racer it did so without turning the latter into a symbol of working-class resistance to capitalist exploitation. The paper did, however, deplore the commercial dimension of events like the Tour and invited 'true sportsmen' to join the Socialist *Fédération Sportive et Gymnique du Travail*, which was the 'only way of achieving pure sport, freed of all commercial and advertising contingencies'.[55]

Explaining the divergence between Communist and Socialist views of the Pélissier incident requires reviewing the state of French left-wing politics in the aftermath of First World War. Participants in the Socialist Congress of December 1920 arrived discouraged by the inability of international Socialism to prevent the butchery of First World War, by their poor performance at the 1919 legislative elections, and by the failure of the general strike of May 1920. Impressed by the successful Russian Revolution, a majority voted to form the French Communist Party (PCF) and join Lenin's Communist International. *L'Humanité* became the organ of the new party. The polarization of the French Left was exacerbated in 1924 when the Socialists – but not the Communists – participated in the centre-left coalition that won the legislative elections. Especially after 1924, the PCF subordinated its autonomy to Moscow's directives. From 1928 to 1934, consistent with the class warfare strategy imposed by the Comintern, the French Communists targeted the Socialists as their principal political enemies, accusing them of leading the working class in a strategy of class collaboration.[56] This exacerbated tensions between the two camps, whose rivalry was played out in the *forçats de la route* controversy. The terms of that debate – the language of work – virtually obligated self-identified representatives of the working class to react, whether to embrace the racers as emblematic proletarians or to reject that comparison as illegitimate. *Le Populaire* saw the debate about the Tour as an opportunity to attack the French Communists' credibility, dismissing the reporters covering the Tour for 'the paper inspired by Moscow' as hopelessly prejudiced puppets contaminated by the Soviet doctrinal line. Determined to distinguish itself from its rival, *Le Populaire* rejected *L'Humanité*'s depiction of the Tour as harsh industrial labour and the racers as convict labourers.[57] As a result, for a decade or so the Socialist paper's stance was difficult to distinguish from that of many conservative and extreme-right-wing papers.

The Nazis' rise to power in Germany in January 1933 and the ominous if unsuccessful attempt by the French Far Right to overthrow the Third Republic in February 1934 led to a dramatic strategic shift by the PCF. Following Stalin's new Popular Front strategy, the French Communists now united with the Socialists and other progressive forces to block the momentum of antidemocratic extreme right-wing movements. Both parties contributed to the victory of their electoral coalition in 1936, the Socialists with about 20 per cent of the vote, the Communists exceeding 15 per cent for the first time. The resulting Popular Front government was led by a Socialist, Léon Blum, a first in the history of the Republic.[58] The new coalition strategy of the mid-1930s apparently influenced *Le Populaire*'s Tour coverage, which became indistinguishable from the Communist critique. Echoing Pélissier's language of 1924, the paper now described the Tour as the deadliest 'hard labour' and criticized the 'at times superhuman labour' demanded by Desgrange of the racers, who, like manual labourers confronted with harsh daily work, expended their energy with great care. Celebrating the 'rebellions of the "giants of the road"', *Le Populaire* embraced the worker-racer comparison.[59]

The fatal crash of the Spanish racer Cepeda during the 1935 Tour confirmed that the French Left was now united in its critique of the Tour as dangerous and exploitative work. *Le Populaire* described Cepeda as 'a humble worker of sport', *L'Humanité* as 'one of those who make the fortune of the great profiteers of capitalist sport'.[60] Both held the organizers responsible for his death. *Le Populaire* faulted them for not obliging racers to wear helmets, which were required in races organized by the Socialist sports federation, and attributed Cepeda's fatal fall to wheel rims of poor quality.[61] *L'Humanité* launched a front-page attack on the Tour's organizers and sponsors for exploiting racers, in this case to the death. The Communist paper implicated 'the ever more brutal regulations' by which Desgrange was seeking to increase 'productivity', 'in other words speed', and argued that Desgrange had been paid by a constructor of wheel rims to use its products on the bicycles provided to Tour racers.[62] The Communist case against the Tour was clear: seeking to maximize sponsorship income, the capitalist organizers had provided racers with defective equipment that had led to 'work accidents', including a fatality. Never had the Tour's participants been so self-evidently *forçats*.

L'AUTO DEFENDS THE TOUR

Given the high profiles of Henri Pélissier and Albert Londres and the attacks launched by *L'Humanité* in particular, *L'Auto* had no choice but to respond immediately and forcefully to charges that the racers were brutalized, exploited *forçats*. For the balance of the inter-war period it would continually seek to restore the Tour's image and defuse the controversy, which the race's critics were forever reigniting. Desgrange fined Henri Pélissier a total of 600 francs for verbal insults and threats towards Tour officials, for dropping out, and for convincing his brother to do the same.[63] In the years that followed, the organizers added articles to the race's regulations to discourage racers from following Pélissier's example. The 1925 regulations warned that any racer harming the race's image by dropping out and encouraging others to do likewise would be banned from the following year's Tour and that 'any understanding among the racers in view of protests of any kind, or against the officials' decisions, any understanding to delay the finish, etc. will be rigorously punished'.[64] The Tour's regulations in the 1930s continued to prohibit racers from constituting 'a little soviet' – a highly charged phrase given the political context – in order to protest or rebel collectively, and promised to penalize any racer who created offensive, harmful, or untrue publicity about the organizers.[65]

In forbidding collective action by racers, Desgrange denied them a right enjoyed by French workers since 1884, when the Third Republic formally recognized their right to form unions, which had been tolerated since 1868.[66] The organizers were especially fearful that racer solidarity and unionization would lead to slowdowns, which suggested racers were rebelling against excessive requirements, eroded Desgrange's authority over the contestants, and undermined *L'Auto*'s depiction of the racers as hard-working, uncomplaining 'pedal workers' to be emulated by workers nationwide. Slowdowns also made for a less spectacular event and increased the public's wait along the itinerary. While collective initiatives by racers were forbidden, Desgrange permitted individual racers to lodge complaints with the race director within 48 hours of the end of the stage in which the incident had occurred, but they had to pay a fee for each complaint lodged. Desgrange may thus have hoped to discourage frivolous complaints and bad publicity, but the fee involved meant that racers had to pay simply to seek justice. Racers could also appeal to the *Commission Sportive* of the French cycling federation, but if they had been expelled from the Tour for a flagrant violation they could not continue to compete while awaiting its ruling.[67] Desgrange thus maintained considerable leverage in meting out punishment.

Beyond these practical measures, *L'Auto* sought to discredit the very notion of Tour racers as slave labour. Noting that Henri Pélissier had dropped out of the 1919 and 1920 Tours complaining that the race was a *'forçat*'s job', the paper acknowledged that it 'may seem the job of a convict for those whose muscles are insufficient or who lack courage'. Success in cycling, as in other professions, was determined by will power and disciplined training: any task, however simple, would seem like hard labour if one did not apply oneself.[68] *L'Auto* parodied Tour coverage *à la Albert Londres*, characterized by what it claimed were the emotional allusions of 'literary journalists' to convicts of the road, human livestock, martyrs, and victims of capitalism and the organizers' sadism. Desgrange dismissed these 'literary exaggerations' and urged his critics to study cycling before they unjustly accused him of sadistically exploiting these martyred *forçats*.[69] Cartoons in *L'Auto* ridiculed the notion of the Tour as exploitative 'hard labour' and of racers as convicts, presenting the event as a month of vacation for the contestants.[70] Racers were quoted thanking the organizers for the opportunity 'to go on a beautiful trip for a month in the most diverse regions of our superb France'. *L'Auto* concluded that they did 'not appear to take the Tour de France for a penal colony'.[71] The paper's portrayal of the Tour as working-class cyclotourism, which contradicted its classic depiction of the Tour as very hard work, indicates the extent to which the organizers had been stung by criticism following the Pélissier incident.

Particularly sensitive to accusations that the race exploited poor workers, Desgrange dismissed the Pélissier brothers as poorly prepared millionaire racers who now claimed that capitalist society exploited them.[72] He drew a sharp distinction between professional cyclists who had chosen 'this honorary profession' and 'workers in mines, coal-bunkers, [and] polders, who struggle their entire lives, and for what profit?'[73] Desgrange listed the Tour's prize money to prove that racers were not *forçats*, describing them at the end of the race as fresh and looking forward to translating their Tour celebrity into lucrative racing opportunities in France, Belgium and Italy.[74] Noting disingenuously that the Tour had existed for 20 years without references to the racers as *forçats*, he pointed out that no racer had ever died during the race (a claim he could no longer make after 1935), and suggested that there was nothing wrong with taking drugs to complete the race. Desgrange no doubt feared that if representations of the Tour as exploitative labour and racers as rebellious workers prevailed, sponsors and communities along the itinerary would no longer support the race. He quoted a letter from 'a poor crank' who, having read Londres's articles, considered Desgrange 'a dirty sports profiteer and a sinister swindler' and promised to prevent the next Tour and Desgrange 'from debasing the French race'.[75]

CONCLUSION

From the sport's earliest years in the late nineteenth century, French physicians, politicians and other commentators expressed concern about the toll that long-distance bicycle races took on contestants. Many of these critics argued that the sport was both a symptom and a source of a broader degeneration afflicting French society at a time of acute anxiety about France's position in an increasingly tense and polarized Europe. Emphasizing its repetitive, unskilled nature, observers also frequently associated endurance cycling with modern industrial labour. Influenced by these concerns and the industrial image of the race, opponents of the Tour through the inter-war years accused *L'Auto* of exploiting racers to increase its profits and those of the race's commercial sponsors. Pointing to pace requirements, fines and the Tour's many regulations, they undermined *L'Auto*'s presentation of the race as the honourable, efficient labour of disciplined 'pedal workers' with an apocalyptic vision of the Tour as a grossly unjust and repressive event. The Communists in particular, joined in the mid 1930s by the Socialists, argued that the race both reflected and reproduced capitalist exploitation of workers in modern, rationalized factories nationwide. In so doing, they and others charged the Tour with dehumanizing racers. These accusations were facilitated by widespread depictions of racers as mechanized automata, which were themselves grounded in recent, influential theories about the human body and its capacity for work.

Ironically, *L'Auto* failed to recognize the extent to which it had, as the leading purveyor of such images, contributed to the rhetorical arsenal of the Tour's opponents, even as it dismissed their 'literary exaggerations'. In seeking to sell the Tour and help fans conjure up images of their heroes, the sports daily had developed representations of racers as respectable workers *and* indomitable machines. The problem for *L'Auto* was that, as evocative as they were, these portrayals were contradictory: human beings – even bicycle racers and factory workers – were not machines. Seizing on this tension, critics cast the Tour and industrial modernity in an unfavourable light: dehumanized by exhausting, dangerous, and repetitive work, the Tour racer – like the factory worker – became a convict labourer.

References to Tour racers as 'pedal workers' and 'convict labourers' generally did not survive Second World War. The new journalists and editors at *L'Auto*'s successor, *L'Equipe*, and other newspapers simply did not share the sensibilities and concerns of their predecessors. They were writing in a nation experiencing extraordinary change as it shifted to an economy shaped by a rapidly expanding welfare state and increasingly dominated by service sector jobs. Condemning the race for exploiting 'slave labourers' was no longer a viable rhetorical strategy in a society in which the percentage of blue-collar workers was declining even as shorter working weeks, safer work places, earlier retirements, automation and, later, computerization were dramatically improving their work experiences and quality of life. Born of the economic modernization and political polarization that characterized pre-First World War and, particularly, inter-war France, the *forçat de la route* seemed less relevant to the nation's new circumstances, no longer lent itself to ideological exploitation and receded into history.

NOTES

1. C. Thompson, 'Regeneration, *Dégénérescence*, and the Medical Debate about Cycling in Fin-de-siècle France', in T. Terret (ed.), *Sport and Health in History* (Sankt Augustin: Academia Verlag, 1999), pp.339–45.
2. *L'Auto*, 9 June 1903.
3. *Arrêté relatif aux courses vélocipédiques à grande distance*, 28 May 1903, Sens Municipal Archives.
4. A. Rabinbach, *The Human Motor: Energy, Fatigue, and the Origins of Modernity* (New York: Basic Books, 1990), pp.23, 72.
5. R. Price, *A Social History of Nineteenth-Century France* (New York, Holmes and Meier, 1987), pp.212, 245; J.F. Stone, *The Search for Social Peace: Reform Legislation in France, 1890–1914* (Albany: State University of New York Press, 1985), pp.124–5; G. Cross, *A Quest for Time: The Reduction of Work in Britain and France, 1840–1940* (Berkeley: University of California Press, 1989), pp. 37, 39, 42–3; R. Price (ed.), *Documents on the French Revolution of 1848* (London: Macmillan Press Ltd, 1996), p.50.
6. The Radicals came to power in 1899 at the height of the Dreyfus Affair, when revelations that the Jewish officer Alfred Dreyfus had been framed by the army, which had then engaged in a cover-up involving high-ranking officers and government officials, united progressive forces on the Left.
7. Cross, *A Quest for Time*, pp.48, 49, 51, 56–7, 71–2, 82–3, 98, 235; Price, *A Social History of Nineteenth-Century France*, pp.210–11, 214; Stone, *The Search for Social Peace*, pp.62–5, 90, 96, 101, 103–22, 124–7, 129, 132–9, 147–59; E. Shorter and C. Tilly, *Strikes in France, 1830–1968* (Cambridge: Cambridge University Press, 1974), p.67; C. Charle, *Histoire sociale de la France au XIXe siècle* (Paris: Editions du Seuil, 1991), p.303.
8. Stone, *The Search for Social Peace*, p.134.
9. *L'Auto*, 9 June 1903. See also *L'Auto*, 8 Aug. 1911.
10. See *L'Auto*, 27 July 1909, 19 Aug. 1909, and 8 Aug. 1912. The Belgian critics quoted were a newspaper in Tournai, a Socialist on the Brabant Provincial Council, and *La Jeunesse Progressiste*.
11. *L'Auto*, 13 July 1923.
12. See, for example, *L'Auto*, 3 July 1903, 20 July 1912, 23 June 1928, 28 May 1929, 3 June 1929, 21 July 1929, 28 June 1931, 20 July 1931, 7 July 1932, 11 July 1932, 30 June 1934, and 26 July 1938; *Le Matin*, 28 July 1913; and *Le Petit Parisien*, 4 July 1935.
13. See, for example, articles by Dr Ruffier in *L'Auto*, 18 July 1911 and 8 Aug. 1939.
14. *L'Auto*, 15 July 1936, 16 July 1936, 21 July 1936, 26 July 1936, 29 July 1936 and 30 July 1936.
15. *L'Auto*, 28 Aug. 1936.
16. J. Hoberman, *Mortal Engines: The Science of Performance and the Dehumanization of Sport* (New York: The Free Press, 1992), pp.5–6, 9, 13–14, 19, 25, 68, 189. For more on Marey's career, see Rabinbach, *The Human Motor*, pp.87, 90, 93–5, 119.
17. Rabinbach, *The Human Motor*, pp.1–4, 10, 44, 59, 60, 133, 137, 183.
18. *L'Auto*, 27 July 1906.
19. Jules Amar, a French industrial ergonomist and fatigue expert and the author in 1913 of *Le Moteur Humain*, was convinced that 'a scientifically predetermined optimum speed and position achieve a maximum amount of work with a minimum amount of fatigue' and tested his theory in sports (Rabinbach, *The Human Motor*, pp.48, 188).
20. For a discussion of Desgrange and his social philosophy of sport, see C. Thompson, 'Controlling the Working-Class Sports Hero in Order to Control the Masses? The Social Philosophy of Sport of Henri Desgrange', *Stadion*, 27 (2001), pp.139–51.
21. The account of the Pélissiers' withdrawal is drawn from P. Chany, *La fabuleuse histoire du Tour de France* (Paris: Editions Nathan, 1991), pp.196–200. A summary of their racing careers can be found in J. Augendre, R. Bastide, G. Marchesini and J.-P. Ollivier, *Le Dictionnaire des Coureurs* (Paris: La Maison du Sport, 1988), pp.987–8.
22. *Le Petit Parisien*, 27 June 1924.
23. Guyana became a French penal colony in the mid-nineteenth century (see J.-G. Petit *et al.*, *Histoire des galères, bagnes et prisons, XIIIe–XXe siècles: Introduction à l'histoire pénale de la France* (Toulouse: Editions Privat, 1991), pp.227–59).
24. For Londres's series on the Tour see *Le Petit Parisien*, 23 June 1924, 27 June 1924, 29 June 1924, 2 July 1924, 3 July 1924, 5 July 1924, 7 July 1924, 9 July 1924, 13 July 1924, 19 July 1924 and 20 July 1924.

25. *L'Humanité*, 1 July 1924.
26. *L'Auto*, 30 June 1924.
27. M. Pierre, 'La transportation (1848–1938)', in Petit *et al.*, *Histoire des galères, bagnes et prisons*, pp.253–4.
28. M. Perrot, 'On the Formation of the French Working Class', in I. Katznelson and A.R. Zolberg (eds), *Working-Class Formation: Nineteenth-Century Patterns in Western Europe and the United States* (Princeton: Princeton University Press, 1986), pp.90, 100; M. Perrot, 'Le regard de l'Autre: les patrons français vus par les ouvriers (1880–1914)', in M. Levy-Leboyer (ed.), *Le Patronat de la Seconde Industrialisation* (Paris: Les Editions Ouvrières, 1979), p.295; M. Perrot, 'The Three Ages of Industrial Discipline', in J.M. Merriman (ed.), *Consciousness and Class Experience in Nineteenth-Century Europe* (New York: Holmes and Meier, 1979), p.16; M. Perrot, *Les ouvriers en grève, France 1871–1890* (Paris: Mouton and Co., 1974), p.295; S. Edwards, *The Paris Commune, 1871* (Chicago and New York: Quadrangle Books, 1971), p.40; R. Palme Dutt, *The Internationale* (London: Lawrence and Wishart Ltd., 1964), p.11; R. Tombs, *The Paris Commune, 1871* (London and New York: Longman, 1999), pp.220–3.
29. *L'Humanité*, 27 June 1924, 28 June 1924, 29 June 1924 and 21 July 1924.
30. Ibid., 25 July 1921, 24 June 1923 and 11 July 1923.
31. Ibid., 21 June 1924.
32. Ibid., 7 July 1932 and 22 July 1935.
33. Ibid., 17 July 1935, 19 July 1935 and 21 July 1935.
34. Ibid., 1 July 1924, 2 July 1924 and 6 July 1932; R. Holt, *Sport and Society in Modern France* (Hamden: Archon Books, 1981), p.204.
35. *L'Humanité*, 15 July 1932, 17 July 1932, 31 July 1932, 11 July 1935 and 12 July 1935.
36. Ibid., 31 July 1932. This was unrealistic: stars did not wish to jeopardize the fortunes they could make by antagonizing Desgrange, while lesser racers lacked the clout to confront him successfully.
37. Ibid., 6 July 1932 and 26 July 1932.
38. *L'Auto*, 1 July 1903.
39. Ibid., 19 July 1903, 1 June 1929, 25 July 1929, 7 June 1930, 12 July 1931 and 22 July 1933.
40. H. Braverman, *Labor and Monopoly Capital: The Degradation of Work in the Twentieth Century* (New York and London: Monthly Review Press, 1974), pp.90–91, 118, 131, 133–4; Cross, *A Quest for Time*, p.106; D.S. Landes, *The Unbound Prometheus: Technological Change and Industrial Development in Western Europe from 1750 to the Present* (Cambridge: Cambridge University Press, 1969), pp.321–2; C.S. Maier, 'Between Taylorism and Technocracy: European Ideologies and the Vision of Industrial Productivity in the 1920s', *The Journal of Contemporary History*, 5, 2 (1970), 29; G. Friedmann, *The Anatomy of Work: Labor, Leisure and the Implications of Automation*, translated by W. Rawson (New York: Heinemann Educational Books Ltd., 1961), pp.86–7.
41. Rabinbach, *The Human Motor*, p.2.
42. Braverman, *Labor and Monopoly Capital*, pp.88, 97, 100.
43. A. Moutet, 'Les origines du système de Taylor en France. Le point de vue patronal (1907–1914)', *Le Mouvement social*, 93 (Oct.–Dec. 1975), 15, 19, 21, 23–33, 38–41, 43, 48; G.G. Humphreys, *Taylorism in France 1904–1920: The Impact of Scientific Management on Factory Relations and Society* (New York and London: Garland Publishing, Inc., 1986), pp.4, 10, 13–14, 49, 76–81, 93–102, 105–11, 113, 116–23, 127–30; M. Levy-Leboyer, 'Innovation and Business Strategies in Nineteenth- and Twentieth-Century France', in E.C. Carter II, R. Foster, and J.N. Moody (eds), *Enterprise and Entrepreneurs in Nineteenth- and Twentieth-Century France* (Baltimore: The Johns Hopkins University Press, 1976), p.116; Cross, *A Quest for Time*, p.106; R.F. Kuisel, *Capitalism and the State in Modern France: Renovation and Economic Management in the Twentieth Century* (Cambridge: Cambridge University Press, 1981), p.28; Rabinbach, *The Human Motor*, p.241. For an overview of workers' reactions to industrial rationalization in early-twentieth-century France, see also G. Cross, 'Redefining Workers' Control: Rationalization, Labor Time, and Union Politics in France, 1900–1928', in J.E. Cronin and Carmen Sirianni (eds), *Work, Community, and Power: The Experience of Labor in Europe and America, 1900–1925* (Philadelphia: Temple University Press, 1983), pp.143–72.
44. Moutet, 'Les origines du système de Taylor en France', 33–4, 44, 46; Humphreys, *Taylorism in France 1904–1920*, pp.3–4, 13, 130–34, 172–4, 221–4, 230, and Ch. 5; S. Van de Casteele-Schweitzer, 'Management and Labour in France 1914–39', in S. Tolliday and J. Zeitlin (eds),

The Automobile Industry and its Workers: Between Fordism and Flexibility (New York: St Martin's Press, 1987), pp.58–60, 63; Rabinbach, *The Human Motor*, pp.260–61, 271; Cross, *A Quest for Time*, pp.105–11, 151–2, 157–9, 195, 200–204, 209, 211–12; Maier, 'Between Taylorism and Technocracy', 38, 50–1; Kuisel, *Capitalism and the State in Modern France*, pp.77, 83, 86. On wartime scientific management in France, see Humphreys, *Taylorism in France 1904–1920*, Ch. 4. For the impact of Taylorism in Europe in the 1920s, see Maier, 'Between Taylorism and Technology', 27–61. For Communist attitudes towards rationalization during the inter-war period, see Van de Casteele-Schweitzer, 'Management and Labour in France 1914–39', p.71.

45. P. Fridenson, 'Automobile Workers in France and Their Work, 1914–1983', in S.L. Kaplan and C.J. Koepp (eds), *Work in France: Representations, Meaning, Organization, and Practice* (Ithaca: Cornell University Press, 1986), pp.523–7. For a different view, which argues for less worker resistance to rationalization while acknowledging high turnover rates and voluntary departures, see Van de Casteele-Schweitzer, 'Management and Labour in France 1914–39', pp.64–5. Van de Castelle-Schweitzer argues that by the late 1920s, 'Taylorism had become part of people's mentalities' in the French automobile industry (p.68).

46. Cross, *A Quest for Time*, p.212.

47. *L'Humanité*, 9 July 1932, 22 July 1932 and 28 July 1935.

48. *Paris-Soir*, 21 July 1937.

49. *Le Canard Enchaîné*, 2 July 1924 and 9 July 1924.

50. *L'Intransigeant*, 19 July 1937.

51. *La Bretagne Sportive*, 19 Oct. 1935, 16 July 1936, 15 July 1937; *Voici*, 4 July 1936, quoted in *La Bretagne Sportive*, 9 July 1936; *La Province* (Rennes), 7 July 1937, 28 July 1937; *Les Nouvelles de l'Ouest* (Rennes), 30 July 1937; *Les Nouvelles Rennaises et de l'Ouest*, 20 July 1933.

52. André Reuze, *Le Tour de Souffrance* (Paris: A. Fayard, 1925), pp.153, 172–7, 230–32.

53. *L'Action Française*, 30 June 1924 and 31 July 1935; *L'Intransigeant*, 29 June 1924, 30 June 1924 and 20 July 1924; *L'Echo de Paris*, 27 June 1924 and 30 June 1924.

54. *Le Peuple*, 27 June 1924.

55. *Le Populaire*, 8 July 1928, 17 July 1928, 6 July 1929, 25 July 1929 and 1 July 1937.

56. M. Winock, *Le socialisme en France et en Europe, XIXe–XXe siècle* (Paris: Editions du Seuil, 1992), pp.82–5.

57. *Le Populaire*, 17 July 1928 and 25 July 1929.

58. Winock, *Le socialisme en France et en Europe*, pp.85–6.

59. *Le Populaire*, 29 July 1935, 19 July 1937 and 27 July 1937.

60. Ibid., 22 July 1935; *L'Humanité*, 16 July 1935.

61. *Le Populaire*, 29 July 1935 and 30 July 1935.

62. *L'Humanité*, 13 July 1935, 14 July 1935, 15 July 1935 and 17 July 1935.

63. *L'Auto*, 29 June 1924.

64. Ibid., 1 June 1925 and 22 May 1925. See also the 1926 regulations in *L'Auto*, 1 June 1926.

65. Ibid., 10 June 1930, 10 June 1931, 6 June 1932 and 14 June 1932.

66. Price, *A Social History of Nineteenth-Century France*, pp.245–6. By 1913, there were just over one million union members, representing about 10 per cent of the French industrial labour force. The anomalous position of the racers did not escape André Reuze, one of whose characters complains that Tour racers are the only workers denied the right to unionize (Reuze, *Le Tour de Souffrance*, pp.212–13).

67. *L'Auto*, 3 June 1925. The fee of 50 francs was reduced to 5 francs for racers in the modest *touriste-routier* category.

68. Ibid., 30 June 1924.

69. Ibid., 20 July 1924, 20 June 1925 and 8 July 1929. See also *L'Auto*, 17 July 1924. For two examples of such parodies see *L'Auto*, 8 July 1924 and 15 July 1924.

70. Ibid., 18 July 1924 and 21 June 1927.

71. Ibid., 30 June 1924 and 28 July 1924.

72. Ibid., 20 July 1924.

73. Ibid., 22 July 1931.

74. Ibid., 12 July 1924 and 20 July 1924.

75. Ibid., 20 July 1924.

The Economics of the Tour, 1930–2003

ERIC REED

INTRODUCTION

The 100th anniversary of the Tour de France provides an ideal opportunity to examine the evolving relationship between business, sport, and culture during the last century in France.

From the moment that Parisian journalists created the Tour, it was a commercial, for-profit event. The business needs of the event's primary stakeholders – Parisian race organizers, the media, corporate sponsors, provincial host-towns, and the race's professional stars – shaped the Tour as an entertainment spectacle from its inception. The stakeholders' practical business decisions had important cultural ramifications: their interests and influence forged the event's underlying business philosophies and determined how the Tour was organized, who became sports celebrities and heroes, what areas of France the race visited, how the event's myths were perpetuated, and how the average fan experienced and participated in the spectacle. Over the decades, the race evolved from an event staged in order to spur sales of bicycles and sports newspapers in France into a globally televised spectacle that generated publicity for a wide range of corporate sponsors in France and from around the world. The success and popularity of the Tour undoubtedly spurred the professionalization and commercialization of other sports in France, and the event helped to acclimatize the French to key trends in twentieth-century mass culture such as mass corporate publicity and the commercialization of leisure. Because of its central position at the intersection of business and culture, the Tour's evolution illustrates how commercial interests shaped France's popular culture in new ways in the twentieth century.

THE PRE-SECOND WORLD WAR TOUR

The primary commercial function of the Tour up to 1929 was to sell newspapers and bicycles. Henri Desgrange, editor-in-chief of the fledgling sports daily *L'Auto*, concocted the event in 1903 as the ultimate stratagem in the circulation battle with his newspaper's main competitor, *Le Vélo*.

The Commercial Function of the Pre-1930 Tour: A Marriage of the Bicycle and the Press

Almost immediately after its creation, the Tour became the linchpin of the commercial marriage of the sporting press and the bicycle industry. Bicycle industrialists and newspapermen worked together to fashion the Tour into a spectacular and profitable sports entertainment event. Journalists chose the race participants and sponsors, created the itinerary and rules of the competition, and provided the equipment necessary to stage the event. Bicycle manufacturers sponsored teams of professional cyclists to compete in the Tour, and the publicity generated by the race allowed them to capture larger shares of the ever-growing mass market for bicycles. Furthermore, the popular appeal of the Tour spurred newspaper sales for *L'Auto* and other titles. Desgrange and his colleagues continually transformed the race in order to allow *L'Auto* and the event's corporate partners to profit in new ways from sports-related publicity and advertising. For example, in order to maximize competitiveness, media coverage, sponsor exposure and spectator enjoyment, the journalist-organizers revised the rules and itinerary of the race nearly every year and introduced such innovations as the 'yellow jersey' competition (1919), time trials (1922) and radio coverage (1929). So powerful was the Tour's popularity and commercial impact before the Second World War that the event helped to 'democratize' the bicycle in France, transforming the machine into an object of consumption affordable to almost every social and economic stratum of French society.[1]

The Publicity Caravan: Widening the Tour as an Advertising Vehicle from 1929

The Tour's initial business formula worked marvellously for more than two decades. Desgrange transformed the event in 1929, however, in response to the new difficulties faced by the Tour and *L'Auto* during the

1920s, not the least of which was that the wealthiest cycling teams monopolized the best professional riders and, in effect, controlled the outcome of the race.[2] After 1929, the Tour became a prime publicity vehicle for a wide variety of business interests, not just bicycle manufacturers. Desgrange instituted the national team formula, in which *L'Auto* invited all-star teams from Europe's top cycling countries to compete in the Tour, and replaced the bicycle builders with a broader and continually changing body of advertisers by opening the event to general corporate sponsorship.

Desgrange radically altered the Tour's business structure and financing. To rid the Tour of the manufacturers' meddling, *L'Auto* undertook to pay for all aspects of the race. *L'Auto*, rather than the team sponsors, provided and paid for the bicycles, food, mechanics and lodging for Tour competitors.[3] Although his reforms increased dramatically the cost of staging the Tour for *L'Auto*, Desgrange coupled his innovations with a novel mode of financing the race through corporate sponsorship and increased *subventions* (subsidies) from the host-towns. Desgrange aimed to craft the Tour into a promotional event open to all interested parties, not only to bicycle industry sponsors. In doing so, the Tour evolved into a spectacle that combined even more closely and overtly entertainment, sport and commerce.

The creation of the publicity caravan and of corporate-sponsored prizes were the most significant of Desgrange's 1930 innovations. The publicity caravan was a motley assortment of vehicles that paraded before the race from town to town. Businesses provided the vehicles and paid a fee to *L'Auto* to join the caravan. Membership in the caravan accorded businesses the right to publicize their products to roadside spectators during the passage of the race. The first publicity caravan in 1930 was tiny – only ten enterprises were represented, each with one vehicle.[4] Thereafter, the size of the publicity caravan increased tremendously and quickly: in 1935, 46 firms participated in the publicity caravan.[5] Fees from the publicity caravan, in addition to larger *subventions* demanded by Desgrange from host-towns after 1930, helped *L'Auto* pay for the organization of the Tour for the next 30 years.

The publicity caravan probably enhanced the fun and enjoyment of the roadside fans, as well. The sheer variety of participants made the procession of Tour sponsors interesting. Desgrange allowed just about anyone who was willing to pay a fee to join the publicity caravan, including the 'Fakir Birman', a Parisian magician and fortune teller, the

Holo-Electron company, which produced an electric wrinkle-removal machine, and 'La Vache qui rit' (Laughing Cow), a processed cheese maker. Desgrange concluded that the publicity caravan was a powerful advertising tool and that it greatly enhanced the Tour's carnival-like atmosphere. '[When the caravan passes] it holds the public spellbound. ... If the publicity caravan did not exist, we would have to create it. ... Not only does it facilitate sales, but it provokes them.'[6]

Desgrange also encouraged businesses and other interested entities to sponsor the race's prizes. Because of the immense interest on the part of private sponsors in this opportunity, the amount of prize money to be won on the Tour rose markedly after 1930. The prize money sponsored by *L'Auto* totalled 150,000 francs in 1929, including a 10,000 franc first-place award.[7] By 1937, total prize money had grown to 800,000 francs, and the first-place award to 200,000 francs,[8] all of which was sponsored by businesses, organizations or other entities.

In addition to helping pay for the race, corporate sponsors bolstered *L'Auto*'s advertising revenue. Many sponsors of the Tour purchased advertisement space in *L'Auto*. In return, Desgrange often provided these clients with free, seemingly unsolicited advertising. *L'Auto* usually coupled descriptions of businesses' cash contributions to the Tour with publicity or product plugs. For the company's contribution of 12,000 francs in prizes to the 1931 Tour, *L'Auto* plugged Cointreau as the 'marvel of marvels of the after-dinner liqueurs ... that the entire world knows and loves'.[9] Desgrange and his writers sometimes incorporated sponsor publicity directly into their race narratives. For example, amid *L'Auto*'s reporting on the third day of racing during the 1931 Tour, Desgrange dubbed the Brest-Vannes stage 'The Stage of "La Vache qui rit"', producers of 'the most delicious crème de gruyère cheese that one can find ... a veritable dessert as well as a first-rate, nutritious staple'.[10]

A look at the estimated budget of the 1938 Tour de France demonstrates how the event's financing shifted after 1930. The total budget for the 1938 Tour was two and a half million francs.[11] Corporate-sponsored prizes that year amounted to 900,000 francs, or 36 per cent of the budget. Prior to 1930, *L'Auto* financed all prizes. In 1938, the stage towns provided approximately 525,000 francs, or 21 per cent of the budget, if one assumes an average *subvention* of 25,000 francs to the Tour from each of the 21 stage towns.[12] Although *subventions* varied greatly from town to town before 1930, it is safe to say that in the 1930s *L'Auto* demanded contributions that were between five and 25 times higher than in the 1920s.[13] The fees paid by businesses to join the publicity caravan that year are unknown, but can be estimated conservatively at 10 per cent of the budget, or 250,000 francs. Thus, town *subventions* and corporate sponsorship accounted for at least 70 per cent of the Tour's budget by the end of the 1930s.

The Tour de France, with its nationwide audience of roadside spectators, newspaper readers and radio listeners, provided a wide range of eager sponsors with a media-saturated stage upon which to promote themselves. The story of how France's most visible national sporting event became even more commercialized in the 1930s also illustrates how a growing number of French businesses embraced new styles of publicity and sought to promote themselves in novel ways during the inter-war years. After the Second World War, the Tour and its sponsors experimented with new, even more potent forms of commercialism and promotion.

THE POST-WAR PERIOD UP TO 1982

The resumption of the Tour de France, which was not staged between 1940 and 1947, was not inevitable after the Second World War.

Business of the Tour, 1947 to 1961: How 'Commercial' Should the Tour Be?

In light of the supply shortages of the immediate post-war period, staging the Tour de France was an impossible task. In addition, the radical restructuring of the press by the new French government after the Second World War created the most formidable obstacle to the Tour's renewal: competing political factions fought heatedly over who possessed the right to stage the race. Not until 1947 did Jacques Goddet succeed in establishing himself and *L'Auto*'s successor, *L'Equipe*, as the acknowledged heirs of the pre-war event. Goddet's *L'Equipe* formed a partnership to stage the Tour with press mogul Emilien Amaury's *Le Parisien libéré* in order to lessen *L'Equipe*'s financial burden and to assure the reborn race a large publicity impact.

The formula of the first post-war Tours closely followed the competitive model employed by Desgrange in the 1930s. The post-1947 event remained a spectacle in which sport, commercialism and publicity mingled. Goddet decided to resurrect the national team formula, but, as a concession to the bicycle manufacturers, the racers competed on the brand-name road bicycles of their sponsors rather than on generic machines supplied by the race organizers. Goddet also launched a publicity caravan in which 15 businesses participated.[14] The 1947 Tour was an immense popular success: the lead changed hands several times during the three-week race, and the victor, the acerbic, combative Breton Jean Robic, won the race with a dramatic breakaway on the last day of competition.

After the Second World War, France's changing commercial and cultural milieu offered new opportunities for an enterprise like the Tour. The post-war consumer 'revolution', fuelled by rising incomes, population growth and increasing leisure time, initiated a sustained economic boom that the French refer to as the Thirty Glorious Years (*Les Trente Glorieuses*). Unprecedented prosperity and population growth, rising standards of living and increasing leisure time fuelled the consumption that was at the heart of France's post-war economic expansion. As their incomes rose, the French purchased enormous volumes of manufactured goods and appliances such as automobiles, televisions, radios, refrigerators and washing machines. They devoted their increasing leisure time to vacations, playing sports, shopping, going to the cinema, and to spending time at home listening to the radio and watching television.

The reborn Tour was well positioned to exploit the new opportunities presented by France's evolving consumer culture and economy after the war. The Tour's dual character as both a long-standing institution of French popular culture and a modern, publicity-generating spectacle allowed the event to act as a bridge between traditional and new forms of commercialism and mass promotion, especially television, as will be discussed later. Nevertheless, although the popularity of the race was not in question, the business structure of the Tour, as well as the event's exact blend of commercialism, publicity and pure sports competition, had yet to be determined. Significant internal and external factors and considerations, such as the needs and desires of the publicity-hungry business community, the financial crisis facing the sport of cycling and the press industry, the advent of television, and the debate among the Tour organizers over how 'commercial' the Tour should be, helped determine the new business philosophies and commercial *raison d'être* of the Tour during the decades after 1947.

The Tour, the bicycle industry and French professional sports in general endured several decades of financial and commercial difficulties after the Second World War despite the onset of France's economic boom. The French bicycle industry remained one of the world's largest but entered an acute crisis in the early 1950s. After the war, the automobile replaced the bicycle in the French eye as the primary symbol of personal freedom and mobility. Household consumption grew 40 per cent between 1950 and 1957, but the French, once they equipped their homes with appliances, preferred to spend their rising incomes on automobiles rather than on bicycles.[15] Demand for bicycles slackened and production plummeted from 1.3 million units in 1949, which matched the total output of the industry in 1939, to 790,000 units in 1956.[16] As their financial situations deteriorated, many individual firms found it more and more difficult to finance professional teams and began to retreat from sponsorship.[17] The teams were expensive. Jean Bobet, a professional cyclist and brother of three-time Tour champion Louison Bobet, estimated that the cost of assembling and paying the expenses for a top-echelon cycling team for a year had risen to at least twenty million francs by the mid-1950s.[18]

The Tour de France also faced financial difficulties throughout the 1940s and 1950s. As the Tour's organizers feared, expanding radio and television coverage of the race eroded the readership of *L'Equipe* and *Le Parisien libéré*. The Tour ceased to be the powerful sales booster that it had been before the Second World War, and the spike in circulation that the event generated for the two dailies gradually flattened. In 1961, *Le Parisien libéré* even experienced, for the first time, a marked drop in circulation during the race.[19] Fewer people followed the race in the daily newspapers and the French relied more and more on the broadcast media for coverage of the Tour. In the two decades after 1947, the annual event consistently lost money. Although no complete budget statistics exist, the organizers indicated that the race ran deficits in 1947, 1948 and 1949.[20] The race's budget deficit in 1953 amounted to 12 million francs.[21] Presumably, the race operated in the red in other years as well.

The Tour struggled to find a solution to its financial shortfalls, but the event's organizers were reluctant to take advantage of new promotional possibilities. Commercialization – how to limit, manage and channel it – was the thorniest problem for the Tour organizers in the 15 years after 1945. In particular, Jacques Goddet resisted the pressure of professional cycling's biggest corporate backers to resurrect the pre-1930 corporate team race formula. He and other Tour officials feared that altering the event's financial arrangements and publicity structure would lead to uncontrollable commercialization of the event and to a degradation of the race's cultural character.

At first glance, it would seem difficult to imagine how the Tour could become a more 'commercial' spectacle. As in the pre-war era, the Tour freely allowed promotion-seeking firms to enter the publicity caravan and aggressively courted businesses to sponsor the event's prizes. The financial contributions of businesses figured highly in the Tour's post-war budget. In 1948, for example, private enterprises accounted for roughly a third of the Tour's budget of 45 million francs.[22] This percentage rose in the 1950s, as did the budget of the event. In 1952, businesses accounted for nearly 60 per cent of the Tour's 120 million franc budget.[23] Because of the highly visible presence of the race's sponsors, many observers criticized the publicity-oriented character of the Tour spectacle. Nevertheless, the event's organizers embraced the role of the race as a promotional machine, at least to a certain degree. Goddet proclaimed, 'As the organizer of the Tour de France, I affirm that all forms and all modes of publicity can express themselves during the race'.[24]

In France and elsewhere, the sport of cycling eagerly sought out new, wealthy corporate sponsors. A growing number of enterprises outside the cycling community's traditional business circle (*extra-sportifs*) hungered to generate nationwide and international publicity for themselves, and recognized the promotional power inherent in sponsoring athletes, teams and sporting competitions. Bicycle firms that continued to sponsor cycling teams sought out these *extra-sportif* businesses in order to lighten their own financial burdens. In 1955, the Fédération Française de Cyclisme (FFC), French cycling's governing body, changed its statutes and allowed *extra-sportif* advertising to appear on riders' jerseys and racing shorts. Throughout the mid- and late 1950s, more and more *extra-sportifs* entered into partnerships with established cycling businesses.

The arrival of the *extra-sportifs* in the 1950s brought to the fore the issue of whether (and how) to restructure France's national bicycle race. Undoubtedly, the Tour would have benefited from the financial participation of the *extra-sportifs*. Nevertheless, for nearly 15 years, Goddet steadfastly refused to revert to the corporate team format and maintained a strict division between the Tour's competitive and publicity structures. The Director and his lieutenants pointed out, as had Desgrange in the late 1920s, that commercial sponsorship of the teams in the Tour could lead potentially to collusion among riders, attempts by sponsors to manufacture victories for certain teams and racers, a general degradation of the competitiveness and combativeness of the race, and, ultimately, a dampening of public interest in the event.[25]

Even more, Goddet redefined the cultural imperative of the Tour after the Second World War and employed the race's new 'mission' as a weapon against the advocates of the corporate team format. He characterized his opposition to the *extra-sportifs* as a struggle to preserve a cultural institution from an invasion by commercial interests. The Tour, Goddet argued, was a powerful symbol of French heritage and must be a bulwark against the encroachment of vulgar promotionalism into traditional culture. In Goddet's vision, the Tour embodied a certain historic 'moral' and 'mystique', and the event's rebirth in its 'traditional' form – the national team format, which was less than two decades old – in 1947 represented a return to normal for the French nation after the Second World War.[26] Goddet believed that the national team formula endowed the race with a sporting character, style and international feel similar to the Pierre de Coubertin-inspired Olympic Games.[27] Furthermore, Goddet contended, the prestige, glory and lustre of the Tour rested on the 'solid framework' of the national team formula, which he considered the event's 'essential principle'.[28] As pressure for a return to the corporate team formula mounted in the 1950s, Goddet argued that the battle over the *extra-sportifs* in professional cycling was a crucial facet of the wider struggle to safeguard the character of French sport and its heroes. 'To see French champions transformed into sandwich-board men (*hommes sandwiches*) by *extra-sportif* interests … we cannot let that happen.'[29] Goddet recognized that his position as Director of the Tour, the most prestigious race in the world, made him a pivotal influence in shaping the French bicycle industry and professional cycling. '[We Tour organizers] are conscious of the fact that we are defending more than just the Tour, that we are defending the entire sport of cycling.'[30]

The Tour de France's struggle against the *extra-sportifs* ended in the early 1960s. Powerful interests both inside the Tour's management and in the camp of the *extra-sportif* groups forced Goddet to accept a return to the corporate team format. Goddet's second-in-command, Félix Lévitan, publicly backed Goddet during the battles over the *extra-sportifs* throughout the 1950s, but he privately favoured reinstituting the pre-1930 formula.[31] Since Lévitan, editor-in-chief of *Le Parisien libéré*'s sports section, was the *de facto* voice of *L'Equipe*'s major financial partner in the Tour, his opinion possessed considerable weight. More importantly, the *extra-sportif* team sponsors possessed a crucial weapon that, by the early 1960s, forced Goddet to re-evaluate his opposition to the corporate team formula. The head-to-head battles that transpired on French country roads among cycling's biggest stars fuelled the drama of the Tour and maintained its popular appeal. Beginning in the late 1950s, several of the most powerful *extra-sportif* teams pressured their featured riders to forgo participation in the Tour de France. The dominant cyclists of the late 1950s and early 1960s, Belgian Rik Van Looy and Frenchman Jacques Anquetil, avoided competing in the Tour in order to honour contracts with their *extra-sportif* sponsors. The decision of Anquetil, the world's leading rider between 1957 and 1965, to participate in the 1960 Giro d'Italia but not in the Tour de France delivered a particularly strong blow to Goddet's position. France's 1960 national team found itself with no top-rank star riders. The following year, Antonin Magne, the former Tour champion and manager of the Mercier-BP team, convinced his rising star, Raymond Poulidor, to skip the Tour because racing in the national team format would undermine his young champion's 'commercial value'.[32] The lack of competitiveness during the 1961 Tour – termed a 'fiasco' by Goddet[33] – forced the organizers to reverse their stance on the *extra-sportifs*. After the race, Goddet and Lévitan agreed to reinstitute the corporate team formula the following year.

In retrospect, Goddet characterized the return to the pre-1930 formula as 'necessary' and 'inevitable', since by the late 1950s bicycle businesses alone could no longer effectively 'nourish' the sport of cycling.[34] Nevertheless, Goddet effectively defended the Tour's national team formula for nearly two decades during a period in which *extra-sportif* sponsorship became the major source of financing for professional cycling in most of western Europe. After 1962, the Tour evolved into an even more formidable mechanism for generating large-scale commercial publicity, and scores of new enterprises entered into the business of sponsoring cycling teams and competitions. The return to the corporate team formula was not the only, or the most important, factor in the Tour's evolution thereafter. The Tour's traditional promotional structures – the publicity caravan, advertising campaigns in the pages of *L'Equipe* and other newspapers, and radio advertising on France's peripheral broadcasting networks – could not generate the volume or style of publicity sought by cycling's new business partners. As will be discussed below, after the return to the corporate team formula, television coverage of the race increased exponentially the promotional power of the event.

Post-1962: Tour Economics in the Television Age

The evolution of the Tour from an annual 'journalistic' event into a televised sports spectacle that dominated the French airwaves during the months of July and August altered the commercial *raison d'être* of the Tour de France. The change occurred on several fronts. For the race organizers, the Tour ceased to be a crucial circulation prop, since more and more French men and women followed the event on their television screens and relied less and less on newspapers for the race narrative. The Tour evolved from a sporting event primarily underwritten by and benefiting the print media into one financed directly and indirectly by audio-visual media. After 1962, the Tour de France continually transformed itself in ways that allowed its organizers and sponsors to profit from the changing marketplace and from new modes of communication and advertising. As television coverage of the event grew, the Tour evolved beyond its original mandate as a circulation prop for its parent newspapers and emerged as the cornerstone of a media and sports empire, the Amaury Group, that owned a vast network of specialized and general-interest publications and created or organized numerous for-profit, televised sporting spectacles, not just the Tour. The Tour's new commercial structure enabled a wide variety of business concerns – not only bicycle manufacturers and *extra-sportif* team sponsors – to capture larger shares of France's burgeoning consumer market. The Tour helped corporate interests to penetrate state-controlled, commercial-free radio and television and thus instigated the commercialization of the most dominant post-war media. In the process, the post-war Tour solidified its place at the intersection of commerce and culture, and influenced the shape of both. With its spectator audience of between one-fifth and one-third of the French population on the roadside, and additional tens of millions of French and European fans on the airwaves, the growing commercial power of the Tour helped to spur the broader symbiosis among business, television and sport that characterized the last three decades of the twentieth century.

From the perspective of corporate sponsors, the televised Tour offered the possibility of generating an unprecedented volume of publicity. The demand by enterprises for publicity – both in traditional

sectors like the press and in new media – increased significantly. In broad
terms, the amount of money devoted to publicity by French businesses
increased from 320 million francs in 1950 to 2.6 billion francs in 1962,
according to a publicity industry trade journal.[35] Traditional venues of
advertising – the press, radio and the cinema – could not accommodate
the growing demand for publicity, since the audiences of these three
media stagnated or declined during the 1960s and 1970s. The television
audience, on the other had, expanded rapidly in the 1960s.[36] Many
businesses shifted the focus of their promotional efforts to this emerging
and rapidly-growing media. Prior to 1968, when the government
changed its policy and allowed advertising in public media, businesses
sought to generate 'clandestine publicity' (*la publicité clandestine*) by
placing their brand names and product images on television in ways that
circumvented official prohibitions. Sporting events like the Tour de
France provided the perfect opportunity to generate such publicity and
spurred many enterprises to purchase cycling teams or to otherwise
participate in sponsoring the race. The Tour's organizers continually
reshaped the event to accommodate the increasing demand for sports-
related, televised publicity. To facilitate the French business
community's growing desire to join the televised spectacle, Tour officials
created new types of sponsorship. Goddet and Lévitan slightly increased
the average number of teams in the race after the institution of the
corporate team formula in 1962,[37] created new prizes and awards for
purchase by interested sponsors, and even sold the right to become
'official suppliers' of the event.[38]

The Amaury Years: Sport, Money and Media

Between 1962, when the race returned to the corporate team format, and
the early 1980s, the race organizers gradually abandoned the founding
precept of the Tour, that is, that the race served primarily to boost the
circulation and advertising revenue of the newspapers that organized it.
In fact, *L'Equipe* faced shrinking circulation numbers throughout the
early and mid-1960s, which prompted Goddet to sell the newspaper and
its subsidiary components (including the Tour) to his friend Emilien
Amaury in 1965.[39] In return, Amaury promised Goddet that he would
retain complete editorial control over *L'Equipe* for as long as Goddet
wanted, as well as his position as the Tour's co-director.[40]

After 1965, the Tour emerged as the crown jewel of a publicity
empire that serviced the promotional needs of a wide variety of business

interests throughout the year. The event served as the linchpin of the commercial union of two concerns, the Amaury Group and the Société Nouvelle de Publications Sportives et Industrielles (SOPUSI), a consortium of newspapers, magazines and sporting events managed by Goddet.[41] Between 1965 and the early 1980s, Goddet and Amaury transformed the new Amaury Group from a loose confederation of publications into a multimedia publicity empire built around a large number of periodicals, several televised sporting events, and the French capital's premier sports and entertainment venues. Thanks to the union with SOPUSI, the Amaury Group also controlled many of the biggest sporting events and venues in Europe. The Group organized most of the great French cycling classics, including the Tour de France, the Tour de l'Avenir (the amateur version of the Tour de France, created in 1961), the Paris–Roubaix, Paris–Tours, Paris–Brest–Paris, Bordeaux–Paris, and Paris–Tours classics, and the Grand Prix des Nations. Goddet, as the legal successor to the property of Henri Desgrange and *L'Auto*, also owned or managed several major arenas and fairgrounds in the Paris region, including the Parc des Princes, Vélodrome d'Hiver, the Palais des Sports and the Parc des Expositions. These venues became parts of the Amaury Group after 1965. The Amaury Group also owned and operated a full-service publicity firm.

Riders, Media Celebrity and Corporate Sponsorship

The celebrity of professional riders became an even more important publicity tool in the television age. As television coverage of the Tour expanded in the late 1950s and early 1960s, the new medium began to play an important role in shaping and disseminating the public images of famous cyclists. An analysis of the television coverage of Raymond Poulidor, who became a professional racer in 1959, illustrates how television magnified a cyclist's popularity, and how star cyclists used the medium to shape their own public images and increase their marketing power. Poulidor became one of the most popular French cycling stars of the post-war era, even though he never won the Tour. So famous and popular was Poulidor, whose adoring fans referred to him as 'Poupou', that the term 'poupoularité' – a play on the word 'popularity' – entered French slang in the mid-1960s.[42] Poulidor's fame was based on his 'peasant' image and 'everyman' character, which journalists helped to create and to which the media constantly referred. In a television piece after he won the 1961 Milan–San Remo race, French reporters visited

Poulidor at his family's home in rural Limousin. The piece stressed Poulidor's continued connection to the soil and to farming, and several video clips of the racer working in the fields followed the kitchen shots. The narrator commented, 'After visiting his family, Raymond immediately goes out to the fields to make sure that the strawberries are growing well after spring's early arrival'.[43] In a television interview prior to a stage of the 1962 Tour, the first question posed to Poulidor – 'You understand perfectly the techniques and methods of sheep breeding, right?' – concerned farming rather than racing.[44] Television allowed cycling fans to see and hear Poulidor's provincial mannerisms, which served to underline his 'peasant' identity and popular appeal. French television informally polled roadside spectators during the 1972 Tour and asked them to comment on why French fans identified so strongly with Poulidor. An elderly woman replied, 'He's a provincial. ... He [speaks with] the Midi accent'.[45]

The case of the Groupe des Assurances Nationales (GAN), an insurance company based in south-western France, illustrates the important place of celebrity riders in the publicity strategies of *extra-sportif* firms. GAN joined the Tour's publicity caravan in 1968, and the race's promotional power and massive television audience impressed the company's marketing executives.[46] The firm decided, in order to increase its brand-name recognition, to expand its exposure in the sport by sponsoring a racing team led by one of cycling's top celebrities. In December 1971, after three years of searching for the right partnership, GAN joined forces with Mercier, the team led by Raymond Poulidor.[47] Poulidor's presence in a GAN jersey justified the insurance company's investment in the team. In 1972, Claude Sudres, GAN–Mercier's public relations agent, pointed out that after only a year of team sponsorship the firm's name had become synonymous with Poulidor. 'When spectators see a GAN car drive by [during a race], they think, "That's Poulidor's team", and they applaud spontaneously.' Sudres concluded that Poulidor's celebrity was so valuable that it would be 'inconceivable' for GAN to allow Poulidor to join another team before his retirement.[48] When 37-year-old Poulidor announced that the 1976 Tour de France would be his last, and that he would retire from cycling the following year, GAN ended its sponsorship of the team.

ECONOMICS OF THE TOUR SINCE 1982

After 1982, when the Mitterrand administration began the process of radio and television deregulation, the Tour gradually transformed itself into an even more formidable publicity machine.

Media Deregulation, Competition for Broadcast Rights and Corporate Sponsorship

The Tour's television audience and on-air coverage expanded tremendously as deregulation progressed. Antenne 2 and FR3 (renamed France 2 and France 3 in 1994), public service stations that were forced to compete with new private channels and networks by the mid-1980s, combined their resources to cover the Tour and to retain the race's French television rights. They devoted a significant portion of their sports-related airtime to the race. Between 1986 and 1996, the two stations' coverage of the Tour grew from 38 hours to more than 112 hours, or approximately 7.5 per cent of all sports-related programming time that year on non-subscription-based French television.[49] Tour coverage increased because the race drew a large viewing audience and generated substantial advertising revenues. By 1994, between five and six million French viewers watched France 2/France 3 each day for Tour coverage, which represented, on average, more than 50 per cent of the audience.[50] In addition, television stations from around the globe sought to purchase television footage of the race for their domestic audiences. By 1986, the Tour de France had emerged as the world's largest annual televised sporting event, and the third-largest television spectacle overall behind the Olympics and soccer's World Cup. The race's worldwide viewing audience increased from approximately 50 million in 1980, to more than 150 million in 1983, and to more than a billion people in 72 countries by 1986.[51] In 1997, television viewers in 150 countries watched the Tour.[52]

The deregulation of television revolutionized the Tour's financial structure. Public and private broadcasting companies competed fiercely to secure broadcast rights contracts for major sporting events such as the Tour. As a result of this competition, France 2/France 3 and international broadcasters paid large (and ever-growing) sums of money to the Tour's organizers. The television rights fees paid to the Société du Tour de France (STF) grew from 12 million francs in 1990, to 32 million francs in 1992, to 50 million francs in 1994, and to 85 million francs in 1998. These payments represented an increasing portion of the race's overall budget. In 1960, French television's payments to the race organizers accounted for only 1.5 per cent of the Tour's projected budget. Rights fees, however, accounted for 26 per cent of the budget in 1992 and for more than a third of the budget in 1998.[53] In 1998, France 2/France 3 was the largest single contributor to the Tour's income. As television-generated revenues rose, the Tour relied less and less on the *subventions* paid by the host-towns. As a percentage of the event's overall budget, host-town *subventions* peaked in the decade after 1947, when those funds represented between 40 and 50 per cent of the Tour's budget.[54] By 1999, host-town *subventions* accounted for only 11 per cent of the Tour's budget.[55]

Businesses that had eschewed sports-related mass publicity turned to the Tour as the race's television coverage grew in France and around the globe. Crédit Lyonnais bank, for example, chose to pursue cycling sponsorship because of its powerful publicity generating capabilities and also out of the desire to undermine the successful sports-related promotional campaigns of its major competitor, the Banque Nationale de Paris (BNP). The BNP was one of the first large, service-sector firms in France to engage in sports-related publicity when it became the exclusive sponsor of the French Open tennis' championship in 1973. The BNP's involvement at Roland Garros made the bank's image synonymous with one of the premier events in tennis. In 1980, *L'Equipe* presented the BNP with the newspaper's annual 'Most Sporting Enterprise' award. The success of the BNP's publicity campaigns forced Crédit Lyonnais to seek sports sponsorship opportunities. As Luc Derieux, a young Crédit Lyonnais executive who participated in his bank's first negotiations with the Tour de France, pointed out, 'The BNP had its sporting event [the French Open]. ... Crédit Lyonnais needed one to call her own'.[56]

In early 1981, Félix Lévitan and Crédit Lyonnais' advertising managers created an entirely new, season-long competition, the Crédit Lyonnais Gold Challenge (*Les Challenges d'Or du Crédit Lyonnais*). The competition became an integral component of races organized by the Amaury Group. Riders won Gold Challenge prize money in each of the eight sanctioned races, including the Tour de France, and earned points toward the season's overall Gold Challenge championship according to how they finished in those events.[57] Crédit Lyonnais agreed to sponsor the competition for three years at an initial base cost of 600,000 francs per year.[58] Through the Gold Challenge, Crédit Lyonnais basked in the publicity that professional cycling's star power and massive media coverage generated. The contract stipulated that the STF organize a televised press conference at the beginning of the 1981 season that included special appearances by French cycling hero Bernard Hinault and Joop Zoetemelk, the winner of the 1980 Tour. *L'Equipe* and *Le Parisien libéré* agreed to print stories on the Gold Challenge throughout the seven-month cycling season. The Tour's organizers also used their connections in the French sports and entertainment industries to gain Crédit Lyonnais special advertising privileges, including special access to billboard advertising in the Palais Omnisports de Bercy, a new sports arena that was being built and funded by the City of Paris, and which would be managed by Jacques Goddet.[59] Crédit Lyonnais' first foray into large-scale sports sponsorship left many of her competitors in the banking industry 'concerned' about the success of the Gold Challenge. The massive television coverage of the Gold Challenge races provided exceptional visibility on the national airwaves. One bank executive concluded emphatically that Crédit Lyonnais' sponsorship of cycling competitions afforded 'excellent [publicity] quality for the price!'[60] The bank fulfilled its contract and renewed its sponsorship of the Gold Challenge competition for another three years in 1984. In 1987, Crédit Lyonnais expanded its sponsorship of the race by becoming the exclusive sponsor of the Tour's central symbol, the yellow jersey.

The example of Crédit Lyonnais bank as a Tour sponsor illustrates how, by the late 1970s and early 1980s, sports sponsorship and television publicity emerged as central components in the promotional strategies of large French enterprises, even those that had been apathetic to mass publicity. Crédit Lyonnais formed part of a new generation of sports sponsors – wealthy service-sector firms like banks and insurance companies – that emerged in the 1970s and 1980s as some of the most important *extra-sportif* benefactors of athletic competition. By the late 1970s, many businesses like Crédit Lyonnais embraced a three-pronged marketing strategy in which sports sponsorship occupied a place equal to that of the traditional venues of promotion, media advertising and patronage of the arts.

Internationalization of the Tour's Commercial Spectacle Since the 1980s

During the 1980s, television emerged as the primary commercial engine of the Tour de France and of many professional sports throughout the western world. Race organizers employed the large war chest of capital generated by broadcast rights fees to mould the Tour into a televised sporting spectacle of global importance. The Tour's organizers altered the race's business structure, as well as the tone and style of its marketing mechanisms, in order to accommodate a new generation of domestic and international corporate sponsors. These initiatives enhanced the event's promotional power and helped its sponsors to profit in new ways from the emerging national and global television economies. Furthermore, the event's new commercial strategies helped the Tour to generate an even larger volume of sponsorship revenue and to turn in consistent profits. The race's organizers and sponsors scrambled to profit from the Tour's growing international appeal and marketing power.

The growth of the international television marketplace, as well as a changing of the guard in Tour management, led to significant shifts in the Tour's financial structure and to a refocusing of the event's commercial strategies. After 1980, Félix Lévitan emerged as the Tour's primary decision-maker and began to transform the race into a global commercial spectacle. Lévitan experimented with the event's itinerary and invited competitors from new countries to participate in the Tour in order to enhance the spectacle's international appeal. In 1987, his last year at the Tour's helm, Lévitan formulated his most audacious itinerary. He added three stages to the schedule – for a total of 25, the most in the event's history – in order to allow Berlin to host the Tour's *prologue*. In addition, Lévitan expanded the Tour's global television audience, which helped the Tour to court more international race sponsorship.

The Tour's emergence as a major international television spectacle in the 1980s presented the race's organizers with enticing business opportunities. As the Tour's worldwide television audience grew, Félix Lévitan spearheaded several initiatives meant to 'globalize' the event's sponsorship, fan base and racer composition.[61] His first major initiative was gradually to alter the competitive structure of the Tour. Between 1980 and 1987, the STF expanded the number of teams and riders invited to compete in the race. The Tour invited 13 teams and 130 riders to compete in the 1980 race. By 1987, the number had expanded to 23 teams and 207 cyclists.[62] As the number of teams grew, the peloton's cross-section of sponsors and riders changed. The preponderance of French-sponsored teams and riders declined markedly during this period, while the percentage of foreign sponsors and riders in the competition increased. In 1973, French firms funded six of the 12 teams in the race, and nearly 40 per cent of the 132 riders were French. By the late 1980s, however, a much smaller proportion of competitors were French. In 1990, only three of the 22 teams (14 per cent) and 34 of the 198 riders (17 per cent) were French. The Tour organizers maintained roughly the same proportions throughout the 1990s. In 1996, for example, four of the 22 teams (18 per cent) and 38 of the 198 riders (19 per cent) were French.[63]

International team sponsorship increased significantly, as did the presence of foreign riders in the race. Tour organizers invited more teams from 'peripheral' nations where the sport of professional cycling was beginning to take root. During the 1980s, the STF invited teams from Colombia, Portugal, Britain, Japan and the United States.[64] In 1990, the Soviet Union sent a team to compete in the race. Racers from cycling's peripheral nations competed on an equal footing with professionals from France, Italy and Belgium, cycling's traditional powers. American Greg LeMond won the Tour three times (1986, 1989 and 1990), Irishman Stephen Roche won in 1987, and American Lance Armstrong won from 1999 to 2002. In addition, the race's growing global popularity and television coverage attracted new, international corporate sponsors to the Tour, which diversified the Tour's sponsorship. Although French companies continued to account for the largest percentage of Tour sponsors after 1980, their share declined significantly. In 1980, for example, French companies sponsored nearly 70 per cent of the Tour's largest prizes (*dotations*). Overall, 25 of the 39 firms that funded prizes or that purchased the right to be 'exclusive providers' to the 1980 Tour were French.[65] By 1995, French firms accounted for slightly more than half of the Tour's official sponsors (*partenaires* and *fournisseurs*). But two of the four members of the 'Tour Club' (*Club du Tour*), the major corporate underwriters of the race, were foreign companies.[66]

As the Tour's global television presence grew, the event became an even more effective tool for mass publicity. The mere fact that the race's television coverage expanded to global proportions made the Tour an extremely attractive advertising venue for international businesses, which began to use sports sponsorship as a means to increase their brand-name recognition in both new and existing markets. Tour sponsorship helped American companies Coca-Cola, the Tour's 'official drink', and Nike, whose 'swoosh' logo appeared on the sleeves and lapel of the yellow jersey, to increase their recognition in France. Coca-Cola was placed first and Nike fifth in a 1995 poll that asked consumers to rank the most recognized brand names in French sports sponsorship.[67] The event's global reach also appealed to multinational corporations that sponsored the Tour. During the 1996 event, for example, massive Asian consumer markets China, India and Indonesia each received 13 hours of televised Tour coverage.[68] The Tour allowed sponsors like Coca-Cola and Nike to disseminate their brand images in France and around the world.

The Tour also remained a preferred sponsorship vehicle for French businesses. The Tour fitted perfectly into the marketing plans of domestic firms like Crédit Lyonnais, since the event produced enormous amounts of national and international television publicity yet it maintained its quintessentially French, provincial character. Although Crédit Lyonnais, for example, hoped to generate national and international promotion through sponsorship, it viewed itself as a bank with firmly-planted provincial roots, since the large majority of the bank's 2,000 branch agencies were located outside Paris. Since most of the event took place on France's country roads, the Tour partnership allowed Crédit Lyonnais to maintain its provincial character while increasing its national and international exposure.[69] In recognition of the Tour's important role in the bank's promotion strategies, Crédit Lyonnais became one of the founding members of the *Club du Tour*, which comprised the event's four largest corporate sponsors, in 1994.[70]

In the 1980s and 1990s, the Tour forged new commercial relationships with television and private industry that helped the Tour, broadcasters and the race's sponsors to profit in new ways from the national and international sports economy. The event served as a model for how to exploit the commercial possibilities of television, sports-related sponsorship and publicity. The Tour integrated corporate publicity into the race's spectacle even more thoroughly in the 1980s and 1990s than in the preceding decades.

CONCLUSION: THE BUSINESS OF THE TOUR AND
FRANCE'S CULTURAL TRANSFORMATION AFTER THE
SECOND WORLD WAR

Paradoxically, the forces that resisted the penetration of business concerns into popular culture after the Second World War – the conservative State determined to maintain a monopoly on France's commercial-free broadcast media and a public and business elite wary of mass publicity – also helped to establish the cultural and commercial infrastructure in which enterprises like the Tour de France flourished. The event helped corporate interests to penetrate into television, and thus instigated the commercialization of the most dominant post-war media. In the process, the post-war Tour forged for itself an important place at the intersection of commerce and culture, and influenced the shape of both.

Television coverage of the race allowed commercial interests to engage French people in new ways. While watching the Tour at home on their televisions, French spectators took in the images of competition, of the cyclists, and of the enterprises that supported the two. As the race's television audience grew, viewers watched much of the race in real time, direct from the race course, with no mechanism to separate images generated by the sponsor from those of the riders or of the spectacle. Through television, the French sporting public came to know the Tour, its cyclists and the race sponsors on an unprecedented level of intimacy.

Public spectacles like the Tour reshaped private leisure and popular culture in new, unanticipated ways in the post-war era. Thanks to the proliferation of radio and television, fewer men and women followed the Tour in the newspapers. Although millions of men and women continued to line France's roads to witness the race in person, increasingly the French experienced sporting events like the Tour in the privacy of their homes as they watched on their televisions. By the 1960s, the race's viewing audience dwarfed the number of roadside spectators. In this sense, the transformation of the post-war Tour into a television event was representative of how an older public culture was waning in France, with leisure shifting away from cafés, public spaces and the church to within the family household. In his ethno-history of a provincial village that he visited in 1951 and in 1959, Lawrence Wylie documented how television began to erode long-standing modes of sociability after the war. As more of the local residents purchased televisions, the village's social life began to change. One farmer, whom Wylie described as a fixture at the village's weekly *boules* tournament in 1951, explained in 1959 that he had stopped competing on Sundays because he preferred to stay at home and watch television. A café owner also complained that fewer men played cards in his café-bar after work because they chose instead to watch television at home. Wylie noted that television viewing seemed to be replacing after-dinner conversation in the village's households.[71] Wylie's insights, although based on anecdotal evidence, nevertheless highlight the subtle but powerful influence of television in shaping French community life and leisure practices after the war. The transformation of the Tour into a televised spectacle illustrates how the audio-visual media forged for themselves a powerful place in post-war popular culture. The popularity of televised sport in France undoubtedly helped the new medium to flourish and to gain acceptance.[72] Millions of men and women watched hours of Tour coverage on television during the months of June and July, and the event became an important component of France's emerging audio-visual culture. Television also blurred the line that separated the public and private realms. Television transported the Tour's publicity-laden spectacle from town squares into millions of living rooms, and thus provided a portal through which commercial culture entered into France's private sphere.

The more recent transformation of the Tour into an international commercial phenomenon illuminates the broader evolution of French popular culture's relationship to cultural and commercial globalisation. The establishment of an international television economy led to an expansive, multidirectional exchange of Tour-related commerce, sponsorship and images of the race and its champions. For example, Tour winners Greg LeMond and Lance Armstrong were not merely exported American athletes who dominated a French competition. Rather, they were cyclists trained in Europe, forged into champions on French country roads, and returned as heroes to the United States, where their victories helped to popularize the race. All the while, Tour organizers sold television coverage of their triumphs to American television networks and used sponsorship funds from American companies like Coca-Cola and Nike to expand the race's budget. In this sense, the Tour's increasing participation in the international television economy was symptomatic of the globalisation of a quintessentially French cultural phenomenon.

NOTES

1. Bicycle sales per year in France grew from 203,026 units in 1894 to 1.7 million in 1905 and to 6.4 million in 1924. 'Une industrie capricieuse ... mais structurée', *Journal de Véloscopie/CRACAP*, special edition, 'Tour de France d'une exposition consacrée à la bicyclette' (April 1976), 5.

2. In the late 1920s, as bicycle sales levelled off and as some bicycle manufacturers focused more heavily on automobile production, bicycle industry profit growth slowed. Sponsors sought to maximize the publicity impact of their investments in the Tour by attempting to control the outcome of the event. This trend somewhat dampened the public's interest in the race and hurt *L'Auto*'s circulation at a time when Desgrange's newspaper faced increasing competition from large-circulation, general-interest dailies like *Paris-Soir* and *Le Petit Parisien* for readers and advertising revenue.

3. The savings for team sponsors were significant. André Leducq estimated that by 1929 it cost his Alcyon team 200,000 francs to sponsor a professional team in the Tour. A. Leducq, *Une fleur au guidon* (Paris: Presses de la Cité, 1978), p.143.

4. J. Augendre, *L'histoire, les archives: le 85ème Tour de France* (Issy-les-Moulineaux: Société du Tour de France, 1998), p.30.

5. Archives départementaux des Basses-Pyrénées (ADBP) 4 M 102, Dossier 'Tour de France 1925–39', document 'Caravane officielle du Tour 1935'.

6. *L'Auto*, 23 June 1937, 4.

7. Augendre, *L'Histoire, les archives*, p.29.

8. Ibid., p.37.

9. *L'Auto*, supplement 'Le 25e Tour de France', 26 June 1931, 7; *L'Auto*, 1 April 1931, 1.

10. Ibid., 4 July 1931, 3. Desgrange sometimes allowed companies to pay for the right to be the 'official sponsor' of a stage. It is unclear whether Desgrange incorporated the product plug for La Vache qui rit cheese into his narrative because the company was the stage's 'official sponsor' or because it was a publicity caravan participant and a sponsor of prize money.

11. Letter from Goddet and Desgrange to Mayor of Brest, 17 Oct. 1938, Archives municipales de Brest (AMB) 1 I 5(3), dossier 'Tour de France, 1910–54'. Jacques Goddet was the son of *L'Auto*'s co-founder, Victor Goddet, and became *L'Auto*'s editor-in-chief and Director of the Tour de France after Desgrange's death in 1940.

12. The *subvention* to the Tour by the town of Brest that year totalled 25,000 francs. Minutes of Chambre de Commerce de Brest meeting, 15 Dec. 1938, AMB 1 I 5(3). The town of Strasbourg, which habitually promised smaller subventions to the Tour organizers than other towns, offered 21,000 francs the same year. Letter and attachment from L. Henri Weber to Mayor of Strasbourg, 13 Dec. 1937, Archives municipales de Strasbourg (AMS) Service des Cérémonies 30/270, dossier 'Tour de France 1938'.

13. In 1928 and 1929, Strasbourg offered the Tour a subvention of 560 francs, while Caen offered an annual subvention of 1,500 francs beginning in 1927. 'Motion Woehl: Tour de France cycliste 1936', 16 July 1935, AMS 30-269, dossier 'Tour de France'; Archives municipales de Caen (AMC), 'Dix ans du comité Caennais du Tour de France cycliste', 1935, Ch. 1.

14. *L'Equipe*, 28 June 1947, 2.

15. R. Kuisel, *Seducing the French: The Dilemma of Americanization* (Berkeley: University of California Press, 1993; paperback edition, 1996), pp.104–105; K. Ross, *Fast Cars, Clean Bodies: Decolonization and the Reordering of French Culture* (Cambridge, MA: MIT Press, 1995), p.29.

16. 'Une progression économique', *Cyclisme Magazine*, 84 (Nov. 1974), 7.

17. J. Marchand, *Le Cyclisme* (Paris: La Table Ronde, 1963), p.94; C. Tillet, 'Une page d'Histoire', *Cyclisme Magazine*, 7 (4 June 1969), 3.

18. J. Bobet, *Louison Bobet: une vélobiographie* (Paris: Gallimard, 1958), p.77.

19. '*Le Parisien libéré*', *Presse-actualité*, 8 (June–July 1963), 22–3.

20. J. Choffel, 'Une grande entreprise commerciale: Les secrets financiers du Tour de France', *Vie française*, 1 July 1949, 14.

21. *Le Miroir des Sports*, 29 June 1953, 4.

22. J. Henry, 'En suivant les caravaniers du Tour de France', *Journal de la Publicité*, 61 (30 July 1948), 3.

23. E. Reed, 'The Tour de France: A Cultural and Commercial History', Ph.D. dissertation, Syracuse University, 2001, Appendix I, Table 5.

24. Jacques Goddet, interview by P. Vernier, *Journal de la Publicité*, 213, Numéro spécial de fin d'année (31 Dec. 1954), 87.

25. *L'Equipe*, 10 June 1947, 1; 4 July 1950, 1, 6; Jacques Goddet, interview by J. Marchand,

Cyclisme Magazine 1960, 5 (April 1960), 96; Félix Lévitan, interview, *Le Miroir des Sports*, 18 June 1962, 4.

26. J. Goddet, 'Un acte de foi', *L'Equipe*, 25 June 1947, 1.
27. J. Goddet, interview by author, tape recording, Issy-les-Moulineaux, 2 July 1999.
28. *L'Equipe*, 10 June 1947, 1.
29. J. Goddet, interview by P. Vernier, *Journal de la publicité*, 213, Numéro spécial de fin d'année (31 Dec. 1954), 87.
30. J. Goddet, interview by J. Marchand, *Cyclisme Magazine*, 5 (April 1960), 96.
31. J. Goddet, *L'Equipée belle* (Paris: Robert Laffont/Stock, 1991), p.221.
32. A. Magne, *Poulidor et moi* (Paris: del Duca, 1968), p.81.
33. *L'Equipe*, 23–24 June 1962, 3.
34. J. Goddet, interview by author, tape recording, Issy-les-Moulineaux, 2 July 1999.
35. P. Soisson, 'En France, la publicité n'est pas ce qu'elle devrait être ... Pourquoi?', *Journal de la publicité*, 470 (14 Jan. 1966), 51.
36. The number of television sets in France increased from 3,794 in 1950 to more than 12 million in 1972. C. Brochand, *Histoire générale de la radio et de la télévision en France. Tome II: 1944–74* (Paris: La Documentation Française, 1994), pp.501–502.
37. On average, the organizers chose 11 teams to participate each year from 1958 to 1961, all of which competed under a national or regional flag. From 1962 to 1965, they chose an average of 13, all of which were sponsored by businesses (and usually several businesses).
38. Tour officials created several categories of 'official providers', including *grands supporters* (major sponsors), *principales exclusivités* (exclusive providers), *fournisseur officiel* (official provider) and *service officiel* (official service provider).
39. *L'Equipe*'s printing numbers shrank from an average of 307,888 copies per day in 1957 to 282,067 per day in 1959 and to 253,481 per day in 1962 before rebounding slightly in the mid-1960s. 'Tirage et Diffusion des Quotidiens de Paris, 1957 à 1964', *Presse-actualité*, 24 (Feb. 1966), 31.
40. Upon signing the deal, Amaury proclaimed, 'Jacques, the only way you are going to leave *L'Equipe* is in a coffin'. (*'Jacques, vous ne quitterez la maison que les pieds devant.'*) Goddet, *L'Equipée belle*, p.314.
41. The Amaury Group purchased 70 per cent of the capital of the SOPUSI in April 1965. Archives de la Préfecture de Police de Paris (APPP) L-11/92512, police inquiry, Feb. 1968, dossier 'Lévitan, Félix'.
42. R. Poulidor, *La Gloire sans maillot jaune* (Paris: Calmann-Lévy, 1968), p.12.
43. Documentary piece by French television on Raymond Poulidor after the 1961 Milan–San Remo race, excerpts from INAthèque de France, television clip compilation videotape 'Raymond Poulidor'.
44. Documentary piece by French television on Raymond Poulidor during the 1962 Tour, excerpts from INAthèque de France, television clip compilation videotape 'Raymond Poulidor'.
45. French television coverage of the 1972 Tour, excerpts from INAthèque de France, television clip compilation videotape 'Raymond Poulidor'.
46. *Stratégie*, 107 (26 Jan.–8 Feb. 1976), 41, cited in P. Biojout, *Le Sponsoring: Analyse économique du comportement des entreprises en matière de parrainage sportif* (Limoges: Centre de Droit et d'Economie du Sport de Limoges, 1983), pp.26–7.
47. C. Sudres, *Poulidor, Guimard, Zoetemelk ... et les autres* (Paris: Editions PAC, 1981), p.8.
48. C. Sudres, interview, *Cyclisme Magazine*, 57 (13 Dec. 1972), 16.
49. Reed, 'The Tour de France: A Cultural and Commercial History', p.400 and Appendix I, Table 6.
50. *Les Echos*, 25 July 1994, 8.
51. J.-M. Leblanc, 'Le vélo et la télé,' *Vélo Magazine*, 218 (Feb. 1987), 10; W. Andreff and J.-F. Nys, *Le Sport et la télévision* (Paris: Editions Dalloz, 1987), p.144.
52. *Le Monde*, 14 July 1997, 2.
53. Reed, 'The Tour de France: A Cultural and Commercial History', Appendix I, Table 6.
54. Ibid., pp.248–9.
55. J.-M. Leblanc, interview by C. Penot, *Jean-Marie Leblanc, gardien du Tour de France. Entretiens avec Christophe Penot* (Saint Malo: Editions Cristel, 1999), p.232.

56. L. Derieux, interview by author, tape recording, Paris, 12 Nov. 1998.
57. 'Challenges d'Or du Crédit Lyonnais. Le règlement, saison 1981', Archives du Crédit Lyonnais (CL) 58 AH 23.
58. The total cost of Crédit Lyonnais' sponsorship of the Gold Challenge amounted to 1.1 million francs in 1981. 'Points sur les activités de sponsoring de 1981. Propositions pour 1982', 3 Nov. 1981, CL 58 AH 23.
59. Draft contract between Crédit Lyonnais and the STF, attached memorandum, 'Préparation de votre entretien avec Monsieur Félix Lévitan du 10 février 1981', 9 Feb. 1981, CL 58 AH 23.
60. B. Normand, 'Points sur les activités de sponsoring de 1981. Propositions pour 1982', 3 Nov. 1981, CL 58 AH 23.
61. *Libération*, 1 July 1987, 25; CL 91 AH 102.
62. P. Chany, *La Fabuleuse Histoire du Tour de France* (Paris: Editions de La Martinière, 1997), pp.933–47.
63. Ibid., pp.922–3, 970–71.
64. Teams are categorized according to the nationality of the majority of the riders or of the team's primary corporate sponsor. Ibid., pp.933–55.
65. *Programme officiel du Tour de France 1980*, Bibliothèque Nationale (BN).
66. The members of the *Club du Tour* in 1995 were Crédit Lyonnais, Champion (a chain of French supermarkets), Fiat (the Italian car manufacturer) and Coca-Cola. Official Tour de France Internet site www.letour.fr/tour95/services.html>.
67. Nike gained six places in the annual poll between 1992 and 1995. *L'Evénementiel*, March 1996, CL 150 AH 19.
68. Official Tour de France Internet site, <www.letour.fr/tour/guide_tv1.html>.
69. L. Derieux, interview by author, tape recording, Paris, 12 Nov. 1998; Daniel Isaac, interview by author, tape recording, Paris, 17 Oct. 1998.
70. Crédit Lyonnais paid 15 million francs for the right to become the exclusive sponsor of the yellow jersey in 1987, and paid 20 million francs as a member of the *Club du Tour* in the mid-1990s. *Tendances*, 2 July 1987, CL 91 AH 102; *La Tribune de l'économie*, 26 Aug. 1997, CL 162 AH 13; *Les Echos*, 20 Aug. 1997, CL 162 AH 13.
71. Wylie remarked that after a Sunday dinner with friends in the village in 1959, the host insisted on watching a televised international swimming meet rather than chatting over coffee, as was the tradition. L. Wylie, *Village in the Vaucluse*, rev. ed. (New York: Harper Colophon, 1964), pp.347–8.
72. J.-P. Rioux and J.-F. Sirinelli (eds), *Histoire culturelle de la France. 4. Le Temps des masses, le vingtième siècle* (Paris: Seuil, 1998), pp.265–6; R. Hubscher (ed.), *L'Histoire en mouvements: Le sport dans la société française (XIXe-XXe siècle)* (Paris: Armand Colin, 1992), pp.520–21.

The Tour de France as an Agent of Change in Media Production

FABIEN WILLE

'The Tour de France was to remain, throughout the whole subsequent history of television, a field of experimentation.' (Sauvage and Maréchal)[1]

INTRODUCTION

On Wednesday 29 July 1998, a few days after France had won the soccer World Cup, Tour de France riders stopped after 32 kilometres on the stage to Aix-les-Bains. For the first time in the history of televising the race, the television crews went in the opposite direction to the race, and went back through the peloton so that they could broadcast the event. The riders' protest followed the questioning by the police of several members of the TVM team. A climate of suspicion had hung over the 1998 Tour since the start because of the so-called 'Festina Affair'. Sporting matters had taken second place to issues of public health and the French CID's interest in the Tour had put a question mark over sporting ethics, which had been flouted by the drug-taking that had apparently been discovered.

The Tour de France cycle race, a spectacle that brings in large media audiences, is not only the third biggest media event in the world, but also the greatest free sporting event in the world. Might not the Tour be considered a victim of a system that it has itself helped generate, since the economic issues linked to sport appear responsible for this abuse?

The period of purgatory seemed to be over by July 2002 as the Tour enjoyed around 122 hours of coverage on French public service television over five regular programmes. The 'grande boucle' appeared on two of France Télévisions' channels (France 2 and France 3 – its other channel being France 5). The programme *La Légende* on France 2 at 1.50pm, a few minutes before live coverage of the race began, showed a retrospective of great cycling champions using archive footage and interviews. *Vélo Club* on France 2 at 5.30pm, that is, just after the finish of the stage, gave a review of the race, live from an outside-broadcast studio with guests including riders and their team managers. Coverage then continued on France 2 with a post-race analysis. France Télévisions also used its France 3 channel. At 10.50am, before the race, *Sur la route du Tour* showed the route to be covered and the spectators at the roadside, and *Le Journal du Tour* at 8.20pm continued the coverage of the event, emphasising how the organization's two channels complemented each other.

Live coverage was increased in 2002 and captured 20 per cent of market share, with 79 hours of coverage, 70 hours of it on France 2. It was the most largest coverage of any Tour, and outdid the French Open tennis championships at Roland Garros, and Champions League football. It also equalled the 1997 record as the most heavily 'consumed' Tour in terms of viewers. France 2's average audience was doubled by the Tour, its audience going up by 6 per cent compared to 2001.

The Tour de France is also an event with an international dimension. Europe is still the continent that offers the biggest share of live coverage, with 1,200 hours. Great Britain, with 64 hours of coverage on ITV1 and ITV2, appears in ninth place, after Channel 4's long-running coverage of 30 minutes a day. With its worldwide presence, 385 hours in Africa, 336 hours in America and 280 hours in Asia, the Tour is also a global event.

Today it is an obvious remark to say that television is the dominant media: it invades private space, and sports programming is an important share of programme supply.[2] Originally a medium of culture, entertainment and news, television today has taken on a commercial dimension, and televised sport is part of this trend. As a cultural product, televised sport is responding to technical demands and economic and social constraints associated with the field of television production.

In looking at the evolution of sport on television, we should not fall into the trap of common prejudices regularly aimed at television that attempt permanently to discredit the nature of the relations between sport, the media and the business world. The criticisms are based, on the one hand, on the attacks on the dominance of financial issues and, on the other, on the denunciation of the power exercised by television over sport. These affirmations emerge at times of crisis such as when drug-taking becomes visible, in discussion of corrupt practices, and over abuses coming from the signing of exclusive TV rights.

This is not to deny the importance today of economic forces, but to orient our analysis towards the meeting point of two driving forces, those of promotion and innovation.[3] The Tour de France is a fine example of this. Jean Durry[4] reminds us that the event has accompanied, indeed stimulated, technological change in television. He even calls the 'grande boucle' 'a travelling laboratory that provides Eurovision in particular with televised "coverage" of the Tour de France'. The point of this chapter is to define one way in which sports television has evolved from its beginnings, where the Tour de France appears as an important example.

FROM RACE TO MEDIA PRODUCTION

For over a century the specialist written press has been structured by an innovative process leading to a transformation of the journalistic apparatus that goes to the site of events, thus reducing the time it takes to transform the event into news.[5] The innovation lies also in the creation of narratives allowing the reconstruction of the event. This process is in the interests of promoting the event itself and enhancing its attractiveness in order to favour the sale of newspapers or to promote an industrial product.

The Beginnings of Commercial Logic

Work by Gaboriau,[6] Boury,[7] Léziart,[8] and Vigarello[9] has shown that the first Tour de France, which was created by journalists from *L'Auto* and began on 1 July 1903, combined aspirations both of riders in search of glory and of cycle brands in search of success.

Vant[10] points out that, in the late nineteenth century, the cycle manufacturing industry was based, above all, on the existence of an old tradition of iron and steel working and on the fact that, 'the demand for bicycles was felt from February to August, in other words the dead period for armaments corresponded to the active period for the bicycle. Many arms manufacturers positioned themselves very early as cycle manufacturers without having to create separate specialist workshops, since their lathes and milling machines served for making parts for both arms and bicycles.' Whereas, originally, cycling competitions were above all aristocratic and upper-class social events, they became part of popular culture thanks to the economic logic linked to the development of the bicycle. Taking the example of the Tour de France, the original prize for each stage win was 3,000 francs, which was 20 times greater than an industrial worker's average monthly salary at the time. Maurice Garin, the first winner of the Tour, received the sum of 12,000 francs, the equivalent of six years' salary of an average worker. But the 1903 Tour only had six stages and the expenses involved in the competition, without any financial guarantees, led many professional racers to think twice before agreeing to take part.[11] It was therefore decided to offer the first 50 finishers, in addition to the finishing bonus, a standard compensation of five francs, corresponding to the average day's pay of an industrial worker. This remuneration was afforded through the increase in newspaper and advertising sales. The democratization of the bicycle became effectively entwined in market logic and each manufacturer had to prove the quality of their product. This promotion was done through poster advertising campaigns, since posters were the main medium used in public places frequented by ordinary people. By taking up these advertising campaigns newspapers gained substantial income. Sporting exploits thus became an ideal and effective means of publicity, and the inadequacies of the general news press led to the emergence of a specialist press. It was in this context that newspapers became the organizers of cycling competitions with the help of industrial groups. This relationship brought together the interests of cycle manufacturers, who used competitions to promote the value of their product, and the interests of the press, who increased their income thanks to improved sales of newspapers and advertising space. As Vigarello describes, as racers became professional, social advancement and industrial development came together on French roads.[12] The Tour de France is a good example of this development since it was created by two journalists, Victor Goddet and Henri Desgrange, with the support of the industrial sector, the race thus allowing *L'Auto* to compete with Pierre Giffard's sports daily, *Le Vélo*.

Journalistic Style in the Service of Selling Newspapers and TV Programmes

Transforming the race into narrative goes beyond simple recounting of the sequence of events during a stage. Christian Pociello[13] suggests that journalistic accounts include both real, objective sporting facts and imaginary and polysemic representations of that reality. The roadside spectacle of the Tour was fleeting and the competition's consequent lack of visibility was conducive to the creation of emotion. Roland Barthes[14] adds that the origins of these narratives lay in the nature of effort and the creation of figures of speech for the riders who became the actors and sometimes the heroes of the story; and also in the evocation of the French landscape that was metamorphosed into multiple and varied backdrops against which the scenes of the drama took place. The newspaper *L'Auto*, whose interest lay in attracting the greatest number of readers possible, promoted the value of the race not only by adding an epic, legendary and dramatic dimension to the narratives, but also by a new time frame and a new form of accessibility to the event through the illusion of a shared experience. The reader participated artificially in the action though the use of a new type of communication: the 'live' or on-the-spot report. In this way the press appropriated and reconstructed the event.

Although the race soon began to appear diabolical and inhuman, the Tour de France rapidly became an event that stirred the masses, and newspapers contributed to the creation of its legendary character. As Vigarello[15] reveals, *L'Auto* was the first newspaper to invest quite specifically in the sports narrative, in order to give the spectator something extra. Cycling is a good example of this since the roadside spectator catches only a fleeting glimpse of the riders. The paper creates the story, the saga, the epic. Television too, in its own way.

There are many books written by journalists or former champions recounting the great moments of the race, its heroes and its dramatic events. They are generally illustrated by press photographs. Television also frequently uses pictures from the archives, thus constructing its own story of the race in pictures without mentioning the conditions of production of these images. How did television, in constructing its visual account of the event, adapt to the media inheritance of the Tour? Did not the possibility of being visually present at the day's stage run the risk of modifying the narrative by destroying the imaginary dimension that had helped construct the event's celebrity?

THE CONSTRUCTION OF A TELEVISION SPECTACLE

As early as 25 July 1948, for the second time in its history,[16] French television showed a live outside-broadcast report. The finish of the Tour de France made its first appearance live on the small screen. There were many constraints to producing a live outside broadcast.[17] Video cameras with 'periscope'-type lenses were not mobile. They could show the riders going past, and could follow them going round the track and do interviews at the finish. Only the few Parisians who had television sets could watch the programme, which was above all an experiment and not common practice in the industry. Yet there was much at stake in the broadcast. Primarily, television's credibility. The project's initiators wanted to enhance the status of the new medium that was television and also to promote the French standard to other European countries. 1948 was the year of the new 819-lines standard and its everyday use in France.[18]

In the early 1950s live television was a rare event because of technical inadequacies. So the Tour appeared on the small screen on news programmes. The items were summaries of the race, recorded on 16mm film and shown the next day. The press was here using the tools of the cinema.

The Event as Media Text: Television's Appropriation and Reconstruction of the Race

The mobility of cine-cameras allowed the racing to be presented from multiple and diverse points of view, through a combination of tracking shots, pans and shots from a fixed point. With the tracking shot following riders along the road, the television news camera not only moved around the site of the event to give an account of it to the largest possible audience, it also got involved in the heart of the action. This added to the process of constructing a media event that was developed around the race and the spectacle, but which offered its own unique representation of the event. The point of view changed. Everybody watching the race on their TV screen were 'viewers' of an event that was specific to a news programme. The exploit was perceived in its totality and in its continuity; we were allowed to discover the rider at the heart of the action. The wide-angle shot, on the other hand, offered a point of view similar to being present at a live spectacle. The camera scanned actions happening under the eyes of the 'tele-viewer'.[19]

Making the race visible by a combination of these two camera movements broadened our view of the stage, also endowing us with the gift of being in different places at the same time. This point of view is a distinctive feature of television; moreover the chronological order of shots was not respected in the editing of the report.

Narratives and Stories: The Inheritance of the Newspaper Press

Television also constructed a new frame of reference to time. Identically to the newspaper press, the language used was that of 'live coverage'. The viewer shared the moment through the use of the present tense. TV's search for authenticity and realism led to a paradox: the report transformed the competition's real time into recorded television time.

The essential point of the commentary remained the description of what was happening in the race. The pictures regularly allowed the commentator to identify the riders and give distances covered or remaining and gaps between different riders. Commentators were not shy of using effects of contrast, that Pociello mentions,[20] which allow the audience to project itself instantly into contests that are all the more exciting for being of uncertain outcome. But TV journalists also regretted not having at their disposal an appropriate set of signs, figures of speech and 'style' for easily dramatizing the narration of sporting stories. In sports broadcasting, television reproduced the model of the newspaper press by also constructing figures of speech, which pictures did not seem to distort; just the opposite in fact, they reinforced them.

We find the same heterogeneity of narratives. To effects of authenticity, the journalist explicitly added the enactment of duels. The riders thus became the actors in the story that we were being told. Over and above the announcement of objective data about the conditions of the race and its development, the commentator kept alive the representations coming out of the competition. The report resembled a news item using simple discourse, while, on the other hand, the narrative uses social metaphors in a search for rhetorical effects. Breakaways became stories with their own setting, their actors and their moral: one of respect for the established order and for merit. Equally worthy of attention is the polysemic nature of the narratives that allow multiple and varied projections and identifications by the viewer.

This illusion of sharing in an event should not make us forget the totally anticipatory nature of the discourse. The announcement of the circumstances of the race or what was at stake was conditioned by knowing what had really happened in the stage. Emerging from work prior to their broadcast, the commentary and editing of the pictures were anticipated and constructed. In such cases, the uncertainty was recreated and fictional. Bernard Jeu[21] has pointed out the difference in tragic dimension between the theatre and sport. In the theatre, the actor (and sometimes the spectator) knows the outcome of the play; in sport the players are not playing a role, they are simply themselves. Sports competitors do not know the outcome of the story. In television reporting the journalist knew the outcome of the stage. The pictures had a double purpose: they were part of the construction process of the report through the choice of shots used, and were a guarantee of the credibility of the discourse.

The Race as Promoting and Increasing the Standing of Television

The construction of the televised sports programme in general and of the Tour de France in particular was also characterized by its role of increasing the standing of television production. Through unusual or aesthetically attractive representations of the race, television did more than just add variety to the coverage of the competition; it linked the report to a valorization process that took different forms: this concerned the race and the riders who remained the main actors of the event and who were presented in the heat of their exertions. Their exploits thereby grew in stature. The grandeur of the sites offered the riders a stage and a backdrop that gave added value to the race. The décor was an important contextual element in the construction of the report. It brought an edifying effect to the representations linked to the race. The level of danger and the risks taken transformed the riders' efforts into exploits. The promotion of the event also included showing the organization of the race, which appeared systematically in every report. The valorization process emerged too from the promotion and the quality of the programme produced. The presence of roadside spectators showed the public's interest in the event, thus contributing to its renown. Finally, television was not shy of self-promotion, by filming itself and thus showing the TV news crews and equipment.

However, the small screen's success upset some people and attracted criticism. Disagreements arose between the sports federations and television. The defenders of sports broadcasting as being good publicity for sport found themselves in opposition to those who believed television alone benefited from its programmes. In the year of the dispute, 1957, television had a disagreement with the Tour de France. With no agreement being reached, the French public had to console themselves with the day's commentary over pictures from the previous day. For a number of years viewers were deprived of the Tour.

The first broadcasts of the whole of the Tour de France were due to begin in 1962, but a conflict arose between the professional body representing the regional daily press (SNPQR[22]) and the Tour's organizers, the *Société du Tour de France*.[23] The SNPQR was against television broadcasting of the Tour, on the grounds that the organizers' establishment of commercial brand teams[24] ran the risk of too many advertising brands appearing on the small screen. Their real fear was, as a consequence, the possible withdrawal of the newspapers' financial partners to become sponsors of the Tour de France, which would cause a sharp drop in income to newspapers. At the time France had only one TV channel (State-controlled) and this dispute led the Minister of Information to ban the broadcasting of the event. The ban was lifted some time later, but the TV crews were elsewhere; they had been mobilized for an outdoor game show called *Intervilles*.[25] It was not until 1963 that there were true live broadcasts of the Tour.

Live Broadcasting of the Tour, Between Reality and Imagination

Media sport in general feeds on the communion between the event and its telling. In producing sports images, television relied on the event's legend and thereby perpetuated it, thus reproducing the process of promoting the standing of the television coverage. So far, in the case of the Tour, we have seen the construction of a spectacle peculiar to television that was only made possible by the time available between the race taking place and the moment of broadcasting. When live broadcasting became the norm in the early 1960s, what form did sports programming take?

From the 1960s onwards, television became a medium of live pictures. On the creation of the first TV news programme, under the authority of Pierre Sabbagh, which showed the start of the 1949 Tour de France, Jean d'Arcy, a major figure in the history of French television, declared: 'Live television is all about the continuity of an event broadcast via several cameras, which makes faking images very difficult and gives a great impression of authenticity. Live broadcasting means being able to look around you at life as it is.' Live broadcasting is the very essence of television; it is what reveals the truth of a situation. This is why television sports programming is structured around a paradox. Through live pictures television allows access to the reality of an event that has constructed its legitimacy in the media through the imaginary dimension it generated.

In 1959 technical innovation brought helicopters into broadcasting. A double constraint brought a distinction between two different time sequences in broadcasts. When the spatial aspect is known in advance, television can put its equipment in place; however, it is difficult to ensure in advance the exact time riders will pass a given point to coincide with the transmission time, since the speed of the riders depends on how the race is evolving. Added to this uncertainty of time is the constraint of the potential duration of the live broadcast. The brief period of airtime possible, which was about ten minutes, perhaps did not merit such high investment. This explains why the live programme was not limited to the actual broadcasting of the race: it was structured in two distinct parts: waiting for the riders and the race live.

The prelude to images of the race was often the time for lyrical and poetic evocations appealing to the imagination. The journalist would describe the landscape, as the background for the broadcast and the race, the spectators, who sometimes became involuntary actors in the story that we were being told, and the race that we could not see. This waiting time also allowed pre-prepared shots to be shown, playing on the unusual or the aesthetic. All these aspects contributed to the process of increasing the prestige of the broadcast, a high point of which was the description of the outside-broadcast equipment.

Helicopter pictures increased the race's visibility, which remained nonetheless limited, since the pictures suffered a loss in quality. The pictures were far away, lacking in clarity and unstable, which tended to recreate a new imaginary dimension. The race was more suggested than shown: when the riders passed in front of the cameras near the finishing line, the spectators present would get in the way of the shots.

Commentary became essential to viewers' making sense of the broadcast, especially to interpreting poor images with low informational power. This was also the moment at which to mention the technical equipment needed to produce the broadcast; the greatest exploit was achieved not by the sportsmen but by television, as the commentator sought to give standing to the pictures shown.

From the Unavoidable Wait to Constructed Live Broadcasts

Increasing autonomy and the development of high frequency broadcasting equipment led to increased lengths of live broadcasts, which allowed more scope for adapting to the uncertainties of the race in terms of time. This era saw the reduction in the size of cameras;

miniaturized and lighter, from 1963 they allowed the filming of the last 30 kilometres from motorbikes. What was at stake for the electronics industry, the essential partner in this evolution, was to improve picture quality in order to sell more television sets. The arrival of colour at the end of the 1960s[26] stimulated sales and the renewal of sets. Improved performance of ground relays, increased autonomy of helicopters and the appearance of the motorbike also added variety to the images produced. Technological improvements reduced waiting times between coming on air and receiving live pictures. In July 1967 coming on air became the privileged moment for introducing the race. There was a wait of less than five minutes before live pictures of the race took over from the introductory commentary by Robert Chapatte (a former rider who had become a Tour commentator).

These few minutes of introduction were used simultaneously to sketch the background décor, mention the TV equipment in place and the newspapers organizing the event, praise a breakaway, recall the previous day's race details, and, finally, to describe the stage that was going on, without forgetting to refer to the history of the event.

The arrival of the motorbike in the peloton changed the way people saw the race. The point of view was specific to television. The viewer had access to an event that the roadside spectator could not see. Further, the commentary team grew in number. In 1967 Robert Chapatte was more or less the only race commentator, using pictures on his monitor. Richard Diot (another journalist member of the commentary team) gave the results at the end of the programme. As a former competitor, Chapatte tried to communicate his own passionate interest and would tell a story starting from the sporting facts. In 1969 three commentators shared the air time. Léon Zitrone, a huge figure in French television history as he presented the evening news programme and hosted major television game shows, managed the programme's continuity with his usual florid exuberance. He handed over to each commentator and they handed back to him in the studio. Another journalist, Jean-Michel Leuliot, was at his side to take over commentary in the climbs. His role was to cast a more distanced eye over the race. He positioned himself as an expert summarizer. With the added presence of Richard Diot, broadcasting from a motorbike, the commentary was not solely on the basis of the pictures on screen but from 'inside the race'. This human and technical broadcasting team lent greater authenticity and expertise to the programme, without the images being an obstacle to constructing

*Henri DESGRANGE à tricycle en 1895
lors de ses tentatives de records*

1. Henri Desgrange, founder of the Tour de France, in his racing days, 1895 (Les Amis du Tour de France; Henri Simoni, after Carrere).

ANDRÉ
Premier de la Course Paris-Bruxelles sur Bicyclette **PAPILLON**

2. The rider André, winner of the Paris–Brussels race of 1893, with a Papillon road-racing machine typical of the mid-1890s (*Le Véloce-Sport*, 24 August 1893).

ARTHUR LINTON   RIVIERRE   MEYER

3. Begun in 1891, the Bordeaux–Paris road race sponsored by *Le Véloce-Sport* was the most important of the 1890s road races, with the start of the 1896 edition shown here (H.O. Duncan, *Vingt Ans de Cyclisme Pratique*, Paris, 1897).

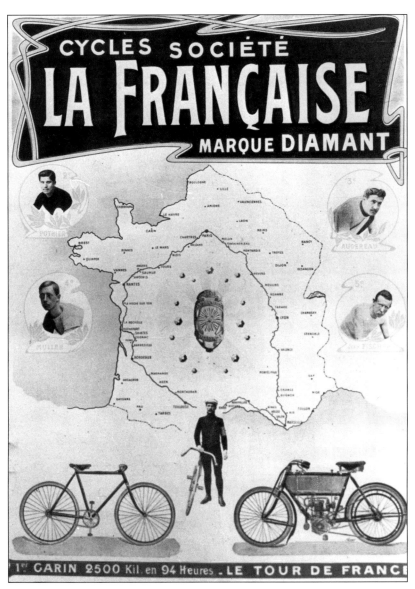

4. The route of the first Tour de France in 1903, and its winner, Maurice Garin, are shown here in publicity for the La Française bicycle which he rode.

Y Année N 411   50 centimes   4 Août 1906 Tous les Samedis

LA VIE AU GRAND AIR

*D A N S
C E   N U M É R O :*

Le Tour de France
La traversée
de Paris à la nage

5. The early Tours de France were widely covered in the sporting and general press; the 1906 winner, René Pottier, is shown here on the cover of the mass-circulation weekly, *La Vie au Grand Air*, 4 August 1906.

6. Signing on at the beginning of a stage provides a regular moment of contact between officials, riders and spectators. Here Belgian Philippe Thys, winner in 1913, 1914 and 1920, signs on at the start of the 1921 race (note spare tyres around the riders' shoulders).

7. Georges Speicher, winner in 1933 and a spectacularly fast descender, is drawn by a press artist during the Tour of 1934 while sitting on a press vehicle.

8. The peloton tackles a typical rolling hill in northern France in the first stage of the 1928 Tour, Paris – Caen (207 kms), won by Nicolas Frantz.

9. The Tour de France brings modern sport to profoundly agricultural areas of France, such as this on the La Rochelle – Rennes stage of the 1933 event, won by Georges Speicher.

10. In the two Tours won by Fausto Coppi (1949 and 1952), one of Coppi's main rivals in the mountains was Jean Robic, who had won the first post-war tour in 1947. Here Robic leads Coppi on the Col de Peyresourde.

11. French hero Louison Bobet, the first rider to win three Tours in succession (1953, 1954, 1955), won decisively in the mountains to claim his victories.

12. Before the current stage finishes on the Champs Elysées began, the Tour finished in Paris at the Parc des Princes, where after his third victory in 1955 Louison Bobet rode a lap of honour before a capacity crowd of spectators.

13. In the 1956 Tour, won by Roger Walkowiak, King of the Mountains Charly Gaul (winner in 1958, second from left) was challenged by Federico Bahamontes (winner in 1959, third from left).

14. The Tour de France has been contested since its beginning on roads which are closed throughout France as the race passes, while millions of spectators stop their normal daily activities to see the race pass.

15. The sauve French champion, Jacques Anquetil, the first cyclist to win five Tours de France (1957, 1961–64), clinched his victories with his total domination of the time trials and outstanding climbing abilities. His rivalry with French rider Raymond Poulidor, 'the eternal second', was lionized in the popular media.

16. Raymond Poulidor.

17. The Tour de France has always offered close contact between the riders and the millions of spectators who line the route. The peloton in the 1966 Tour, with Tom Simpson and Rik van Looy (third and fourth from left).

18. Spectatorship is not confined to fans of cycling, but involves the entire populations of towns through which the race passes. Here the peloton passes through Villedieu, on the 6th stage (Caen – St. Brieuc) of the 1958 race.

19. Industrial workers take time off to watch the Tour pass by on the 4th stage of the 1964 Tour, from Forest (Belgium) to Metz.

20. Intense competition, a large field of nearly 200 riders and unpredictable road and weather conditions make the Tour de France a dangerous event.

21. The Tour de France ends with a fiercely contested criterium on the Champs Elysées in the heart of Paris. Here, Bernard Hinault, five-time winner (1978, 1979, 1981, 1982, 1985) leads.

22. The entire race is followed by TV and still photographers riding on the backs of motorcycles. Here Laurent Fignon (winner 1983, 1984) protests by throwing a drinking bottle.

23. On the stage from Nice to Pra-Loup in the 1975 Tour, Bernard Thévenet (winner 1975 and 1977) catches Eddy Merckx (winner 1969, 1970, 1971, 1972, 1974) and takes the yellow jersey from him.

24. The sport of cycling is heavily influenced by the principle that a cyclist gains advantage and shelter by riding behind another, and that the one in front works harder, because of the impact of wind-resistance.

25. An exhibition marking the tenth anniversary of Louison Bobet's death.

26. The Tour dominates newspaper headlines.

an imaginary and lyrical discourse. On the contrary, they encouraged grandiloquence and exaltation, depending on each different commentator's personality.

The Establishment of a Market in Sports Programmes

French television's public service mission was to attract and satisfy the viewer. The appearance of a second and then a third channel was a response to a desire to offer more diverse programmes and more choice. The 1980s represented a break in the relationship between sport and money. One of the main reasons is that television became interested in this cultural phenomenon that until then had been promoted by the written press and radio. Sport brings high audiences, and for exceptional events the audience is exceptional. Sport generates the highest market share of all the different programmes on television. The increased number of channels has amplified the economic dimension of sport-media relations, since it has been at the origin of the inflation of sports budgets since the 1980s.

The relationship between sport and television is a double one and it is organized around two markets.[27] The first is between the television company and the viewer (air time devoted to sport, audience figures, cost of access to these programmes); the second is between the channel and the sports event organizer (number of events bought, cost of rights). Broadcasting rights and number of hours transmitted are important criteria to evaluate how this market has been changing. The increase in rights can be explained by the creation of new channels basing their programming partially (Canal+) or wholly (Eurosport, Equipe TV and others) on sport, and by a radical change of television regime that has transformed sport into a veritable programming industry.

Televised Sport: A Programming Industry

From 1984 onwards a 'competitive' system has forced the different channels to rationalize their production costs and to go after market share (audience ratings, advertising income). The birth of Canal+ in 1984, of a fifth and sixth channel (both commercial) in 1986 and the privatization of the largest audience channel TF1 in 1987, the opening of thematic cable networks (with channels TV Sport in 1988 and Eurosport in 1989), the digital multiplexes (CanalSatellite, TPS and ABSat in 1996), marked a new era in sport-TV relations. The general audience channels had to become competitive and think about audiences in order to justify investment. This concerned not only the purchase of rights, but also production costs. Television channels had thereafter to be managed like businesses with profitability as an issue. They are now television programme industries: sports events have become consumer products.

Promotional logic takes the form of marketing strategies guided by two imperatives: firstly, the cost-audience relationship, which is very favourable to television sports programmes compared to other programme genres, and secondly, the benefit in terms of image brought by the sport broadcast. These both exercise great attraction for the broadcaster and the advertiser. In 1987, Jacques Carbonnel[28] declared:

> A new age of sport has begun because the economic, media and symbolic circumstances have changed with the integration of sport into mainstream society. As a fantastic reflection of society, sport is experiencing in return the consequences of its brutal and rapid modernization. Because sport today is also and perhaps above all an entertainment. An all-out show, intensified by the most sophisticated marketing techniques. A spectacle systematically shaped for pictures and for broadcasting.

As Bourdieu[29] wrote in 1994, that amounts to saying that every 'television sports programme is, in some way, produced twice', once for the event's multiple organizers and managers and a second time for all the professionals in charge of the production and transmission of pictures of the competition. So television has a double relationship with the broadcast event. It broadcasts it and takes it over, appropriates it. In the case of the Tour de France this 'take-over' happens nowadays at three levels.

Firstly, French public service television is today the Tour's main financial partner, as both producer and transmitter of the event. France Télévisions owns, moreover, the broadcasting rights, and this double role would allow it to influence the running of the event or its rules. It would be moving in the direction of making the spectacle more telegenic. But for the Tour de France this power relationship does not operate, even if, in 1994, the race prologue was held for the first time in the evening, in prime-time,[30] after pressure from the official sponsors of the competition.[31] On the other hand, the same year, for the first time, stages were broadcast from start to finish using both public service networks, France 2 and France 3. The event is now sandwiched in a broadcast that includes the 'pre-' and 'post-race', punctuated by advertising breaks that are never allowed to interrupt the transmission of the race itself. France Télévisions, in this case, is trying to exploit the event as best it can. As for the organizers of the 'grande boucle', they too have at their disposal *promotional* strategies. The promotional strategies of the broadcaster must not conflict with these. The broadcaster is not simply a supplier of capital but a service provider. In 1992, on the renewal of the rights contract, France Télévision (its original name) was preferred to TF1 (the major private terrestrial channel) despite a financially more advantageous offer, because of the benefits that the public service channel was offering (transmission on both networks – France 2 and France 3). At the same time, Jean–Marie Leblanc, organizer of the event, makes no secret of his attachment to the public service, bearing in mind the specificity of the competition that takes place on public roads and requires help from different public service professions (police, *gendarmerie*, highway maintenance, etcetera).

The second way in which television has appropriated the race is that technical improvements have enabled the filming of the race to be optimized by multiplying the different camera angles from fixed equipment. Super-slow-motion, miniature cameras ('paluches'), and articulated arms ('louma') all renew and diversify production.

Equally, mobile equipment has improved in flexibility and quality. Not only are motorbikes more reliable, but also an innovation in use since 1992 is the Wescam. This allows a TV camera suspended from a helicopter to be controlled from the cockpit with constant stability and very high focal lengths, giving the advantage of filming the race from above, and also and above all of 'showing France', thereby participating in the promotion of the sites the race passes through. The pictures produced today by helicopter contribute to the positioning of France Télévisions as a general audience channel with a special interest in the regions (the original name of France 3 was France Régions 3).

Improvements in (off-air) communication between the different actors of the broadcast (commentators in the commentary box, mobile commentators, directors, fixed cameramen, motorbike cameramen or helicopter) also help the director orchestrate the live broadcast and helps the commentators anticipate their commentary.

Increased on-air time imposes a new management of the continuity of the programme. The waiting time has been recreated and managed to ensure the transmission of important moments of the race as and when they appear in the course of a stage.

Thirdly, television has taken over the event in the sense that the evolution of television pictures gives access to new information, which calls for a new type of commentary. Indeed, commentaries are becoming more varied by becoming more intimate, more expert, and by stressing the spectacular. Increased airtime allows other types of news that come from outside the strict framework of the event. Diversity also comes from the increase in the number of speakers. France Télévision's journalistic team up to 2001 consisted of two commentators in the commentary box (a journalist and a consultant or expert summarizer) and two commentators on motorbikes, whose function and comments were quite distinct from their two colleagues.

Patrick Chêne, who replaced Robert Chapatte in 1989, managed on-air continuity and sometimes organized the live coverage. The commentators in the commentary box now have a bank of monitors showing them pictures coming from the different cameras – only the director and his assistant directors had access to this previously. We are seeing an evolution of roles. Exchanges between the different production staff, the motorbikes and the commentators have the effect of giving more authenticity to the commentary, as the journalist can better anticipate his comments and be more in control of them.

When Patrick Chêne asked a question of Bernard Thévenet, the channel's expert consultant and a former winner of the Tour, the latter's point of view gave credibility to his comments. It allowed the broadcast to respond to the different expectations linked to the different degrees of expertise among viewers. The expert also has a pedagogical function, to help viewers understand the race. He helps make sense of the sporting action, helps structure emotions and testifies with all the legitimacy of a former champion. Jean-René Goddart, from radio, the commentator on Motorbike Number 1, was positioned at the head of the race, which allowed a wider coverage of the event, sometimes resulting, however, in pictures being 'out of sync' with the sound commentary.

Finally, Jean-Paul Ollivier, nicknamed 'Paulo la science' ('the Knowledge') by his colleagues, is the historical guarantor of the event. The imaginary dimension, which is the strength of the written press, was being weakened by today's pictures. With his historical evocations, Ollivier[32] admitted to creating a new area of suggestion that operates in two directions. On the one hand, he maintains the race's legends by talking about different victories, exploits and dramas; on the other, he refers to different events that have marked the history of the places the riders pass through, outside the context of the race. This is also the opportunity, from Motorbike Number 2, to mention local gastronomic specialities, to fill a virtual basket of regional produce, or indeed to recall cultural and other curiosities of interest to tourists, which local authorities have sometimes taken the trouble to expand on in their press releases. Tour de France commentaries go beyond a simple evocation of the circumstances of the race; France Télévisions tries to orient the broadcast towards showing landscapes, sites and the tourist heritage. Today this choice is strengthened by an institutionalization of Jean-Paul Ollivier's role as he now find himself in the commentary box seated beside Bernard Thévenet and Christian Prudhomme, a new commentator in 2001. France Télévisions also makes available to foreign press and commentators a 'Road Book', giving stage-by-stage details of local peculiarities likely to be shown on screen. From 2001 the whole commentary team has been changed round. Jean-René Goddart has kept his function at the head of the race. He is accompanied by another commentator, Thierry Adam, at the rear of the peloton, who gives news of the race that television does not show.

Sport-media relations are still structured around promotional processes, which are taking new forms. Sport in general, as a source of audiences, allows channels to develop various marketing strategies. The event's top-level partners or sponsors appear as the programme comes on air (France Télécom and Champion supermarkets for the Tour de France). Local politicians and local councillors, as representatives of the local authorities making financial contributions for the award of a stage finish or departure, are often looked after particularly carefully. For its partners, be they private companies or representing public authorities, the Tour is an opportunity to engage in public relations operations. The adverts, that France Télévisions shows before and after the programmes that accompany the live coverage, are part of the whole broadcast. Television, finally, by permanently highlighting its broadcasting team and the technical means deployed, proves its effectiveness. In this context, the commentators also have the task of ensuring the continuity of the broadcast, by inscribing the event in a whole that includes the advertising breaks and the self-promotional strategies, and by praising the technical teams as well as the quality of the broadcast. The broadcasting of an event now attracts spectators to the site of the event. Sports broadcasting thus has the effect of promoting a live event which is above all a media event.

CONCLUSION

The Tour de France has kept pace with or indeed stimulated many innovations in journalists' professional practice. Journalists went out to where the event was happening, which saved time in news gathering. This was clear progress for the press, and this reduction in time and space brought about a renewal and a spectacularization of news. The Tour's specificity as a cycling event is that it is an itinerant competition, and watching it at the roadside is a very fleeting experience. The race's lack of visibility thus encouraged accounts based on imagination, legend or epic.

The sport-press relationship was also characterized by the fact that it encouraged different forms of *promotion*. Initially, the media promoted itself, since organizing and narrating sports events sold more newspapers. This effect of sports writing also brought investment by industrialists (cycling, motor cars) in the organization and support of sports events.

Television obeyed the same logic in its capacity as a media of live pictures. Broadcasts have been transformed under the influence of technological innovation and media promotion that generate changes in the construction of the visible. The essential aim of these innovations has been to expand the television crews and equipment to extend the visibility of the race. The progress achieved later allowed greater mobility of equipment and better quality live pictures. The images put the viewer in the privileged position of being close to the action and everywhere at the same time. This increased visibility of the race also enhanced the status of television, which was not slow to use these technical innovations, extra broadcasting equipment and improved quality of coverage to promote itself. The pictures also acted as 'evidence' for the discourse: they served as a medium for recreating the adventure that the commentators were narrating.

The birth of private channels marked an important break in the sport-television relationship. Broadcasters were now in competition with each other and worried about their audience. The issue became one of constructing a new form of broadcasting, a programme made 'for and by' television. But it appears, in reality, that the Tour de France was a precursor in this respect, since from its inception it was a media product with economic connections. Further, the particular nature of the event (itinerant and fleeting as a spectacle) led to the creation of a sports television spectacle offering its own particular point of view.

The current era has changed the promotional rationale, which takes the form of marketing strategies. Television gets most of its income from private sponsors and by broadcasting commercial advertising. Improved visibility of the race enhances both the status of the event and the media coverage of the various financial partners: those sponsoring the competing teams, the organizing company or France Télévisions. The multiple promotional strategies must not compete with each other. The publicity caravan was born in the 1930s, to cover the loss of income when brand teams were replaced by national teams. Today the peloton fulfils this function, since it is an advertising medium in itself, no longer aimed at the roadside public, but for the television viewer.

The Tour de France appears therefore as a bringer of change to media production, essentially for the written press and for the early period of television. Other sports have played the same role. British television was the first to offer a new way of watching football matches, an innovation taken up by Canal+ from 1984. The recent appearance of digital TV channels brings in a new dimension. We are entering the era of virtual reality. Indeed, the viewer can now choose matches *à la carte* through pay-per-view, but above all, he or she can, for certain events, take an active part in the broadcast by choosing channels that correspond to particular cameras covering the event. The Kiosque channel on CanalSatellite allows subscribers to construct their own production of Formula 1 broadcasts.

Sport now serves as a promotional medium for new image broadcasting systems. Internet also fits this pattern and furthermore allows new forms of access to the broadcasting of certain sports. Today, sailing has its share of adventures and its drama on offer; races that we cannot see allow for the writing of new legends. Will the Internet be an appropriate medium for this sport?

The Tour de France was once a precursor in structuring the links between sport and the media. Can it remain a driver of development and innovation?

NOTES

1. M. Sauvage and D. Maréchal, 'Les racines d'un succès', in J.-N. Jeanneney and M. Sauvage (eds), *Télévision, nouvelle mémoire, Les magazines de grand reportage 1959–1968* (Paris: Seuil/INA, 1982), p.37.
2. J.-F. Bourg, *L'Argent fou du sport* (Paris: Table ronde, 1994).
3. F. Wille, 'Une diachronie du spectacle sportif télévisé: des logiques d'innovations et de

promotions', in P. Gabaston and B. Leconte (eds), *Sports et télévision. Regards croisés* (Paris: L'Harmattan, 2000), pp.427–42.

4. J. Durry, 'La télévision prend le pouvoir, l'histoire en mouvement', in R. Hubscher (ed.), *Le Sport dans la société française (XIXe–XXe siècle)* (Paris: Armand Colin, 1992), pp.520–24.

5. F. Wille, 'Le spectacle sportif médiatisé ou l'appropriation reconstruction de l'information', *Les Cahiers du journalisme*, 7 (June 2000), pp.212–25.

6. P. Gaboriau, *Le Tour de France et le vélo. Histoire sociale d'une épopée contemporaine* (Paris: L'Harmattan (coll. Espace et temps du sport), 1995).

7. P. Boury, *La France du Tour. Un espace à géographie variable* (Paris: L'Harmattan (coll. Espace et temps du sport), 1997).

8. Y. Léziart, *Sport et dynamique sociale* (Joinville-le-Pont: Actio, 1989).

9. G. Vigarello, 'Le Tour de France', in P. Nora (ed.) *Les Lieux de mémoire*, Tome III, Les France, Vol.2 : Traditions (Paris: Gallimard, 1992), pp.887–920.

10. A. Vant, *L'industrie du cycle dans la région stéphanoise* (Lyon: Editions Lyonnaises d'art et d'histoire, 1993), p.9.

11. Riders' objections related to two further points: the absence of trainers on the course and the length of the event.

12. G. Vigarello, 'Le Tour de France'.

13. C. Pociello, 'Spectacles, Images et représentations', in *Les Cultures sportives. Pratiques, représentations et mythes sportifs* (Paris: PUF, 1995), pp.111–34.

14. R. Barthes, *Mythologies* (Paris: Points, 1956).

15. G. Vigarello, 'Le Tour de France'.

16. The first one was on 6 June 1947 when a soirée de gala was broadcast from the Théâtre des Champs-Elysées to commemorate the D-Day landings.

17. J.-M. Bertrand, 'Histoire du direct sportif', *Accès n°4*, Carrefour international de la communication, Paris, June 1986. (A chronology of great technical and sporting events.)

18. François Mitterrand, Junior Minister of Information, signed a ministerial order (arrêté) on 20 Nov. 1948 establishing the standard for the French broadcasting network at 819 lines.

19. The author differentiates between the terms 'téléspectateur' (viewer) and 'télé-spectateur' (tele-viewer) with respect to the nature of the programme produced by the media compared to the live event.

20. C. Pociello, *Sport et société. Approche socioculturelle des pratiques* (Paris: Vigot, 1985).

21. B. Jeu, *Le Sport, la mort, la violence* (Lille: Edition universitaire – Université Lille III, 1975). See also B. Jeu, *Le Sport, l'émotion, l'espace* (Paris: Vigot, 1983).

22. Le Syndicat national de la presse quotidienne régionale, an association whose purpose is to defend the interests of the French regional daily press.

23. Interview with Jean-Paul Ollivier, Tour commentator on Motorbike number 2, 24 Feb. 1998.

24. Up to 1961 the peloton was made up of national teams.

25. The French *It's a Knockout*. Each programme set two French towns in competition with each other in a series of events in similar fashion to its successor of a few years later, *Jeux sans frontières*, on a European basis.

26. The first worldwide colour broadcast was the Mexico Olympic Games of 1968. It was not until 1970 that the Tour de France was first broadcast partly in colour and partly in black and white.

27. J.-F. Bourg and J.-J. Gouguet, *Analyse économique du sport* (Paris: PUF, 1998).

28. J. Carbonnel, 'Le nouvel âge du sport', *Esprit*, numéro spécial (April 1987).

29. P. Bourdieu, 'Les Jeux Olympiques. Programme pour une analyse', *Actes de la recherche en sciences sociales*, 103 (1994), p.103.

30. Prime-time (the time of the broadcasting day most highly prized by advertisers) in France is the slot between 8.45pm and 10.30pm. It corresponds to high audience ratings, and is therefore the most profitable.

31. Interview with Jean-Marie Leblanc, Managing Director of the Société du Tour de France, June 1998.

32. Interview of 24 February 1998 with Jean-Paul Ollivier.

MEANINGS, METAPHORS AND VALUES

Beating the Bounds:
The Tour de France and National Identity

CHRISTOPHE CAMPOS

The Tour de France has, since the late 1960s, made brief inroads into neighbouring countries. (It came briefly to the south of England in 1974 and 1994.) In 2002 it began in the Duchy of Luxembourg. The first two stages (7–8 July) took it south-eastwards from Luxembourg to Saarbrücken in Germany, and the third stage back westwards to Metz, in France. The sporting daily *L'Equipe*, which descends from the newspaper that first sponsored the Tour, still provides the most extensive coverage (up to five broadsheet pages a day) and perhaps best represents the popular spirit of the event. On 9 July it celebrated the return to France:

> Le Tour s'exporte bien, mais aujourd'hui, retour au pays. En passant par la Lorraine jusqu'en Champagne, le Tour de France retrouve la mère patrie. Après toutes ces chutes depuis trois jours, espérons que ça va arrêter de tomber à Gravelotte, haut lieu de la guerre de 1870, tandis que, de Metz à Reims, c'est un peu d'histoire de France qui défilera sur l'itinéraire: Verdun, l'Argonne, Valmy.[1]

La mère patrie, the motherland. The French language (unlike German, which talks of 'fatherland') feminizes the word *patrie* (literally, place of the father, or *pater* in Latin) so that it stands, in a sense, for both parents. In emotional moments like this, the word *mère* is added, stressing the maternal role of France in relation to her wayward sons, now back at their mother's breast, or on her lap, or what you will. The two days in foreign parts had been difficult: several prominent runners had suffered bad falls in the first two stages. But now we are back in mother France, says the unidentified journalist ('notre envoyé spécial', our special correspondent, a phrase usually applied to foreign correspondents), we hope all will be well.

There is even more subtext to this extract. Since the Revolutionary period, France has been divided into administrative units called *départements*, bearing the names of natural features (mostly rivers or mountains). More recently, the Fifth Republic (founded in 1958) has created larger economic *regions*, often referred to in the economic or political context. Given the yearning of De Gaulle, the inspirer of the Fifth Republic, to remind France of its pre-Revolutionary monarchic past, these *regions* were, in most cases, given the names of the old French *provinces*, abandoned by the Revolution because of their associations with the monarchy. So over the next two stages (Saarbrücken to Metz and Metz to Reims), the Tour was to cross the *départements* of the Moselle, the Meurthe et Moselle, the Meuse, then the Marne, but the journalist instinctively goes for the regional names, Lorraine and Champagne-Ardennes, shortening the latter to its most authentically French part, for the Ardennes hills are partly in Belgium.

Nor do Lorraine and Champagne lack significance. The latter gives its name to what is, worldwide, France's most famous product. Thus the Tour's own exportability – *le Tour s'exporte bien* – gains from the reflected glow of the drink that is certainly one of France's best-known commodities internationally. The former is perhaps the most historically and politically charged of all names of French provinces, and for two reasons. First, it is the homeland of Joan of Arc, who famously hung up her clogs (*sabots*) and helped to rally the forces of the king, Charles VII, in his armed struggle against the English and the Burgundians in the 1320s, and get him crowned at Reims, before being captured, sold to the English and burned at the stake for sorcery, to become, from the nineteenth century, France's most prominent patriotic martyr and, for some, its patron saint. One of her names, in popular tradition, is Jeanne la bonne Lorraine. Lorraine is associated, in the minds of many former French schoolchildren, with a song, derived in a complex way from the Jeanne myth, of which the first line, *En passant par la Lorraine avec mes sabots*, is hinted at above by our anonymous journalist.

Secondly, Lorraine, already charged with the Joan of Arc association, was one of the two former French provinces annexed by the new German state after its victory over France in 1870. The Third Republic, founded in France as a result of the humiliating defeat of 1870, spent the following 40 years purposefully reinforcing the sense of national identity (the conception of the bicycle Tour belongs to that period). It did so in part by shaping French history into a national curriculum, known as *l'Histoire de France* (also named in the above extract), designed to show every schoolchild how the founding fathers, kings and others, had built up the national heritage; and also by teaching French geography to all, with the message that France was a land unit having a strong cultural tradition supported by natural frontiers and therefore destined from the start to become a nation.

More overtly, many politicians of the Third Republic built their stance on the premise that France had been mutilated by the outcome of the 1870 war, and must attempt by all means to retrieve the two lost provinces, Alsace and Lorraine – an aim eventually achieved, at a cost of two million dead, by the First World War. No wonder, then, that the journalist also mentions Gravelotte, one of the fiercest battles of the 1870 war before the French collapse, then Verdun, l'Argonne and Valmy. The first two are amongst the French victories (the first with a gigantic death toll) of the First World War. The third dates back to 1792, when the new popular Revolutionary army, under Dumouriez, successfully repelled a Prussian army commanded by the Duke of Brunswick, which was attempting to restore royalist order in France – the poet Goethe, who was present, was so impressed by the citizens' army that he wrote in his diary that he had just witnessed the start of a new era in history.

The return of the cycling sons to their motherland (no matter if many of the riders are not French and the favourite is an American) is thus symbolically associated with the places where that land was first defended, then mutilated, then reunified. No wonder, either, that so many riders fell from their bicycles in the first two stages, pedalling over what was not only foreign tarmac, but also the hostile territory of the Prussian and German, against whom French identity was constructed in the late nineteenth century.

Our journalist goes on to admit that one or two cyclists are German:

> Erik Zabel was inspired and feeling at home yesterday, for three quarters of the stage were in German territory, once they had left Luxembourg and crossed the Moselle at Schengen. Jan Ullrich was not missed much by the Tour de France. There were still people along the roadside, and the sunny weather had encouraged the young ladies to dress lightly, even though, it must be admitted, we did not meet the impressive and memorable crowds that had gathered to watch the Tour two years ago in the Fribourg area.[2]

However, he does not fail to remind his readers that another of these, Ullrich, had notoriously failed a dope test. Furthermore, support from the lightly dressed young ladies along the way, was not as great as it would be in the motherland, or, indeed, in Fribourg, presumably somewhat de-Germanized by being in Switzerland.

Admiration by the young ladies for those magnificent heroes on their pedal machines has, since the 1920s, been a favourite 'take' for photojournalists following this intensely masculine event. At the photocall for the winner of each stage, there was regularly a kiss from a specially chosen local beauty, followed by the symbolic explosion of the bottle of champagne (though in recent years some of the champions have favoured a somewhat less buccaneering image by having their wives in the van). There was even, as one sees from nostalgic picture books on the Tour, a little orchestrated flirting with country lasses in their summer dresses on the edge of fields. In the photographic history of the twentieth century these images resemble nothing so much as those of French women embracing and festooning the heroic crews of the Allied tanks as they rolled into France in 1944. The symbolic reward of the warrior at the end of the battle is an iconic feminine role. Here, the campaign is programmed to embrace the score of beauties who encompass the beauty and variety of France. In the Tour, indeed, every stage is a struggle and a victory for some hero. In the hyperbolic language of journalists, it is a war of endurance, consisting of daily pitched battles strung out along the waystages, to which there have recently been added minor skirmishes to conquer the tops of slopes or mountain passes. 'Conquer' is the key word. The Tour is a series of conquests adding up to the whole of the national territory: a ritual annual reoccupation of France from within, blessed by the provincial feminine godmothers, until the final return to the mother of all mothers, the Champs-Elysées.

The Elysian Fields is a pre-Christian phrase for Paradise, and the ritual of the Tour has always had its religious undertones in a country that has traditionally associated its nationhood with religious beliefs. The itinerary has been compared to Christ's ascension of Golgotha, the waystages being the Stations of the Cross ('of which there were only 14', implying that the cyclists have an even harder time).[3] To this day, *L'Equipe*, true to the macaronic style of much reporting on sport, is both an orchestrator and a revealer. On 10 July 2002, our 'special correspondent' remembers that 'a year ago, the men of the US Postal had a nasty time on the shiny tarmac of the *Sacred Way*'.[4] The following week another journalist writes of Jalabert, the leading French rider, 'Jalabert is a born crusader',[5] and later a sub-editor adds in a subtitle, 'Jalabert est devenu un personnage indispensable à la grande messe cathodique du Tour'.[6] The play on *catholique/cathodique* suggests that, while the Tour has been appropriated by television (born of cathode-ray tube technology), it is still 'catholic' in the grand mass it celebrates annually for the nation. It is, indeed, part of a veritable liturgy leading to Bastille Day on 14 July.[7] The first celebration of Bastille Day, in Paris in 1790, was called the 'Fête de la Fédération', and it brought together representatives of the National Guard of the whole nation. Nowadays, it is the role of the heroic cyclists to symbolically federate France and bring it home to Paris.

THE ORIGINS OF THE PHRASE 'TOUR DE FRANCE'

The association of the Tour with national identity is thus not only a contemporary fact, but an historical intention on the part of its founders. They carried this out by giving it a name embedded in the nation's collective memory.[8]

The phrase *tour de France* was originally used as early as the sixteenth century. Then, more than 300 years later, France was sorely in need of consolidation. Its then main royal and Catholic identity was threatened by the resistance to royal authority from western and southern Protestant-dominated areas. In the European context, it was hemmed in by the interests of Spain, then the major continental European trading and colonial power, which also controlled the Low Countries to the north and had active links with parts of Italy. Catherine of Medici, the French king's mother and the real power behind the throne, sent her son Charles IX on a two-year tour of his kingdom from 1564 to 1566. The growing complexity of diplomatic, administrative and economic aspects of government meant that the kings had stopped transporting their entire retinue from province to province as they had done in earlier times. The visits by the itinerant monarch to the courts of far-flung vassals were intended (however poorly endowed he was as to brains, another reason for his mother sending him out of the way) to consolidate their support, and map out for each of them the geographical extent of the network of allegiance they belonged to.

The meaning of the word 'tour' was somewhat different from its most common contemporary one. Since the development of leisure travel, in Britain and in France, it has become associated with 'tourism' in its more diluted and pleasureful aspects. For Charles IX the word had a more political meaning: it was more a 'tour of inspection' such as a military commander might carry out in his camp, or a government representative in visits to key officials and installations. Indeed, even for the precursors of modern package-holiday tourists, a tour of the Continent or of such-and-such a country was still a sort of inspection, a dutiful personal or collective appropriation and assessment of a cultural heritage.

Histories of the Tour rightly point to the commercial interests of the bicycle trade as the immediate causes of its birth, but its linguistic and ideological background gave it, from the start, far more importance than a cycle race. The tour of Charles IX was, by 1903, no more than a distant reference, but the idea of an inspection or assessment of national unity was very much a feature of the late nineteenth century. Three prominent references belonging to that time will go a long way to explaining it. The first is the historian Jules Michelet (1796–1874), one of the grandfathers of the modern French nation. Michelet, who wrote the most comprehensive history of France seen at that time, and was also instrumental in retrieving the Joan of Arc myth from the scattered bric-à-brac of the royal past, felt it necessary, as part of his History, to describe the French provinces. This description, entitled *Tableau de la France*, is presented in the form of a journey starting and ending in Paris.

For all the prominent French historians of the early and mid-nineteenth century, history was about consolidating national identity. The foundation myth available to earlier ages, which explained the existence of France according to the chronicles of kings' reigns, had been exploded by the Revolution and the Romantics. Other, wider, perspectives were sought by historians, groping their ways through documentary sources towards the history of the French people as we know it today. France's geographical identity was also ideologically crucial, for without it the Third Republic, born of the defeat of 1870, would not have been able to construct a virulent form of patriotism around the mutilation of France through the loss of Alsace and Lorraine.

The geographical image of France as we know it was relatively new. Not until the 1880s was it imprinted in people's memory by being hung up on the walls in primary school classrooms. Nor was it, until then, that neat at the edges. Up to the eighteenth century Continental states were defined more by a series of local allegiances to the monarch and his governance than by a physical frontier line. Even though Louis XV had made it his business to move towards a more modern map by bargaining for allegiances in some of the marginal territories, this work was far from complete by the time of the Revolution. Once the Congress of Vienna (1815–18) had re-drawn the map of the spheres of influence which were to develop, in the course of the century, into the nation states, it fell to the intellectuals to construct bonding devices for national territories, together with national cultures and national histories. Michelet was aware of the close links between history and geography, and with these in mind he conducted his readers on an imaginary tour so that they could visualize the unity and variety of the national territory whose history he was about to tell.

Michelet lived and wrote in Paris, so it seemed natural to him, as it did a generation later to the founders of the Tour, to begin and end the *Tableau* in the capital city. Since the Revolution, centralization, which is so much a feature of modern France, had been increasing. The railways being planned and built radiated from Paris, as did the main national highways. Intellectual and academic life was clustered there. The growing national press, which was to spawn the sporting journals, one of which founded the Tour, was also based there. Michelet, unlike the later organizers of the race, did not need to plan his tour in relation to the factors which affect cycling, but he did face two problems which have always been in their minds: how to start and end a tour in Paris, which is neither really central nor peripheral, and how to skirt around the country while still accounting for the central parts.

Michelet's readers are first taken down the River Seine from Paris to the trading ports of Rouen and Le Havre. They then delineate Normandy and Brittany with a short dash inland to Rennes, travel up the Loire to Tours and follow one of the main medieval trading routes to La Rochelle via Poitiers (which survives to this day in the TGV train link from Paris to La Rochelle). At this point, Michelet is in something of a quandary, because if he continues along the coast he will miss the main central area (le Massif central), and if he penetrates this, he will need to retrace his steps at some point, so he compromises in taking the reader to Brive and mentioning that it is typical of the whole central *massif*, then turning south towards the Pyrenees. The tour then resumes its boundary route as far as Grenoble and Lyon, where a second quandary awaits. This he solves by forking the route (bicycle races can't), in order to

MAP 1

MICHELET'S IMAGINED TOUR (1833)

explore the north-eastern frontier regions as far as Metz, Toul, Verdun and Sedan, though leaving out the province of Alsace because 'few people speak French there', then returning to Lyon to start off again in a north-westerly direction towards Burgundy and Champagne. This second loop takes in the famous sites of Joan of Arc's progression towards Reims and beyond, and, because of his own attachment to this figure, he cannot resist a dogleg to Orléans.

Organizers of the first bicycle tour also certainly had in mind the title of a book they had all studied in primary school, *Le Tour de la France par deux enfants*.[9] This was a work designed to introduce children to an awareness of French geography and history through the story of an initiatory journey by two boys who set out, on the death of their father, to find an uncle whose probable whereabouts is uncertain and constantly removed. This leads them to travel round most of the country, discovering its natural features, significant industrial and commercial activities, and the names and brief biographies of the worthy citizens hailing from the towns where they stay. Whereas Michelet had set out mostly to discover the surprising variety of France, Mme Fouillée, the authoress, had a political intent: to assert the necessary links between parts of a territory that was in danger of being split by the mutilation of 1870. Accordingly, the two orphaned boys are made to start off in Lorraine (now also orphaned of its mother, France, and forcibly adopted by Germany) and to seek, together with their maternal uncle, the mother country they yearn for, which they explore with passionate interest before finally tracking down the elusive man in the heart of hearts of France, the rich agricultural countryside west of Paris. These two ideas, variety and unity, recur in all the presentations, lyrical or political, of the Tour to this day.

The third reference in the notion of a 'tour de France' is an equally popular one, associated, not with learning or education, but with traditional crafts. Since the prosperous twelfth and thirteenth centuries, which had seen the building of France's great cathedrals, craftsmen of the various trades involved in such projects (carpenters, stonemasons and others) had organized themselves into semi-secret societies, known as *devoirs* ('obligations' is a rough translation). They performed various functions, some akin to those of modern trade unions: the main one was to provide their members, known as *compagnons*, with a legitimate basis of training and qualification, to protect their interests against poor craftsmen or impostors, and, associated with this, to facilitate travel from town to town so that the *compagnons* could learn various methods and practices associated with different provinces. The itinerant training, which could (and still does) last upwards of five years, came to be called *le tour de France*. Here again, the word tour implies a journey of information, a completing of knowledge of one's craft, not a trip taken for pleasure.

In the mid-nineteenth century, with incipient industrialization and its reliance on new concentrations of unqualified labour threatening traditional societies of this kind, there was a great deal of interest in the *devoirs*. It was taken up most famously by the novelist George Sand, in a novel based on the published memoirs of one of them, which she entitled *Le Compagnon du Tour de France*. Here she attempts to dismantle the reputation the *compagnons* had acquired in the eyes of the middle classes, for rivalry and brawling, and paints a romantic picture of their traditional country morality and humble decency (a similar attitude was to be demonstrated in England a few years later by John Ruskin). Indeed, though Mme Fouillée's two orphaned boys in *Le Tour de la France par deux enfants* are not involved in a specific craft, they too show an unfailing willingness to learn about anything practical, which makes them the heirs of the George Sand character. Its model for this character, according to Sand's Foreword[10] to her novel, went on a 500-league pilgrimage around France to spread the good principles he had preached. The religious term is worthy of note: a pilgrimage usually takes the faithful to a holy place and back, whereas here it is the whole of the country that is, by implication, sacred.

The link between the *compagnons* and the bicycle was reinforced in popular memory by the fact that several *compagnons* were celebrated by the media in the mid-nineteenth century for accomplishing their tour, not on foot, but with a predecessor of the pedal bicycle, the *draisienne* (the original 'push-bike').

This brief prehistory of the phrase *tour de France* and of the political and social connotations it had for the inventors of the cycle race should help to understand why it was to become so rapid and so popular a success. The bicycle was cherished as a French invention: it was the first really popular and cheap means of transport. It was made and used by workers who were moving to towns and away from the orbit of the traditional crafts but who still understood the attitudes associated with them. The bicycle race was one of the first popular sports: it initially involved not trained professional athletes, but lusty workers who could propel 20 kilograms of metal over poor roads all day and all night, who knew how to weld a broken frame in a blacksmith's forge, and who often gained fame and modest wealth starting from the humble beginnings that most of their spectators understood. (As late as the 1970s, when only 15 per cent of active Frenchmen worked on the land, half of the riders were sons of farmers. If by chance the route took them near to the birthplace of one of them, he was always allowed to lead the race at this point.) A bicycle race around France not only linked the various towns and provinces symbolically; it also brought the technology of the industrial town back into the countryside, the new city workers in touch with their rural cousins, and, in addition, could be seen as a patriotic event with sacred connotations at a time when the unity of French territory was a crucial political issue.

TERRITORIAL RITUALS AND NATIONAL NETWORKS

In my village of Saint-Gervais-les-trois-clochers, in central France, one of the schoolmasters organizes, every year in June, a one-day outing for all the classes. No coaches are hired, no theme parks visited. Everyone brings a packed lunch, and the schoolchildren make their way to the edge of the three former parishes (now one civic *commune*), then spend the day walking around it, following roads and paths situated close to its boundaries, noting, with the help of their master, the names of the various areas and landmarks, and calling in on outlying farms.

Though they do not use the term, these schoolchildren are, in fact, 'beating the bounds', as their forefathers have probably done for the past three thousand years. This ritual, which must have begun when the first sedentary agricultural communities spread over Europe from the valley of the Danube and displaced or absorbed the earlier semi-nomadic hunters and gatherers, is primarily a collective proprietorial gesture. The area claimed from woodland or heath, and the boundaries ('bounds') between the territories of one's community and the neighbouring ones, or between agriculture and wilderness, are checked and marked afresh, as one might trim a hedge or mend a fence regularly. Established divisions of woodland, pastureland and cultivated land are surveyed by the inhabitants, who traditionally (until two centuries ago) held communal rights over much of it. Trespassers or new settlers are identified. More important, the bonding of the community, and its self-awareness, are reasserted by visits to all homesteads. And, because practical considerations and ritual ones are always associated, the exercise is often conducted in semi-religious mode. Symbolic chanting or anointing confirms possession and civilization of the land, excludes foreign or evil forces, and, hopefully, paves the way for a good harvest the following year. The early Christian church reclaimed many pagan practices, and one can find in a number of early modern ceremonies the remnants of the beating of the bounds: thus, Christmas carols taken around the homesteads, or the midsummer ritual described by Thomas Hardy at the start of *Tess of the d'Urbervilles*.

Our initial quotation from *L'Equipe* shows that the symbolic values attached to the marking and transgression of frontiers are still alive. Nation states have, by a variety of methods, endeavoured to transpose the idea of territory from the scale of the traditional agricultural community to the larger scale of the nation. In the former, the community consists of people who all know each other as individuals, and are bonded by the shared knowledge of their local landscape which they all know in detail, and which contains their shared livelihood. In the latter (recently called 'an imagined community'[11]) people too numerous to ever meet and know each other live from varied activities in a country that few or none of them will ever explore fully. The national ideology needs to find ways of transposing local values onto a larger scale. It also needs to create or develop channels of communication between various parts of its territory and landscapes that can equate to the well-known local roads, paths and natural features of the traditional environment.

The need for emblems of transposition was fulfilled in France under the Third Republic (1870–1940) in the context of what was still a predominantly agricultural country. 1903, the year of the first Tour, was also the one in which the famous *Marianne semeuse*[12] first appeared on postage stamps (she survives to this day on the reverse of the French 10, 20 and 50 cent euro coins). The beautifully flowing gesture of the sower accords with the hope of the time that the national future was being sown, like a harvest from grain. It was also in the minds of our incorrigible hyperbolists, the sporting commentators, who could cite a famous novelist of their time in support of the notion that the Herculean cyclists were about to spread their energy like grain throughout the nation:

> Du geste large et puissant que Zola, dans *La Terre*, donne à son laboureur, *L'Auto*, journal d'idées et d'action, va lancer à travers la France, dès aujourd'hui, les inconscients et rudes semeurs d'énergie que sont les grands routiers professionnels.[13]

The other need – for consolidation through networks of communication – was also addressed by the Third Republic. For instance, a law enacted in 1879 (the *plan Freycinet*) was intended to harness the previously commerce-driven railway lines in the interests of a national grid. One of its aspects was that all (then private) railway companies, in their applications for franchises, were to plan a grid of double main lines linking all the *villes préfectures* (main administrative towns) to their neighbours and to Paris, and a secondary grid of branch, single and often narrow-gauge lines linking the *villes préfectures* to the *villes sous-préfectures*. The founders of the Tour participated, from their Parisian offices, in this aspect of the building of the nation. A keynote emark attributed to Géo Lefèvre, main bicycle correspondent of *L'Auto-Vélo*, in 1902, is that the Tour should follow 'a circuit linking all the French towns'.

Geographically, this ideal had to be adapted in various ways to other factors, commercial, promotional and political, and has continued to be so, though the factors have evolved over the century. Initially, the main commercial aim underlying Lefèvre's pious statement was to visit the areas where there was the largest existing or potential market for bicycles and related equipment, and where, consequently, there were active cyclists' associations liable to support the event. *L'Auto* (which called itself for a time *L'Auto-Vélo*, until its main rival *Le Vélo* took court action to make it change its name) was in the business of promoting the revolutionary invention which, over the second half of the nineteenth century, had made a convenient and relatively cheap mode of individual transport available to the urban working man. At the turn of the century, France had completed the first phase of its industrialization, which had led mainly to the growth of existing large trading towns (Bordeaux and Nantes on the Atlantic seaboard, Rouen on the Channel, Marseille on the Mediterranean, Lyon and Toulouse situated on important pivots of traditional river transport), and, secondarily, to the development of new urban centres in areas producing the raw materials of heavy industry (Clermont-Ferrand, Lille). There lay the largest markets for the bicycle and, indeed, for sporting newspapers.

The first Tour accordingly embraced most of these towns, as it progressed from Paris (then with a population of 2.5 million) to Lyon (560,000) via Nevers and Moulins; from Lyon to Marseille (490,000); from Marseille to Toulouse (190,000) via Narbonne; from Toulouse to Bordeaux (330,000) via Montauban and Agen; from Bordeaux to Nantes (150,000) via Cognac; and from Nantes back to Paris. Of these six stages, all followed traditional trading routes, mostly running along river valleys, as indeed, because of the need to avoid high gradients, did the recently developed railways.

What it did not embrace is also of interest. Of the major towns of the time, Clermont-Ferrand, Lille and Rouen were not visited. Of the provinces, the north-west, the north and the north-east (Brittany, Normandy, Picardy, Flanders, Champagne, Burgundy, Dauphiné) were left out of the loop, as were the Alps, the coast of Provence and the Pyrenees. The bounds were only really beaten between Marseille and Narbonne and, very roughly, between Bordeaux and Nantes. The whole of the central core between the Loire, the Rhône and the Garonne was circumscribed but not penetrated: indeed, this first route (due to be repeated in the centenary 2003 race) has been called a *Tour du Massif Central*.[14]

There were both political and commercial reasons for this imperfect itinerary. Because of the loss of Alsace and Lorraine, the northern areas were rather out on a limb, and to visit, say, Nancy and Dijon while

MAP 2

THE 'TOUR OF THE MASSIF CENTRAL' (1903)

leaving out Metz and Strasbourg would have been tacitly abandoning the wider frontiers the Third Republic was committed to restore at the earliest possible moment. On the other hand, *L'Auto* and its main rival, *Le Vélo*, had already successfully organized races from Paris to Brest and back (1891), from Paris to Roubaix (in the Lille conurbation, 1896), and from Paris to Brussels, through Flanders (1893), and from Bordeaux to Paris (1891). The 1903 '*Tour du Massif Central*' was to a large extent an exploitation of new areas.

The itinerary of the third Tour (1905) began to resemble a beating of bounds, though boundary provinces rather than frontier towns were visited: Nancy, Besançon, Grenoble, Rennes and Caen were added to the staging towns. Roads are not necessarily made up to encircle frontiers, but rather to link frontier areas with foreign ones, so even the most frontier-hugging tour resembles a polygon circumscribed by frontiers, rather than a wheel. This is particularly true of mountainous frontier areas (particularly the Alps and the Pyrenees, where valleys point outwards and upwards), which can only be included if the waystage is at the high frontier post (where there is no accommodation for the riders), or in the foreign town at the bottom of the valley on the other side. This feature, and commercial interests, rather than a pure spirit of internationalism, explains most of the foreign stages incorporated over the years. On the other hand, sea coasts are often hugged by roads, so that the Mediterranean and Normandy coastlines have often been part of the circuit. Some attempts were made in the 1930s and 1940s to follow military 'strategic roads' along the northern and north-eastern frontiers. These had the added 'value' of being cobbled bone-shakers and thus posing particular problems to the riders, who dubbed them *l'enfer du nord* (the northern hell).

The national territory does not only need to be retraced, it also has to be reconquered ritually by men of heroic stature. During the first few Tours, when the riders left one town and were expected one or two days later at another, every stage was an individual trial of strength and initiative (including even – for the less heroic – snatching an illegal ride on a train between two checkpoints). As the length of stages was brought down to more reasonable proportions from 1910 onwards, other heroic feats needed to be introduced if the superhuman stature of the champions was to be preserved in the eyes of the media-fed public. The most successful one was to incorporate mountain stages, which break up the tendency of more modern riders to spend the stage in a bunch, and provide both the need for physical stamina to get up, and daring to get down, the other side at high speed. These routes sometimes had to be created for the purpose. The first time the Tourmalet pass, in the Pyrenees, was incorporated in the Tour, *L'Auto* negotiated with the local authorities to subsidize the making up of a relatively safe road out of a series of mountain paths. And the victory of the champions over the difficulties of the terrain became another aspect of the annual reconquest.

Henri Desgrange's famous lyrical report of 1911 on the ascension of the Galibier pass illustrates this battle of the heroes over the Titans:

> In the history of mankind, is not the bicycle the first successful effort of intelligent beings to rid themselves of the laws of gravity?
> 'These are eagles,' Maurice Leblanc told us more than 15 years ago, and are these men of ours not winged, since they have now managed to rise to heights where eagles do not venture, and cross the highest peaks in Europe?

Their slim and all-conquering muscles carried them so high that they appeared, from up there, to dominate the world! Meanwhile the mountain, that apostle of secular beliefs and also of fine health, acclaims them with the adorable song of its pearly springs, the crashing of its iridescent waterfalls, the thunder of its avalanches, and the frozen stupor of its everlasting snowfields!

Smiting slowly with the strength of their thighs, our men had pushed themselves up, and the valleys had rung out with their fearsome grunts!

And way down there, the town of Saint-Michel-de-Maurienne, shrinking as we watched, was wondering whether some avalanche would not fling back down to it all these miscreants intent on violating the mountain.[15]

Further on in the same report, he tells how Georget, the leader, dismounted for an instant at the top of the pass, 'to rest his foot on the monster's head'. The combination of modern technology and human courage is thus seen to be asserting the enslavement of the forces of nature. This imagery is still prevalent. The cartoonists of *L'Equipe* represent the Pyrenees, the Alps, and, especially, the Mont Ventoux (a particularly gruelling mountain to climb, swept by frequent high winds) as threatening Titans awaiting to entrap the riders as they progress through the plains.[16] Anyone can now drive up to these passes effortlessly by car, but their attractiveness for the media remains, as events liable to bring variety to what is, for part of the time, a predictable and uneventful competition.

Once the eastern and southern mountainous areas had been incorporated into the Tour, it fell into regularly circling the boundaries of the national territory. This was reinforced from 1919, when Strasbourg and Metz, now returned to France as a result of the Treaty of Versailles, were symbolically reintegrated into the motherland by the bicycle.

The inter-war period was one when French integrity and independence were somewhat fragile, given the human price it had had to pay for the First World War and the increasing threat posed by Germany, and it was also one when the Tour was at its most nationalistic. Foreign teams were only welcome if they could provide an occasion for the French riders to demonstrate their own superiority: otherwise they risked penalty points and even manhandling by spectators.[17]

The relationship to national territory underwent considerable change from the late 1950s, with the growth of interest in the Tour on the part

MAP 3
HUGGING THE FRONTIERS (1919)

of the tourist industry. In the second half of the twentieth century, a large proportion of the population of industrial towns was to be found elsewhere during the statutory July holiday, and so the organizers responded increasingly to commercial bids from tourist centres to act as staging towns. League tables of stages up to 1940 show Bordeaux, Metz, Grenoble, Nice, Marseille and Toulouse in the lead, together with smaller towns favoured by their peripheral positions (Metz, Belfort, Cherbourg, Brest, Bayonne, Montpellier, Perpignan, Caen). But similar tables for the period since 1950 include places such as Luchon (both a spa and a gateway to the Pyrenees), Les Sables d'Olonne (amongst the Atlantic beaches) and Aix-les-Bains (a large Alpine resort). The resultant shape of the Tour (previously matching the hexagon-like shape of France) took on interestingly diagonal features. Thus, in 1959, when the Tour began at Mulhouse, in the north-east, it circled the north-east and north (taking in a bit of Belgium, a country keen on cycling) through

Metz, Namur, Roubaix, Rouen, Rennes; then followed the Atlantic coast (with its many developing holiday beaches and camp-sites) down to Bayonne; then, after the traditional Pyrenean passes, sliced straight through the *Massif Central* (sparsely populated in winter, but a tourist area in summer) via Albi, Aurillac, Clermont-Ferrand and Saint-Etienne; then cut across the Rhône valley to the Alps, through Grenoble, Aosta (in the French/Italian valley of the same name), Annecy (another tourist centre); then repaired to Chalon, Dijon and Paris.

Purists (like myself, and possibly the ghost of Michelet) may be shocked by the most recent development (starting in the mid-1970s), which consists in breaking the continuity of the symbolic ribbon, and organizing train and even plane transportation from the end of one stage to the start of the next. National and regional commercial interests have weighed increasingly in the choice of itinerary. In the 1970s France made strenuous efforts to develop its ski tourist industry, going as far as modifying the traditional school holiday dates to guarantee maximum custom, and so the new mountain resorts needed to be celebrated by the Tour. Other holiday centres, wine-producing regions, theme parks in need of media support (such as the Futuroscope, near Poitiers) pitch in their bids, while the television companies put pressure on the organizers to hop over uninteresting (flat, or less populated or picturesque) areas which will not provide good footage.[18] Thus the 1977 Tour (an extreme example) was cut into as many as nine discontinuous segments.

Nevertheless, the official rhetoric surrounding the event has always continued to emphasize, like its great uncle Michelet, the fact that it encompasses the whole of the variety and the beauty of France. In 1938, Henri Desgrange, its 1902 conceiver, now Director both of *L'Auto* and of the event, and 'grand old man' of the Tour, read this lyrical statement out over the radio:

> There is another aspect of the race that interests me as much as the sport, and that is the route of the Tour, which criss-crosses all the beautiful provinces of our country, and gives me considerable emotion every year. I am proud to be a Frenchman who adores his country and is sensitive to the emotions that arise from the beautiful landscapes, from the various customs and practices of our different *départements*. I have been and I still am touched each year by various country sights encountered. It may be a wine-grower, it may be a woodcutter in the forests south of Bordeaux, it may be a

MAP 4
INTRODUCING DIAGONALS (1959)

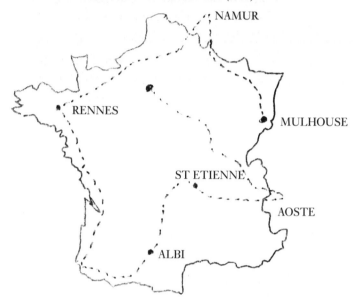

MAP 5
TRUNCATED CIRCUITS (1977)

shepherd, it may be a green and fertile landscape or it may be a dried-out landscape in the south. Each and every year, I look forward with great pleasure, and indeed passion, to the emotions I shall meet along the way.[19]

From the earliest days, the journalists in the van of the Tour filed reports on the provinces they were crossing, in parallel with the progress of the race. For a nation as yet innocent of daily weather maps, this was in a sense a return to primary school, where one had learned to draw the outline of France and recite the resources of its different areas. Sophisticated photographic equipment was used to provide pictures of the regions in the days before the picture postcard imagery associated with more modern tourism. In the 1920s the magazine *La Vie au grand air* offered explanations on monuments, towns and other sites (particularly mountains) which were as yet largely unexplored by the majority of French people, who, until they were allowed an annual paid holiday, had no occasion to travel.[120]

CELEBRATION OF COMMUNITY AND NATION

In 1903, 60 brawny part-amateurs, watched by half a dozen journalists, set off at the crack of dawn from a suburb of Paris on a variety of makes of bicycle, equipped with maps, spare tyres and starter's pistols (to clear the roads of cattle, wild boars and sundry locals liable to obstruct them). Their adventures through the various stages were wired to Paris by provincial correspondents, while members of local cycling associations manned checkpoints and refreshment stands along the route. Otherwise, they were lone riders. Spectators did not line the roads. Their clocking-in times were reported in *L'Auto-Vélo* the next morning in Paris and the day after in the rest of France. In the following few years extra checkpoints were established to avoid cheating (by hopping onto a car or train), the competition between federations of associations became keener, and the cyclists had to watch out for ambushes laid by associations supporting their rivals. *L'Auto-Vélo* did not hesitate to announce, when the Pyrenees were first included in the route, that there was the extra danger of their being attacked by bears.[21]

In 2003, 200 highly trained professionals will take to the road at the end of a morning, wearing colourful team shirts associating them with national and international sponsors, protected by crash helmets and goggles, and wired up with radio receivers for the instructions given by their team managers accompanying the race in cars. Their route will be marked out and protected by crash barriers, bales of straw, and thousands of police and stewards and they will be accompanied throughout by a hundred or so vehicles of all sorts, watched from helicopters, cautioned and fined for jostling or hemming-in tactics, and both celebrated and tested for drugs at each staging town. They will be wondering whether it will ever be possible to break the stranglehold established in the last four years by the US Postal team, who have carried professional training and support of the team leader into a new dimension. The differences between their performances will be measured in seconds and not, as in the first Tours, in hours or even days.

There will be, as in every Tour, national rivalries, but these will be far from as virulent as in former years. There will be media support for the most successful French riders, but these will not be easy to identify under the colours, helmets and goggles and on the practically identical bicycles. Nevertheless, more than five million spectators will line the roads, twenty million will follow the television coverage in France and many more abroad.

France has now known stable frontiers and a considerable uniformization of national territory through improved communications for three-quarters of a century. The political undertones of the first itineraries have given way, since the 1940s, to a more celebratory form of nationalism. The introduction of statutory workers' holidays in 1936 created a live audience for what had until then been mainly a serialized narrative in newspapers and on the radio. The Tour takes place in July, which was the second most popular month for such holidays, and the start of the two-month summer break for schools. It was timed, from the 1920s, to end on the French national holiday, 14th July. In the second half of the twentieth century, the festival side of the event has been emphasized. Louis Aragon, the communist poet and spokesman for popular opinion in the 1930s and 1940s, wrote:

> The Tour is the festival of a man's summer, it is also a celebration of our whole country, through a specifically French passion. Too bad for those who are unable to share its emotions, its follies, its hopes. It is a lesson, renewed every year, which shows that France is alive and that the Tour really is the tour of France.[22]

In 1990 Claude Sudre, a member of the Tour management, echoed this on the radio, saying: 'The Tour is a national monument. It's the Eiffel Tower, it's the Arc de Triomphe, it's the Champs-Elysées.'[23] In 1960, shortly before extended television coverage brought the public even closer to the event, Cavanna and Massonnet published a 'faction' (fictionalized history), including a chapter on the original conception of the Tour. Such works often tell us more about the time when they were written than about the historical episode, and these authors read back into the editor's office of *L'Auto-Vélo* their own feeling that the enterprise is essentially patriotic. They imagine the following enthusiastic proposal made in 1902 by the journalist Géo Lefèvre to his editor:

> Do you realise? The most novel, the most thrilling, the most Titanic race … And also the most popular, dear chap! Try saying it aloud: the Tour of France … What a red, white and blue sound! It cracks like a banner in the wind, it resounds like the *Marseillaise*! A national monument, or rather a world monument, like everything French … I can see the crowds drawn out of their villages, scattered along the roads, the towns decked with flags, the brass bands in full uniform, an immense festive feeling running all around the country like a firework display.[24]

Though this description is only accurate if one telescopes the three-week event snaking around the roads of France into one continuous ribbon, it does capture the sense in which people go out as much to share in a national celebration as to see the riders. A bicycle race on non-looped roads sits somewhat uncomfortably between a linear spectacle (such as a carnival procession or a street demonstration) and a dramatic event (such as a play or a football match). In a dramatic event, spectators gather to watch a series of scenes in meaningful chronological sequence taking place within one designated unmoving area. In linear spectacles practically nothing new happens once the start has been given: essentially static or repetitive elements move along a route that will give them maximum exposure to the spectators. At most, the route itself may be symbolic, linking districts of a town or ending for instance at a war memorial or a seat of government. During the five or six hours that a stage of the Tour takes, things are supposed to happen, as in any competitive event, though these days precious little does. Watching tactics prevail amongst the professional teams, and there will be at most two or three attempts to gain a lead on the main group of riders, a sprint to win the stage, and three or four minor sprints to gain points at specified landmarks or, for the sake of the label sponsors, once the time has come for the continuous afternoon television coverage to start. But none of these can be witnessed, except by a stroke of luck, by the spectators along the route. The dramatic function is still fulfilled by the media, which inform the public of events so far and of the identities of riders in the lead or left behind. Only the crowd massed along the last two or three hundred metres of a stage, or at the top of a mountain pass, can be relatively assured of seeing something meaningful.

But the estimated five million French citizens who turn out to watch something that they could see better on television are well aware that they are participating in a national celebration as much as in a sporting event.

The Tour passed through Saint-Gervais-les-trois-clochers on a Sunday afternoon in July 1999. Three-quarters of the 600 inhabitants were out lining two of the four main streets, the roundabout, and one of the approaches to the village down a hill. A couple of hundred more had come from neighbouring villages less favoured by the route. The three locally-stationed policemen were prominent, and, together with reinforcements from farther afield, busy warning the children to keep well back from the road, especially at the roundabout. The crippled and the lame in the row of senior citizens' bungalows at one end of the town had been wheeled out, or their front doors opened so that they could see the event. A field up the hill had been requisitioned as a helicopter staging post, and attracted some of the expectant attention.

At a quarter to four, the advance parade of 70 or so publicity floats began, advertising everything from washing machines to package holidays. For a good 15 minutes, strategically placed children (and adults) were showered with sweets, souvenirs, samples, sugar-plums and sundries sprayed from the lorries. A first helicopter roared overhead to take up an advance 'cultural' position over a neighbouring *château* (never previously revealed to the public before this television broadcast), which the producer keyed in to allow the commentators to depart from the repetitive news that there was still no strategic development within the main bunch of riders. A second helicopter (of the two taking turns in following the race itself) landed to refuel in the field above. After a few minutes' pause, press cars began to stream through, bristling with aerials and placarded with advertisements for channels and newspapers. A second short gap was followed by two police motorcyclists, a group of team HQ cars (also bristling with aerials), then three television motorcyclists displaying various channel emblems, two more police motorcyclists, a large bunch of more than a hundred cyclists strung out over two hundred yards, two further police motorcyclists, a two-minute pause dominated by the noise of the refuelled helicopter taking off, another group of a dozen cyclists, two follow-up television motorcyclists, a stray rider looking exhausted, some more team cars carrying spare bicycles, a final police van, and then nothing.

Half a dozen local worthies, on racing bicycles and in shirts and tights every bit as colourful as those of the professionals, set out behind the disappearing procession to demonstrate that they could more than keep up, at least as far as the next village. The policemen relaxed, some people ventured out into the road to pick up unclaimed sundries, others repaired to one of the two local bars or to their home television altars for close-ups of the champions at the end of the stage. People discussed which of the yellow jerseys had been that of the leader. The time was twenty-five past four. The strange bubble had moved on. Antoine Blondin, one of *L'Equipe*'s prominent cycling correspondents, has aptly described the Tour as 'a moving patch of French territory, neutralized over an area 100 metres wide and 60 kilometres long, moving forward at 40 kilometres per hour'.[25]

The average gap between this passage of the Tour and the next one is 25 years. Saint-Gervais-les-trois-clochers may not wake up every morning in anticipation of the next occurrence, but there is no doubt that in July 1999 it had a communal experience. Even more people were on the streets than for a prominent wedding, a heartfelt funeral, or the Armistice Day ceremony on 11 November. The number most closely matched those who take part in the Bastille Day festivities on 14 July.

The live experience outside was matched by the media experience on the altar indoors. The locals had seen beautiful aerial shots of the familiar townscapes and countryside around, graced by the colourful stream of cyclists snaking along the roads, fanning out and regrouping in response to slopes and winds, their individual rivalries hidden by the group rhythm, as though the earth and the sky had been inverted, and the human eye was looking down on a flight of wild geese. Twenty million others at home, and many more abroad, had seen this too. Saint-Gervais had been included in the 'neutralized', or better perhaps, 'nationalized' patch of French territory which had bonded it that July to the thousand or so other communities strung along the year's route. For the virtual duration of three weeks and the actual span of 35 minutes it had become a live part of the inner bounds of France.

NOTES

1. Where the words of a quotation are important enough to be given in the text in the original French, their translation will appear in the note, as here: 'The Tour is easily exportable, but today we are coming home. Making its way through Lorraine and as far as Champagne, the Tour de France is returning to the motherland. After all the falls over the past few days, let us hope that things will stop coming down at Gravelotte, that heroic site of the 1870 war, whilst the way from Metz to Reims will take us through part of our national history: Verdun, the Argonne, Valmy.' *L'Equipe*, 9 July 2002, 3, col.1.
2. Ibid.
3. F. Cavanna and P. Massonnet, *Le Tour de France* (Charpentier: Lecture et loisir, 1960).
4. *L'Equipe*, 10 July 2002, 2, col.2. (My italics.) The US Postal was the team led by Lance Armstrong, winner of the last four Tours. The reference is only indirectly religious, but all the more patriotic, since *voie sacrée* is a phrase from the First World War, when it was the name of an essential, and specially protected, supply route during the pivotal battle of Verdun.
5. *L'Equipe*, 18 July 2002, 2, col.1. The infidels here would be the all-conquering American team.
6. 'Jalabert has become an indispensable character in the *cathodic high Mass* of the Tour.' (My italics.) Ibid., 26 July 2002, 2, col.1.
7. A point made by P. Sansot, 'Le Tour de France, une forme de liturgie nationale', *Cahiers internationaux de sociologie*, 86 (1989).
8. Vigarello is the first to relate the long tradition of tours of France to Desgrange's cycle race and its title, following the monanlis tours the *compagnons* and Mme Fouillée's school text book, and the Tour's symbolic appropriation of territory. G. Vigarello, 'The Tour de France' in P. Nora, *Realms of Memory: Rethinking the French Past* (New York: Columbia University Press, 1997), pp.469–500. See espec. pp.470–71, 473–76.
9. G. Bruno that is, Mme Fouillée, *Le Tour de la France par deux enfants*, 1877. This book sold 8.5 million copies between 1877 and 1976, and was used to teach geography, patriotism and secular moral values in most French primary schools between 1880 and the 1950s. A centenary edition (1977) is still in print. See the article on the book by J. and M. Ozouf (subtitled 'Le petit livre rouge de la République' – the little red book of the Republic) in P. Nora, *Les Lieux de mémoire* (vol.1) (Paris: Gallimard 1987 repr. 1994).
10. G. Sand, 'Notice sur les compagnons', Foreword to *Le Compagnon du Tour de France* (1859).
12. B. Anderson, *Imagined Communities: Reflections on the Origins and Spread of Nationalism* (London: Verso, 1983).
12. Marianne as sower. Marianne, first conceived in a Revolutionary patriotic song in 1792, became a national emblem, as did Britannia for Britain.
13. 'With the wide and powerful gesture that Zola lends to his ploughman in *La Terre*, *L'Auto*, a journal of ideas and action, is about to send out over France those tough and uncomplicated sowers of strength, the great professional roadsters.' (*L'Auto*, editorial article on the first day of the first Tour, 1 July 1903). *L'Auto* organized the Tour until 1940. It was suppressed in 1944 because it had 'collaborated' during the German occupation of France, but it mutated into *L'Equipe*, now established as France's only sporting daily newspaper, which sponsored the revival of the Tour in 1946. In the early twentieth century, specialized newspapers (sport, racing, finance) used coloured paper to distinguish themselves (as did the *Financial Times* until fairly recently). *L'Auto* was printed on yellow paper, hence, in the 1930s, the invention of the *maillot jaune*, the yellow jersey that identifies the current leader of the race.
14. P. Boury, *La France du Tour: Le Tour de France, un espace sportif à géographie variable* (Paris: L'Harmattan, 1960), p.114. The *massif central* is the name given by nineteenth-century geographers to the region of older hills and mountains delineated by the Mediterranean, and

the valleys of the Loire, the Rhône and the Garonne. The adjective *central* is a political denomination, since it presupposes an established nation around it.

15. *L'Auto*, 10 July 1911:1.
16. *L'Equipe*, 18 and 20 July 2002.
17. In 1937, *L'Auto* complained in a headline: *Les étrangers font la loi!* (Foreigners are calling the tune), and this is perhaps not unconnected with the fact that both the Belgian and the Italian teams complained of harassment and discrimination by the judges, and that the Belgian team withdrew collectively from the race. (This also happened as late as 1951, when the Italians withdrew in protest against an attack on their champion, Gino Bartali, in a mountain stage.)
18. See P. Boury, *La France du Tour*, pp.273–4.
19. Radio Paris, 26 June 1938.
20. The television channel with most regional interest, FR3 (now called France 3), was still following this pattern as recently as the 1990s, with a series of programmes called 'Autour du Tour'.
21. It did not mention that there was also a real danger of being attacked by local peasants, who, in their extreme political incorrectness, resented the appropriation of their countryside by a gang of Parisians.
22. L. Aragon in the daily *Ce Soir*, 12 July 1947.
23. 'Le pays d'ici', France Culture radio, 10 July 1990. He added that if the Tour ever became financially unviable, it should be taken over by the State.
24. F. Cavanna and P. Massonnet, *Le Tour de France*.
25. A. Blondin, *Sur le Tour de France* (Paris: La Table Ronde, 1996), p.27.

8

French Cycling Heroes of the Tour: Winners and Losers

HUGH DAUNCEY

In 1960 the Tour made a detour to pass through the village of Colombey-les-deux-Eglises where General de Gaulle (then President of the new Fifth Republic) had his private home. Although the Tour that year was won by the Italian Nencini, as the riders cruised past the crowds containing the President, one national myth – de Gaulle – encountered another, the Tour de France.¹ Whether or not the Tour de France is a properly 'international' sporting event, or still remains in some ways a 'national' competition, despite the presence of riders from many countries, it often appears that in the Tour, French heroes are defined more by reference to France and other French riders than to foreigners. This chapter outlines the nature of the status of a number of French champions whose careers have been inseparable from the story of the Tour de France in the post-war era. In so doing, it approaches the 'heroic' status of riders from a number of perspectives, including the 'reality' of their sporting achievements and behaviour, the nature of their media presentations, and their cultural significance in different periods of French post-war society.

INTRODUCTION

The importance – in various ways – of the Tour de France as a symbol and generative mechanism of French national identity has already been discussed in a number of chapters in this volume. The Tour is defined by its route and the way this contours the cultural, social and political boundaries of France; the Tour is defined by its organization and funding and the way this structures its status as a national sporting event; the Tour is defined by the fashion in which it is reported and the way in which this represents the competition to those who follow it. But perhaps most of all, the Tour is defined by the riders and the ways in which their success and failure – circumscribed within the conditions alluded to above – have through the decades been transformed into a narrative and discourse of sporting performance.

Mignon's analysis of the Tour and performance-enhancing drugs also touches on the status of competitors in the Tour de France as 'heroes'. Over recent years in particular, there has been a complex re-assessment by the public of how cyclists such as the Italian Pantani (winner of the 1998 'Tour of Shame' and later revealed as a drug-taker) and the hugely popular French five-times King of the Mountains Virenque (a member of the infamous Festina team in 1998) should be viewed. In 1999, Wieting suggested that the 'crisis of trust' in the integrity of the Tour as a sporting event was producing what he described as the 'twilight of the hero'.[2] Wieting's analysis of the Tour identifies two normative frameworks operating within the Tour whose conjunction explains the distribution of opprobrium and honour amongst competitors: instead of a single normative framework established by the Tour organizers, French society and politics, and increasingly, globalized influences on sport and performance-enhancement, a second normative framework, that of the competitors themselves, interacts with the first.

Thompson and Marks especially have addressed the analysis of some of the sporting personalities produced by the Tour since 1903. Thompson's study of the scandals surrounding the Pélissier brothers in the 1920s locates their cycling prowess firmly within the sociocultural context of the economics and politics of France in the inter-war years, whereas Marks' treatment of the ways in which foreign riders have been represented locates their identities in relation to French perceptions of (foreign) national identity and France's evolving perception of herself as part of a modern Europe, and more recently as part of a globalized world. For Marks, whereas the French saw their integration into Europe as leadership of a modern supra-national unit, they are less happy about their relationship to the forces of globalization, often equated to a dominant American economic and cultural model.

This chapter investigates the ways in which French cyclists have been portrayed as they have succeeded (and failed) in France's national cycle race. Sporting popularity is a phenomenon determined by a variety of factors. More than in other sports, mediatization is the key to the creation of the Tour's heroes, especially as the Tour (as Wille points out elsewhere in this volume) is such a fleeting experience for the roadside spectator. In the early days, coverage by the written press, then press and radio, then television was what created heroes in the eyes of fans. Whannel has recently examined how sporting exploits have been gradually incorporated into the pantheon of the heroic, as, for example, unproblematic war heroism has been undercut by the dominance of technology. Whannel points out that the notion of 'heroism' requires a degree of consensus in the audience, a consensus that needs to be produced by the media.[3] What precisely makes a sportsman or woman a star is often a mystery, but any level of popularity must depend on: admiration of sporting success; admiration of courageous behaviour in adversity; admiration of correct behaviour in adversity; 'attractiveness' of personality. To these 'basic' factors can be added many other characteristics, which in various ways may contribute or detract from an individual's status as a hero or star (such as, for example, whether or not they contribute the mastery of a new technique or technology in their given sport).[4] In essence, we can say that the popularity of competitors depends on the synthesis of expectations and reality and on the ways in which individual sportsmen and women negotiate this synthesis.

HEROISM AND HEROES OF THE TOUR:
THE NATURE OF THE TOUR AS A SUPERHUMAN FEAT

The term 'hero' in the context of sport – as in other fields – can be an ambiguous one, and for critics of the ideology of modern sport, such as Brohm and Redeker, it is regressive or infantilizing. Whannel explains that in this perspective, 'celebrity [...] is intrinsically vacuous' but rejects the distinction some writers make between sporting heroes and sports stars. What sports heroes/stars come to signify (to their fans, through the media) is socially shaped, and tells us something about the society and culture of their era.[5] At its simplest, heroism is of course a simple matter of 'emblematic' success, achieved in ways which are approved by the normative frameworks applying within and to the activity in question. But heroism can also be more complicated, in the sense that heroes may also be 'tragic', grasping success at costs which appear too heavy, or failing to succeed, but doing so in ways which reinforce the validity of normative expectations. Cycling, and arguably, the Tour de France in particular, have probably always entertained a special relationship with the concept of heroism. In a sense, in the Tour de France, sporting heroism can only truly be expressed in failure, since, almost by definition, winners are superhuman.

The Tour and the Morality of Cheating

The exceptional nature of the Tour as a physical trial has from its beginnings created the belief among competitors and spectators alike that to succeed (or even simply to complete the course), some bending of the rules (of the race and of the normative frameworks) is not only permissible, but perhaps required. Examples of 'cheating' in cycling in general and in the Tour are abundant, both from the early 'heroic' years and from the modern and 'post-modern' periods. As early as the second Tour in 1904, the first four riders to complete the course, including the winner of 1903, Maurice Garin, were disqualified for having taken short-cuts under cover of darkness (the length of the stages required night riding); in the same year, another rider was banned from competing for life for having taken a train!

The culture of 'cheating' amongst competitors resulted partly from the nature of the Tour itself, rightly perceived as an 'inhuman' physical challenge and the inflexible and 'inhuman' attitudes of the Tour organizers. Henri Desgrange realized that the Tour had to be extreme in its physical demands in order to captivate the attention of the French public, and so the stages were long and arduous; in addition, partly in an attempt to minimize the cheating that was so evident from the beginnings, the Tour organizers developed a draconian system of rules. One of the most infamous rules in the early days of the race was that which prohibited riders from changing bicycles when they suffered breakdowns and also required them to repair the problem unaided; apprehension that riders would find ways of gaining advantage or of causing technical difficulties for their competitors led to bicycles being tagged and kept under lock, key and guard overnight. The technical misfortunes of Eugène Christophe, who lost the chance of overall victory in 1913 and 1919 because of broken frames, brought a change in the rules allowing team members to swap bicycles, so the system of values and rules of the Tour organizers was susceptible to change under pressure from riders and sponsors and in the interests of competition. Likewise, the nature of the route of the Tour and the length of the stages gradually became the object of some compromise between riders and organizers: from the Tour of 1910, when the winner Octave Lapize accused the organizers of being 'assassins' for forcing the riders to cover the Pyrenees, 'rider-power' in the form of strikes, go-slows and other protests has gradually forced the Tour to adapt its most 'heroic' stages, but the physical demands still remain such that survival, as much as success, can often rely on some bending of the rules.

Celebrity and Heroism

The popularity of professional cyclists is a complex phenomenon, which at its simplest must combine elements of simple sporting success (Tours and jerseys won), courage in adversity (Tours and jerseys contested and lost to superior riders), correctness in adversity (Tours and jerseys lost honourably against misfortune), and some measure of 'attractiveness' (image, personality). Success alone is arguably insufficient to achieve popularity – it is possible to be an unpopular hero, especially in an event such as the Tour de France – since overriding superiority or arrogant domination can cause the public to withhold its support and affection. Anquetil in the 1960s was arguably an example of a champion whose nature and dominance of the race over a number of years made him less popular than might have been expected, and Miguel Induráin and Lance Armstrong in the 1990s and 2000s have been multi-winners of the Tour whose status as popular heroes is mitigated by shyness and spectator-fatigue at the predictability of the contest (Induráin) and media antipathy (Armstrong).

In this context, it is interesting to consider the work of the French sociologist/philosopher of sport Paul Yonnet, who has suggested an analysis of contemporary professional sporting activities postulating the existence of two 'systems' of sporting competitions. These two 'systems' are described as those motivated by, on the one hand, 'uncertainty', and, on the other hand, 'identification'. Professional sporting competition, for Yonnet, is defined by the principle of 'uncertainty' (of outcome) theoretically generated by the near-equality of those who take part: the interest of the contest is principally generated by the closeness of the match in terms of performance between contestants. In the second 'system' of contemporary sport, Yonnet places those competitions in which significantly unequal competitors participate for individual reasons and motivations (he cites the examples of mass-participation marathons, or, interestingly the 'Tour de masse' in which amateur cyclists follow the routes of particularly famous stages of the Tour de France).[6]

Another of Yonnet's suggestions is that contemporary sporting competitions of sport as media spectacle (those driven by 'uncertainty') – such as professional cycling in general and the Tour de France – are in reality two competitions in one. To apply Yonnet's observations to the Tour de France, for example, there exist in the Tour both the 'official' (explicit, overt, concrete) competition of the *classement général*, the *classement des sprinteurs, classement des grimpeurs, classement des jeunes coureurs* organized along the measurement of times and points bonuses and marked by the highly visible jerseys of each category, and the competition for popularity. The interaction – sometimes antagonistic and sometimes harmonious – between these two competitions produces the overall story of sporting failure and success. Success in both dimensions of any given competition thus creates the conditions in which a competitor may properly accede to the status of a 'popular champion' recognized by collective memory and representative of collective identity. Although he does not explicitly discuss the situation of 'nearly-men' like Raymond Poulidor, Yonnet's analysis can of course encompass cases in which competitors are more successful in one of the 'systems' than in the other, and in which the overall status of 'popular champion' is achieved by the merging of the capitals of 'popularity' achieved either in the objective contests of times, points and jerseys or in the subjective contest of 'identification'. Significantly, Yonnet points out that the element of a sporting event that concerns 'popular favour', although it does not lead directly to prize money and contracts for other competitions, is not free of financial implications, since 'popularity', even unaccompanied by outright success in the 'technical' competition, can still lead to monetary rewards in the form of engagement as a media commentator. Poulidor, in particular (but also the French double Tour-winner Bernard Thévenet) has been a significant example of this phenomenon.[7]

Whannel's recent study of media sport and sports stars identifies ways in which the development of the media in the UK and US has contributed in the contemporary period to the creation of 'stars' who play sport, alongside the more usual stars of stage and screen.[8] Such figures are 'celebrities' whose images are media and social products, and whose content needs to be understood as textual and social. Whannel's synthesis of perspectives on sporting heroes and stars suggests that an approach combining aspects of Dyer's famous analysis of cinema stardom, and Critcher's study of cultural identity in professional football in the UK, could be a fruitful tool for understanding the 'image and reality' of sporting figures.[9] Critcher's approach proposed a model of footballers' cultural identity describing their social position, social change, the power of the media sport industry and the symbolic power of representation. Thus stars may be 'traditional/located' (retaining roots in their working class communities and values); 'transitional/ mobile' (benefiting from significant financial rewards but retaining cultural values of the working class); 'incorporated/embourgeoised' (self-conscious upward social mobility); 'superstars/dislocated' (resistance to or failure in embourgeoisement and incorporation). A common feature of the French cycling heroes considered here is that they are all from relatively modest social origins (as is generally the case in the – popular – sport of cycling in France), and so the ways in which they negotiate their affluence and celebrity mirror in some ways the issues of Critcher's analysis, but an understanding of the status of 'heroes' such as Bobet, Anquetil, Poulidor and Hinault also requires the study of their role in the context of French Republicanism, post-war economic reconstruction and modernization, the establishment of the technocratic Fifth Republic, France and globalization.

Sporting Style and Conduct

Just as the Tour as a sporting event embodies two normative frameworks which exist in tension and discontinuity (the moral code of the riders and that of French society's attitudes towards sporting activities), to which can be added the more prosaic rules and regulations of the Société du Tour de France governing the conduct of riders and teams, the popularity of riders combines the elements described above with other systems of values, two of which at least are represented by 'style' and 'fair play'. The cycling public and general public in France – better-informed about the sport than, say, the audiences which, until recently, followed the UK's television coverage of the Tour in 30-minute daily programmes on Channel 4 – form judgements about riders on the level of technique as well as combativity, or simple success, to which they add their assessments of the 'ethics' of the competitors' behaviour.[10] On the most basic level, the public follows the categorization of racers as 'rouleurs', 'grimpeurs' or 'sprinteurs' and appreciates them appropriately as they ply their differing responsibilities; additionally, however, the technicity of different styles forms part of the evaluation of the riders' popularity – are the time-trial specialists smooth in their pedalling style, do they favour big or normal gearings, what settings for their bikes do they prefer, are the grimpeurs 'pure climbers' who ride out-of-the-saddle spinning tiny gears, or do they grind up the inclines in as big a gear as possible? Part of Anquetil's reputation, for example, centred on the elegance and fluidity of his pedalling style, whereas for other champions such as Merckx and Induráin their 'heroic' status was predicated essentially on strength (and their other exceptional qualities) and only secondarily on the technical style that such strength allowed them to exhibit.

Appreciation of technical style is combined by spectators with an evaluation of how the riders behave. Such a 'moral' judgement is elaborated from the fans' understanding of the different normative frameworks within which the riders compete. As suggested previously, there are at least three or four (often interdependent but sometimes conflicting) normative frameworks which constrain and direct the riders' sporting performance: the rules of the Tour itself; the rules of the peloton; the rules of French society, culture and politics concerning sport; and 'international' views on sport and ethics. The spectators' 'ethical' analysis of the conduct of their favourite riders is arguably more complex than that of the Tour organizers (limited to the rules of the race) or that of the French state (limited to French law and Republican values towards sport) or that of cycle sport's international ruling bodies such as the Union Cycliste Internationale (UCI). The complexity of the normative framework within which fans accord the status of hero or villain to the competitors resides in the fact that this normative framework is a synthesis of all the others. The most fundamental example of this superimposition of normative systems is provided by fans' reactions to drug-taking: although spectators would prefer their 'heroes' to deliver epic performances unaided by illegal substances, they realize that professional cycling has always involved 'cheating' of this nature, and accept that the physical demands of a race such as the Tour de France probably actually require artificial aids to performance. The perceived 'inhuman' nature of the Tour (imposed by the 'assassins' of the Tour organization) means that 'normal' riders need un-natural assistance: thus the taking of drugs is somehow proof that the riders are simply human (and thus closer to their fans). Since the 1998 'Tour of Shame' and the efforts on the part of cycling authorities to change the culture of performance-enhancement in the Tour and in cycling in general, it has been intriguing that whistle-blowers amongst the peloton (such as Christophe Basson) and champions who take a stance against drugs (even those wearing the yellow jersey such as Lance Armstrong) meet with a mixed reception from the press and public.

FRENCH TOUR HEROES: 'LA FRANCE QUI GAGNE' OR 'LA FRANCE ÉTERNELLE SECONDE'?

There are arguably only four major French cycling heroes in the Tour de France: Louison Bobet, Jacques Anquetil, Raymond Poulidor and Bernard Hinault. Anquetil and Hinault both won the Tour five times, and Bobet was victorious three times in a row in the 1950s, but Poulidor never won the Tour and indeed never wore the yellow jersey. Bobet, Anquetil and Hinault inspired and still inspire mixed feelings amongst cycling aficionados (although they are undoubtedly perceived as 'heroes'), whereas Poulidor was and is still one of France's most popular and affectionately-remembered sporting figures. In the 1970s and 1980s, although both Bernard Thévenet and Laurent Fignon were double Tour-winners (not a common achievement), their status in the pantheon of French cycling heroes is unambiguously inferior to that of Hinault – although generally liked and admired, Thévenet's career was shortened by injury (he is now a well-known television cycling commentator), and Fignon (characterized by the peloton and the media as a Parisian intellectual – he had been a university student) saw his success cut short in the late 1980s by the dominance of Greg LeMond, to whom he famously lost the 1989 Tour by eight seconds, on the final stage into the Champs-Elysées.[11] The careers of Bobet, Anquetil, Poulidor and Hinault spanned the mid- and late-1950s, 1960s, 1970s and 1980s – the major part of the history of the Tour between its renewal after the Second World War and the more recent problems of cycling and drugs – and since Hinault, France has been waiting in vain for another major star to represent her aspirations. Bobet was the victor in the 1953 Tour and celebrated with the surviving winners from the first 50 years of the competition; a French winner in 2003 is highly unlikely. We shall analyze in detail the representations of these riders in a section of this chapter.

The Historical Peloton of French Riders

If we can accept Bobet, Anquetil, Poulidor and Hinault as stars (or in the case of Poulidor, an 'anti-star') of the 'mature' post-war period, there are other representatives of French cycling whose success, failure and popularity in the Tour during the early 'heroic' period, the inter-war years and the immediate post-war period can inform us about the functioning of the 'star system of French riders' in the Tour de France.

Between 1903 and 1911, the Tour was dominated by French riders. Only in 1912 did the Belgian rider Odile Defraye break the succession of French winners. In contrast to the multiple victories of some star riders in later periods, the winners of the early years – doubtless because of the extreme conditions – tended to win only once. Thus the role of honour for 1903–11 is one of nine champions whose heroic status was established by a single year of competition: Maurice Garin (1903); Henri Cornet (1904); Louis Troussellier (1905); René Pottier (1906); Emile Georget (1907); Lucien Petit-Breton (1908); François Faber (1909); Octave Lapize (1910); and Paul Duboc (1911). The fact that each rider was only champion for a single year meant that their celebrity was generated solely by victory and by their exploits during that race, and so, although most of these riders competed in a number of these early stagings of the Tour, it was difficult for a 'cult of sporting celebrity' to develop. During this early period the example of the French rider Eugène Christophe provides an early case of a recurrent 'trope' in the narratives and discourses of success and failure in the Tour de France. Ninth in 1909 and second in 1912, during the race of 1913, Christophe seemed well-placed to gain overall victory until – in an incident which has become a centrepiece of the folklore of the Tour – the frame of his bicycle broke during a stage and he was obliged to mend it himself in a nearby blacksmith's forge, thereby losing so much time that he could only finish seventh overall. Christophe suffered the same misfortune when he was leading in the 1919 Tour, demoting him to third place at the end of the race. Although breaking two frames seems more careless than simply unfortunate, the case of Christophe nevertheless provides an early iteration of the 'unlucky' French rider – in this case betrayed by untrustworthy technology.

Another 'unlucky' French contestant during the 1930s and just after the Second World War was René Vietto. After a debut Tour in 1934 when he made a very strong showing but sacrificed his chances of winning to help his team leader Antonin Magne, Vietto's participation in the race in 1936, 1938, 1939 and 1947 was dogged by medical problems that either caused him to abandon completely, or simply vitiated his chances of taking the overall victory. Known by the public as 'René le Roi', Vietto took over the mantle of the courageous but ultimately unrewarded French talent from Christophe. Vietto's failure to convert his promise into victories during a period in which other French riders such as Leducq and Magne had – happily for France – recently dominated the Tour, prefigured the contrasting images of the successful Bobet, the victorious Anquetil and the losing Poulidor in the 1960s and then the contrast between the plucky Poulidor and the Belgian 'Cannibal' Eddy Merckx in the 1970s. Bobet, Anquetil and Hinault provided France with winners of the Tour in the 1950s, 1960s and 1980s, but during the 1990s and early 2000s, as the Tour was dominated by the Spanish rider Miguel Induráin (1991–95) and by Americans such as Greg LeMond (1989, 1990) and Lance Armstrong (1999–2002), French national hopes rested principally on two competitors: Laurent Jalabert and Richard Virenque. Both Jalabert and Virenque were immensely popular riders to whom the public of the Tour de France became attached as potential French victors, although neither – for differing reasons – ever really came close. The quiet, modest and laconic Jalabert and the extrovert and voluble Virenque were riders of very different natures who became friends towards the ends of their careers because of their experience of misfortune.

Jalabert (affectionately known as 'Jaja') was arguably – until his retirement in 2002 after a career total of 138 victories – France's best candidate for a home win in the Tour since Hinault's last victory in 1985. In the mid- and late-1990s (1995–97, 1999) Jalabert was rated the best racing cyclist in the world by the Union Cycliste Internationale (UCI) for his all-round performance, but was never able to translate his ability into overall Tour de France success. Like Christophe in the early years and Vietto in the 1930s, Jalabert's career was marked by misfortune (a variety of accidents, particularly colliding with a gendarme in a race in 1994 and a fall from a ladder doing DIY) although he collected many wins in one-day classics, the Tour of Spain, Paris–Nice and world time-trials. Although he participated in the Tour de France ten times, he took only five stage wins and the King of the Mountains trophy in 2001 and 2002. Jalabert's special relationship with the French public was complicated by his apparent inability to find a French commercial team for which to ride: he spent three years with the Toshiba team (linked to La Vie claire team managed by Hinault) after turning professional in 1989 and then (disappointingly for the French cycling public) rode for the Spanish team Once until 2000 when, although a possibility arose to sign for the French Bonjour team, he eventually rode for the Danish team of the 1996 Tour winner Bjarne Riis. Despite his five stage wins (including – significantly – Bastille Day victories at Mende in 1995 and Colmar in 2001) and the polka-dot jerseys in 2001 and 2002, Jalabert was a much-liked and much-respected 'nearly man' of the Tour de France for the French, and his statement after retiring that, 'In the Tour, I never shed tears of joy'[12] reinforces the view that his image should be understood as another example of the narrative of plucky French riders riding against superior athletes (in Jaja's case Induráin and Armstrong) and misfortune. Jalabert embodies a number of typical 'tropes' of heroic status in French sport: the public service channel sports programme Stade 2 retrospective on his career emphasized his 'chevaleresque' (chivalrous) behaviour (for example, as race-leader, catching a lone breakaway and then allowing him to win the stage in the Vuelta in 1995). The example of Jalabert presents itself as a contemporary iteration of the working-class sporting hero 'I don't forget where I'm from' – his working-class origins are in Mazamet.[13] Indeed, the theme of French TV's Stade 2 profile was 'Jaja champion populaire' ('Jaja the people's champion').[14]

Louison Bobet: Rebuilding French Confidence in the 1950s

Louison Bobet's treble of wins in 1953, 1954 and 1955 provided the French public with a fillip of pride during years when – as normal politics regained its previous patterns of Left–Right strife and France's problems with colonies in Indochina and Algeria came to the top of government agendas – doubts strengthened about the long-term viability of the young Fourth Republic. Bobet's six previous participations in the Tour from 1947 seemed to reflect France's period of reconstruction and reorganization after the war, and by winning the Tour of the fiftieth anniversary and those of the next two years, Bobet seemed to lay claim again to the Tour as France's national competition, just as Garin, Cornet, Trousselier and the others had done between 1903 and 1909.

France in the mid-1950s was a country which was beginning to move forwards again after the destructions and disruptions of war and occupation. In 1947, the first post-war Tour had been won by the French rider Jean Robic, whose third place at the end of the penultimate stage was transformed into an unexpected victory by a surprise – and irregular, in terms of the riders' code – attack on the final day. Robic's win – at the expense of the Italian rider Pierre Brambilla – was greeted with relief by the public that the pre-war run of wins by Belgians and Italians had been broken (even if through the use of a slightly questionable tactic). Given the enormous difficulties experienced by France in the immediate post-war years – economic reconstruction and the re-establishment of normal politics in the form of the Fourth Republic founded in 1946 – Robic's snatching of victory from the jaws of defeat can be interpreted as another iteration of the Astérix complex, in which the combative French rider (even more appropriately a Breton) employs a ruse to undo the technical superiority of the Italian (who had seized the yellow jersey after the 'technical' stage of an individual time-trial). Robic continued to compete in the Tour until 1959, but never repeated his success.

1947 in particular had been a year of great social, political and economic unrest, and although by the mid-1950s the economy and politics had reached a new equilibrium, French society overall was still both coming to terms with the aftermath of occupation and collaboration and increasingly, being challenged by the socio-economic modernization demanded by the post-war world. The French were looking for signs that France could be successful again, and could put behind her the perceived causes of her collapse in 1940 (technological backwardness, social divisions and political incompetence), so sporting victories were welcomed with great appreciation.

Bobet's Tours – as a reflection of their period – were Tours which saw a number of innovations and changes: in 1953 Goddet introduced the sprint competition (the green points jersey was green because it was sponsored by a French garden equipment company); in 1954 the Tour's first stage started in Amsterdam (the first foreign start); in 1955 German riders returned to the Tour for the first time since the war. Although Bobet was a popular champion, giving the French an impression of pride in France at a time when the loss of Indochina and the rise of unrest in

Algeria undermined confidence in politics and institutions, the fact that he dominated the competition led some to hope for the appearance of challengers (even foreign) who would make the Tours less predictable. It was thus that Charly Gaul, from Luxembourg, was much supported during the 1955 Tour, simply because his climbing abilities made him the only rider able to put in doubt (to use Yonnet's principle of 'uncertainty') Bobet's overall dominance. But a treble of victories for France – even at the expense of Tours that were boring for the general public – was enough, in terms of popular identification with national success, to make Bobet a national hero. In 1954, Bobet was strong enough to win both the Tour and the World Championship later in the same year.

Bobet won his Tours as a member of the French national team – between 1930–39 and 1947–1962 the Tour was run with national teams – so his status as a national champion, rather than simply a winner who happened to be French but riding for a foreign team with foreign team-mates is perhaps even more to be emphasized. Bobet's profile was defined both in opposition to the foreign champions he met – the Italians Fausto Coppi and Gino Bartali, the Swiss Hugo Koblet, the Luxembourger Charly Gaul – and by his relationships with the main French contenders of his era. These relations were by no means always cordial and centred essentially around the rivalry between Bobet and the French champions of the late 1940s (the evergreen René Vietto and Jean Robic) and Jacques Anquetil, whose record in the Tour in the late 1950s and 1960s was to outdo even that of Bobet. In 1947 and 1948, for example, the young Bobet did well in his first two Tours, but struggled to gain acceptance by both Vietto (who had twice nearly won the Tour before the war) and by Robic (also of Breton origin but who portrayed Bobet as 'un Breton de l'extérieur', unfaithful to his roots). The tension in the national team in 1948 was such that the press lamented the situation in no uncertain terms: 'The French team is made up of a ragbag of stars all more egotistical and self-centred than the others. The pity is precisely the team's strength in strong riders, since everyone feels able to win.'[15] Bobet's good showing in 1948 was sabotaged by lack of support from his team-mates and then by illness; in 1949 Robic was left out of the national team because of his inability to work with the rising young star, leaving Vietto to represent the older guard, but feuding broke out between Robic and Bobet again in 1950. The status of 'national' champion for France was also complicated by the existence of regional teams, in which other French riders – not selected for the national team but often strong competitors – also participated in the Tour. The Tour of 1953, eventually to be the first of Bobet's victories, in which Robic competed as a member of the West regional team, provided a clear example of this as this formation attempted to sabotage Bobet's duel with Bartali.[16] The team orders in 1953 gave no special priority to Bobet, but when it became clear that Bobet and his team mate Gemiani were both well placed for possible victory, Bobet claimed the support of the team for his efforts by promising all his winnings to the team.

Bobet's image in the pantheon of French cycling stars is almost unfailingly positive: the criticisms that were occasionally made of him were outweighed by the cycling public's appreciation of his style and racing behaviour, and the general public in France was delighted that confidence in post-war recovery could be bolstered by national sporting success in the Tour. In comparison with the later French champions, Bobet's career was played out in an arguably simpler sporting and media context.

Jacques Anquetil: The Coldness of Perfection in the 1960s

Anquetil died in November 1987 at the early age of 53. The cause of his death – stomach and liver cancer – has often been attributed to the drugs that he readily admitted taking during his racing career simply to enable him to compete. He was the first rider to win four, and then five, Tours, dominating the race and winning in 1957, 1961, 1962, 1963 and 1964. After Anquetil's first Tour win in 1957, the journalist René Dunn of the popular paper *France-Soir* presented his victory in *veni, vidi, vici* terms that combine the atavistic regionalist stereotypes typical of much writing about sport in France with a suggestion of his status, henceforth, as a national cycling hero:

> He came, he saw, he conquered […] Adaptable as a Norman, stubborn as a Breton, cunning as an Auvergnat, easy going as a Provençal, Anquetil now known as 'Young Jack' – the clearest sign of fame – is taking on a challenge much more testing than the one he has just won in five thousand kilometres of racing […] It's harder to wear a suit than to carry the yellow jersey […] It's up to you Jack! France admires you, but is keeping an eye on your behaviour as well.[17]

But the French public never accepted him quite as warmly as other French heroes, watching him for examples of the fatal flaw of 'arrogance' that distances heroes from their fans. Later in 1957, after his Tour victory, Anquetil was awarded the honour of la Coupe de l'élégance sportive, but turned up late at the ceremony because he had over-indulged in champagne. Anquetil was a champion whose 'technical' accomplishments both in terms of races won and pedalling 'style' were beyond question, but his behaviour – as a champion in the public sphere and also (sometimes) in the 'privacy' of the peloton as a competitor – was often perceived as somehow unbecoming. The issue of his attachment to champagne is perhaps a good example of both of these mismatches between expectations and reality. Somewhat paradoxically, given that spectators of the Tour were aware that riders took stimulants to help them through the race, there was also the expectation that as athletes they should eschew everyday pleasures such as alcohol, and Anquetil's predilection for champagne (not just any wine) was perceived as an almost insulting disdain for the principles of 'proper' training. Anquetil's defence was simple, but no more likely to win favour: 'I don't live my life in contradiction of established principles of cycle training on purpose; I just follow my natural inclinations.'[18]

Anquetil's image was that of the champion whose domination was generally so total, and whose public confidence in his abilities were such that they amounted to 'insolent facility'. In 1961, he took the yellow jersey on stage one and kept it until the end of the race.[19] The facility with which Anquetil achieved his Tour wins led to his reputation for 'la froideur de la perfection', and analyses that he had transformed competitive cycling into an 'exact science' in which uncertainty, emotion and suspense had been suppressed.[20] Although Bobet's treble of wins had threatened to produce a similar disaffection of the public in 1955, a situation redeemed by spectators' awe at Bobet's duplication of Thys' three wins in a row and by the champion's generally positive image, Anquetil's calculating approach to racing tactics rendered his successes flawed in some way: in 1962, for example, there were whistles of disapproval as he arrived at the Parc des Princes finish of his third victorious Tour. Anquetil himself once summarized his difference from Bobet in terms that suggest an attitude towards competition that is informed more by pure ego than by sporting racing 'panache': 'Unlike Bobet, losing a race doesn't make me ill – I just work out how to get even, which is what I often manage to do.'[21]

Foreign champions such as Gaul, Bahamontes, Gimondi and Nancini also provided foils against which Anquetil's reputation as 'Monsieur Chrono' (for his invincibility in individual time-trials) or 'Monsieur Millimètre' (for his tendency to do no more than necessary to win) was forged. But essentially, Anquetil as a hero of French cycling was defined by his relations with the French champions of the past – Robic and Bobet – and the nearly-champion of the period of his domination of the Tour, and after, Raymond Poulidor.

Anquetil was arguably the single cycling champion whose career spanned the particularly confused period of the transition between widespread drug-taking in cycling tacitly accepted by the professional cycling community, race organizers, public and State, and the period ushered in by the law on drug-taking which became operational on 14 June 1966 and led to the famous inaugural dope-test in the Tour at the end of the stage from Royan to Bordeaux on 28 June 1966. Although he won his fifth and final Tour in 1964, he continued to compete until 1967 when the new world hour record he had established failed to obtain ratification from the cycling authorities because of his positive dope-test. The implementation of the law was obviously unable to suppress drug-taking amongst professional cyclists, as a series of positive tests, scandals and tragedies – including the emblematic death of the British rider Tom Simpson in the 1967 Tour[22] – demonstrated, but the new attitude of cycling authorities and the French State transformed the culture of drug-taking from an 'amateur' practice managed by riders and *soigneurs* into a 'professional' practice often supervised by doctors. Anquetil's open admissions of his drug-taking represented the feeling widespread amongst the peloton of competitive cyclists that the physical demands of the racing season, and the superhuman scale of individual races such as the Tour, required the riders to obtain artificial assistance. Such an explicit avowal of doping was visibly honest and treated the spectating public as a mature audience with a sophisticated understanding of the mechanisms and processes at work in sporting competitions such as the Tour de France, but, to adopt Yonnet's conceptual framework for a moment, Anquetil's readiness to disabuse any fans of the illusion that professional cyclists could accomplish what they did without drugs was perhaps based too much on his status as a champion of the 'official' competition (five Tour victories) and disregarded any need to appear (or remain) as a truly 'popular' national sporting hero.

Anquetil's popularity was complex, involving public respect for his technical accomplishments (both in terms of races won and pedalling technique – pushing bigger gears than anyone else) tempered by irritation at his domination and the minimization of 'uncertainty' about the final result of the Tour, and, despite his reputation for 'la froideur de la perfection' ('the coldness of perfection'), affection for his 'sens de la fête' ('liking a good time'), Anquetil's fondness for champagne, his pretty blonde wife and his elegant clothes sense helped compensate his reputation as a rider whose objective was always to win, but by the smallest necessary margin (he would generally maintain that '10 minutes lead is 9 minutes 59 seconds too much'.

Raymond Poulidor: Heroic Failure of Social Change in the 1960s and 1970s

Raymond Poulidor is the prime example of a French rider in the Tour de France whose media image and reputation is that of 'l'éternel second'. The name 'Poulidor' has even entered common parlance as a term designating someone who never manages better than second.[23] Poulidor's career was long – 1962–76 – and spanned the France of the early years of de Gaulle's Fifth Republic to the early years of Giscard d'Estaing's modernizing presidency. Despite numerous participations in the Tour, Poulidor never won the race overall and never wore the yellow jersey. Although the latter part of Poulidor's career saw him losing out to Merckx and other *campionissimi*, after Anquetil's retirement in 1967, Poulidor's status as a French heroic failure is inextricably linked with the career and dominance of 'Maître Jacques'.

Poulidor's public image during his racing career and since has always been that of the quiet, modest and honest rider, untainted by suspicions of doping and almost unreservedly admired for his courage and combativity in the Tour and other races when faced with the unbeatable superiority of champions such as Anquetil and Merckx. During the 1960s and 1970s, his nickname 'Poupou' was everywhere, and the public supported his efforts to impose himself against the 'insolent facility' of Anquetil's domination or the 'cannibalistic' competitive spirit of Merckx. As Yonnet has pointed out, popularity (even if unaccompanied by success in the 'technical' competition of times and points) can be translated into financial gain, and this is what Poulidor has done since retirement by working as a television consultant and commentator on cycling.

One of the most famous photos of the post-war Tour is that of Poulidor and Anquetil climbing shoulder-to-shoulder up the Puy-de-Dôme in 1964 – as usual, Poulidor fails to beat a tired Anquetil by enough to wrest the yellow jersey from him.[24] In a brief analysis of the rivalry between Anquetil and Poulidor, Pociello suggests that they exemplify what he terms 'l'effet Carpentier' in French sport, namely a 'dramatization' of the relationship between competitors which is produced when there exist two rivals whose physical, stylistic, tactical and other features are completely opposed.[25] To take this further than does Pociello, Anquetil was blond, thin, northern (from Normandy), a special expert in 'technical' events such as time-trials, a dominant member of the peloton and a multiple champion; Poulidor, on the other hand, was dark, heavier in build, from central France (the Limousin region), a good climber, a rider with no special influence within the peloton and a nearly-man.

The 'duels' between top champions which the French sporting press is keen to narrate and even create – as Pociello reminds us, journalists (particularly some influential cycling journalists, it would seem) are attached to the interplay of signs, figures and styles which facilitate the creation of a dramatized narration of sporting stories – are well demonstrated by the rivalry between Anquetil and Poulidor. It is probably the case that the duel between these two riders was never a 'true' reality, given the long-term disparity in their records (can Poulidor really have been 'unlucky' for 15 years?). In the same way that the 'duel' between Bobet (at the end of his career) and the young Anquetil in the late 1950s was 'more theoretical than practical',[26] it is possible that the rivalry between Anquetil and Poulidor was more an artefact of the fevered imaginations of sports journalists and the product of the two riders' desires to create public images that benefited them, than a real physical contest of near equality. As Ichah and Boully have pointed out, as early as the 1961 Tour de France, Poulidor was aware of the strategies required to build rivalries and success, since he declined to compete in the national French team where he would have been obliged to ride in support of Anquetil. Only from 1962 and the return of commercial teams was the fruitful rivalry in popularity between Anquetil and Poulidor able to flourish. Ichah and Boully describe in telling terms how by 1963 the antagonism between the two riders had become 'a product which sold well' and suggest that 'Poulidor well understood that it was in his interest, as long as he won races from time to time (because that's what champions do), to appear as the victim of a devilish opponent. Sporting France loves to mother the unlucky, and gives herself more easily to nice losers than to insolent winners. At best, Poulidor is loved, and Anquetil respected.'[27]

Such a perspective on public images and the heroic status of riders in the Tour de France reflects the idea developed by Yonnet that the riders in a competition such as the Tour have a set of values which is their own, and which they operate often in opposition to those of the 'official' race, as defined by the Tour organizers and the French state. Jacques Calvet, whose economic study of cycling champions is pointedly entitled 'The Myth of the Giants of the Road', is one of the few analysts to address the vexed issue of the true nature of Poulidor as a competitor. Whereas the myth that still has popular currency 25 years after his retirement is that Poulidor was loved for his open and courageous nature by the French public and fellow riders, while Anquetil was respected and at best liked, according to Calvet, Poulidor was in reality disliked by the peloton for his ill-humour and selfish tactics, whereas Anquetil was appreciated for his fair-play and courtesy. Thus the public image confected by Poulidor and Anquetil together was in fact a 'product' for consumption by followers of the Tour based on a myth which was the opposite of sporting reality. Calvet reports that when two journalists wrote articles exploding the Poulidor myth in the mid-1960s, their magazine received such outraged mail from fans that they were asked by the editor to revert to the usual presentation of the rider.[28]

One sociocultural and sociopolitical interpretation of the symbiotic rivalry of Anquetil and Poulidor is that they implicitly represented two antagonistic trends in French society in the 1960s, whose interplay found expression in France's national sporting event.[29] One characteristic of true champions is sometimes claimed to be 'innovation', in the sense that they redefine the nature of the sport itself, and in this perspective, Anquetil's greatness is confirmed both in terms of sporting records (he was the first to complete the double of the Dauphiné–Libéré and Bordeaux–Paris) and in terms of his approach to racing. Despite his idiosyncratic approach to training he was still profoundly influenced by the meticulous ('scientific') approach of Coppi, and his technical mastery of the time-trial ('man against machine') reflected French society's technocratic and technological modernization under the later Fourth Republic and under de Gaulle. Poulidor, in contrast, although of rural extraction like Anquetil, represented much less the new confident France of the Fifth Republic advancing towards technological and sociopolitical modernity under the guidance of national planning and a new constitution, than 'la France profonde' of Poupou's native and still archaic Limousin. This interpretation portrays Poulidor as the anachronistic representative – still loved as the underdog, like Astérix, Vercingétorix, Roland, Joan of Arc and Charles de Gaulle[30] – of the France of the Fourth Republic's uncertainties and weaknesses, and casts Anquetil as the embodiment of Gaullist 'grandeur' and as the harbinger of 'la France qui gagne'.

Bernard Hinault: French Cunning and Panache against the World in the 1980s

Bernard Hinault is still considered by many to be the greatest of the Tour champions, outdoing even Merckx and Induráin. His run of five victories in 1978, 1979, 1981, 1982 and 1985 was ended by a retirement which seemed premature, such was his ability apparently to win further Tours, and the puzzling circumstances of his final Tour, when he finished second behind his American team-mate Greg LeMond, authorize suggestions that he should have won more than his eventual tally of Tours. Hinault's career was 'unfinished', in a way that those of Merckx and Induráin were not; Hinault's 'heroism' was that of a hero who seemed still able to return. The Hinault era provided France with one of her most dominant periods of national victories. It had been another French rider, the farmer's son Bernard Thévenet, who finally put an end to Merckxism by winning in 1975 and 1977, and during Hinault's heyday in the mid-1980s, the young rising French star Laurent Fignon took two Tours in 1983 and 1984.

Hinault's status as superchampion of the French star-system of national riders of the Tour de France is perhaps explained by the fact that he seems – in reality, as well as in media presentation – to fulfil the criteria required by the French cycling public to fashion a true 'hero'. Calvet's analysis of professional cycling as a system of interlocking and superimposed 'markets' (sporting 'spectacle', advertising and promotion, riders) leads him to develop a three-fold classification of competitors: champions, good riders, team-mates. In this framework, Hinault in the early 1980s was the only champion present in the French market, and could therefore capitalize on his 'scarcity' both in terms of financial reward and in terms of his media image. Hinault appealed to the French cycling public because of his origins, because of his behaviour in racing both ethically and athletically and because of his resourceful and charismatic personality, often linked by spectators to that of his flamboyant team owner, the controversial Bernard Tapie. Hinault came from modest origins in a village in Brittany, thus fulfilling the first requirement for true French champions, namely that they are 'popular' (that is, working-class men-of-the-people, and generally rural). Although from a rural and agricultural area, and thus attuned to what the French describe as 'la France profonde', Hinault was not from an agricultural family (unlike many of his predecessors), since his father was a railway employee, and he himself was intended for a career as a fitter. Thus he appeared as someone with whom both rural/agricultural and urban/industrial France could proudly identify.[31]

As a rider, Hinault distinguished himself both through his superiority as an athlete (he was an all-round champion, able to climb and time-trial), through his combativity and sense of fair-play, and through his willingness to play the role of *patron* of the peloton. He combined physical prowess with a mental strength and resourcefulness that earned him the famous (and essentially complimentary) nickname of 'le Blaireau' ('the Badger'). Hinault's technical and moral qualities as a racing cyclist in the Tour de France were thus of a nature to favour his popularity with riders and spectators alike: as a rider of class and ability and as an aggressive but essentially honourable competitor he had the respect of his peers and the admiration of the public. The role of boss of the peloton involved on the one hand regulating the internal moral code of the riders, and on the other hand, managing the peloton's relations with the Tour organizers and the sporting authorities. The first example of Hinault's importance to his fellow-riders as a spokesman and leader came as early as the 1978 Tour, when, in a classic example of friction between the competitors and the race organizers, the peloton crawled along the stage between Tarbes and Valence d'Agen at 12mph and walked across the finish line in protest against long stages and difficult transfers. As French national champion and a respected rider, Hinault represented the riders' views and then a week later took the yellow jersey, followed by final victory – his first – in Paris.

Victories in 1979 and 1981 (he withdrew from the 1980 Tour because of injury) and in 1982 brought Hinault to the verge of equalling the five victories of Anquetil and Merckx, but, established as he was as a respected rider and leader, new concerns and new challenges to his career began to arise. It is arguably these new dimensions of Hinault's role in the development of professional cycling that reveal the most about his status as a sporting hero. During the period 1982–86, Hinault found himself at the centre of rapidly developing changes in professional cycling in the Tour de France involving the nature of the teams, and the arrival of influential English-speaking riders, who would eventually end Hinault's own career and come to dominate the Tour itself. Hinault's early success had been achieved with the Renault-Gitane team, but in 1982 tensions were developing within the team around two French riders – Madiot and Didier – employed to support Hinault, and the young Australian Phil Anderson began to show a promise which undermined Hinault's primacy. Anderson wore the yellow jersey during the early stages of the Tour, only giving it up to 'le Blaireau' after two time-trials in which Hinault re-established his control of the race and his team. Although Hinault provided a prime example of racing 'panache' by out-sprinting the specialist sprinters on the Champs-Elysées in the final stage (he claims this as his most precious victory), he felt he had outgrown the Renault-Gitane team, and was keen to work with the controversial entrepreneur Tapie in a new team completely at his orders.

The La Vie claire team built around Hinault in 1983 was a sporting and commercial machine designed to maximize the popular celebrity of Hinault. Compared with the traditional image of the Renault-Gitane team – jointly sponsored by France's major state-owned automobile company and the long-established bicycle producer – La Vie claire's dietary products provided a resolutely more 'modern' representation of what cycling was about. Team-owner Tapie declared that associating cycling and Hinault – as a symbol of health and as a great champion – was quite simply a good idea for selling La Vie claire's ecologically-branded products.[32] The team jersey of La Vie claire team was designed by Benetton around a Mondrian painting, further to reinforce the modern and novel image of the sporting and business venture. La Vie claire was in competition with the Renault team, now led by Laurent Fignon, who would win the Tours of 1983 and 1984, but Tapie, in anticipation of the future success of the American, and conscious of the importance of US markets, enticed Greg LeMond from Renault to become Hinault's team-mate. The fact that LeMond's salary deal over three years with La Vie claire gave him a larger annual pay cheque than Hinault illustrates Tapie's desire to tap in to the coming trend in professional cycling, namely its globalization, through successful US and other international riders.

In the 1985 Tour, although Fignon did not participate, the threat of the younger generation of riders to Hinault was represented by his own team-mate LeMond. Although apparently initially prepared to support Hinault as the team leader in search of his fifth Tour victory, LeMond's reaction to an accident which left Hinault injured and particularly dependent on team support led to bitter discussions as to which rider should be allowed to win the Tour. LeMond finally agreed to let Hinault win his fifth Tour, being compensated financially by Tapie, and obtaining the promise that Hinault would help him win the 1986 Tour. Thus in 1986, the scene was set for a tragic confrontation between generations, between France and the US, between team leader and team-mate, between a rider attempting to win an unprecedented sixth Tour and one trying to win his first.[33] For once, unarguably, the 1986 Tour was a real tragic epic of competitive cycling. In 1986, there was no need for journalists and commentators to invent the convenient metaphors of heroism, treachery and athletic prowess in search of glory. It is doubtless Hinault's very failure in the 1986 Tour that has done much to seal his enduring popularity with the French public. An iconic image of the contemporary Tour de France is still that of Hinault and LeMond hand-in-hand crossing the finish line at L'Alpe d'Huez – the Tour's most famous stage, in 1986. This was where, according to LeMond, Hinault finally agreed to honour his promise of the year before and allow the American (who had battled to win the yellow jersey from Hinault only the previous stage, after Hinault had worn it for five days) to take final victory. LeMond hung back a few centimetres to give Hinault the win at L'Alpe, but four days later became the first American Tour winner.

Yonnet has analysed the conflict of interests between Hinault and LeMond in terms of what he calls the 'bi-competitive' nature of professional sports.[34] In this perspective, the Tour is both a competition for technical, measured, quantified results (wins, times, classifications, etcetera) and a competition for 'faveur populaire'. To adapt Yonnet's framework of analysis, we can say that the status of true hero/star can only be achieved when success in these two competitions is balanced so that the winning of sporting contests is done in such a way as to maximize popular support. For example, dominating a race totally with either complete athletic superiority or a masterfully calculating limitation of risk is unlikely to produce enthusiastic favour, but a champion who wins in a context of 'uncertainty' over the final result and by demonstrating 'panache' in his manner of winning, combines success in bi-competitive sport. Thus, just as Tapie maximized the interest in his La Vie claire team by employing both Hinault and LeMond, despite the frictions this would provoke, Hinault 'manufactured' the final element of his public image by bowing out of cycling as an *heroic* 'failure' (beloved by France) who had missed out on a sixth Tour win despite riding with aggression, style and panache because he had to honour his agreement of 1985.

CONCLUSION

Bobet, Anquetil-Poulidor and Hinault can be seen both as representative of their eras in socio-cultural and socio-political terms and as examples of the media frameworks in which their careers were played out. Bobet is arguably the simplest of the case-studies, reflecting the 'modern' preoccupations of France during the Fourth Republic, as French society and sport renewed itself after the war, but still operating within a cultural and media framework markedly inherited from the 1930s and the early years of the Tour. Although the Tour during Bobet's era did try to modernize itself, Bobet remained – in Critcher's terminology – essentially a 'traditional/located' or 'traditional/mobile' star. The Anquetil-Poulidor 'tandem' provides a somewhat more complicated symbiotic pair of sporting stars, on whom much further work would seem useful, but the reputations of the champion and the nearly-man as they were forged in the media of the 1960s suggest an intriguing relationship between an 'incorporated/embourgeoised' Anquetil and a 'traditional/located' Poulidor. Anquetil and Poulidor offer more for analysis than Bobet simply because of the greater media coverage of the Tour during their era, and also, as French society began to feel the stresses of modernization, these two riders began to represent different social and cultural values, as well as their sporting meaning.

Hinault is an example of a Tour rider who succeeded in managing his career in such a way as to maximize his popularity with fellow competitors, the organizers of the Tour, his team owners and the spectating public. As a variant of the 'transitional/mobile' type of athlete, Hinault exemplified the ways in which in the 1980s, an exceptional sporting figure could negotiate the markets of professional cycling (to use Calvet's terminology) and forge a career and image which adopted the affluence and social mobility allowed by financial gain, while at the same time remaining true to his origins. In this, he is an intriguing example of France's attachment to equality of opportunity and the possibility of social advancement, French cycling's attachment to its working-class roots, and France's love-hate relationship between urban and rural cultures. Further study of Hinault should investigate his sporting, cultural and media relationship with the 1983 and 1984 Tour winner Laurent Fignon (almost forgotten in France) whose social origins, character and image ill-fitted him to compete with Hinault and LeMond outside the roads of the Tour itself.

NOTES

1. According to someone who was in the race director's car, at the last minute, hearing that de Gaulle was in fact waiting for the race to pass, the organizers decided to stop the Tour. In the village where the President was waiting with other spectators, race-director Goddet said through a loud hailer (from the race director's car), 'Monsieur le President, le tour a tenu à s'arrêter pour vous saluer' (Mr President, the Tour wishes to stop to salute you) and de Gaulle responded: 'Il ne fallait pas' (There was no need). He shook hands with Anglade whom he recognized from his tricolour (champion de France) jersey and congratulated Nencini, who looked as though he would win (as he did). See J. Marchand, *Jacques Goddet* (Anglet: Atlantica, 2002), pp.187–90.
2. S. Wieting, 'Twilight of the Hero in the Tour de France', *International Review for the Sociology of Sport*, 35, 3 (2000), pp.348–63.
3. See G. Whannel, *Media Sports Stars: Masculinities and Modernities* (London: Routledge, 2002), pp.44–5.
4. See, for example, the comprehensive listing of what makes up a 'champion' given by the French sociologist of sport Jean-Marie Brohm in *Sociologie du sport* (Nancy: Presses Universitaires de Nancy, 1992).
5. See Whannel, *Media Sports Stars*, p.46.
6. P. Yonnet, *Systèmes des sports* (Paris: Gallimard/NRF, 1998), p.89.
7. Whatever the criticisms that can be levelled at Yonnet's analysis – it could perhaps be argued that 'mass' marathons are not 'mass' in any real sense since firstly they have élite competitors and secondly, that they are also driven by 'uncertainty' in the sense that the other runners participating for personal reasons very often measure their performance in comparison with those they perceive as their athletic peers – his thinking does shed some light on how success and heroic status can be generated.
8. Whannel, *Media Sports Stars*.
9. R. Dyer, *Stars* (London: BFI, 1979); C. Critcher in J. Clarke, C. Critcher and R. Johnson (eds), *Working Class Culture* (London: Hutchinson, 1979), p.47.

10. The Tour organizers have even created a daily 'prix de la combativité' judged by former riders in order to encourage racing.
11. Some cycling journalists and commentators liked to see Fignon as a new kind of cycling champion: see, for example, O. Dazat, *Laurent Fignon: champion d'un nouveau siècle* (Paris: Messidor, 1990). Interestingly, in this perspective, his defeat in the final stage of the 1989 Tour – an individual time-trial – is often ascribed to his refusal to ride a modern aerodynamic bike like that chosen by his American challenger Greg LeMond. LeMond's margin of victory in the time-trial was largely a result of Fignon's technological disadvantage. Thus Fignon was in fact a champion of the 'old style', and in a complex figure of imagery, embodied France's love of the 'éternel second' and her worries about technological backwardness in relation to the US.
12. L. Jalabert, with C. Thomas, 'Ma Vie de A à Z', *L'Equipe Magazine* (12 Oct. 2002), pp.36–46.
13. J.-A. F., 'Les pudiques adieux de Laurent Jalabert, champion qui sait d'où il vient', *Le Monde* (15 Oct. 2002), p.26.
14. Richard Virenque is discussed by Patrick Mignon in his chapter on drug-taking in the Tour. His implication in the Festina drugs scandal of 1998 (and his long-running denial of his obvious guilt) knocked him off his pedestal as a French 'champion' whose popularity at times rivalled that of Jalabert. It was perhaps more Virenque's implausible repudiations of the evidence than his actual taking of the drugs that undermined his public following. Significantly, in terms of the media representations of the images of Virenque and Jalabert after their setbacks (a ban for Virenque and injury for Jalabert) it was Jalabert who was depicted as extending the hand of friendship to a fallen rival by going on daily training rides with him near their homes in Switzerland.
15. Jean Leulliot of *Miroir-Sprint*, quoted in J.-P. Ollivier, *La Légende de Louison Bobet* (Paris: L'Aurore, 1992), p.56.
16. See the contribution of *L'Equipe* journalist Jacques Augendre, '1953 – derrière les volets clos', in M. Milenkovitch, *Cyclisme: 50 histoires du Tour de France* (Paris: Editions du Sport/Editions Fontaine, 1997), pp.21–2.
17. Quoted in J.-P. Ollivier, *Anquetil: l'homme des défis* (Paris: Flammarion, 1986), pp.86–7.
18. Ibid., p.90.
19. A feat only previously or since achieved by the Belgian Romain Maes in 1935.
20. This is how the *Miroir des Sports* journalist Roger Bastide commented on Anquetil's 1961 Tour victory (quoted in Ollivier, *Anquetil: l'homme des défis*, p.130).
21. Ollivier, *Anquetil: l'homme des défis*, p.90.
22. For a treatment of the facts and myths of the death of Tom Simpson on the Mont Ventoux in 1967, see W. Fotheringham, *Put me back on my bike – In search of Tom Simpson* (London: Yellow Jersey Press, 2002).
23. See J. Calvet, *Le Mythe des géants de la route* (Grenoble: Presses Universitaires de Grenoble, 1981), p.24.
24. See '1964 – Le Duel avec "Poupou"', in H. Bossdorf and B. Bossdorf, *100 moments forts du Tour de France* (Aartselaar (Belgium): Chantecler, 2001), p.63.
25. C. Pociello, *Les cultures sportives: pratiques, représentations et mythes sportifs* (Paris: PUF, 1995), pp.114–15.
26. See R. Ichah and J. Boully, *Les grands vainqueurs du Tour de France* (Paris: Criterion, 1992), p.217.
27. Ibid., pp.219–20.
28. Calvet, *Le Mythe des géants de la route*, p.208.
29. This approach is suggested by Michel Winock in 'Le Complexe de Poulidor', in *Chronique des années soixante* (Paris: Seuil, 1987), Chap.10.
30. The list of symbolic figures loved by the French for their heroism in adversity is taken from Pociello, *Les cultures sportives*, p.116.
31. One of the first things Hinault did when he became financially independent was to buy a farm, which was then managed by his brother-in-law.
32. Quoted in J.P. Ollivier, *Bernard Hinault, La véridique Histoire* (Grenoble: Glénat, 1998), p.149.

33. The famous French rider Jean-François Bernard, who was a La Vie claire rider in 1986, has described how the atmosphere in the team was fraught by tensions between Hinault and LeMond. Significantly, he relates that all the French riders supported Hinault, and all the 'foreign' riders supported LeMond. See J.-F. Bernard, '1986 – haute tension', in M. Milenkovitch (ed.), *Cyclisme: 50 histoires du Tour de France* (Paris: Editions du Sport/Editions Fontaine, 1997), p.86.
34. Yonnet, *Systèmes des sports*, p.108.

9

Se faire naturaliser cycliste: The Tour and its Non-French Competitors

JOHN MARKS

INTRODUCTION:
THE POPULAR CONSTRUCTIONS OF THE TOUR

Writing on the Tour de France in 2000, Julian Barnes speculates upon the fact that, despite the 'vast moral taint' of drug-taking and the lack of recent French success, the Tour remains extremely popular in France.[1] As Barnes points out, the last French rider to win the Tour was Bernard Hinault in 1985, and in 1999 not a single stage of the race was won by a Frenchman; in 2000 French riders won two out of 21 stages. Barnes offers two explanations for the continuing French attachment to the Tour. Firstly, he recounts an anecdote relating to France's failure to qualify for the 1994 football World Cup finals. France lost to both Israel and Bulgaria in their final qualifying matches, and Barnes overhears a waiter saying of Bulgaria's last-ditch winner, 'It was a pretty goal'.[2] The French sports fan tends to be, Barnes claims, a 'purist', a devotee of the sport itself rather than a fanatical supporter of a team or nation. This claim, built as Barnes admits on the slenderest of evidence,[3] is, of course, consonant with a more general truism regarding French savoir-faire and style, as opposed to Anglo–Saxon fanaticism and boorishness. Secondly, Barnes claims that although the French may be purists in sporting matters, they are not moralists. On drugs issues, for example, fans of cycling and the Tour seem willing to side with their heroes against the forces of law and order and bureaucracy. Barnes may be building his argument on the national stereotypes of French 'style' and anti-authoritarianism, but it is his claim that the Tour retains a genuinely *popular* aspect that is perhaps the most contentious:

In other sports, fans go to a stadium, where there are entrance fees, tacky souvenirs, overpriced food, a general marshalling and corralling, and a professional exploitation of the fans' emotions. With the Tour de France, the heroes come to you, to your village, your town, or arrange a rendezvous on the slopes of some spectacular mountain. The Tour is free, you choose where you watch it from, bring your own picnic, and the marketing hard-sell consists of little more than a van offering official Tour T-shirts at 60 francs a throw just before the race arrives.[4]

THE 'EUROPEAN' PERIOD

This chapter seeks to challenge Barnes' argument, precisely because many of what he considers to be the popular elements of the Tour have been under threat in recent years. There is today a certain degree of popular suspicion directed towards what many perceive to be a 'mediatized' and 'globalized' Tour. In short, Barnes' reading needs to be historicized.

There is undoubtedly plenty of evidence – despite the fact that hostility has occasionally been directed at non-French riders – that French cycling fans have been ready to accept and admire non-French riders, but this needs to be seen in a historical context. Riders such as the Italian Fausto Coppi in the immediate post-war period, and the Englishman Tom Simpson in the 1960s, were seen to embody a particular set of popular, progressive values broadly associated with the modern 'European' France of *les Trente glorieuses*. (This term refers to the 30 years that followed the Second World War, during which France experienced a remarkable period of modernization and economic growth, and sought to position itself at the heart of the construction of a united Europe in which France and West Germany would be the main players.) These riders were seen to embody some of the distinctive values of the Tour, and were incorporated into the implicit 'European' project of the Tour, which in many ways reflected France's political ambitions in the post-war era. That is to say, the Tour constituted a sporting version of the strategy that France followed with a good deal of success after the war: economic modernization within a 'new' Europe. However, the 'globalization' – sometimes referred to as an 'internationalization' – of the Tour, which has taken place in the past 20 years or so, has constituted something of a challenge to these modes of popular identification.

'Cher pays de notre enfance'

It seems that Barnes, rather than describing the Tour as it *is*, is actually influenced by a certain nostalgia in France for what the Tour once *was*, particularly in the post-war era. Michel Dalloni has recently problematized this particular form of nostalgia for what the Tour once represented, particularly for those growing up in the post-war era. Writing in *Le Monde* in 2001, he expresses a somewhat ironic and melancholy nostalgia for the Tour as 'cher pays de notre enfance'.[5] For Dalloni, the Tour, more than any other occasion in the sporting calendar, brings with it an air of nostalgia. We know, says Dalloni, apparently addressing the 'baby-boom' generation of the *Trente glorieuses*, that doping and corruption exist, but we prefer to forget about them. Instead, this generation of spectators is intent on revisiting the mythical landscape of 'France in July'. They remember the small child holding a father's hand on a sweltering afternoon, watching the Tour from the roadside. This is the generation whose childhood and adolescence are marked by memories of Mickey Mouse, Neil Armstrong, Georges Brassens, Mick Jagger, the Vietnam war and John Wayne. In purely cycling terms, the baby-boomers grow old with memories of Fausto Coppi, René Vietto, Bernard Thévenet and Lucien Van Impe. Dalloni acknowledges that this age of innocence cannot be rediscovered since, for one thing, the French are now more sceptical. However, he still seems to be attached to what he sees as something of a golden age of the Tour.

A Popular Republicanism?

What this chapter does suggest is that the Tour has expressed and crystallized at certain points in its history – particularly in the post-war 'European' years – a certain popular, democratic, generally left-leaning internationalism. That is to say, a pride in what the Tour represents as distinctively 'French', combined with the notion that the Tour can act as a force for integration and international co-operation: in short, a popular Republican universalism. There are several ingredients to this particular cultural construction.

Firstly, as Christophe Campos shows elsewhere in the volume, the Tour expresses a certain attachment to the variety, vigour and beauty of France and the French landscape. Secondly, the Tour has also traditionally been a focus for a popular faith in democracy and modernity, an attitude that is essentially forward-looking. Philippe Gaboriau notes that the Tour has a particular relationship to themes of change and the future: the Tour symbolizes forward movement and popular aspirations. He claims that the Tour points to the future and offers the public a 'vision of its collective immortality'.[6] Thirdly, as Gaboriau also discusses at some length, the Tour, certainly in the first half of the twentieth century, was an important expression of the particularly rich working-class symbolism that surrounds the bicycle. Essentially, the bicycle is associated with a tension that exists in the development of capitalism at the beginning of the twentieth century, whereby industrially produced objects become relatively readily accessible to members of the social class that produces them. In other words, the products of the labour, which imposes harsh working and living conditions on the working class, seem to offer a means of escaping these conditions, opening up new spheres of mobility and leisure.[7] In the course of the twentieth century the bicycle, particularly in European countries such as France and Italy, becomes linked with a whole series of popular, working-class themes. For one thing, it offers mobility, bringing the industrial worker into contact with the rural environment, and the rural worker into contact with the city. It also becomes associated with the freedom of youth and leisure, evoking memories of the working-class aspirations developed by the Front Populaire.[8] The Front Populaire – a coalition of Communist, Socialist and Radical parties led by Léon Blum – came to power briefly in the late 1930s, and is chiefly remembered as a regime which sought to respond to the needs of France's working class. It succeeded in introducing key domestic reforms such as the 40-hour working week, paid annual vacations, and compulsory schooling until the age of 14.

In historical terms then, as mentioned already, the Tour serves as an expression of a particular construction of Republican universalism. In simple terms, the popular pride in the fact that the Tour comes to 'your village, your town' is reflected on a larger scale, in that the greatest riders in the world come to France to race. To illustrate this 'Republican' thesis, the chapter will look in some detail at the way in which two of the Tour's most famous riders, the Italian Fausto Coppi, and the English rider Tom Simpson, were integrated into the Tour.

Working-class credentials were undoubtedly important, particularly in the case of Coppi, as was the general perception of a desire to integrate into the democratic and forward-looking 'European' project that the Tour implicitly supported and symbolized. As the internationalization of the Tour gathered pace in the 1980s, it became increasingly difficult to place, for example, American riders within this framework. In short, France's anxiety and uncertainty in the face of globalization are mirrored in the cultural topography of the Tour.

Merckx, le Cannibale

It does seem, then, that at certain points in time the French press and public are sporting 'purists', as Barnes would have it, in that almost universal respect and admiration are expressed in relation to successful riders such as Fausto Coppi. However, this does not mean that all non-French riders were integrated into the system of values and metaphors that the Tour generated in its 'European' period. Eddy Merckx, for example, the great Belgian cyclist and five times winner of the Tour in the late 1960s and early 1970s, is still widely perceived as both an individualistic and also unsophisticated rider in his ruthless dedication to victory, and his apparent disdain of 'tactics'. *L'ABCdaire du Tour de France* refers to him euphemistically as 'champion de tempérament bien plus que champion de style'.[9] In a typically elegant and punning piece from 1970, Antoine Blondin, the effective poet laureate of the Tour, portrays Merckx as a rampaging Mongol with his high cheekbones, dark hair and hooded eyes, wearing 'le numéro hun' on his back.[10] Drawing on the well-established tradition of military metaphors and the Tour, Blondin talks of the 'cruelty' of Merckx's ambition. He leads his Faema team with an 'implacably dispensed' mixture of charm and terror, knowing just how to subjugate a supporting rider, 'une bête à pédaler, literally 'a pedalling beast': 'In this way, charming kids can be transformed into heavies and made to work for the big heavy himself.'[11] Blondin's piece undoubtedly expresses admiration, but it is also an elegant expression of the popular description of Merckx as 'le Cannibale'.

French spectators occasionally jeered at Merckx in the 1971 Tour, who were apparently resentful of his uncompromising domination of the Tour, and this popular antagonism was encouraged by certain unscrupulous elements in the French press (*Paris-Match* asked whether Merckx might 'kill' the Tour).[12] There may be many reasons for this hostility, including traditional cultural antagonisms between France and Belgium but, as far as the argument here is concerned, it is interesting to note that Merckx was widely considered to have come from a bourgeois rather than a working-class background.[13]

The Tour as Lieu de mémoire

Before looking in some detail at the reception of Coppi and Simpson, it is necessary to consider the cultural pre-history to the European phase of the Tour. The Tour is, of course, a genuinely national institution. More than this, it is a *lieu de mémoire*, a generator and repository of popular national symbols and myths. As we have already seen, Philippe Gaboriau argues that the history of the Tour is intimately connected to evolution of the bicycle as a symbol of 'l'espérance industrielle' of the French working classes.[14] In more general terms, Georges Vigarello shows how the Tour is woven into the French popular imagination, and how it is involved in the construction of the *Hexagone* as a collectively constructed topography. The Tour is instrumental in the construction of the image of a France unified by its geography.[15] In other words, it functions as a popular supplement to the Republican project of national unity that dates back to the Revolution. It is implicated in the great Republican project of popular pedagogy, which gained momentum particularly during the Third Republic. The Tour, almost in spite of itself, takes on the classic Republican role of educating the nation.[16] The image of France as a 'natural' unity, protected by the sea and mountains, feeds into the collective 'appropriation du sol'. In addition to this, the Tour is also involved in the process of the 'physical regeneration' of frontiers by, for example, including a stage in Alsace-Lorraine from 1906 until 1911.[17]

Travelling Armies and International Diplomacy

The extent to which the Tour established itself over a period of several decades as a national ritual is captured in Louis Malle's short documentary *Le Tour* (1962). The documentary lingers on shots of the spectators – nuns, elderly people, schoolchildren – emphasizing that the arrival of the Tour in a town or village engenders a festival atmosphere. The documentary also illustrates some of the 'quainter' customs of the Tour that were still practised at the time. These include 'la chasse à la canette', whereby *domestiques* (support riders) would raid cafés, taking whatever liquid refreshment – including alcohol – that came to hand. (The film shows riders carrying bottles of beer and eating ice creams.) Another section of the film shows spectators on a mountain stage indulging in the tradition of *la poussette*, pushing stragglers as they struggle to climb steep inclines. In this way, the Tour reinforces a national sense of identity and collectivity, but at the same time creates its own enclosed world of ritual and custom.[18] Time and time again, the Tour is described by commentators as a friendly travelling 'army', consuming all that lies in its path, and briefly imposing its own rhythms and customs on the territory it passes through.[19]

However, as has already been suggested, it would be wrong to think of the Tour as entirely inward-looking, merely reinforcing the shared national sense of the hexagon. Nor should it be seen as essentially conservative and backward-looking, concerned with preserving its own particularities whilst at the same time conserving a vaguely folkloric national identity. By virtue of its broad connections with the Republican project of education and citizenship, the popular faith in modernity and industrial advances, and the fact that from the beginning it was a commercial affair, the Tour, in different ways over time, looks outwards from the hexagon at a wider world. As Vigarello outlines, the creation of national teams of riders in 1930 had the result that the Tour is represented in terms of the language of diplomacy; it recreates the world of pacts and national oppositions that characterized Europe in the first half of the twentieth century. In this context, the Tour provided a reassuring transposition of the fraught European situation of the inter-war period.[20]

Europeanization and Globalization

The participation of non-French riders in the Tour also inevitably means that it has, almost from its inception, a dimension that goes beyond the national. In broad terms, the history of the Tour and its riders might be split into two eras: a 'European' era, which reached its height in the 1950s and 1960s, and a 'global' era, which definitively gathered momentum in the 1980s. 'European' means here a fairly small group of western and southern European nations who provided the majority of riders and winners of the tour. Up until the mid-1980s winners had come from France, Italy, Spain, Belgium, Holland, Switzerland and Luxembourg, with a predominance of French and Belgian winners. Since 1986, the USA, Ireland, Spain, Denmark, Italy and Germany provided winners, with a total of seven victories going to the USA. It is arguably in the European era, and particularly in the 1950s and 1960s, that the national and 'international' dimensions of the Tour coexisted most harmoniously, precisely because 'international' here effectively means European. The later phase of globalization proved harder for the French to deal with in cultural terms, precisely because the national and the international elements could no longer be so easily reconciled.

FAUSTO COPPI

The Italian Fausto Coppi epitomizes the 'European' phase of the Tour, and his positive reception in France is in many ways an expression of an emerging European spirit. Amongst other things, Coppi appears to facilitate, at a popular level, something of a *rapprochement* between France and Italy, after being effectively at war with each other for the duration of the Second World War. Coppi was born into a farming family from Castellania in Piedmont in 1919, and turned professional in 1937. He won the Tour de France twice, the Giro d'Italia five times, the Tour of Lombardy five times, two world pursuit championships, along with Paris–Roubaix and Milan–San Remo. Coppi is certainly one of the most celebrated riders ever to have competed in the Tour de France. His distinctive physical appearance – extremely long legs, an almost cylindrical upper body, along with a lean, angular face dominated by a large nose and globular eyes – earned him the nickname the 'heron'. Even Roland Barthes, in *Mythologies*, his ironic and acute analysis of France in the 1950s as the *Trente glorieuses* begin to pick up speed, seems seduced by Coppi. His 'Lexique des coureurs (1955)' simply describes Coppi as: 'Héros parfait. Sur le vélo, il a toutes les vertus. Fantôme redoutable.'[21] Coppi's two victories in the Tour in 1949 and 1952 do not in themselves compare with the record of multiple non-French winners such as Merckx, LeMond, Induráin and Armstrong. His fellow Italian and great rival Gino Bartali also won the Tour twice, in 1938 and 1948, but Coppi appears to have captured the imagination of the French enthusiasts of the Tour and commentators alike. One reason for this fascination with Coppi, apart from his obvious talents as a rider, was the tragic and complex trajectory of his life. He spent two years as a prisoner of war after being drafted into the Italian army and captured by the British 8th Army in Tunisia, lost his brother in a cycling accident in 1951, and was involved in a widely-reported affair with a married woman, Giulia Locatelli, referred to as 'la dame blanche'. He continued to ride past his prime, and died at the age of 40, having contracted malaria.

A 'European' Hero: 'Arriva Coppi!'

More importantly, the fascination with Coppi has much to do with his emergence as an Italian rider in the period immediately after the Second World War. Through the figure of Coppi, the popular imagination of the Tour is developed on a 'European' as opposed to purely national level, and the fact that Coppi is adopted by the French press and public reflects and expresses the reconstruction of French pride and nationhood via the nascent European project. Coppi becomes synonymous primarily with a 'modern' progressive way of thinking. He fulfils the traditional criterion for any hero of the Tour, in that he is from working-class stock, but he also conforms to the popular preoccupation with the bicycle as a symbol that combines working-class pride with technological advancement.

Pierre Chany's well-known book on the development of European cycling in the aftermath of the Second World War is, significantly, entitled *Les rendez-vous du cyclisme ou Arriva Coppi*.[22] Chany starts his book with a detailed description of the scene at the Turchino Tunnel at the halfway point of the Milan–San Remo race in 1946, as spectators and journalists waited for the emergence of the riders. The *passo del Turchino* is, Chany emphasizes, a place of pilgrimage and popular sporting celebration, 'le point fixe' of Italian sport.[23] On this particular day, 19 March 1946, however, the Tunnel had an added significance. Although only 50 metres long, it was as if it were 'six years' long, referring of course to the involvement of Italy in the Second World War. The foreign observers in the crowd of pilgrims, Chany claims, were hoping that the Tunnel might deliver some sort of hope for reconciliation after the war.[24] Giuseppe Ambrosini, standing Pope-like on the last car to emerge from the tunnel before the riders, informed the 'pilgrims' by means of a loudspeaker that, 'Coppi is coming!' This cry, '*Arriva Coppi!*', which he was to hear many times in the future, has a particular significance for Chany. Firstly, in cycling terms, Coppi significantly changed the *modus operandi* of the press pack. Before Coppi, the Italian press would follow the peloton, waiting for incidents and accidents, only overtaking when a rider or riders decided to attack.

However, as Coppi's domination grew, the press pack took up the habit of going in advance of the peloton. It is a matter of record, Chany claims, that Coppi was never defeated once he had attacked and left the peloton between 1946 and 1954. Secondly, the cry of '*Arriva Coppi!*' is significant because he represents a new, forward-looking mentality. As far as Chany is concerned, Coppi 'rewrites the book' of modern cycling, investigating the most up-to-date methods of diet and training, and, significantly, shows great generosity, along with a strong awareness of the wider cycling community. He manages, almost single-handedly, to replace the rather 'rough and ready' ['quelque peu empirique et très artisanal'] sport of the past with a sport 'conceived of on an industrial scale'.[25] In terms of competing, Coppi combines an awareness of his own prestige with a restless intelligence, whereas away from the arena of competition he is accommodating to the point of vulnerability. In short, he embodies the popular, progressive, humanistic values that cycling has traditionally been associated with. For Chany, cycling represents a 'passionate and vivid snapshot of humanity in movement'.[26]

Ladri di biciclette (Bicycle Thieves)

In his recent *Fausto Coppi, l'échappée belle*, Dominique Jameux puts forward a similar argument concerning Coppi.[27] Jameux sees Coppi as representative of Italy's re-integration into a developing Europe after the Second World War. In 1946, 90 per cent of the electorate voted in a constitutional referendum, with a clear majority in favour of a republic. As Jameux points out, this vote in favour of an Italian republic expresses the desire of a majority of the electorate at this moment in time to place Italy firmly in the progressive and democratic European mainstream. It also represents something of an act of contrition towards France, betrayed by Italy in 1940. Coppi, who in his professional life is committed to modern, rational, scientific methods, comes to be seen as 'the most French of Italians'.[28] The theme of Coppi as a 'European' figure, particularly appreciated in France, which, as already mentioned, begins to conceive of itself as being at the heart of Europe in the post-war era, is crucial for Jameux. He points out, for example, that Coppi's years of greatest success correspond to the great years of Italian neo-realist cinema. The bicycle, and by extension Coppi, is associated with the positive, collective and democratic popular values.

To illustrate the importance of the bicycle, Jameux offers a short synopsis of the 'film quasi-manifeste' of Italian neo-realism, De Sica's *Ladri di biciclette* (1948). Jameux perceives links between the emergence of Italy as a dominant force in the 'petite Europe du vélo', which prefigures the post-war European project ['la grande Europe de l'histoire'], and the supremacy of Italian neo-realist cinema at this time. Just as Coppi was arguably more popular in France than in Italy, so neo-realist films were often better received in France.[29] Jameux himself appears to subscribe to the view that cycling is an inherently progressive activity, when he claims that there was very little possibility of Coppi, given his intelligence and curiosity, being seduced by the discourse of Italian fascism. Any professional cyclist is, Jameux claims, essentially *poliphile*, looking to 'escape' from the constraints of 'la terre' in favour of the city and foreign countries.[30]

Coppi and Bartali

As Jameux, along with other commentators, shows, the widespread notion of Coppi as a politically progressive figure is reinforced by the construction of an opposition with the other great Italian rider of the era, Gino Bartali.[31] The opposition between Coppi and Bartali becomes emblematic of Italy in the immediate post-war era. As riders, Bartali and Coppi had much in common, both favouring mountain stages as opposed to sprinting, but Bartali came to be seen as a sort of model Christian athlete by the Catholic Right, whereas Coppi was popularly mythologized as a Communist, representing the democratic attachment to anti-clerical and secular values. His affair with the 'white lady' was important in this regard, given that the moral values generated by Catholicism were still very strong in Italy at that time. In general terms, Bartali represented the 'old', the traditional and the conservative, whereas Coppi represented the 'young', the progressive and the modern. Ultimately, Jameux suggests, the Coppi–Bartali opposition offered a semi-fictional division, which helped Italy to devise a narrative of national rebirth and reconstruction after the war within a European context.[32] Coppi's victory in the 1949 Tour is particularly significant in this respect, partly because this Tour is markedly 'European' in tone. After the first post-war Tour, 'le Tour franco-français de 1947' as Jameux puts it, the Tours of 1948 and 1949 become more cosmopolitan in flavour.[33] In 1949 the Tour passes through Brussels (the first foreign stage was introduced in 1947), San Sebastian, Aosta and Lausanne, and the presence of Italians, Belgians, Swiss and Luxemburgers in the peloton means that a genuine 'Europe cycliste' is born in this era, expressing a friendly European national rivalry.

TOM SIMPSON

In the 1960s the British rider Tom Simpson was very much part of the 'European' era of the Tour. His success on the European cycling scene was remarkable, given the low profile of the sport in Britain at the time. But Simpson's decision to cross the Channel and establish himself as a professional cyclist on the European circuit was seen, in France, at least, as having more than merely sporting significance. It was considered to be an act of openness, almost a desire to be a 'European' that was uncharacteristic of a famously insular nation. In this way, the generally warm reception of Simpson in France seems to spring from a French confidence in what the Tour represents. Simpson was seen as bringing a touch of English style and eccentricity to the Tour, but also as a Briton who was willing to become part of the distinctively European institution that was the Tour. However, Simpson's role is ambiguous: as the first English-speaking rider to make a real impact in European cycling,[34] he also pointed forward to a later 'international' era. At this stage in the Tour's history, Simpson could be accepted as a 'naturalized' cyclist, whereas later riders such as Greg LeMond and Lance Armstrong would find it more difficult to discover this sort of acceptance.

Although his record is slight compared to that of Fausto Coppi, Simpson still holds a unique place in the history of the Tour. This has much to do with the fact that he is one of only three riders to have died whilst competing in the race, the others being the Spaniard Francisco Cepeda in 1935, and the Italian Fabio Casartelli in 1995. Simpson died, at the age of 29, on Mount Ventoux, the thirteenth stage of the 1967 Tour. Speculation and controversy still surrounds his death, but it is generally accepted that he had taken amphetamines, which enabled him to push his body to dangerous limits. Added to this, he had been suffering from stomach problems throughout the Tour, and the heat experienced by the riders on this unforgiving stage was particularly intense on that day. He collapsed twice in attempting to reach the summit, and the second time it was impossible to revive him. The monument to Simpson on Mont Ventoux remains a place of pilgrimage for fans of cycling to this day. Simpson was the first British rider to wear the *maillot jaune* in 1962 (it was not until 32 years later that Chris Boardman became the second British rider to wear it), and his record of victories in four of the one-day Classics plus the world championship in 1965 is impressive. He eventually finished sixth in the 1962 Tour, which was the best British result for 22 years.

For William Fotheringham, whose recent book on Simpson takes as its title Simpson's alleged last words, 'put me back on my bike', Simpson's early death and record of achievement have meant that he has played an 'occult role' [sic] in British cycling akin to that of Fausto Coppi in Italy.[35]

Cycling as it is Spoken

However, as far as the Tour is concerned, the tragic circumstances of his death and his solid record as a professional cyclist are not the only reasons that Tom Simpson is a significant figure. In fact, an indication of this significance is provided by the monument on Mont Ventoux, which refers to him as a 'sporting ambassador'. Simpson surpassed all other British cyclists in the impact that he made on 'European hearts and minds', as Fotheringham puts it. This impact can be gauged from Antoine Blondin's report – effectively an obituary – in *L'Equipe* the day after Simpson's death.[36] When he became the first Englishman to wear the *maillot jaune*, his victory became, Blondin claims, 'our victory'. He had added a touch of Englishness to the cycling mix: 'We liked to think that he had tied the Eton school tie to the handlebars of a machine that many still see as a means of transport for a postman.'[37] Blondin is clearly influenced by Simpson's conscious marketing of himself as 'Major Tom', the eccentric bowler-hatted Englishman abroad.[38] The image was at odds with Simpson's working-class roots, but the connotations of eccentricity and difference were more important than the class implications of Simpson's image. This faintly stereotyped view of the 'English', evident elsewhere in Blondin's playful and allusive pieces, constitutes a fascinating reminder of the physical and cultural gulf that still existed between Britain and continental Europe at that time. However, even more revealing in terms of the cultural construction of 'le cyclisme' is the notion of the British rider who has 'naturalized' himself as a 'cyclist'. The implication is that European cycling in general, and the Tour in particular, represent a sort of 'rainbow' (Blondin uses the term 'arc-en-ciel') proto-internationalism. If one ignores the contemporary 'multicultural' connotations of this particular term, there is more than a hint of 'le creuset républicain', 'the Republican melting pot', in Blondin's formulation. The Tour may be a form of cycling internationalism, but it is played out in a French – and by extension European – context, and Simpson integrates himself as a 'citoyen', whilst maintaining his own eccentric distinctiveness. Blondin had used a similar formula in an earlier piece on Simpson's elevation to the *maillot jaune* in 1962.[39] He is impressed and charmed by Simpson's idiomatic grasp of French spoken with an English accent,[40] and conflates this with his integration into the cycling world: 'cycling as it is spoken' holds no secrets for Simpson.

Blondin's piece on the Hercules squad, the first English team to compete in the Tour in 1955, contains similar ideas on integration.[41] He opens with a description of the Tour as it progresses from Lens to Bruay. Between the peloton and the star riders out in front a single English rider (Brian Robinson) makes his way, in silence and solitude, like a 'musical pause' in the tumult. He knows that he will not be able to catch the handful of stars leading the race, but neither does he want to return to the anonymity of the pack. The suggestion is that this insistence on maintaining a sort of splendid isolation is in itself a 'thoroughly' English way of behaving. However, although he is at pains to portray the difference of the English squad, Blondin also praises the efforts that the English riders make to integrate. They are led by Sydney Cozens, a former sprinter, a stout and bespectacled 'Mr Pickwick' figure, and have the air of 'displaced persons'. Blondin portrays them as a series of English stereotypes: a 'clergyman', a character from *David Copperfield*, a cockney barman, and a City gent, all carrying travellers' cheques in their *musettes*. However, he admits that appearances can be deceptive. Their accents may sound strange against the 'Mediterranean' and Flemish banter of the peloton, but they have integrated well. They have even received praise from a Dieppe hotelier, who claims that it is the first time he has received English tourists who have not 'called attention to themselves' ['qui ne se singularisent pas'] in some way. Given their relatively positive experience of the 'melting pot' that constitutes the Tour, and the fact their exploits will receive little attention at home, it seems possible, Blondin speculates, that they might find in the Tour a 'spiritual' home. (Again, Blondin uses the French term 'se faire naturaliser'.)

'He was our pride'

One should of course be wary of reading too much into Blondin's pieces, which obviously seek on one level to play with established stereotypes. However, the notion of the Tour as 'un creuset', a melting pot, is a recurrent theme, and Fotheringham's biography of Simpson reinforces the notion that a British cyclist in the 1950s and 1960s who wished to break into European cycling was required to integrate into a 'European' way of life. In many ways, Simpson's story is a familiar one of working–class ambition and social mobility in post-war Britain. (His Nottingham upbringing, ambition and desire to travel bring to mind the novelist Alan Sillitoe.) He realized that his horizons were limited in terms of cycling, and was willing to move to continental Europe in order to further his career. Simpson initially lived in France, and moved to Ghent in Belgium in 1961. For some time, visits to Britain were constrained by the fact that he had avoided National Service and the still relatively long travelling times involved. As Fotheringham shows, referring to Blondin's obituary piece in *L'Equipe*, Simpson's success as a cyclist cannot be separated from his equally skilful ability to integrate himself into the European cycling fraternity:

> Simpson's achievement in getting to the very top of cycling can be put in simple perspective. The sport was as distant and alien to the Harworth miners among whom Simpson grew up as Test cricket would be to a fisherman in Saint Brieuc. Five years after welcoming him with '*Roule* Britannia', Blondin summed up in his obituary the pleasure and satisfaction Europeans had gained from watching Simpson's progress: 'He was our pride'.[42]

VERS UN TOUR MONDIALISÉ?

As William Fotheringham points out, Tom Simpson was in many ways the first indication of a growing trend which was to make its impact felt in the 1980s. Simpson was one of the first English speakers to make a significant impact on the Tour, and a direct line can be traced from Simpson through to Lance Armstrong. Simpson's success in the Tour was arguably the very first step in a process of evolution that would end with its internationalization. Fotheringham quotes the Tour's official historian Jacques Augendre who argues to this effect:

> When English riders arrived at the Tour they gave it an extra
> dimension, broadened the race's international appeal. Simpson's
> winning the yellow jersey [in 1962] was a turning point. Today,
> Armstrong's victories stem from all that. It was a long evolution
> but Simpson was a pioneer of something which ended with Greg
> LeMond and Armstrong. The Tour de France was Flemish and
> Latin, now it belongs to the Anglo-Saxons as well.[43]

It can be seen in retrospect that the 1960s, Simpson's era, were a
point of transition, both in the Tour and in European life in general.
The fact that Simpson was welcomed as an Englishman who appeared
to disprove the widespread notion of English insularity, whilst at the
same time he was nicknamed 'Tommy', a term used to refer to British
soldiers, is telling in this respect. The war was still a recent experience
and Europe was still under construction, but the process of
globalization was also slowly beginning to accelerate. The Tour was
slowly but surely taking on a new, genuinely international, potentially
global, dimension. In his book on the Tour of 1990, Geoffrey Nicholson
addresses directly the issue of its growing internationalization.[44] He
recalls being struck by the size and extravagance of the first Tour he
covered in 1965. On the one hand, there was the familiar friendly self-
sufficient 'invading army', with a small cycling battalion between two
motorized divisions, welcomed by the local 'civilian' population with
banners and bunting. On the other hand, Nicholson was struck by the
commercialization of the Tour. The presence, since the war, of non-
cycling team sponsors such as Nivea, and the general sponsorship of the
Tour by companies such as IBM, Poulain[45] and Outspan[46] was still
unfamiliar in the 1960s. Louis Malle's short 1962 film is again
illustrative here, in that the popular festival aspects of the Tour are
accompanied by hints of what is to come: schoolchildren are wearing
Poulain sun hats, promotional 'freebies' are distributed by the *caravane
publicitaire*, and international journalists are beginning to talk of 'le
dopage'. 1962 was also the first year in which the Tour returned to
trade, rather than national teams, which had been the format since
1929. In terms of the development of cycling itself, 1962 represents the
culmination of a period of modernization and professionalization
which, as has already been discussed, began in 1947. Training and diet
had improved significantly, as had the technology of the bicycle itself.

Although the Tour of the 1960s was still long by today's standards (the Tour of 2002 was exactly 1,000 kilometres shorter than the Tour of 1967), shorter stages had been progressively introduced since 1947. In short, the Tour had undergone a period of sporting, technological and commercial modernization.

Toujours la petite Europe du vélo

However, despite this size and extravagance, Nicholson realises in retrospect that in some ways the 1965 Tour was still in fact quite a parochial affair, and to that extent somewhat 'exotic' for an English journalist. Only riders from a bloc of five adjoining European countries (France, Spain, Italy, Belgium and Holland) were present in any numbers, with only a sprinkling of individual riders from other nations. Vin Denson and Tom Simpson, for example, were the only British riders, and the language of the peloton was predominantly French and Flemish. The attempt to placate those opposed to the intense commercialization of the Tour by returning to national – rather than trade – teams in 1967 was inevitably short-lived. For one thing, this move only served to emphasize the relatively closed nature of the Tour since four countries had to be allocated nine of the 13 teams. France, for example, had three teams: France, Bleuets and Coqs. Also, the pressures of commercialization meant that the trade teams would inevitably return. The European focus of the Tour was to last a little longer, but the spirit of a friendly European rivalry, 'la petite Europe du vélo', was no longer relevant if the Tour was to respond to a changing world.

By the mid-1970s – the era of Merckx – the Tour had still apparently changed very little, and with Thévenet, Hinault and Fignon, France would enjoy one of its best spells of success until the late 1980s. However, in the course of the 1980s the Tour, certainly in terms of its competitors, was rapidly internationalized. Nicholson locates the turning point in the 1981 Tour, when Hinault attacked on a stage in the Pyrenees, and was unable to shake off the Australian Phil Anderson. This was the first time that an Australian had worn the *maillot jaune*. There had always been what might be termed 'international' competitors, which is to say riders who came from outside the 'inner circle' of European nations. These riders were occasionally successful, such as Tom Simpson or to a lesser extent the Irish rider Seamus Elliott, who briefly wore the *maillot jaune* in 1963.

However, as the 1980s progressed, the success of 'international' riders increased dramatically.

Le Tour du monde

A crucial stimulus to the globalization of the Tour was the 1982 football World Cup in Spain, in which France reached the semi-finals. The way in which the World Cup captured the imagination and reached a global audience impressed Jacques Goddet, co-director of the Tour with Félix Lévitan, so much that he proposed, in an editorial for *L'Equipe*, the concept of an equivalent 'World Tour' ('un Tour mondialisé'). Goddet divided the cycling world into 'traditional' and 'new' cycling nations. The traditional nations were all European countries, including Great Britain and the Commonwealth, and the new nations were an African grouping, Canada, Colombia, USA, Poland, Portugal, East Germany, Czechoslovakia and the USSR. Goddet proposed that every four years these countries should compete in a World Cup-style Tour with mainly professionals from the first group of countries and amateurs from the rest. The race would keep France as its main geographical point of reference, but a whole series of stages in other countries would be developed. The prospect was raised of the Tour opening in New York, followed by a transfer by Concorde back to Paris. Of course, Goddet's plans were never adopted in the form he proposed, and the centenary 2003 Tour will remain entirely within the hexagon, in an attempt to recreate something close to Desgrange's original vision. However, changes were to take place in terms of the provenance of the riders. The 1983 Tour was opened to amateurs and professionals, and it was initially thought that five or six amateur nations would compete. In the end, Colombia was the only amateur nation to send a team. However, a corner had been turned, and riders from 'non-traditional' countries began increasingly to compete and enjoy success in the Tour. Colombian riders, for example, returned as professionals and in 1985 Lucho Herrera set a record points total for the *Grand Prix de la Montagne* (polka-dot jersey) and came seventh overall, whilst in 1988 Fabio Parra finished in third place.[47] The Irish riders Sean Kelly and Stephen Roche built on earlier success, and Roche won the Tour in 1987. In the same year Lech Piasecki became the first Polish rider to wear the *maillot jaune*. By 1990, although the older European nations – France, Belgium, Spain, Italy and Holland – still provided roughly two-thirds of the peloton, there were 19 nationalities in all represented in the Tour. Only Miguel

Induráin, from Villava in northern Spain, who achieved a remarkable string of five consecutive victories in the 1990s, stood out against this trend. He was frequently portrayed as a taciturn, tough but modest product of a traditional rural region, a reminder, in other words, of the popular European heritage of the tour.

The Americans Arrive

The single most significant change in this period was the emergence of the USA as a major force in the Tour. In 1986, with Greg LeMond's victory, *L'Equipe* announced the new, international era of the Tour with the headline *Le Tour du nouveau monde*.[48] For Pierre Chany, writing on LeMond's victory also in *L'Equipe*, an American winner and four nations sharing the first five places confirmed the 'complete internationalization' of the Tour.[49] He reminded readers that it would have been practically unimaginable in the 1970s for the *maillot jaune* to be won by anybody but a European. Evoking the earlier success of the Colombian Herrera, he looked forward to a time when 'all barriers will have been removed' and the current process of 'intermingling' ['brassage'] would accelerate to such an extent that no nation would be able to presume dominance of the sport. The language is clearly that of international fraternity and co-operation, and is all the more significant in the light of the controversial circumstances surrounding LeMond's victory. The tension between LeMond and the French rider Hinault in the 1986 Tour inevitably became associated with more general anxieties in France over the emergence of American riders. Both Hinault, five times winner of the Tour and firm French favourite, and LeMond, from Nevada, were riding for Bernard Tapie's La Vie claire team. There was apparently an agreement between the two that Hinault was riding to help LeMond, since LeMond had ridden in a supporting role to Hinault the previous year. However, Hinault seemed to be tempted by the idea of winning a sixth Tour. Consequently, tension and confusion characterized the relationship between the two riders throughout, and it was inevitable that sympathy would be divided along national lines. To complicate matters further, there was a widespread feeling that LeMond, and particularly a LeMond victory, served primarily Bernard Tapie's business interests. Robert Ichah and Jean Boully, in their generally hagiographic *Les grands vainqueurs du Tour de France*, are at times less than complimentary about LeMond (although they do acknowledge that a more likeable side to the rider emerged over time).[50] The promotion of Tapie's products was not, they claim, the American rider's primary preoccupation, but it was undeniable that the interests of the businessman and the rider coincided.[51] There are suggestions here of a tension between the 'official' construction of the Tour as a genuinely global spectacle and, for example, popular attitudes of anti-Americanism.

LeMond went on to win the Tour three times, and Lance Armstrong has become the latest star of the Tour, having won it four times, starting in 1999. It is highly significant, in terms of the cultural construction of the Tour, that American riders do not, as a general rule, come from the 'conventional' working-class background required for a hero of the Tour. One reason for this is that there is no 'popular' tradition of cycling in the USA, with cycling being associated with the middle-class pursuit of fitness and leisure. But also, as Nicholson points out, many in France see the 'candidly businesslike approach to money and ambition' of a rider like LeMond as typically American. Similarly, the involvement of LeMond's family, particularly his father, in his sporting and business affairs was viewed with suspicion.[52] In general terms, a certain amount of hostility has been directed against LeMond and Armstrong for what is perceived to be their individualistic, 'calculating' and overly 'businesslike' approach to cycling and the Tour. Ichah and Boully emphasize that LeMond was the first major cycling champion to have concentrated uniquely on the world championship and the Tour de France, and they pull no punches regarding his main motivation: 'His watch-word: winning. Winning races to make money, first and foremost. Earning money and possibly winning a few races as well.'[53]

Lance Armstrong has faced hostility in France for similar reasons. As Yves Bordenave reports in *Le Monde* in 2001, although Hinault considers Armstrong to be the inheritor of the great tradition of Coppi and Merckx, Jacques Augendre 'relativizes' this judgement in view of the fact that Armstrong concentrates almost solely on the Tour. For Augendre, he is the best 'businessman' (Augendre uses the English word) in the world of cycling.[54] Armstrong may be at pains to point out in his autobiography that his concentration on the Tour is the result of a greater 'maturity' in his cycling, as well as respect for the uniqueness of the Tour, but this does not seem to convince all French commentators.[55] The tone of *L'Equipe* in 2002 might be described as one of slightly grudging respect.[56] Armstrong is not, Philippe Brunel claims, in the great tradition of Coppi, Hinault or Induráin, but his professionalism and 'killer instinct' must be respected. After a period of hostility between Armstrong and the French press, including accusations of drug-taking, his 2002 victory has marked something of a truce. According to Brunel, he should be admired for what he is, an 'admirable fighter' ['un admirable combattant']. Given the semi-epic tone of much reporting on the Tour, there is more than a suggestion of faint praise here.

CONCLUSION

The tensions and uncertainties that France has experienced, and continues to experience, in the face of the pressures of globalization, have been mirrored in the cultural construction of the Tour. The post-war 'European' period of the Tour might now be viewed as a relatively golden era, during which it was able to consolidate its position as a much-loved national institution whilst at the same time drawing on its associations with progressive, popular attitudes, enabling it to look towards a wider, European society. This stance expressed itself in a positive embrace of non-French riders such as Coppi and Simpson. Coppi was welcomed as a forward-looking son of the Italian rural working class, an innovator in sport, and Simpson was seen as an 'eccentric' English rider who went against the trend of British insularity and 'naturalized' himself as a European cyclist. Coppi and Simpson were undoubtedly both what might be commonly called 'working-class heroes', and it should not be forgotten that this in itself means that they might be considered as prototypes of the sort of professional cyclist that LeMond and Armstrong are seen to represent. Both Coppi and Simpson benefited from the increasing social mobility of the post-war era, establishing cosmopolitan lives for themselves, and Simpson in particular was acutely aware of the business potential that success in the Tour represented.

In the 1980s, the Tour consciously 'globalized' itself, partly in response to the global success of events such as the football World Cup. This might be seen as one sort of distinctively 'French' solution to the problems posed by commercialization and globalization in sport. Rather than attempting to protect the Tour from these pressures, the idea was to globalise on the Tour's own terms, retaining a distinctively French core and flavour to a genuinely global event. These grand projects did

The Tour de France, 1903–2003

not come to fruition, but the numbers and success of international riders have increased dramatically, and the popular cultural tradition of the Tour has at times struggled to accommodate these changes. In France, there has been a widespread suspicion of the process of economic globalization that has gained momentum in recent years, which has drawn on an already existing anti-Americanism in French culture. Globalization is associated with American capitalism and American multinationals, and is seen as damaging to the European social project. If the Tour functioned for a certain amount of time as a sporting representation of France within a modernizing Europe it can no longer fulfil this representative role in an era of American-led globalization. The defensive attitude towards globalization is mirrored in a sort of crisis of representation in the Tour. Many in France find it difficult to accept the perceived value system that underpins economic globalism *à l'américaine*, and it is therefore not surprising that a rider like Lance Armstrong is viewed with suspicion by many in France who are unwilling to accept the values associated with what they perceive to be unfettered global capitalism.

1. J. Barnes, *Something to Declare* (London: Macmillan, 2002), pp.90–91.
2. Ibid., p.91.
3. The claim is shared by analysts such as C. Pociello, *Les cultures sportives: pratiques, représentations et mythes sportifs* (Paris: PUF, 1995), and is discussed in terms of football in H. Dauncey and G. Hare (eds), *France and the 1998 World Cup: The National Impact of a World Sporting Event* (London: Frank Cass, 1999).
4. Barnes, *Something to Declare*, pp.91–2.
5. M. Dalloni, 'Tour de France, cher pays de notre enfance', *Le Monde*, 2 Aug. 2001, 1. This is the second line from the famous French singer-songwriter Charles Trenet's song *Douce France*.
6. P. Gaboriau, *Le Tour de France et le vélo: histoire sociale d'une épopée contemporaine* (Paris: L'Harmattan, 1995), p.60.
7. Ibid., p.136.
8. Ibid., pp.136–7.
9. J.-P. Ollivier, *L'ABCdaire du Tour de France* (Paris: Flammarion, 2001), p.91.
10. A. Blondin, 'Un despote à sciatique' ('An Asian Despot/Despot with Sciatica'), in *L'Ironie du sport: chroniques de L'Equipe 1954–1982* (Paris: Editions François Bourin, 1988), p.287.
11. Ibid., p.288. 'Ainsi peut-on transformer de charmants bambins en gorilles et les enrôler pour la plus intransigeante des "gorillas".' ('Thus can the loveliest of children be transformed into gorillas and mobilized for the harshest of guerrilla combats'.)
12. See G. Fife, *Tour de France: The History, the Legend, the Riders* (London and Edinburgh: Mainstream, 1999), pp.45–6.
13. See R. Ichah and J. Boully, *Les grands vainqueurs du Tour de France* (Paris: Criterion, 1992), p.265.
14. Gaboriau, *Le Tour de France et le vélo*, p.199.

15. See G. Vigarello, 'Le Tour de France', in P. Nora, *Les Lieux de mémoire, III, La France, 2 Traditions* (Paris: Gallimerd, 1992), pp.885–925.

16. Vigarello, 'Le Tour de France', p.887.

17. Vigarello, 'Le Tour de France', p.898.

18. See Gaboriau, *Le Tour de France et le vélo*, pp.27–8, on the *Tour* as a total 'institution'.

19. See Gaboriau, *Le Tour de France et le vélo*, pp.29–30, on the 'suiveurs'.

20. Vigarello, 'Le Tour de France', p.902.

21. R. Barthes, *Mythologies* (Paris: Seuil, 1957), p.120. 'The perfect hero. On the bike, he has every virtue. A redoubtable ghost.'

22. P. Chany, *Les rendez-vous du cyclisme ou Arriva Coppi* (Paris: La Table Ronde, 1960).

23. Ibid., p.11.

24. Ibid., p.12.

25. Ibid., p.19.

26. Ibid.

27. D. Jameux, *Fausto Coppi: L'échappée belle, Italie 1945–1960* (Paris: Edition Austral/Arte, 1996).

28. Ibid., p.56.

29. Ibid., p.78.

30. Ibid., p.26.

31. See also S. Pivato, 'Italian Cycling and the Creation of a Catholic Hero: The Bartali Myth', *The International Journal of the History of Sport*, 13, 1 (March 1996), pp.128–38.

32. Jameux, *Fausto Coppi: l'échappée belle*, pp.81–2.

33. Ibid., p.95.

34. See W. Fotheringham, *Put Me Back on My Bike: In Search of Tom Simpson* (London: Yellow Jersey Press, 2002), p.12. As Fotheringham points out, Brian Robinson had preceded Simpson in making an impact upon the Tour. However, Simpson was the first British rider to make a significant breakthrough and establish himself as a respected rider (p.12).

35. Ibid., p.9.

36. A. Blondin, 'On court toujours seul', in *L'Ironie du sport*, pp.264–5.

37. 'On se plaisait à penser qu'il avait noué la cravate d'Eton au guidon d'un engin où beaucoup voient encore le gagne-pain du facteur.' Ibid., p.264.

38. 'Major Tom' plays with a reference to a famous character of humorous fiction 'le major Thompson' invented by Pierre Daninos in the 1950s in *Le Figaro*, whose old-school British attitudes to France and the French reflect various stereotypes of national identity. See P. Daninos, *Les Carnets du Major Thompson* (Paris: Hachette, 1954).

39. A. Blondin, 'Roule Britannia!', in *Tours de France: chroniques intégrales de 'L'Equipe' 1954–1982* (Paris: La Table Ronde, 2001), pp.280–2.

40. See Fotheringham, *Put Me Back on My Bike*, pp.97–8. Fotheringham emphasizes Simpson's facility with French, including the ability to make sophisticated puns, along with adequate Italian and Flemish.

41. A. Blondin, 'L'Anglais tel que l'on le court', in *Tours de France*, pp.27–9.

42. Fotheringham, *Put Me Back on My Bike*, p.98.

43. Ibid., p.12.

44. G. Nicholson, *Le Tour: The Rise and Rise of the Tour de France* (London: Hodder & Stoughton, 1991). See, in particular, Chapter One, 'The Foreign Legion', pp.11–26.

45. Poulain is associated with chocolate products.

46. Outspan is associated with oranges and orange juice.

47. See M. Rendell, *Kings of the Mountains: How Colombia's Cycling Heroes Changed Their Nation's History* (London: Aurum Press, 2002).

48. *L'Equipe*, 28 July 1986, 1.

49. P. Chany, 'La voie tracée par LeMond', *L'Equipe*, 28 July 1986, 3.

50. R. Ichah and J. Boully, *Les grands vainqueurs du Tour de France* (Paris: Criterion, 1992), pp.343–63.

51. Ibid., p.353.

52. Nicholson, *Le Tour*, pp.73–4.

53. 'Son maître mot: gagner. Gagner des courses pour gagner de l'argent, tout d'abord. Gagner de l'argent et éventuellement quelques courses, ensuite', Ichah and Boully, *Les grands vainqueurs du Tour de France*, p.345.
54. Y. Bordenave, 'Un géant qui n'a pas encore rejoint les héros', *Le Monde*, 24 July 2001, 16.
55. L. Armstrong (with S. Jenkins) *It's Not About the Bike: My Journey Back to Life* (New York: G.P. Putnam's Sons, 2000), pp.221–2.
56. P. Brunel, 'L'as Armstrong', *L'Equipe*, 28 July 2002, p.2.

The Tour de France and the Doping Issue[1]

PATRICK MIGNON

The Tour de France's economic and symbolic importance has turned it into a distorting mirror of how cycling works, particularly regarding doping and its treatment. There are indeed a lot of good reasons that cause one to find doping in the Tour de France because it is such a hard race that it pushes the sport of cycling – more generally – to extremes. But doping is not just taking products to enhance performance or maintain one's position. It is also a scandal or a social or health problem once these performance-enhancing practices become subject to rules, when a sport decides to ban certain products out of concern for equity between competitors, or once they become subject to the law when the State considers it must ban the consumption of certain products because they are dangerous to individuals' health or because it gives a bad image to an activity that should set a good example. The relationship of doping and the Tour de France is not simply one that links a demanding competition and the means employed by riders to face up to that. It is one where a sports event, because of its popularity, is a site where the problem will be aired in public. The Tour de France is the occasion when doping is defined and when the array of measures to deal with it will be set in train. It is therefore where the ability of sports governing bodies and political authorities to deal with it and resolve it will be judged, in dramatic fashion.

THE TOUR AS THE CYCLING EVENT *PAR EXCELLENCE*

The Tour de France is undoubtedly *the* cycling event *par excellence*. The race, organized nowadays by the Société du Tour de France, a subsidiary of the Amaury press group, has a budget of £18 million. It offers more than £1.5 million-worth of prizes (including £220,000 to the winner). Millions of spectators line the route each July to watch the riders and the publicity caravan of 250 vehicles representing 40 brands. Millions of television viewers spend several hours in front of their sets watching the daily broadcasts. The Tour de France is also the shop window of world cycling, the most popular and the most followed sports event because, from Albert Londres's 'convict labourers' in the 1920s through Antoine Blondin's 'giants of the road' in the 1960s, today it offers three weeks of real drama.

Georges Vigarello's founding text[2] on the history of the race shows clearly that its introduction into the world of cycling and its inscription into the national collective memory came about not only because of its systematic exploration of the resources of the whole of the national territory, its plains and its mountains, but also because of the race's duration and length necessary to fulfil its objective of covering the national space and its range of summer climatic conditions, scorching heat and the rain and cold of climbs. Riders repeat their efforts every day, employing different types of effort, testing the body in different ways: short-lived effort to gain time in a stage; solitary efforts in time trials; falls caused by the bunching of riders in the peloton, the vagaries of the road surface, and by sudden accelerations, etcetera. The Tour de France involves a permanent mobilization of the riders, of their body and mind.

> The riders reckon that a good Tour takes one year off your life, and when you finish in a bad state, they reckon three years … You can't describe to a normal person how tired you feel … In 1987, when I finished in a really bad way it took until the end of November to recover; by that I mean until I could wake up and not feel tired as if I had already done a day's work.
>
> The fatigue starts to kick in on the Tour after ten days if you're in good shape, and after five days if you're not in your best condition physically. Then, it all just gets worse and worse, you don't sleep so much, so you don't recover as well from the day's racing, so you go into your reserves, you get more knackered, so you sleep less … It's simply a vicious circle.
>
> The best way of describing how you feel is that it's as if you were a normal person doing a hard day's work, you've got flu, and you can just about drive home and fall into bed. By the end of the Tour, you need sleeping tablets.
>
> You can't divide the mental and the physical suffering; you tend to let go mentally before you crack physically…

Riding up one of the mountains in the Tour if you're feeling bad is like being sick. Physically, your body has a limit every day, there's only a set speed you can go at and it might not always be enough. The pain in your legs is not the kind of pain you get when you cut yourself, it's fatigue, and it's self-imposed...

It takes two weeks to recover from a good Tour, three months to recover from a bad one.[3]

This account by Robert Millar, the Scottish professional, echoes all those descriptions by riders of their experience of the event. We have, here, to imagine the notion of mental strength, both the moral strength to finish the event, but also the moral qualities that a rider needs to bring to bear to live up to the expectations of organizers, media and public. This is because the accumulation of difficulties, whether unavoidable, like the necessary transfers from one place to the next, or deliberately calculated, in order to make the event more spectacular, produce the heroic nature necessary to the popularity of the Tour. And its more or less instantaneous commercial success has long been an attraction to champions, thus structuring competition between riders and generating increasing challenges and exploits. It is a confrontation with other competitors, but also with the public who expect riders to show the moral qualities of effort, hard work and solidarity, but also those of unselfishness and 'class'. Moreover, as an object of media coverage from its beginnings, the Tour de France cannot avoid seeing an increase in the demands on competitors with the ever-growing importance of television, whose systematic coverage of every stage has also brought in, on top of the necessary battle for the stage win, the necessary battle for permanent presence in front of the TV cameras, therefore making races ever faster.

A HISTORY OF DOPING IN THE TOUR DE FRANCE

The long-standing presence of doping in the Tour brings us back to the excessive nature of the race. Cycling was one of the first professional sports and the exploits of track racers, notably competitors in the Six Day events, and of the first competitors in the early 'classics', excited the interest of journalists curious to know how they could manage these exhausting events and wanting to understand their mysterious entourage of *soigneurs*, *masseurs* and miracle-worker doctors.

There are good reasons to believe that competitors in the early Tours used what track-racers used. The confessions of the Pélissier brothers to the great investigative journalist Albert Londres (see also Chapter 4 above) may be considered as the first doping *affaire*. The scene took place on the evening of a Tour stage in Coutances on 27 June 1924:

> 'You have no idea what the Tour de France is like,' said Henri. 'It's a Calvary. But Christ had only 14 stations of the cross. We have 15. We suffer from start to finish. Do you want to see what we run on? Look.' From his bag he took out a phial: 'That's cocaine for the eyes, that's chloroform for the gums.' 'That,' said Ville, also emptying his *musette*, 'is a cream to warm up my knees.' 'And the pills, do you want to see the pills? Look, here are the pills.' They each took out three boxes. 'In short,' said Francis, 'we run on "dynamite".'

This scene, which has been replayed hundreds of times since, was first recounted in *Le Petit Parisien*. It is the scene that popularized the image of 'the convict-labourers of the road', of the Tour de France riders seen as workers who have to use whatever is in their power to complete their task. But is it a doping issue? Probably not, since the point was not, either for the journalist or for the riders, to denounce an illicit practice, but to show how cycle racers were exploited by organizers who not only impose on them terrible workloads, but who also make the racers submit to harassing controls over their clothes and their attitude during the race. The Pélissier brothers were in fact making revelations about their working conditions and about Henri Desgrange's authoritarianism. But this example also has the virtue of relating the issue of doping to that of the respect afforded to the riders: going through cases looking for doping products or monitoring modes of dress come from the same spirit of wanting to control everything and are always bound to be received with hostility as an intrusion. This points us in the direction of understanding a difficulty in anti-doping policies, which, to the world of cycling, look like constraints on workers' freedoms.

Other incidents followed, more explicitly linked to the doping issue. First, in 1955, Jean Malléjac, a good Tour rider, fainted during the climb of the Mont Ventoux. There were fears for his life and the rider only came to some 15 minutes later. He was delirious in the ambulance. Other well-known riders like Ferdi Kubler or Charly Gaul fell victim to huge weaknesses in the same stage. The new Tour doctor, Dr Dumas, encouraged the organizers to make an official complaint; cases of riders and *soigneurs* were searched, and one of the latter was excluded from the race.

But the most dramatic incident was of course the death of Tom Simpson on 13 July 1967, when he collapsed on the slopes of the Mont Ventoux. Despite the efforts of Dr Dumas, still Tour doctor and an activist in the fight against doping, Simpson could not be saved. The Tour doctor refused permission for burial and the autopsy was to reveal traces of amphetamines that, while no doubt not the direct cause of the British rider's death, nevertheless led him to go beyond his limits. What interpretation can be put on these cases? They have been seen as accidents by numerous followers of the Tour, whereas other close observers have interpreted them as the most dramatic examples of common practices.

A study by Dr de Mondenard reported in *Le Nouvel Observateur* and *Le Monde* has presented elements that allow us to judge the scale of the problem.[4] First of all he recalls the list of riders who have tested positive since 1966, the first year anti-doping tests were carried out in the Tour de France. Among them were former or future winners, such as Zoetemelk, who tested positive in 1977 and won the Tour in 1980, Gimondi, winner in 1965, who tested positive in 1975, and more recently Delgado, winner in 1988, who tested positive the same year on the thirteenth stage, but who was in the end declared winner on procedural grounds and after political pressures. On the list too were recognized top racers, stage winners or winners of the points classification, such as Pollentier, Altig, Guimard and Bellone. In particular, on the basis of a study of 667 former competitors in the Tour de France, Mondenard upheld the thesis that riders have a higher mortality rate than average, especially those whose career came after 1961, whom he called 'modern' riders.

Thus he showed that the longevity of 'modern' riders is lower than 'old' riders: 85 per cent were still alive at 60, compared to 93 per cent of their predecessors. He cited the early deaths of Rivière, Coppi, Nencini, Bobet, Anquetil and Oosterboch, from cancer or cardio-vascular illnesses, but also the fatal road accidents of Robic and Koblet, and the suicide of Luis Ocaña, which he argues may be understood as effects of psychological disturbances, such as less good perception of risks while driving, or, in the case of Luis Ocaña, as a solution to suffering caused by the consequences of absorption of doping products. He could also have referred, in the same vein, to the mental troubles of riders such as Freddy Maertens or Henk Lubberding and the difficulties they had reintegrating into society at the end of their careers. One may also recall how the Dutch PDM team dropped out of the 1991 Tour de France when their riders were supposed to have fallen victim to food poisoning. Starting from the comments of Jacques Anquetil, who justified his own consumption of doping substances as necessary in order to do his job, without ever having tested positive during a Tour, many others have come under suspicion, from Laurent Fignon and Stephen Roche to Bjarne Riis; the Italian Marco Pantani celebrated victory in 1998, but was excluded from the Giro, the Tour of Italy, in 1999 with a red-blood-cell count of more than 50 per cent. The same year the American, Lance Armstrong, won the Tour, but the victory of a champion who had suffered from cancer in 1996 was bound to raise suspicions. In 2000, the American repeated his success, while the Frenchman Richard Virenque admitted taking drugs during the Festina trial. The greatest cycle race in the world is an event where victory is increasingly accompanied by doubts over the conditions under which it has been achieved.

THE TRANSFORMATIONS OF DOPING

A history of its products and mode of organization of the Tour de France can stand in parallel with this chronicle of cases of doping. The different authors[5] previously mentioned agree on how doping products have evolved and how they have been extended to different sports. At all events, cycling was one of the first involved. There was the period of consumption of stimulants and pain-killers during the first century of the history of sport from 1850 to the 1960s. These products have not disappeared and are present in the form of anti-asthmatic treatments, for example, which are over-consumed by riders, but taking over from them we find cortisones and especially EPO (erythropoietin) in the 1990s.

The introduction of this product leads us to pull on the thread of the history of the organization of doping. It is tempting to contrast two periods in the history of doping in sport. The first relates to the 'home-made' stage where doping is the equivalent of kitchen recipes that are transmitted from rider to rider, and from *soigneur* to rider, a period of experimentation rather than setting up systematic programmes. In a period when rules were vague concerning doping, that is up to the 1960s, this kind of doping did not necessarily appear as a problem for competitors or sports organizations: it may be imagined that everybody saw themselves on an equal footing with each other. The second period corresponds to a more rational stage – the model being the systematic doping practised in East Germany or in the USSR: within the framework of a sports programme, the latest advancements of science were applied to the preparation of sportsmen and women.

Doctors became involved in sport at an early stage, but initially from a health perspective or because champions were seen as marvels who should be studied and who did not need to be improved. The reversal of curiosity towards applied research came about more or less everywhere in the 1960s. The problematizing of doping may be seen as part of the long process of civilization of behaviour that manifested itself in the medicalization of western societies.[6] Health values underpin the medicalization of society and encourage doping along the lines of the equation: a problem = a product. One of the consequences of this change was of course the medicalization of sport, where the sports doctor tended to act as an agent for a club or a team. The doctor therefore became part of a rationale of rapid recovery and of support for the performance potential of the sports entity for which he was acting.

Sports medicine of the 1960s saw the emergence of a new type of individual, 'the trained athlete', different psychologically and physiologically from the man in the street. There also developed medical routines specific to the sports person, with specific treatments for specific injuries, but also specific care for preparation. This went hand in hand with the development of medical staff as a necessary condition of sports preparation: bio-mechanics for exercises and massages; nutritional scientists for vitamins and complements; psychologists for personal discipline and meditation; pharmacologists for the use of different medicines available on the market. This rationale could also come to encompass non-medical uses of medicines such as steroids, analgesics, stimulants or tranquillisers. Good reasons for taking drugs are therefore contained in the properties of different products that can be listed according to their relationship to competition, but also to the organization of training. Cyclists did what everyone else did, they sought shortcuts to manage the different difficulties of a life in sport.

In cycling this type of organization appears to have developed in the 1980s, and the Tour de France, because of its physical demands and its rules (anti-doping tests), no doubt became especially affected by this.

The current sophistication of doping (the complexity of programmes, of the doping calendar in relation to detection, the value of the newest molecule in a world where the difference between winning and losing is minuscule) gives weight to the hypothesis of a constant coming together of innovators and entrepreneurs from the worlds of sport and medicine. This is the case of Dr Ferrari and Dr Belloc who we come across in all the doping affairs concerning Italian cycling teams or in the entourage of various champions.

The problem that is no doubt specific to cycling is the coexistence/competition between doctors and self-appointed specialists like 'Dr' Sainz and more generally *soigneurs* who have come up through the ranks as shown by the table of 'qualifications' of cycling *soigneurs* implicated in doping *affaires* (from the former cyclist to the driver, and from the shopkeeper to the pharmacy assistant).[7] For Waddington[8] contemporary doping may be seen as the meeting between two rationales, the development of sports medicine and demand from athletes through the innovative or entrepreneurial elements from both worlds. That is what happened, notably, in some Italian cycling teams from the end of the 1980s: it was no longer individuals resorting to 'tricks of the trade', but companies getting organized in order to dominate collectively. Thus, in 1998, Willy Voet, the Festina team's *soigneur*, was intercepted by the French Customs and found to be in possession of 500 doses of doping products, including EPO and growth hormones. This was the start of the Festina *affaire*. Bruno Roussel, the team's sporting director, admitted that his riders were taking drugs under medical supervision that he had personally organized, and he presented himself as the organizer of a system of a rational use of doping, claiming in this way to be following a strategy of risk reduction.[9]

The team was thereupon excluded from the Tour by the director of the Société du Tour de France, Jean-Marie Leblanc, and the rooms occupied by the Dutch team TVM were searched by the police, which led to its withdrawal from the event, along with the Spanish teams who abandoned out of solidarity. The trial and the enquiries brought to light the system that, it is thought, is the one adopted by cycling teams in general. The Festina *affaire*, in the 1998 Tour, has taken on the status of inaugural moment of what appears to be a new attitude towards doping.

THE TOUR BECOMES AN *AFFAIRE*

Having appeared as a witness in the affair on 30 October 2000, Hein Verbruggen, President of the UCI (International Cycling Union), declared on leaving the court that his 'conscience was clear'. But how can he justify the fact that, while he knew about the circulation of EPO in the peloton as early as 1990, he did not encourage testing for it until 1995? And the fact that, for five years, the sums of money allocated by the UCI to anti-doping measures were only raised to 1.8 million francs [£180,000] out of a budget, over the same period, of 250 million francs [£25 million]? The discredit that fell on the ICU President stained the whole of cycling. On 9 December 2000, Daniel Baal, President of the French Cycling Federation, announced he would not be standing for re-election, officially for reasons of 'unavailability'. His retirement, as someone who had made the fight against doping his priority, was certainly not good news for the sport of cycling.[10]

The above may be read as a summary of the Festina *affaire*, posing the question of the delays by the sports governing bodies in implementing a real fight against doping and, in a country like France, of the part played by the State in this issue.

Despite the commotion caused by various revelations such as those cited above by Albert Londres on the 1924 Tour de France, notwithstanding the efforts of Dr Dumas, who had treated Malléjac in the 1955 Tour, the impression may be formed that nothing happened before the 1998 Tour. How can this periodization be explained? No doubt because the problems posed by the struggle against doping, which have yet to be overcome, reflect the relations between the different levels of the organization of sport: its international nature and at the same time the existence of national sovereignties; the conflictual relations between international federations and the IOC (International Olympic Committee); the demands for independence by the different national federations, not to mention the reticence of the sporting world to talk openly and publicly about its internal difficulties. There are similarly different levels at which we see expressed rivalries over control of sports policy between states wishing to intervene and the world of sport. There are also those conflicts that inevitably occur between internal sports governance and civil justice. In this way the three themes that define anti-doping policy are all areas of conflict: the list of prohibited substances and practices (there is no agreement between the sports governing bodies, the federations); the principles of testing (who carries out the tests? what means do laboratories have at their disposal? what are the officially agreed procedures?); the regime of sanctions, their nature, their duration and who carries the blame (the athletes, the federations, or the suppliers?).

In fact, a law was passed by the French parliament in 1965 that may be seen as the result of the earliest organized struggle against doping. Indeed, after his first experience of the effects of doping on a cyclist, the Tour doctor had shared his ideas with the French Medical Association for Physical Education and Sport. He recommended that the federations as a whole explicitly condemn doping, that they each appoint a doctor to their governing body, that they require their coaches and trainers to follow medical, pharmaceutical and dietary training courses, and that they educate their athletes about the dangers of doping. The *L'Equipe* journalist reporting these comments concluded: 'Let us hope that, now the impetus has been given, the struggle against this scourge will be pursued in an increasingly concrete fashion.'[11] For at the same time as medicalization supports the search for a product corresponding to a given problem or allows the emergence of performance medicine, it also allows the questioning of practices that would not be healthy or ethical, such as doping, which can then be denounced. Whether this double movement is seen as an effect of the contradictions inherent in medicine or as a strategy to assert authority over a given field of activity, a change did happen in the 1960s when the world of medicine began to criticize doping.

Sports governing bodies did begin to express their concerns about doping, for example on the occasion of the Rome Olympics in 1960. Sports medicine conferences were devoted to doping, and in particular there was a European colloquium held at Uriage (Isère) in January 1963, on the initiative of the same Dr Dumas, where the first definition of 'le doping' was proposed (the English term was still used in France at the time): 'doping is defined as the use of substances or of all means designed to artificially enhance performance, in preparation for or on the occasion of competition, and which can prejudice sports ethics and the physical and mental integrity of the athlete'. At this time, early in the 1960s, the Council of Europe also proposed a definition that it hoped would be valid for all European countries. The IOC voted a resolution against doping in 1962 and set up a Medical Committee in 1967 to develop a strategy against doping, and notably to establish a regularly updated list of banned products. Similarly, in 1967 the UCI established its own list of banned products and set up monitoring mechanisms, which was followed by different national federations. But already part of the problem had become visible: the federations' list and that of the IOC can differ, thus opening the way to procedural battles. In this way, when in 1988 the Spaniard Pedro Delgado tested positive for probenecide (a masking agent for anabolic steroids) his victory in the Tour de France was not challenged because the product, while banned by the IOC, was not yet on the UCI's banned list.

One of the results of this regulatory activity was the adoption in France of its first anti-doping law, called the *loi Herzog*,[12] in 1965. The implementation of a national sports policy after the failure of French athletes in the Rome Olympics of 1960 and the rising suspicions concerning doping among athletes from the sporting superpowers, are sports-related reasons that may explain why doping was highlighted in France at this time and led to the 1965 law. In addition to concerns that France had to compete on equal terms with Eastern bloc countries, there was the health side of the issue which came along with the extension of the Welfare State, worries about the scourges affecting (or which might affect) young people, worries that could win general support, just as did the idea that sport was a fundamental educational tool, or indeed the action of doctors asserting their position within sport.[13]

However, this law was never really applied. Why not? Promoted in the name of defending sporting ethics, the content of the law was based on the defence of athletes' health. It set out criminal penalties for anyone, during a sports competition, knowingly using substances that artificially increase their physical capacities and endanger their health. For sportsmen and women the penalties were fines; for those supplying or encouraging doping, the penalty was imprisonment. To these criminal penalties could be added sporting sanctions such as bans from taking part in or organizing competitions. But the frontier between sports authorities and police authorities was not clearly defined. Penalizing cheating, that is measuring the damage done to sporting ethics, should be up to the different federations. Matter relating to health or trafficking should be the responsibility of the State. The 1965 law gave the State the power to punish, no doubt because it was felt that the process needed to be kick-started, but the judges did not appear well placed to judge offences that were too specific: why condemn sports people for consuming products that were quite legal elsewhere? One of the most spectacular difficulties of applying the law concerned appeals to civil courts against decisions made by sports bodies. The latter lost highly publicized cases where athletes condemned for doping obtained decisions from civil courts finding federations at fault on procedural technicalities, or guilty of infringements of personal freedoms or of employment law, or by throwing scientific doubt on the term doping being applied to their case.

Thus, when the Public Prosecutor asked the presiding judge in the Lille magistrates court in November 2000 to drop the case against Richard Virenque in the Festina *affaire*, he felt that Virenque as a citizen had done nothing wrong as regards French law, whereas Virenque the rider had just come round to admitting that he had been taking doping products, that he had cheated in practising his sport, having declared, like others before him, that he had been 'doped unbeknownst to his wishes'.[14]

So the Buffet law of 1999 did not change the situation very much, even though, if we look at it from the rationale of the balance between prevention and repression, it has considerably developed the health axis (creation of medical centres, regular monitoring over time) and has created, in the form of a *Conseil de Prévention et de la Lutte contre le Dopage* (Council for the Prevention and Fight against Doping), an independent administrative authority to centralize all data concerning doping, which can also make recommendations to sports federations or indeed require them to take measures. Indeed, knowing how the Festina affaire was triggered during the 1998 Tour (the actions of Customs and police seizing doping substances and the charges that followed),[15] it would seem that the way to make everyone face up to their responsibilities was by a *coup de force* and the creation of an *affaire* obliging people to break the law of silence. The arrival of a new Minister for Youth and Sport, Marie-George Buffet, less sensitive than other Sports Ministers to the priority given to elite sport, no doubt for ideological reasons (she is a member of the Communist Party), and hardly minded to do favours for the Amaury Group as organizer of the Tour de France because of conflicts between this press group and the publishing union and the Communist Party, allowed these unceremonious, strong-arm tactics and the triggering of the *affaire*.

WHY TURN THE TOUR INTO AN *AFFAIRE*?

So, whereas doping was not a new phenomenon in cycling, the law of *omertà* governing the peloton was lifted only through the intervention of the police and the courts. One of sport's challenges is indeed to be able to control doping and all forms of deviance that comes from unreflecting socialization into the values of sport and competition. But the problem posed is precisely that of sport's ability to enforce respect of its own rules. For, if sport has gradually won its own autonomy and the freedom to run its affairs in its own way free from outside interference, nearly two centuries later the issue is less about guaranteeing its autonomy against its opponents, but preventing its uncontrolled and limitless development.

The reason is that sports authorities have too much difficulty in protecting the monopoly of legitimately defining sport when, firstly, professionalism and, secondly, media involvement are bringing in new stakes (for sports people, earning their living) or new definitions (from the public of cognoscenti to the general public who want entertainment and spectacle). In sport today, the power to give awards or distribute sanctions is moving away from the federations and going to events organizers and the courts, and the various protagonists are seeking to assert their own interests: players and athletes are seeking glory and are pursuing their own financial interests; medical companies want to offer more and more treatment; journalists want news and want to create events; judicial authorities want to enforce respect for the law, and so on.

The Festina trial has shown that sports organizations have long facilitated doping practices, across the board, as, earlier, did the Dubin Report on Ben Johnson or the Delgado affair when the decision not to exclude the Spanish rider was taken under joint pressure from the President of the UCI, Mr Puig, and the Spanish government.[16] Some people stress rising economic and commercial stakes to explain the difficulties of combating doping: but it is just as much in the interests of the UCI and the Société du Tour de France to develop an anti-doping policy, to defend sporting ethics and to avoid losing sponsorship, as to cover up cases of doping for the same reasons.[17] For Georges Vigarello,[18] it is sport's claim to make itself into a virtuous 'alternative society' that is preventing it from recognizing the problem.

This alternative society of sport defines its purity by setting up boundaries: in the past, it was professionalism and money, today it is doping. However, this frontier is difficult to draw, because the criteria that allow doping to be defined are eminently debatable: take, for example, the definition of doping as recourse to artificial means to gain an unfair advantage – what is that worth when the whole of sport is based on the exploitation of increasingly sophisticated technology? How can it be recognized that doping may be a consequence of competitive sport when sport is defined as a virtuous world *par excellence*? Hence, the fact that you can only run 'trials for witchcraft' and that it is impossible to get the 'guilty' to admit their guilt. However, morality – right and wrong – is not enough to combat the problem, as doping is a health issue, since doping has been medicalized, and it is a public health issue, because the phenomenon has gone wider than elite sport. And it is a criminal issue because of the existence of large-scale organized trafficking. Public intervention is therefore necessary since health and the resources that need to be devoted to it are at stake, and because the independence of the regulator, the sports federations, is not guaranteed.

The present context is one of a crisis of legitimacy of sporting institutions, marked by the move from a unified sporting ethic to a pluralization of norms defining what is a sports person's identity and what is legitimate behaviour. Doping is one example of this. Sport is under suspicion because of the limits of dope testing or the limits of surveys and research that find it hard to quantify and describe the phenomenon. This situation is producing a theatrical model of doping affairs[18] in which the people carrying out the study (usually journalists) hunt for evidence to interest the public, while the accused seek to save their sporting reputations. Signs are looked for, such as gaining a few pounds, physical changes, links between sports people and people of dubious reputation, unexplained performances. In the meantime, the guilty, according to the degree of guilt admitted, deploy defensive strategies that deflect the accusations onto others (they deny it and cast doubt on others and their doubtful performances or on their envy or jealousy), they present themselves as persecuted, push the accusation onto a third party (a dishonest trainer), play down the seriousness of the phenomenon ('everybody does it'), turn the stigma round into a sacrifice they willingly accept as the price of the grandeur of the sport, or, finally, convert to the moral struggle against doping. Other writers[20] have identified further ways of legitimizing attitudes in defence of doping or a desire not to bring out doping affairs into public view: the defence of a total engagement with sport, loyalty to the family of sport, the defence of transparency and truth, virile conduct able to resist pressure from the press or the police, and respect for one's employer. This explains why Virenque, like Anquetil before him, remains a hero.

The first dope-tests were carried out in 1966 and they triggered a riders' strike, just as in 1998 the searches triggered protests. Jacques Anquetil, in a series of interviews in 1967,[21] declared that 'the anti-doping law is idiotic', adding: 'Yes, I have taken doping products.' Similarly, two years before his death, Tom Simpson had said in *The People* that he used doping in order to do his job. And as a defence of Richard Virenque and the other cyclists in the Festina *affaire*, the question is asked how they can do their job without resorting to doping.

Doping has long been seen as legitimate among cyclists, because of the nature of the job and the thin line between treatment and doping. The development of doping can therefore be analysed in relation to a physically demanding sport like cycling,[22] which is also a sport that has been professional for a long time. It has therefore become familiar with competition on the labour market, the volume of work involved (as we have seen), and the system of constraints that surround the cyclist (staying in the peloton in order to build a career and accepting the rules of the world of cycle racing).[23] The meeting of innovators and entrepreneurs was made possible by the increase in competition, which produced the emergence of specialists and professionals devoting their time to sporting activity and its preparation. The possibility of generalised competition, of professionalism (meaning paid work) and the rise in various economic stakes, produced a system of increasingly high rewards for winners or appearance bonuses for well-known riders, in addition to income from sponsorship and television. All this created more and more reasons for not wanting to come second.

Doping appeared as a means of overcoming the pain that a professional needed to endure to win. It was therefore another performance material that allowed the rider to cope with the pressures and demands produced by the internal logic of performance. It was also an aspect of the new culture of sensation, based on the general acceptance of the idea of the unlimited possibilities of an infinitely malleable body. The body came to be seen as a tool of the trade, and suffering, a part of the physical experience of the cyclist who rides for a living. Thus doping, or treatment, appeared a legitimate means to do it as well as possible for as long as possible. The Tour de France racer was a worker managing the length of his career, the intensity of his work, his injuries and his stress, using the means at his disposal.

In this framework, riders who use doping are not bad or corrupt elements, but are individuals exposed to the contradiction between the requirements imposed on them and the use of illicit means to achieve them. The sportsman using doping belongs to the category of innovative deviant who accepts the general aims but rejects the legal means in favour of illegal means. But he is not alone since this behaviour is learned, through interaction with other people from whom rudimentary or sophisticated techniques are discovered, and where riders become skilled at rationalizing their behaviour in the face of judgements from the outside. Thus, doping is the result of co-operation not only between cyclists but also doctors and trainers, and has produced a cycling sub-culture in which recourse to different types of 'treatments' is legitimate.[24]

This sub-culture is formed in the interplay between internal constraints, that is internalizing sporting norms, and external constraints, in other words the action of organizations to enforce respect of the rules. And it is the weakness of these external constraints (tolerance of doping and/or lack of credibility of the tests and sanctions) that can explain the greater development of doping in cycling than elsewhere, along with the difficulty society has had in recognizing doping and its quasi-legitimation through the place occupied by medicine and the emergence of sports medicine. These two factors come together to confuse the line between treatment and doping. These are modes of legitimization of doping in so far as they give the possibility of rationalizing its use by the manner of winning, by the service given to the team or the nation. Furthermore, with the increasing condemnation of doping, this social group has to defend itself against people from the outside who do not know the rules of the game, and has to be able to keep the secret, since outsiders do not know how hard a rider has to work just to stay in the race.

Cyclists know that riding a Tour de France is not good for their health; they know too that opponents use doping products, and they also know that so do people who do not take part in sports competitions. They think that the constant marketing of new substances for performance or treatment (whether Viagra or Prozac or any other medicine) makes using these substances normal. These automatic reactions, and the feeling of being individuals outside the mainstream, allow them to think that the desire to play the game, to stay in the peloton, is stronger than the desire to win and make money. Even those who have no chance of winning the Tour want to stay in the game and respect the norms of the performance ethic and of the peloton. This desire supports the law of silence that protects the group against accusations from the outside and makes it reject people who, like Gilles Delion or Christophe Basson, want to promote the idea of dope-free cycling: Basson was driven to drop out of the 1999 Tour. The law of silence is reinforced and protected by the incredulity of admiring spectators who reject accusations of doping like any other accusation that highlights riders' deviance.

THE TOUR DE FRANCE IN POPULAR CULTURE

The public believes, so we learn from opinion polls, that cycling is the sport most affected by doping, but it is estimated that a third of people understand and accept this phenomenon. In spite of the revelations and the dramas, the public remains loyal, on the roads and in front of the TV screens. Is the public a victim of the media? Do they refuse to believe because they want to be entertained? Perhaps there exists a strong link between cycling culture and popular culture. Cycling, as one of the most popular sports in France, is a model of individual advancement, at the same time as it offers a reading of how to achieve this advancement. When you are small, when you come from the bottom of society, you understand cheating, just as you admire the physical courage or the grace of an Anquetil surpassing himself at critical moments.

Faced with the uncertainty of definitions, members of the public balance their attitude in the same way as sports philosophers. Why should doping be banned or combated? Because there is a counterpart of sports justice and the breaking of the rules of fair play: the doped rider is giving himself an unfair advantage in a world based on the principle of organizing fair competition. Also, resorting to doping is expensive and so can bring in a difference between those who can afford the products and those who can't. The latter are also likely to be the ones who would not be able to benefit from medical help to control the effects of the product. This point opens up a series of arguments about doping damaging the health of those taking it in so far as the dangers of these products are too well known or, conversely, their precise effects on the body are not known.

Recourse to doping products thus implicates the integrity of anyone who ingests foreign substances into his own body that will make his body function beyond its natural aptitudes: doping is therefore the artifice that goes against the principle of using natural abilities. As an attack on the physical integrity of the individual, it is also morally reprehensible because it seems a form of coercion: the athlete who wishes to remain faithful to sporting ethics, but who wants to regain the equality he has lost, has a different set of rules imposed upon him by those who use doping, without taking into account that coercion can also be exercised by members of his entourage. Furthermore, doping, since it is seen as cheating, damages the image of the sports player and of sport in general as a model for the education of young people or as a means of integration that can be held up as a model.

However, these arguments come under criticism when the boundary between drugs and doping is questioned: one might ask in what way is cannabis a doping product? Or, regarding the boundary between doping and treatment, why is Ventolin, a medical treatment for asthma, banned for sports people? Additionally, it might easily be thought that doping is not just about improvement of performance, but it could also be about restoring the sports person's health. Furthermore, pointing the finger at doping as a danger to health is challenged because of the lack of knowledge of the real effects of products, and, indeed, if the issue was about damaging sports people's health, then elite sport as a whole would have to be questioned. And it is looking at elite sport that highlights the debatable arguments of the defenders of natural sport or fair sport. Indeed, elite sport is based on all sorts of artificial aids to enhance performance or improve the comfort of athletes: fibreglass poles, track surfaces, dérailleur gears and training. So why exclude the artificial aid of doping? All the more so because there are techniques considered as doping which are based on the use of natural products such as testosterone, or blood transfusion techniques, including transfusions of an athlete's own blood. In fact, condemning doping as an artificial aid is, in the end, challenging a fundamental principle of sport, one which attaches it to modernity, namely its relation to the idea of human progress. And what becomes clear when thinking this way, and what we know to be true, is that cycling, especially the Tour de France, is the hardest of sports.

NOTES

1. The French language distinguishes between terms for doping in sport ('le dopage', 'se doper') and words to do with drug-taking ('la drogue', 'un drogué', 'le stupéfiant', 'la toxicomanie'). The English translation follows the author in retaining this distinction.
2. G. Vigarello, 'Le Tour de France', in P. Nora (ed.), *Les Lieux de mémoire, III* (Paris: Gallimard, 1997).
3. Interview with Robert Millar, *Guardian*, 31 July 1998, cited by Ivan Waddington, in *Sport, Health and Drugs: A Critical Sociological Perspective* (London: Spon Press, 2000), p.161.
4. See J.-P. de Mondenard, *Dopage: l'imposture des performances* (Paris: Chiron, 2000); 'Quand le sport tue', *Le Nouvel Observateur*, 19 Nov. 1998; and 'L'aveu', *Le Monde 2*, Oct. 2000, n°1.
5. Waddington, *Sport, Health and Drugs*; de Mondenard, *Dopage*.
6. See Waddington, *Sport, Health and Drugs*, pp.114–34.
7. See de Mondenard, *Dopage*, pp.191–3.
8. Waddington, *Sport, Health and Drugs*.
9. See, on the affaire Festina, in English, Waddington, *Sport, Health and Drugs*, pp.153–69, or, in French, Fabrice Lhomme, *Le Procès du Tour: Dopage, les secrets de l'enquête* (Paris: Denoël, 2000).
10. Entry on 'Le cyclisme' in *Encyclopedia Universalis* (Paris: Encyclopaedia Universalis, 2001).
11. Reported by de Mondenard, *Dopage*, p.267.)
12. French laws are usually referred to by the name of the Minister proposing the bill to parliament, here the Sports Minister Maurice Herzog.
13. In O. Le Noé, 'Comment le dopage devint l'affaire des seuls sportifs', in La Fièvre du dopage, *Autrement*, 197, pp.77–91.
14. Virenque's tortuous phrase in French was that he had been 'dopé à l'insu de mon plein gré'.
15. For details see Lhomme, *Le Procès du Tour*.
16. See Paul Yonnet, *Systèmes des sports* (Paris: Gallimard, 2000), pp.155–220.
17. See the analyses of V. Simson and A. Jennings on the IOC, in *The Lords of the Rings: Power, Money and Drugs in the Modern Olympics* (New York: Simon and Schuster, 1992).
18. Georges Vigarello, 'Le sport dopé', *Esprit*, 1 (1999), pp.75–91.
19. Pascal Duret, 'Juger les pratiques sportives', *Esprit*, 1 (1999), pp.92–109.
20. Pascal Duret and Patrick Trabal, *Le sport et les affaires. Une sociologie de la justice de l'épreuve sportive* (Paris: Métailié, 2000).
21. *France-Dimanche*, nos. 1089 to 1092, July 1967.
22. Christophe Brissonneau, 'A chaque sport sa formule magique', in La Fièvre du dopage, *Autrement*, 197 (2000), pp.109–119.
23. Jacques Calvet, *Le Mythe des géants de la route* (Grenoble: PUG, 1981).
24. See texts on the sociology of deviance and its application to sport, for example, Jay Coakley, 'Deviance in Sports: Is it out of Control?', in *Sport in Society. Issues and Controversies* (Boston: McGraw Hill, 2001).

A côté du Tour: Ambushing the Tour for Political and Social Causes

JEAN-FRANÇOIS POLO

On 7 July 1982 a stage of the Tour was halted by the steelworkers of the Usinor company protesting against the closure of their factory. On 5 July 1988 the passage of the Tour caravan through the toll barriers of the Loire bridge was impeded by workers from the Saint-Nazaire shipyards demonstrating in support of increased wages. On 3 July 1990 sheep farmers erected barricades on the route of the Tour in order to protest against falling prices for lamb.

INTRODUCTION

For some 20 years – in the wake of increased media coverage of the race – the Tour de France has become the scene of a range of interventions varying from the unfurling of banners to attempts to interrupt stages.

The Tour de France holds a special place amongst French sporting competitions. More than simply a bicycle race, the Tour is a reflection of the France through which it moves, passing along roads and through regions and towns. The Tour attracts to its roadside hundreds of thousands of spectators and its television coverage is watched by millions of viewers. The Tour's mediatization – which has contributed and will continue to contribute to its success – has also proven to be a notable platform for statements from individuals or more or less well organized groups intended to publicize their social or political concerns.[1]

This chapter will investigate the uses of the Tour as a platform for the expression of grievances and the ways in which the Tour deals with them, in order to learn about the Tour's own meaning. In effect, studying the Tour in this way reveals how truly this sporting event belongs – socially and politically – to the French nation, and also how the Tour, embedded since its invention in 'popular' (or working-class) values, is at the same time the mirror of a 'national' France and its social and political agitations.

The study of the collective actions elicited by the Tour provides a new perspective on this sporting competition, and, we hope, facilitates a better understanding of its multiple sociological significance.[2] We shall firstly consider how and why the Tour de France has become the object of such activities, and secondly, the chapter will examine how the ways in which the Tour organizers deal with such incidents demonstrate the special nature of the Tour de France as a sporting competition uniquely contained within its political and social context.

A SPACE FOR PROTESTS ON A NATIONAL SCALE

The reasons which lead groups within French society to exploit the Tour de France for the expression of social or political demands are mostly linked to the Tour's media coverage, but these reasons are also influenced by other processes connected to the national nature of the event, both in terms of geography and of culture and imagination. Through its location within a national space and through its embodiment of a 'popular' France, the Tour evokes both interest and respect.

Using the Tour as a Platform for Airing Grievances

The success of the Tour de France since its very invention is inextricably linked to its media coverage. Created in 1903 by the newspaper *L'Auto* in order to revive its sales, the race produced an increase in circulation figures and stifled competing papers. From a circulation of 20,000 in 1903, ten years later *L'Auto* was selling 120,000 copies, and during the month of July – during the Tour – its average print-run was 284,000 copies.[3] Nor was this media success lost with the appearance of radio and television reporting, since from the first radio coverage in 1929, the first live TV coverage in 1948 and then the live broadcasting of the final 30km of each stage in 1962,[4] and the current coverage of the concluding three hours of each day's racing, the Tour has become one of the most intensively followed sports competitions in France and in the world. This close link between the sporting competition and its representation in the media has only served to intensify the incredible popularity of the event.[5]

Public interest in the Tour and its broadcasting on TV has certainly been one of the factors that have attracted groups who want to use the Tour's media platform to get a political message across or to communicate a social demand. For those who demonstrate, 'the Tour allows demands to be passed on', and, if the message is taken up by the written press or by television, they consider this to be 'a good media coup'.[6] This strategy is an example of a new kind of 'répertoire d'action' ('repertoire of action'). The idea of repertoires of actions was invented by Tilly[7] in order to describe the existence of codified registers of action which groups 'choose within "repertoires" varying according to the period, and the place, according to the group involved, the benefits expected of the action, and also the attitude of the authorities and the organizations targeted towards these consecrated forms of collective action'.[8] Nowadays, access to the press seems generally to be one of the repertoires of action most sought after by demonstrators.

> In many fields, groups – trades unions, associations, etcetera – implement actions which aim to produce a 'press-review-effect', in other words to interest journalists. It is thus that it has been shown that the real place where thousands of people demonstrate is less the street than the press in the widest sense.[9] Alongside this traditional register within the repertory of actions intended to attract the interest of reporters, there are others which can be used by small groups (or even occasionally by individuals) as is shown by examples from the work of Greenpeace, Agir contre le chômage (Act against unemployment) or Droit au logement (Right to housing). The actions specifically designed to be taken up by the media are generally the occupation of somewhere, the disruption of the speech of someone known by the media, etc.[10]

The passing of the Tour close to people's workplaces therefore represents an opportunity for action, and can even encourage it: 'we had no particular intention of doing anything, but we said to ourselves that since the Tour was coming right past us, we should do something. And when the TV commentator said "and there are the supporters of José Bové" we'd got what we wanted.'[11]

Since the end of the 1970s, facilitated by France's economic and social crisis,[12] the Tour has been the target of many actions aiming to publicize grievances. The 1982 Tour, for example, was disturbed on a number of occasions by steelworkers whose industry was in much difficulty in France at this period.[13] During the third stage, after discussions with the race organizers, the Tour took a detour through the Longwy steelworks in order 'to hold up a mirror to the situation in this sector of industry'.[14]

As the peloton passed by, the striking workers handed out flyers while applauding the riders and wishing them 'Welcome'.[15] Two days later, the steelworkers at another works, Usinor, blocked the Tour's route at Denain, thereby leading the race organizers to cancel the fifth stage, the first time this had happened in the Tour's history.[16]

In this way, since the 1980s, the Tour is targeted almost every year by demonstrators. It is not easy to establish a list of these actions, because given that they do not all lead to an interruption of racing, the press does not always mention them. Moreover, the Tour organizers have put into place a number of procedures intended to nullify these undertakings, as we shall see later in the chapter. Relying on the recollections of organizers, reporters and riders for a list of these actions is problematic, since they mostly have imprecise – if not confused – memories of who, where and when people were demonstrating.[17]

The demonstrations are very diverse in nature, and therefore do not all have the same impact on the race. Displaying a banner or waving placards alongside the route or at the start or finish of a stage does not, for example, produce any major difficulty for the race. Nevertheless, other groups may be more determined to disrupt the smooth running of a stage by blocking the race route temporarily or by slowing the riders (for example, the Saint-Nazaire shipyard workers in 1988 and the farmers in 1992). More infrequently, more radical actions have been undertaken: for example in 1996, when demonstrators obstructed the route with felled trees and nails scattered on the road. Other demonstrators still have expressed their grievances through 'provocations', such as the Basque nationalists, who, pretending to be riders, managed to slip amongst the members of a breakaway group in a mountain stage in 2000.

These demonstrations are thus designed to draw the attention of the Government to the problems and difficulties of various groups and may well express anger or despair. Their frequency and their regularity – during the month of July – lend them a routine aspect. Thus, the various demonstrations to which the Tour has been subjected reflect the three categories of demonstration identified by P. Favre, namely: the initiating demonstration targeting the recognition of a grievance thus far unrealized; the crisis demonstration (for example, May 1968); the routine demonstration (trades union marches on 1 May).[18]

These groups choose the Tour – specifically – for their actions because of the ease with which it can be targeted. Taking place as it does over 3,500km of road, the Tour cannot be protected by its organizers over its entire route.[19] Moreover, the Tour is a free spectacle characterized by its closeness to a spectating public entitled to choose any location on any part of the route. Such demonstrations would be much more difficult to undertake in a stadium where entry is checked and where access to the field of play is restricted by fences and moats. Even if it is still possible to display a banner in a stadium, it is more difficult to stage a demonstration, unless it is a violent one.[20] Admittedly, all stadiums are not equipped with protective features, nor have rigorous entry controls, but whenever the sporting event that is taking place is of high media interest – and it is precisely this media coverage that is sought by demonstrators – such protective measures are implemented.

The press reports of these demonstrations vary according to the newspaper and to the ways in which groups intervene in the running of the Tour. Generally, reporters are sympathetic to the demonstrators, especially when their actions do not interfere with the race. When the demonstration is more radical – for example when the route is blocked – reactions can be sharper. The sports newspaper *L'Equipe* ran headlines after the cancellation of the stage on 7 July 1982 of 'The Tour taken hostage' and 'Usinor closes down the Tour'[21] and roundly condemned this kind of action, even if the editorial writers understood the despair that motivated the steelworkers (it should be remembered that this newspaper belongs to the Amaury Group which also owns the Tour de France). Covering the same incident, the Communist newspaper *L'Humanité* was more inclined towards generosity and reminded its readers of the difficult working conditions of the steelworkers.[22] Commenting on the interruption of a stage of the Tour by farmers in 1990, a *Le Monde* journalist adopted a more mocking style in referring to 'rural desperados'.[23] However, quieter protests scarcely give rise to even the shortest of articles in the following day's press.

A 'Popular' Representation of France

For Georges Vigarello, the Tour de France is a 'national institution'. The Tour lives with its times, 'reflects them, and in so doing, illustrates some of the significant changes in popular culture during the twentieth century'.[24] Philippe Gaboriau, for his part, considers that 'the principal quality of the Tour is that it is linked, more closely and more deeply than other sporting events, to its working-class origins. The Tour appears as a strong symbol of the popular cultures of our societies.'[25] The epic of the Tour de France thus writes a history with its own heroes and myths,[26] in resonance with the living conditions of the working classes. To a certain extent, demonstrations 'around the Tour' represent – through the diversity of the groups attempting to express their social and political grievances – the reflection of a 'mobilized working-class France'.

These demonstrations are principally led by professional associations or by trades unions. Many actions have been launched by workers' trades unions, like that of the steelworkers in northern France in 1982, the shipyard workers in Saint-Nazaire in 1988, or the cigarette-paper factory workers at Cintegabelle in 2001. It should be noted that these demonstrations are organized in collaboration by numbers of trades unions working together in a context of considerable weakness.[27] Within the context of economic crisis affecting France, of industrial restructuring and competition from the Far East, the Tour has appeared as the means of last resort for expressing deep social malaise.

The actions of the working class should also be linked to the place of the Tour, and more broadly, the place of the bicycle in the sporting practices and imagination of workers.[28] As Pierre Bourdieu has suggested: 'sport has all the greater chance of being adopted by the members of a given social class when it does not contradict an individual's relationship with his body in its deepest and most unconscious aspects, namely the bodily scheme in its role as repository of a whole social vision of the world, a whole philosophy of the individual and of the body.'[29] During the twentieth century, 'the bicycle becomes the first useful means of transport which allows people to distance themselves from the factory, brings the urban workers of office and factory in contact with the countryside and the *paysans* and agricultural labourers of the countryside in contact with the town. The bicycle opens the door on vacations and on the right to paid holidays.'[30]

The working-class dimension of the Tour de France even led – at the end of the Second World War and after the banning of *L'Auto* for its ambiguous attitudes during the Occupation[31] – the communist newspaper *L'Humanité* to demand the right to organize the race on the grounds that it belonged to 'national working-class heritage'. Criss-crossing the national territory and rural France, the Tour has also been the target of numerous actions undertaken by farmers and livestock breeders, notably during the Tours of 1982, 1990, 1991 and 1996.[32] Moreover, in 2002, within the context of anti-globalisation protests of recent years, new incidents were led by members of the Confédération paysanne in order to support their spokesman José Bové, who was embroiled in a number of

court cases.[33] At Alençon (the sixth stage) and at Lavelanet (the thirteenth
stage) banners were waved displaying slogans of solidarity with the
media-celebrity leader of the Confederation.

More infrequently, other professional groupings have sought to
exploit the passing through of the race to draw media attention to their
problems, for example, shopkeepers' trades unions (la Confédération de
Défense des Commerçants et Artisans in 1996), nurses' unions (2002) or
fire-fighters' unions (2000).[34]

Additionally, the Tour de France is – more marginally – the target of
agents belonging to what are called 'les nouveaux mouvements sociaux'
(new social movements) such as environmentalists and regionalists.[35] In
1989 (at La Bastide near Toulouse) and in 1997 (at La Chapelle-Bâton in
the Vienne department) environmentalists demonstrated along the
Tour's route. In this latter demonstration they worked together with an
association of locals unhappy with the creation of an underground store
of radioactive waste beneath their fields.[36] In 1992, the peloton's crossing
of the Parc de la Vanoise gave rise to unease and protest from the Rhône-
Alpes regional Nature Protection Federation concerning the
environmentally harmful effect of the passage of the advertising caravan
and the presence of thousands of spectators. It should be noted that this
is one of the rare cases where it was the Tour itself that was criticized.[37]

Demonstrations by regionalist movements mainly involve the Basque
independence activists in France and in the Spanish Basque country, for
instance, when the Tour visited the Basque areas in 1992 and 1996. On
the occasion of the Tour prologue in San Sebastian in Spain in 1992,
Basque nationalists demanded that the Basque language should be given
the status of official language of the race alongside French, and the Tour
organizers accepted the request.[38] French Basques have also produced
similar requests.

·These demands concerning regional identity have an even greater
resonance because of the Tour's own location within a conjugation of
local and regional territories where everyone finds personal memories,
family links or a corner of France that is known. Commentators of the
written, TV and radio press remind us that such-and-such a rider is 'the
regional rider of the day's stage'. TV coverage and shots from the air of
the Tour display a rural France, a France fixed by its historic
monuments[39] and the regional and local symbols embodied by
cathedrals, bridges and ports.

In contrast to what happens in other sports, demonstrations of
protest in the Tour are essentially the work of organized groups

expressing well-defined social and political grievances. The Tour de France is not affected by phenomena of social deviance such as hooliganism or excessive nationalistic fervour. There have admittedly been examples of stages – notably after the Second World War – when French supporters spat on and abused Italian riders such as Coppi and Bartali (1949 and 1950).[40] But since these events, no other incident of this nature has been noted to our knowledge. On the contrary, victories of non-French riders in recent years have been celebrated with enthusiasm and popular excitement, whereas other international sporting competitions – such as the 1996 Atlanta Olympics – have been criticized for involving unhealthy national chauvinism.[41]

Above and beyond their diversity, the different characteristics of the various exploitations of the Tour for media interest underline the Tour's image as a sporting event which is both rooted in a social world marked by the working class and a strong linkage to local identities.

A Popular Race which Demands Respect

Demonstrators who attempt to publicize their demands by intervening in the Tour de France mostly express a deep respect for the race and its riders. This is particularly true for protesters from working-class groups. The demonstrators from the Saint-Nazaire shipyards on 4 July 1988 intended that their protest would simply slow down the progress of the advertising caravan: 'it was important for us that our demonstration would not make the peloton stop'.[42] This concern derives from the strikers' sensitivity to the effort of the riders: 'The shipyard workers admire and respect the riders.' This respect is born of an identification on the part of the workers with the suffering of the riders and their strength of character and the demands of the race.[43]

The analogy with the workers' social condition is also to be seen in struggles against institutions and power – that of bosses as well as of the race organizers. The rider Lapize's exclamation of protest at the summit of a Pyrenean col in the 1910 Tour,[44] the withdrawal from the 1924 Tour of the Pélissier brothers in refusing to become 'forçats de la route'[45] have stayed in people's minds and laid the foundation stone of a legend of resistance. Similarly, the leaders of the workers' sports association, the FSGT (*Fédération sportive et gymnique du travail*, founded 1935), rejected 'the over-exploitation of competitors in the interest of show and commerce' and spoke of the 'Tour de (souf)France' (the Tour of suffering).[46] Likewise, in order not to equate the suffering of riders with that of workers, the reporter for *L'Humanité* covering the stage's passage through the Pompey steelworks wrote that the Tour 'has for a few wheel-lengths entered a world where sweat is of another nature, where, as in the race, giving up is not an option'.[47]

The origins of such respect for the race and riders is perhaps to be found in the working-class roots of the majority of competitors: Bernard Hinault, son of a Breton railway-worker; Louison Bobet, apprentice baker; Eddy Merckx, son of a Belgian grocer; Raymond Poulidor, *paysan* from the Creuse department.[48] For their part, the riders show a generous attitude towards the demonstrators, even though they are less indulgent concerning incidents that lead to the cancellation of stages. 'I'm sorry it happened, but I understand',[49] was the comment of Bernard Hinault after the blockage of the race by the steelworkers of Usinor.

Notwithstanding social and economic change over the years, the importance of the bicycle is still to be seen in discourses prevalent today. For the shipyard workers of Saint-Nazaire, respect for the race and for the riders is matched by that for cycling itself: 'you just have to see the number of bikes in the yard'.[50]

When strikers decide on more extensive action such as the interruption of the Tour, a sense of guilt is to be discerned in the justifications they provide. Thus for the trades-union official of the Usinor steelworks, the decision to disrupt the fifth stage at Fontaine-au-Pire on 7 July 1982 was not easy to make: 'Every year when the Tour goes nearby, the lads ask for an hour or two off so they can go and watch it. We love the Tour.'[51] But this area has 'the yellow jersey of unemployment [...] No-one pays any attention to us, and the passing of the Tour was a golden opportunity'. And, asking for public understanding: 'We know that what we've done is not popular. But what we're living through is too serious. The people of the Tour have got to try to understand.'

Awareness of the counterproductive unpopularity of actions against the Tour is clear in the minds of strikers and integrated into their strategies. For José Bové's supporters in 2002: 'we limited ourselves to showing banners and placards along the roadside because we knew that we couldn't do anything more without prejudicing our interests and image.'[52] Moreover, the Tour de France is perceived and lived as a popular festival during the summer period and holiday journeys. Even when they are legal and legitimate, uncontrolled actions against the Tour would spoil the delights and simple pleasures of the spectators.

Therefore, actions aiming at disturbing the race without any consideration for the riders have been infrequent. Actions that do not take the riders into consideration are typified by those which endanger the safety of the peloton. This was the case, for example, in 1996 when nails were strewn on the route of the Tour. In this particular case, the gendarmerie (rural police force) suspected the Confédération de défense des commerçants et des artisans (CDCA – a shopkeepers' and artisans' association of Poujadist leanings)[53] which engages in violent protest against compulsory social security contributions.

Demonstrations around the Tour de France thus assume different forms, but the desire to use the race as a media sounding-box is partnered by a respect for it as a sporting competition that demands admiration and that, because of its popularity, creates respect even amongst those whose aim is merely to use its media coverage.

MANAGING THE IMPACT OF PROTESTS

Confronted with the many attempts to use the Tour to assist the media coverage of social and political grievances, the organizers of the Tour de France have been obliged to deploy a whole range of strategies. An analysis of these strategies reveals a certain empathy between the Tour organization and the various demonstrating groups, but also a veritable mastery of the race and of its potential dysfunctions.

The Tour Threatened by Protesters

From the late 1970s onwards, the Tour organizers have learned to anticipate potential risks to the smooth running of the race. They recognize nowadays that one of the major tasks of the Tour organization is to guarantee the security of the riders, of the advertising caravan, the reporters and spectators. This leads to the need to forestall all kinds of incidents and to anticipate all kinds of threats. The organizers bear in mind previous problems encountered in past Tours and – in preparatory meetings – try to envisage ways of avoiding them in the future.

Demonstrations occurring during the competition do not represent a threat to the Tour as long as they are limited to a peaceful expression of their message through banners and do not interfere with the smooth running of stages. On the other hand, the blocking of a stage can distort the result of the race by disadvantaging individual riders or teams. After the cancelled stage in 1982, the race organizers rescheduled a new stage of the same kind (a team time-trial) during the following days, as a stage of this nature is often liable to bring a change in the ownership of the yellow jersey. Thus for the organizers, the main damage brought by demonstrations is to the race itself rather than to the financial interests at stake, which also rely on a variety of other activities. But it is obvious also that more and more numerous disturbances to the race would damage the seriousness and quality of the competition and, eventually, produce damaging consequences.[54]

More serious are those actions that endanger the safety of the riders, such as the nails thrown on the road in 1996. It should be noted that this is the only occasion on which the Société du Tour de France has taken legal proceedings.[55]

Finally, the organizers mention the moral wrong incurred by all those who have invested time and energy in the stage such as the many unpaid helpers who help organize their town's welcome of the Tour. The cancellation of the stage on 7 July 1982 produced much bitterness in the stage town – itself a town which had suffered much from the economic recession – despite a certain empathy with the motives of the strikers: 'we felt drained, but things will get better […] I understand the guys who did this – they've got problems. But they shouldn't have done it when the Tour came to Fontaine.'[56] Jacques Goddet and Félix Lévitan – the then organizers – undertook to reschedule the stage the following year, which was what eventually happened.

The danger of demonstrations is not taken into account when the overall route of the Tour is drawn up a year in advance of the race, since it is impossible to foresee incidents except general political threats such as Basque nationalism. According to Jean-Marie Leblanc, when the decision was taken to go through the Basque region, the good running of the stages seemed to be guaranteed by a number of factors. In effect, in 1992, the visit of the Tour de France allowed the Basque country to host an international sporting event in the same way that its Spanish rivals had done (Barcelona with the Olympic Games; Seville with the Universal exhibition and Madrid as European capital of culture). In 1996 the stage finish in Pamplona (and the necessary crossing of the Basque country to reach the town) had been decided in honour of the stage's regional rider, the Spaniard Miguel Induráin (who lost the Tour that year after having won the previous five). Although there were no major incidents on the route of the Tour that year,[57] Leblanc accepts that today he would not take the peloton back into this region. One can also wonder whether the absence of any visit of the Tour to Corsica (the only department never to have welcomed the Tour) is really simply due to logistical problems, as is claimed by the Tour's organizer. A counter-argument to this is that the Tour stayed for two days in Ireland (the prologue and one stage), but Leblanc maintains that he has never been made aware of a desire on the part of the Corsicans to host this competition.

In order to forestall this kind of incident, the Tour organizers do all in their power to keep informed of potential strike threats along the route of the Tour and are provided with information by the Préfecture, gendarmerie, police and Renseignements généraux (the French MI5). Every morning during the race the organizers meet to discuss potential risks, and if threats to the competition are present, it is Jean-Marie Leblanc himself and Daniel Baal (the second-in-command of the race) who go in person to meet the union officials in charge of the strikes and try to persuade them not to undertake any actions which could interfere with the proper running of the stage.

This strategy for avoiding problems and for allowing the race to follow its normal course is also informed by a certain empathy with the difficulties of the demonstrators. Leblanc, as someone who comes from the north of France and as a former rider and journalist with *Voix du Nord* regional newspaper, admits to being 'sensitive to social grievances, because perhaps of some vestiges of Christian socialist convictions'. Concerning the demonstrators, he states that, 'They are people who are in distress. They are hoping we can do something for them. How important is a cycle race compared with the predicament of fathers of families who risk finding themselves out of a job?'[58] It is interesting to note that Jean-Marie Leblanc is often described as a moderate man who is open to discussion. Analysing his reaction to a barricade erected by farmers in 1990, a reporter for *Le Monde* wrote that, 'Faced with this aggression born of despair, Jean-Marie Leblanc [...] refused confrontation. Rather than the intervention of riot police advised by the Préfecture, he preferred to side-step and bypass the obstacle. The wisdom of one man, always attentive to the problems of others, calmed the situation.'[59]

But empathy does not mean acquiescence. The Tour organizers are skilled in negotiating techniques. They do not reject the demands of demonstrators, but rather attempt to find ways in which they can express their grievances without interfering with the race.

A Culture of Negotiation

Throughout the years, the organizers of the Tour de France have in this way put into place means of incorporating protests into the race. Thus, while understanding the real motivations of protests, they attempt to adapt them to the needs of the Tour.

From the position of strength afforded by their empathy with the strikers, they initially deploy the persuasive argument that an unwelcome action aiming to disrupt a stage would do disservice to the cause of the demonstrators and would go against their own interests. As we have seen previously, this is an argument that is taken up and acted upon by the agents involved. The organizers propose in place of this a kind of non-aggression pact and compromises through which groups may benefit from the media platform offered by the Tour de France to get across their demands, as long as the race itself is respected. This conciliatory attitude reflects a 'euphemising of violence' in which the threat of stopping the race is pushed towards other repertories of action that do not disrupt the smooth running of the competition.

The organizers may suggest, for example, that the protesters read a statement from the official Tour rostrum before the start of the stage. Although a certain number of conditions are imposed on the tone of these statements – they must be 'neither aggressive, nor disrespectful' – and on their length, Jean-Marie Leblanc has indicated that he has himself been ready to give his help and skills as a former journalist to distraught demonstrators who have not prepared anything in writing.

Another strategy consists in deviating the stage from its planned route in order to pass by a symbolic place and thus to produce some mention in the press. During the second stage of the 1982 Tour between Nancy and Longwy, the organizers – after discussions with the union officials – agreed to modify the race route to pass through a local steelworks. The strikers were thus obliged to work from 3 am to prepare the new route by sweeping gravel and covering tramlines in order to prevent accidents.[60] It should be noted also that two days previously, the race organizers had refused to deviate the route of the Tour through the Usinor works on the grounds of the danger of tramlines and had suggested instead that the Tour take the main road parallel to the factory. This compromise was at first accepted by the unions, before more radical strikers rejected it in favour of blocking the stage, which then led to its eventual cancellation.

The relaying by the media of a social grievance can also be organized by the race directors. Jean-Marie Leblanc has admitted that he has on occasion undertaken to pass on to the press the problems divulged to him by the leaders of social movements. This may happen directly and personally, during television programmes after each stage,[61] or indirectly, by asking a reporter to cover the problems or to do an interview with the union officials concerned. Obviously, such undertakings are given in exchange for promises not to endanger the race.

'Euphemization of violence' even leads to innovation and the discovery of new ways of expressing grievances. The race organizers attempt to 'defuse potential demonstrations which threaten to jeopardize the calm of the riders by transforming protest into prize-giving ceremonies'.[62] For example, the organizers suggested to the Poitou sheep-breeders who wanted to block the Tour in protest at the falling prices of their flocks that they should donate a lamb to the last team to finish the stage.[63] Similarly, in 2002, the start of the fifth stage between Soissons and Rouen was marked by a small ceremony during which a cup inscribed with the message 'Live and Work in Soissons – Aisne CGT' was awarded to the leading rider from the Picardy region in the general classification. A short message was read after the rider had expressed his support for the protest. In addition, the protesters had been given day-passes to the Tour de France organization which allowed them to circulate amongst the riders, the team stands, the press services and the organizers. Thus, according to a CGT (Communist trades union) official: 'Blocking the Tour would have been a bad protest. It's necessary to be constructive and positive.'[64]

The giving out of visitor passes to demonstrators may also form part of a strategy intended to 'neutralize' potential troublemakers by integrating them into the Tour. This means of integration reflects another practice – institutionalized in the Tour de France almost without interruption since the Liberation – of providing free vehicles for trades unions in the advertising caravan. The initial idea behind this after the German Occupation was that the Tour de France 'belonged to the French people. The newspapers which had participated in the struggle against Germany were therefore invited to join the Tour'.[65] It is probable that the Tour organizers also needed to create a new legitimacy for the Tour after the newspaper *L'Auto* had been banned from publication after the Liberation. It is thus that three major union confederations, the CGT (since 1947), Force Ouvrière (since 1980) and the CFTC (since 1998) benefit from two or three cars provided free in the advertising caravan (it should be noted that the standard tariff for three cars in 2001 was 20,000 euros). In fact, in order to free the trades unions from having to occupy their places in the advertising caravan, they are represented by their newspapers which in this way constitute 'communications links' between the unions and the Tour (the papers involved are *La Nouvelle Vie ouvrière* for the CGT, *FO Hebdo* for Force ouvrière and *La Vie à défendre* for the CFTC).[66]

The union organizations present in the Tour have fully internalized the ways in which the Tour organizers manage protests and demonstrations and have learned to use them themselves, whilst at the same time using them to underpin their own communication. In fact, whereas they are not voicing social demands, they are primarily interested in their own self-promotion. Starting from the principle that 'the Tour's public is [their] own' the unions take advantage of their position within the Tour to publicize their newspapers and activities.[67] Their weekly papers report the race every year or even produce one or two 'special numbers' devoted to the Tour with interviews and reports covering what goes on around the Tour itself. They do not miss the opportunity of justifying their presence by evoking the working-class nature of the competition, as Marc Blondel, in an editorial for *FO Hebdo*, emphasizes: 'Watching the Tour de France pass by is always a moment where childhood memories, pleasure, partying, encouragement mix together … all feelings which correspond nicely with this event which remains a great sporting competition, perhaps the most popular of all in terms of numbers of direct participants and spectators.'[68] During the 2002 Tour the union cars in the advertising caravan relayed the union campaigns for the Prud'hommes elections of early December,[69] as is illustrated by the conclusion to Blondel's editorial: 'So, when the race has gone by, when you're left with memories and commentary in December, put your confidence in the FO candidate. Better still, join FO.'

According to an implicit agreement that satisfies both parties, the race allows the trades unions to communicate, while the Tour organizers benefit from the support of unions which appear as a central element in their apparatus for negotiating with protesting groups. For one journalist of *La Nouvelle Vie ouvrière*, 'the public of the Tour de France being more or less our own public, the Société du Tour would not run the risk of cutting itself off from it'.[70] But the trades union organizations reject the idea that the Tour buys social peace, as has been suggested by one *Le Monde* reporter.[71] The union headquarters don't want the Tour to be disrupted, but feel that the competition can provide a magnificent platform for the expression of workers' grievances. Of course, when there is the risk of a potential demonstration, the Tour organizers ask the union headquarters to negotiate with the local union officials threatening to block the race: 'after the morning meeting, J.-M. Leblanc quickly warns us if there is a risk of a demonstration and we go off to see the comrades to explain that it's better to use the Tour to get their message across rather than to undertake blockages which would only be counterproductive … And, if necessary, I call Paris, and Marc Blondel deals personally with the demonstrators.'[72] But occasionally the union representatives on the Tour take the initiative and negotiate with the protesters without being asked to by the Tour organizers. They always emphasize that the local union officials are free to do as they wish.

Through all these mechanisms, the Société du Tour de France integrates into the Tour a certain form of social protest, whilst at the same time exercising a relatively close control on the ways in which they express their demands.

The Ability to React if Negotiation Fails

Despite their skill in negotiation, the Tour authorities are occasionally unable to manage the protests before they actually occur, and in these cases, they need to have the means to react. Indeed, negotiations can end in failure, as was the case in 1982. Moreover, it sometimes happens that the compromises reached between the Tour and the protesters are not interpreted by both parties in the same way. Thus, for example, in the 2002 Tour, Jean-Marie Leblanc considers that the officials of the Confédération paysanne did not respect their undertakings and abused his confidence.[73] Finally, the problems which arise nowadays arise less from organized union demonstrations – which can be more or less integrated into the competition – than from spontaneous and impromptu collective actions. In order to defend themselves against unforeseeable threats during the racing, the Tour organizers have developed a range of experience that helps them adapt to these imponderable events. For example, a car at the head of the race is entrusted with the task of erasing slogans which are too political on the tarmac of the road. Although such slogans would represent no danger to the workings of the race, this activity seems to represent the Tour's will to maintain a certain kind of political neutrality often claimed in sporting contexts.[74] Moreover, in order to counter the threat of disruption of the race, the lead car is provided with a chain-saw and cables intended to allow it to remove any trees felled on the route of the race, and thus to allow the riders to pass.

They also have the ability to react immediately thanks to the technical and logistical means they have at their disposal: 'nowadays we have very good road maps, the road network in France is excellent, and thanks to radio communication, we can very quickly at the last moment change the itinerary of the race.'[75] The organizers also enjoy the support of the police and the helicopter that can be used to find 'diversionary routes'. Thus in 1990 during the third stage, when some particularly determined farmers had built a barricade on the road using felled trees, bales of straw and burning car tyres, the riders were diverted on a detour route which avoided the barricade at the cost of 15 extra kilometres. 'We warn the team managers but not the riders themselves, in order not to worry them. The race is neutralized and the job is done.' But at worst, for the boss of the Tour de France, 'in no case whatever would we try to force a barricade. It's too dangerous for both the riders and the demonstrators.' And for the image of the race, which could be badly affected.

The management by the Tour organizers of social and political protests on the roads of the Tour reveals a strong wish to maintain control over the race and to monitor its different aspects and forms. By giving the floor to protesting groups they defuse the threat of trouble and delegitimize those who persist in refusing compromise and keep to direct protest. This ambivalence between empathy and close control of the protests sometimes seems to belong to a kind of paternalistic management of the race, and could be understood as a strategic mechanism aimed at extending the control of the Tour organizers and minimizing the inconvenient independence of the protesting groups.[76] But there is a fundamental difference which invalidates this conclusion: the demonstrators have no direct requests to make of the Tour organizers themselves, except that of giving media coverage to their demands. And it is precisely through giving them the platform that they desire that the Tour organizers satisfy this need, whilst simultaneously guaranteeing the smooth running of the race.

The ability of the organizers to respond to the attacks of demonstrators and to allow them to express their protests more peacefully should be considered within the context of the changing forms of protest in France. In effect, the protest of social movements has evolved from a logic of confrontation to a logic of more symbolic action.[77]

CONCLUSION

The Tour de France belongs without doubt to the French collective popular memory of the twentieth century. As a true 'national passion',[78] it brings together along its route generations of family spectators come to share the efforts of the riders and to enjoy the lurid show of the advertising caravan. This closeness to the public feeds an intimate and faithful relationship, orchestrated by an extraordinary media production of the Tour. In this way, the media coverage of the Tour gives rise to a paradox: if the Tour's media coverage makes it an ideal target for protesters keen to communicate their demands, it is at the same time – because of its popularity – directly un-attackable. Unless they are prepared to attract universal criticism, the social movements who want to sensitize the public to their concerns through the Tour have no choice but to agree to the constraints that it imposes.

The strategies of risk prevention deployed by the Tour organizers against possible disruptions to the Tour provide for compromises that satisfy all parties. The media platform offered to social movements to allow them to talk about their problems reinforces the image of a race that is popular. Thus the festival of the Tour de France does indeed appear as a 'magnificent indicator of the life of our country, our regions and our towns'.[79]

NOTES

1. We have chosen not to include in this study the gatherings, demonstrations or strikes organized by the riders themselves, because these are examples of another, more traditional kind of problem, namely that of relations between workers and employers. Such revolts by the riders are quite numerous, ranging from the showy retirement of the Pélissier brothers in 1924 (see the essay by Thompson in this current volume) to the revolt led by the young Bernard Hinault in 1978 and the more recent events of the tribulations of the Tour concerning drugs and the riders' strike in 1998.
2. Protests are not the sole political aspect of the competition. For the towns and regions through which the Tour passes, the race has an importance in local politics, less in terms of political contests than in terms of commercial knock-on effects and of the towns' or regions' images. Cf. J.-L. Le Touzet, 'Quand la caravane passe…', *Les Cahiers de médiologie*, 5 (1998), 239–43.
3. J. Calvet, *Le Mythe des géants de la route* (Grenoble: Presses universitaires de Grenoble, 1981), p.36.
4. W. Andreff and J.-F. Nys, *Le sport et la télévision* (Paris: Dalloz, 1988), p.145.
5. See the interview with Jean-Marie Leblanc, race director, by Dominique Marchetti in this volume.
6. Interview on 2 Oct. 2002 with a CFDT (Confédération française démocratique du travail) union official of the Saint-Nazaire shipyards concerning the 1988 protest around the Tour.
7. C. Tilly, *La France conteste de 1600 à nos jours* (Paris: Fayard, 1986).
8. O. Filleule, *Stratégies de la rue. Les mobilisations en France* (Paris: Presses de Sciences Po, 1997), p.208.
9. See the work of Patrick Champagne, especially *Faire l'opinion. Le nouveau jeu politique* (Paris: Minuit, 1990), Chap.4.

10. D. Marchetti, 'Les conditions de réussite d'une mobilisation médiatique et ses limites : l'exemple d'Act Up', in CURAPP, *La politique ailleurs* (Paris: Presses Universitaires de France, 1998), p.277.
11. Interview on 9 Oct. 2002 with a representative of the Confédération paysanne of the Orne department after a protest around the Tour in 2002.
12. The oil crises of 1974 and 1980 had serious effects on the French economy, bringing rising numbers of industrial closures and unemployment.
13. On the problems of the steel industry in this region see G. Noiriel, *Vivre et lutter à Longwy* (Paris: Maspero, 1980) and *Longwy. Immigrés et prolétaires 1880–1980* (Paris: PUF, 1984).
14. *L'Equipe*, 8 July 1982.
15. *L'Humanité*, 6 July 1982.
16. Throughout its history, the Tour has only seen three stages cancelled. But the other two occasions (1978 and 1998) were brought about by the riders in protest against the organizers.
17. It is for this reason that we have decided not to draw up a listing of different agents and their styles of intervention: such a listing would unavoidably be imprecise and incomplete.
18. P. Favre, 'Manifester en France aujourd'hui', in P. Favre (ed.), *La Manifestation* (Paris: Presses de la FNSP, 1990).
19. Interview with Jean-Marie Leblanc, 17 Oct. 2002.
20. This was the case with the tragic end to the Munich hostage-taking in 1972. Cf. M. Gros, 'Sport et politiques internationales', in P. Collomb (ed), *Sport, droit et relations internationales* (Paris: Economica, 1988), pp.195–218.
21. *L'Equipe*, 8 July 1982.
22. *L'Humanité*, 6, 8 and 21 July 1982.
23. *Le Monde*, 4 July 1990.
24. G. Vigarello, 'Le Tour de France', in Pierre Nora, *Les lieux de mémoire* (Paris: Gallimard, 1992), p.895.
25. P. Gaboriau, *Le Tour de France et le vélo* (Paris: L'Harmattan, 1995), p.20.
26. R. Barthes, 'Le Tour de France comme épopée', *Mythologies* (Paris: Le Seuil, 1970), p.119.
27. French trades unionism has been strongly marked by ideological debate and by the fragmentation and division of unions. The current diversity of unions is explained by the existence of two strands: the first comes out of the workers' movement and gave rise to the Confédération Générale du Travail (CGT), close to the Parti Communiste Français, and Force Ouvrière (FO); the second, a product of 'Christian socialism', gave rise to the Confédération Française des Travailleurs Chrétiens (CFTC) and the Confédération Française Démocratique du Travail (CFDT). Added to this duality has been a trades unionism based on economic sectors. Cf. D. Andolfatto and D. Labbé, *Sociologie des syndicats* (Paris: La Découverte, coll. repère, 2000).
28. On the origins of sport in the working classes, see P. Arnaud (ed), *Les Origines du sport ouvrier en Europe* (Paris: L'Harmattan, 1994). On popular culture, see R. Hoggart, *La Culture du pauvre. Etude sur le style de vie des classes populaires en Angleterre* (Paris: Editions de Minuit, 1986), originally published as *The Uses of Literacy* (London: Chatto and Windus, 1957).
29. P. Bourdieu, *La Distinction. Critique sociale du jugement* (Paris: Editions de Minuit, 1979), p.240.
30. Gaboriau, *Le Tour de France et le vélo*, p.137. The victory of the Popular Front (a coalition of left-wing parties) in the 1936 general election, followed by strikes and the occupation of factories, obliged the employers' organization to approve the government's Matignon Agreement on 7 June by which wages were raised by 7-15 per cent and which recognized the freedom of action of trades unions and collective bargaining. The working week was also reduced from 48 to 40 hours, with no reduction in pay. But of all the reforms instigated by the Popular Front, the most successful was the provision for two weeks of paid holidays. The right to leisure, until then the sole reserve of the rich, was allowed to workers. Workers in their thousands went on holiday, on foot, by train, but also on bikes, and notably on tandems. The Popular Front government was short-lived, but it has endured in French collective memory. P. Ory, *La Belle illusion: culture et politique sous le signe du Front populaire 1935–1938* (Paris: Plon, 1994). For a more critical reading of sport policy under the Popular Front, see F. Auger, 'Sport, culture et fascisme. Pour en finir avec le mythe du Front populaire', *Quasimodo* (Spring 1997), 149–62.
31. C. Penot, *J'écris ton nom, Tour de France* (Saint Malo: Edition Cristel, 2002).
32. On collective protests by farmers' associations, see Duclos, *Les Violences paysannes sous la Ve république* (Paris: Economica, 1998).

33. Founded in 1987, the Confédération paysanne is a left-wing farming union that wishes to return to a more traditional style of agriculture. It condemns GM foodstuffs, the World Trade Organization and globalization. Its spokesman, José Bové, is doubtless the best-known figures of the French anti-globalization movement. He has become known by his stances against world trade organizations, the poor quality of foodstuffs and by direct actions against a McDonalds restaurant and the destruction of GM plants, which have seen him sentenced to prison sentences. Cf. X. Crettiez and I. Sommier (eds), *La France rebelle* (Paris: Editions Michalon, 2002), pp.142–8.

34. Although, as far as we know, the Tour has not been targeted by fishermen, they did however demonstrate during the Tour d'Armor cycle race in 1979.

35. These new movements are new forms of mobilization of protest, led by new agents in the 1960s and 1970s. Such movements mark a break from old movements of protest characterized by trades unions and the workers' movement through the ways they are organized, their style of action, their links with politics, their values and demands, and the identity of their members. Cf. E. Neveu, *Sociologie des mouvements sociaux* (Paris: La Découverte, 2002), 3rd edition.

36. *Le Monde*, 14 July 1997.

37. *Le Monde*, 21 July 1992.

38. Interview with Jean-Marie Leblanc, 17 Oct. 2002.

39. Cf. The interview with Jean-Marie Leblanc, race director, by Dominique Marchetti in this volume.

40. *L'Equipe*, 23 July 1949 and *Le Monde*, 27 July 1950. In the 1950 Tour, the Italian team even abandoned the race after the stage victory of its leader Bartali because of the aggressively chauvinistic behaviour of the French spectators.

41. 'L'irrésistible chauvinisme sportif des Jeux Olympiques d'Atlanta', *Le Monde*, 26 July 1996.

42. Interview with a union official of the Saint-Nazaire shipyards, 2 Oct. 2002.

43. On the social issues linked to sport and their evolution, see J.-P. Clément, 'La représentation des groupes sociaux et ses enjeux dans le développement du sport', in J.-P. Clément, J. Defrance and C. Pociello (eds), *Sport et pouvoirs au XXe siècle* (Grenoble: Presses universitaires de Grenoble, 1994), pp.53–104.

44. Arriving at the summit of l'Aubisque, the rider, exhausted, got off his bike and shouted at the organizers, 'Vous êtes des assassins!' ('You are murderers'). According to Vigarello, this distress reveals 'the humanity of the hero'. G. Vigarello, *Du jeu ancien au show sportif. La naissance d'un mythe* (Paris: Seuil, 2002), p.120.

45. The expression – 'forced labourers of the road' – taken up by Albert Londres, in the interview given to him by the Pélissier brothers for the newspaper *Le Petit Parisien*, has become famous.

46. L. Strauss, 'Le sport travailliste français pendant l'Entre-deux-guerres', in Arnaud, *Les Origines du sport ouvrier en Europe*, pp.216–17. It should be noted that according to Arnaud, 'from 1937, the "Grande boucle" was no longer criticized: the improvements brought to its organization were adjudged to be sufficiently substantial to no longer warrant any radical condemnation of France's most popular sporting event. A major organization such as the FSGT could no longer afford to adopt an elitist critical attitude, incomprehensible for a large part of its supporters.'

47. *L'Humanité*, 6 July 1982.

48. Professional riders mostly came from the Parisian working class before 1914; from 1918–40 they came mainly from the urban working classes in general, and then after the Second World War, from both urban and rural working classes. Cf. P. Gaboriau, 'Les épopées modernes. Le Tour de France et le Paris–Dakar', *Esprit*, *Le nouvel âge du sport*, 4 (April 1987), p.10.

49. *L'Humanité*, 8 July 1982.

50. Interview with a union official of the Saint-Nazaire shipyards, 2 Oct. 2002.

51. 'Usinor ferme le Tour', *L'Equipe*, 8 July 1982.

52. Interview with a representative of the Confédération paysanne de l'Orne, 9 Oct. 2002. Whereas the Confédération paysanne gained much of its reputation through a struggle involving civil disobedience and symbolically violent actions, a kind of tiredness with police repression and the lack of flexibility of the courts are becoming evident amongst its supporters. For the spokesman of the *Confédération de l'Ariège*, over-strong demands by *La Conf'* around the Tour would provoke a disproportionate reaction from the forces of law and order, although these forces have shown themselves more tolerant of attacks led by the right-wing farmers union (the FNSEA) (interview, 3 Dec. 2002).

53. Poujadism is an anti-taxation protest movement which grew around a shopkeeper named Pierre Poujade during the 1950s under the Fourth Republic. Transformed into a political party, Poujadism aimed to defend the interests of artisan (self-employed) workers and small shopkeepers, and criticized taxation and parliament, while praising 'national' values. J.-P. Rioux, *La France de la IVe République. Tome 2, L'expansion et l'impuissance, 1952–1958* (Paris: Seuil, 1983).

54. The expertise with which this race is managed, and the experience thus acquired over many years, added to considerable financial influence, have led the owner of the Tour de France, Amaury Sport Organization, to buy or manage a number of other classic cycle races in France (Paris–Nice, Paris–Tours, Paris–Roubaix) and abroad (Flèche Wallonne, Liège–Bastogne–Liège, Tour du Qatar, Tour of Faso).

55. *Le Monde*, 13 July 1996.

56. Declaration of a member of the organizing committee for the Tour finish at Fontaine-au-Pire, *L'Equipe*, 8 July 1982.

57. The Basque nationalists of ETA had made threats and had exploded several bombs in the region during the month of July 1996. *Le Monde*, 23 July 1996.

58. Interview with Jean-Marie Leblanc, 17 Oct. 2002.

59. *Le Monde*, 4 July 1990.

60. *L'Humanité*, 6 July 1982.

61. The programme '*Le Vélo-Club*', broadcast by France 2 and presented by the popular French reporter Gérard Holtz.

62. *Le Monde*, 13 July 2002.

63. *Le Monde*, 4 July 1990.

64. *Le Monde*, 13 July 2002.

65. Interview with a reporter from *La Nouvelle Vie Ouvrière* who has followed the Tour since 1992, 26 Nov. 2002.

66. The advertising caravan is divided into three sections: commercial; institutional (Gendarmerie, ministry of the Interior, ministry of Equipment, police, etcetera); and the press. The trades unions have vehicles both in the 'institutional' section, and in the press caravan. It should be noted that between 1993 and 1997 the new director within the Association Sport Amaury, Jean-Claude Killy (ex-champion skier, co-organizer of the 1992 Albertville Olympic Games and businessman) prevented the unions from appearing in the institutional caravan because they could not pay for the privilege. During this period, the unions' only presence was via the press caravan. Interview with reporter from *La Nouvelle Vie Ouvrière*, 26 Nov. 2002.

67. They give away their newspaper at the start and finish of stages, but are not allowed to do this inside the caravan, and thus limit themselves to the distribution of all kinds of knick-knacks.

68. *FO Hebdo Spécial Tour*, supplement to No.2572 of 19 June 2002. Marc Blondel is the General Secretary of FO.

69. The five-yearly elections for the Prud'hommes designate magistrates elected from both sides of industry (employers and employees) who deliberate on cases concerning employment litigation.

70. *Le Monde*, 13 July 2002.

71. The *Le Monde* article of 13 July 2002 was entitled 'La présence de syndicats dans la caravane du Tour contribue à la "paix sociale"' ('The presence of trades unions in the Tour caravan contributes to "social harmony"').

72. Interview with an *FO Hebdo* reporter who has followed the Tour since 1982, 28 Nov. 2002.

73. Interview with Jean-Marie Leblanc, 17 Oct. 2002.

74. J. Defrance, 'La politique de l'apolitisme. Sur l'autonomisation du champ sportif', *Politix*, 50 (2000), pp.13–27.

75. Interview with Jean-Marie Leblanc, 17 Oct. 2002.

76. G. Noiriel, *Les Ouvriers dans la société française. XIXème-XXème siècle* (Paris: Seuil, Points, 1986), p.78.

77. J.W. Duyvendak, *Le Poids du politique. Nouveaux mouvements sociaux en France* (Paris: L'Harmattan, 1994).

78. G. Vigarello, 'Le Tour de France. Une passion nationale', in Vigarello, *Du jeu ancien au show sportif*, pp.113–24.

79. *La Nouvelle Vie ouvrière*, 26 July 2002.

Chronology of the Tour 1902–2003

1902   Desgrange, Lefèvre and V Goddet of *L'Auto* decide to organize a Tour de France cycle race, in competition with its rival sports paper *Le Vélo*.

1903   The first Tour de France in six huge stages, including night riding, covers 2,428km. Maurice Garin (France) wins the Tour.

1904   Riders are disqualified for cheating. Henri Cornet (France) is promoted to become the second winner. At 19 years and 11 months he is the Tour's youngest victor. *Le Vélo* disappears as *L'Auto*'s circulation increases.

1905   The Tour includes 11 shorter stages, daytime only. The first mountain stage (the Ballon d'Alsace in the Vosges). A points system is instituted. The race finishes for the first time in the Parc des Princes velodrome, Paris. Louis Trousselier (France) wins the Tour.

1906   The 14 stages total 4,637km. The first stage to go outside France, into Metz in German-annexed Lorraine. René Pottier (France) wins the Tour.

1907   Lucien Petit-Breton (France) wins the Tour.

1908   Lucien Petit-Breton (France) wins the Tour for the second time.

1909   François Faber (Luxembourg) wins the Tour.

1910   The first stage in the Pyrenees and the Tourmalet climb. The first *voiture-balai* (broom wagon) to round up stragglers and retirees. The Tour is won by the climber Octave Lapize (France) who accuses the Tour officials of being 'murderers' for the routes imposed in the mountains.

1911   The Alps are included for the first time as the Tour covers 5,343km. An official doctor follows the Tour. After singing of the *Marseillaise* in Metz by the local inhabitants during the passage of the Tour, the race is banned in future from the town by the German authorities. Gustave Garrigou (France) wins the Tour.

1912	131 starters. The Tour is won by a Belgian rider – Odile Defraye – for the first time.
1913	Return to the classification by time after the experimentation with a points system. Philippe Thys (Belgium) wins the first of his three Tours.
1914	Thys wins his second Tour.
1915–18	The First World War interrupts the Tour.
1919	The yellow jersey (*maillot jaune*) is introduced for the race leader. Firmin Lambot (Belgium) wins the Tour.
1920	Team members can exchange spare parts but not whole bikes. Thys wins his third Tour.
1921	Léon Scieur (Belgium) wins the Tour.
1922	Firmin Lambot (Belgium) wins his second Tour.
1923	Henri Pélissier (France) wins the Tour.
1924	Ottavio Bottecchia (Italy) wins the Tour.
1925	18 stages in the Tour. Ottavio Bottecchia wins his second Tour.
1926	The first time the race starts from a provincial town (Evian) rather than Paris. Lucien Buysse (Belgium) wins the Tour.
1927	A record number of 24 stages. Non-mountain stages are all team time-trials. Nicolas Frantz (Luxembourg) wins the Tour.
1928	Down to 22 stages, and thereafter the Tour varies between 20 and 24, most often 21 stages. Frantz wins the second of his two Tours.
1929	Maurice Dewaele (Belgium) wins the Tour.
1930	National teams replace company or brand teams, with other individual riders taking part. The publicity caravan is born. It is made up of 28 vehicles by end of 1930s. The first live radio reports. André Leducq (France) wins the first of his two Tours.
1931	Antonin Magne (France) wins the first of his two Tours.
1932	André Leducq wins his second Tour. Time bonuses inaugurated.
1933	For the thirtieth anniversary the inauguration of the king-of-the-mountains classification, as both Pyrenean and Alpine stages are included for the first time since 1913. Georges Speicher (France) wins the Tour.
1934	Inauguration of an individual time-trial stage. Magne wins his second Tour.

1935   The first death of a rider during the race (Cepeda) following a fall on a descent. Romain Maes (Belgium) wins the Tour.

1936   H. Desgrange is replaced as Race Director by J. Goddet. Maes (Belgium) wins the Tour.

1937   Derailleur gears are authorized for the first time (replacing three gears). Roger Lapébie (France) wins the Tour.

1938   Gino Bartali (Italy) wins the first of his two Tours.

1939   Inauguration of an individual time-trial in the mountains. Maes wins the second of his two Tours.

1940–46 The Second World War, German Occupation and aftermath prevent the running of the official Tour. German capture of Paris and northern France prevents the 1940 Tour starting. Desgrange dies in August 1940 aged 75.

1942   A short 'Circuit de France' (six stages) is organized by 'La France socialiste'.

1943   'Le Grand Prix du Tour de France' is organized by *L'Auto*, not a stage race, but a classification based on nine classics.

1944   'Le Grand Prix du Tour de France' is interrupted by the Allied push to liberate France.

1945   'La Course du Tour de France' is organized.

1946   The Cycling Federation bans stage races longer than five days, for logistical reasons.

1947   The first real post-war Tour (organized by the Société du Parc des Princes). The first Tour to go to a foreign capital, Brussels. Jean Robic (France) wins the Tour on the final stage. Albert Bourlon (France) of the regional team Centre–South–West succeeds in a lone breakaway of eight hours and ten minutes over 253km.

1948   Television shows the finish of the Tour live. Bartali wins his second Tour, ten years after his first victory.

1949   Fausto Coppi (Italy) wins the Tour.

1950   Ferdi Kubler (Switzerland) wins his only Tour.

1951   The first time the Tour climbs the Mont Ventoux. Hugo Koblet (Switzerland) wins his only Tour.

1952   The first time a Tour stage ends at altitude. The first time l'Alpe d'Huez is included. Coppi wins his second Tour.

1953   The fiftieth anniversary. The inauguration of the green jersey for the best sprinter, initially for stage finishes, and later for intermediate sprints. Advertising is allowed on the yellow jersey. Peugeot is the official sponsor of the Tour. The first *extra-sportif* (that is, not directly linked with sport) company as a sponsor (Nivea). The Tour is won by Louison Bobet (France).

1954   The first time the Tour starts outside France, in Amsterdam. The Tour is won by Bobet.

1955   Two German riders are invited back into the Tour after 17 years' absence. The Tour goes to Cologne. First time a photo-finish is used for stages. Television shows a daily highlights programme. Bobet wins his third successive Tour.

1956   The Tour is won by the French rider Robert Walkowiak.

1957   Riders' jerseys bear commercial advertising for the first time. Jacques Anquetil (France) wins his first Tour.

1958   The first mountain climb shown live on TV. The Luxemburger climber Charly Gaul wins his only Tour.

1959   The end of a stage is shown live on the evening news. The Spanish climber Federico Bahamontes wins his only Tour.

1960   Television pictures come via motorbikes and a helicopter. The first time a German team takes part since 1938. The train is used to transfer riders between stage towns. Nencini (Italy) wins his only Tour. The Tour stops in the village of President Charles de Gaulle.

1961   Anquetil takes his second Tour. Anquetil wears the yellow jersey from Stage 2 until the finish. A Tour de l'Avenir is organized for young riders (in national teams). It is abandoned in 1976.

1962   Creation of the Société du Tour de France to organize the race. National teams give way to private sponsors' commercial teams. Tom Simpson is the first Englishman to wear the yellow jersey. Anquetil wins his third Tour. Poulidor is second – his best result.

1963   Sean Elliott is the first Irishman to wear the yellow jersey. Poulidor is eighth. Anquetil wins his fourth Tour.

1964   New rules allow a change of bike during a stage. Jacques Anquetil wins his fifth Tour.

1965   Felice Gimondi (Italy) obtains his sole victory. Poulidor is second again.

1966   The first official dope test leads to riders' protest. Poulidor is third behind the winner – French rider Lucien Aimar – and the Dutchman Janssen.

1967   The first time the Tour prologue (opening stage) is a time-trial. Simpson dies on the Mont Ventoux after a suspected drugs overdose. The last time the race finishes at the old Parc des Princes velodrome. Victory is taken by Roger Pingeon (France).

1968   The Tour ends at the Bois de Vincennes velodrome. Regular dope tests at stage finishes. The white jersey – in its first form – is inaugurated for the best combined points scorer. Jan Janssen (Holland) wins.

1969   After two years of national teams, the Tour definitively returns to commercial brand teams. First victory by Eddy Merckx. Poulidor is third.

1970   Second victory of Merckx.

1971   The Tour covers 3,584km, and the first use of air transfers between stages. Serious accident eliminates Luis Ocana. Third victory of Merckx.

1972   Fourth victory of Eddy Merckx. Poulidor is third.

1973   The first use of a titanium-framed bike, by Luis Ocana (Spain). 50 million TV viewers watch the finish. Luis Ocana wins the Tour.

1974   A stage takes place across the Channel in Plymouth. Transfer to Roscoff by ferry. Merckx wins his fifth Tour.

1975   First finish on the Champs-Elysées in Paris. Creation of the polka dot jersey (*maillot à pois*) for the best climber and the white jersey now rewards the best placed young rider. First win by Bernard Thévenet (France).

1976   Victory of the specialist climber Lucien van Impe (Belgium). Final participation in Tour of Poulidor (third place overall).

1977   Second win by Bernard Thévenet. Strong performance (he wins the young riders' competition) by Dietrich Thurau (Germany) encourages renewal of interest in Tour de France in Germany.

1978   Riders protest at the number of transfers between towns. First victory of Bernard Hinault (France).

1979   Hinault wins his second Tour.

1980   The Tour starts in Germany, Frankfurt. Henceforward the Tour is organized by the Société du Tour de France from inside the Amaury press group. Joop Zoetemelk (Holland) becomes the Tour's oldest winner.

1981   Phil Anderson (Australia) is the first non-European to wear the yellow jersey. Bernard Hinault wins his third Tour.

1982   Hinault wins his fourth Tour, and also wins the sprint finish on the Champs-Elysées.

1983   The new 'Open' formula allows amateur Colombian riders to take part. Laurent Fignon (France) wins his first Tour.

1984   The red jersey is inaugurated for intermediate sprints. Fignon wins his second Tour.

1985   Hinault wins his fifth Tour. Rivalry between Hinault and his Vie claire team-mate Greg LeMond apparently results in an arrangement that LeMond will allow Hinault to win in 1985, if Hinault helps LeMond to win in 1986.

1986   A record number of competitors start, 210. LeMond is the first non-European winner of the Tour. LeMond's victory prevents his team-leader Hinault from winning a record-breaking sixth Tour. There is confusion concerning the tactics of the two riders.

1987   The Tour starts in a still divided Berlin. First Irish victory (Stephen Roche).

1988   The Tour covers 3,281km. Inauguration of the departure village at each stage. The Tour is won by Pedro Delgado (Spain), who tests positive for a substance banned by the IOC (International Olympic Committee), but not by the UCI. (Union cycliste internationale) Delgado wins the Tour but is snubbed by the French Minister for Sports Lionel Jospin, and the substance he was found to be using is banned by the UCI the following month.

1989   The 18 participating teams are chosen according to FICP (International Professional Cycling Federation) classification. The closest finish to a Tour. LeMond beats Fignon by 8 seconds.

1990   The prize-giving protocol at each stage finish is rationalized to include only the stage-winner and the three basic jerseys: yellow, green and polka dot. LeMond (USA) wins his third Tour.

1991   First victory of Miguel Indurain (Spain).

1992   The year of the Maastricht Treaty sees a European route, with the Tour departure in San Sebastian (Spain). Second victory of Induráin.

1993   Third victory of Induráin.

1994   The Tour goes to England via the Channel Tunnel. Fourth victory of Induráin.

1995   Miguel Induráin wins his fifth successive [and final] Tour (a record). Fatal accident of the Italian rider Fabio Casartelli (Motorola).

1996   First Danish winner – Bjarne Riis (Telekom).

1997   Victory of Jan Ullrich (Germany). The first German to win the Tour.

1998   The Tour starts in Ireland. The so-called Festina 'affaire': two teams withdraw after drugs are discovered. Riis plays role of spokesperson for the riders in negotiations with the Tour organization. The Tour is not cancelled and is won by the Italian climber Marco Pantani.

1999   Lance Armstrong (USA) wins his first Tour.

2000   Second victory of Armstrong.

2001   Third victory of Armstrong.

2002   The *caravane publicitaire* is made up of some 250 vehicles. Armstrong wins his fourth consecutive victory.

2003   Centenary Tour.

Select Bibliography

The Tour de France:
A Pre-Modern Contest in a Post-Modern Context
HUGH DAUNCEY and GEOFF HARE

R. Barthes, *Mythologies* (Paris: Seuil, 1957). Translated by Annette Lavers as *Mythologies* (London: Jonathan Cape, 1972).

H. Dauncey and G. Hare (eds), *France and the 1998 World Cup: The National Impact of a World Sporting Event* (London: Frank Cass, 1999), translated as *Les Français et la coupe du monde* (Paris: Nouveau monde, 2002).

G. Fife, *Tour de France* (Edinburgh: Mainstream, 2002, first edition 1999).

P. Gaboriau, *Le Tour de France et le vélo: histoire sociale d'une épopée contemporaine* (Paris: L'Harmattan, 1995).

R. Holt, J.A. Mangan and P. Lanfranchi (eds), *European Heroes: Myth, Identity, Sport* (London: Frank Cass, 1996).

J. Marchand, *Jacques Goddet* (Anglet Atlantica, 2002).

G. Vigarello, 'Le Tour de France', in P. Nora (ed.), *Les Lieux de mémoire*, Volume II, *Les Traditions* (Paris: Gallimard, 1992). Translated as *Realms of Memory: Rethinking the French Past* (New York: Columbia University Press, 1997).

E. Weber, *France, Fin de Siècle* (Cambridge, MA: Harvard University Press, 1986).

The Tour de France and Cycling's Belle Epoque
PHILIPPE GABORIAU

A. Baugé, *Messieurs les coureurs. Vérités, anecdotes et réflexions sur les courses cyclistes et les coureurs* (Paris: Librairie Garnier frères, 1925).

P. Birnbaum (ed.), *La France de l'affaire Dreyfus* (Paris: Gallimard, 1994).

G. Bruno, *Le Tour de France par deux enfants* (Paris: Librairie classique Eugène Belin, new edition, 1976).

E. Dunning, P. Murphy and J. Williams, *The Roots of Football Hooliganism: an Historical and Sociological Study* (London and New York: Routledge and Kegan Paul, 1988).

N. Elias and E. Dunning, *Quest for Excitement: Sport and Leisure in the Civilising Process* (Oxford: Blackwell, 1986).

E. Gautier, 'Le sport et la civilisation', in Maurice Leudet (ed.), *L'Almanach des sports 1903* (Paris: A. La Fare, 1903).

J. Miral, 'Le cyclisme', in Maurice Leudet (ed.), *Almanach des sports 1905* (Paris: La Fare, 1905).

G. Vigarello, 'Le Tour de France', in P. Nora (ed.), *Les Lieux de mémoire, III, Les France, 2 Traditions* (Paris: Gallimard, 1992).

M. Viollette *et al.*, *Le cyclisme, 1912* (Geneva: Ed. Slatkine, 1912; new edition, 1980).

The Tour in the Inter-War Years:
Political Ideology, Athletic Excess and Industrial Modernity
CHRISTOPHER THOMPSON

G. Cross, *A Quest for Time: The Reduction of Work in Britain and France, 1840–1940* (Berkeley: University of California Press, 1989).

J. Hoberman, *Mortal Engines: The Science of Performance and the Dehumanization of Sport* (New York: The Free Press, 1992).

G.G. Humphreys, *Taylorism in France 1904–1920: The Impact of Scientific Management on Factory Relations and Society* (New York and London: Garland Publishing, Inc., 1986).

A. Moutet, 'Les origines du système de Taylor en France. Le point de vue patronal (1907–1914)', in *Le Mouvement social*, 93 (October–December 1975).

J.-G. Petit et al., *Histoire des galères, bagnes et prisons, XIIIe–XXe siècles: Introduction à l'histoire pénale de la France* (Toulouse: Editions Privat, 1991).

A. Rabinbach, *The Human Motor: Energy, Fatigue, and the Origins of Modernity* (New York: Basic Books, 1990).

A. Reuze, *Le Tour de Souffrance* (Paris: A. Fayard, 1925).

J.F. Stone, *The Search for Social Peace: Reform Legislation in France, 1890–1914* (Albany: State University of New York Press, 1985).

C. Thompson, 'Controlling the Working-Class Sports Hero in Order to Control the Masses? The Social Philosophy of Sport of Henri Desgrange', *Stadion*, XXVII (2001).

M. Winock, *Le socialisme en France et en Europe, XIXe–XXe siècle* (Paris: Editions du Seuil, 1992).

The Economics of the Tour, 1930–2003
ERIC REED

W. Andreff and J.-F. Nys, *Le Sport et la télévision* (Paris: Editions Dalloz, 1987).

C. Brochand, *Histoire générale de la radio et de la télévision en France. Tome II: 1944–74* (Paris: La Documentation Française, 1994).

P. Chany, *La Fabuleuse Histoire du Tour de France* (Paris: Editions de La Martinière, 1997).

R. Hubscher (ed.), *L'Histoire en mouvements: Le sport dans la société française (XIXe–XXe siècle)* (Paris: Armand Colin, 1992).

R. Kuisel, *Seducing the French: The Dilemma of Americanization* (Berkeley: University of California, 1993; paperback edition, 1996).

J. Marchand, *Le Cyclisme* (Paris: La Table Ronde, 1963).

E. Reed, 'The Tour de France: A Cultural and Commercial History', (unpublished Ph.D. thesis, Syracuse University, 2001).

J.-P. Rioux and J.-F. Sirinelli (eds), *Histoire culturelle de la France. 4. Le Temps des masses, le vingtième siecle* (Paris: Seuil, 1998).

K. Ross, *Fast Cars, Clean Bodies: Decolonization and the Reordering of French Culture* (Cambridge, MA: MIT Press, 1995).

L. Wylie, *Village in the Vaucluse*, rev. ed. (New York: Harper Colophon, 1964).

The Tour de France as an Agent of Change
in Media Production
FABIEN WILLE

J.-F. Bourg, *L'Argent fou du sport* (Paris: Table ronde, 1994).

P. Boury, *La France du Tour. Un espace à géographie variable* (Paris: L'Harmattan (coll. Espace et temps du sport), 1997).

J. Durry, 'La télévision prend le pouvoir, l'histoire en mouvement', in

R. Hubscher (ed.), *Le Sport dans la société française (XIXe–XXe siècle)* (Paris: Armand Colin, 1992).

P. Gaboriau, *Le Tour de France et le vélo. Histoire sociale d'une épopée contemporaine* (Paris: L'Harmattan (coll. Espace et temps du sport), 1995).

Y. Léziart, *Sport et dynamique sociale* (Joinville-le-Pont: Actio, 1989).

M. Sauvage and D. Maréchal, 'Les racines d'un succès', in J.-N. Jeanneney and M. Sauvage (eds), *Télévision, nouvelle mémoire, Les magazines de grand reportage 1959–1968* (Paris: Seuil/INA, 1982).

G. Vigarello, 'Le Tour de France', in P. Nora (ed.) *Les Lieux de mémoire*, Tome III, Les France, Vol.2: Traditions (Paris: Gallimard, 1992).

F. Wille, 'Le spectacle sportif médiatisé ou l'appropriation reconstruction de l'information', *Les Cahiers du journalisme*, 7 (June 2000).

F. Wille, 'Une diachronie du spectacle sportif télévisé: des logiques d'innovations et de promotions', in P. Gabaston and B. Leconte (eds), *Sports et télévision. Regards croisés* (Paris: L'Harmattan, 2000).

Beating the Bounds: The Tour de France and National Identity
CHRISTOPHE CAMPOS

B. Anderson, *Imagined Communities: Reflections on the Origins and Spread of Nationalism* (London: Verso, 1983).

L'Auto, one of France's sporting dailies and sponsor of the Tour, June–July numbers, 1903–1940.

A. Blondin, *Sur le Tour de France* (Paris: La Table Ronde, 1996).

P. Boury, *La France du Tour : Le Tour de France, un espace sportif à géographie variable* (L'Harmattan, 1960).

G. Bruno [i.e. Mme Fouillée], *Le Tour de la France par deux enfants* 1877.

F. Cavanna and P. Massonnet, *Le Tour de France* (Charpentier: Lecture et Loisir, 1960).

L'Equipe, France's national sporting daily and sponsor of the Tour, June–July numbers, 1944–.

P. Sansot, 'Le Tour de France, une forme de liturgie nationale', *Cahiers internationaux de sociologie* 86, 1989.

G. Sand, 'Notice sur les compagnons', Foreword to *Le Compagnon du Tour de France* (1859).

French Cycling Heroes of the Tour: Winners and Losers
HUGH DAUNCEY

J. Calvet, *Le Mythe des géants de la route* (Grenoble: Presses Universitaires de Grenoble, 1981).

J. Clarke, C. Critcher and R. Johnson (eds), *Working Class Culture* (London: Hutchinson, 1979).

O. Dazat, *Laurent Fignon: champion d'un nouveau siècle* (Paris: Messidor, 1990).

M. Milenkovitch, *Cyclisme: 50 histoires du Tour de France* (Paris: Editions Fontaine, 1997).

J.-P. Ollivier, *Anquetil: l'homme des défis* (Paris: Flammarion, 1986).

J.-P. Ollivier, *La Légende de Louison Bobet* (L'Aurore, 1992).

G. Whannel, *Media Sports Stars: Masculinities and Modernities* (London: Routledge, 2002).

S. Wieting, 'Twilight of the Hero in the Tour de France', *International Review for the Sociology of Sport*, 35, 3 (2000).

P. Yonnet, *Systèmes des sports* (Paris: Gallimard/NRF, 1998).

Se faire naturaliser cycliste:
The Tour and its Non-French Competitors
JOHN MARKS

R. Barthes, *Mythologies* (Paris: Seuil, 1957).

A. Blondin, *L'Ironie du sport: chroniques de L'Équipe 1954-1982* (Paris: Éditions François Bourin, 1988).

A. Blondin, *Tours de France: chroniques intégrales de 'L'Équipe' 1954-1982* (Paris: La Table Ronde, 2001).

G. Fife, *Tour de France: The History, the Legend, the Riders* (London & Edinburgh: Mainstream Publishing, 1999).

W. Fotheringham, *Put Me Back on My Bike: In Search of Tom Simpson* (London: Yellow Jersey Press, 2002).

P. Gaboriau, *Le Tour de France et le vélo: histoire sociale d'une épopée contemporaine* (Paris: L'Harmattan, 1995).

R. Ichah, and J. Boully, *Les grands vainqueurs du Tour de France* (Paris: Criterion, 1992).

D. Jameux, *Fausto Coppi: L'échappée belle, Italie 1945-1960* (Paris: Éditions Austral/Arte, 1996).

G. Nicholson, *Le Tour: The Rise and Rise of the Tour de France* (London: Hodder & Stoughton, 1991).

J-P. Ollivier, *L'ABCdaire du Tour de France* (Paris: Flammarion, 2001).

P. Chany, *Les rendez-vous du cyclisme ou Arriva Coppi* (Paris: La Table Ronde, 1960).

The Tour de France and the Doping Issue
PATRICK MIGNON

J. Calvet, *Le Mythe des géants de la route* (Grenoble: PUG, 1981).

P. Duret and P. Trabal, *Le sport et les affaires. Une sociologie de la justice de l'épreuve sportive* (Métaillé, 2000).

F. L'homme, *Le Procès du Tour: Dopage, les secrets de l'enquête* (Paris: Denoël, 2000).

O. Le Noé, 'Comment le dopage devint l'affaire des seuls sportifs', in La Fièvre du dopage, *Autrement*, 197.

J.-P. de Mondenard, *Dopage: l'imposture des performances* (Chiron, 2000).

G. Vigarello, 'Le Tour de France', in P. Nora (ed.), *Les Lieux de mémoire, III* (Paris: Gallimard, 1997).

Waddington, *Sport, Health and Drugs: A Critical Sociological Perspective* (London: Spon Press, 2000).

P. Yonnet, *Systèmes des sports* (Paris: Gallimard, 2000).

A côté du Tour:
Ambushing the Tour for Political and Social Causes
JEAN-FRANÇOIS POLO

P. Arnaud (ed.), *Les Origines du sport ouvrier en Europe* (Paris: L'Harmattan, 1994).

J.-P. Clément, J. Defrance, C. Pociello (ed.), *Sport et pouvoirs au XXe siècle* (Grenoble: Presses universitaires de Grenoble, 1994).

X. Crettiez and I. Sommier (eds), *La France rebelle* (Paris: Editions Michalon, 2002).

P. Favre (ed.), *La Manifestation* (Paris: Presses de la FNSP, 1990).

O. Filleule, *Stratégies de la rue. Les mobilisations en France* (Paris: Presses de Sciences Po, 1997).

P. Gaboriau, *Le Tour de France et le vélo* (Paris: L'Harmattan, 1995).

E. Neveu, *Sociologie des mouvements sociaux*, 3e édition (Paris: La Découverte, 2002).

C. Tilly *The Contentious French* (Cambridge, MA: Harvard University Press, 1986).

G. Vigarello, *Du jeu ancien au show sportif. La naissance d'un mythe* (Paris: Seuil, 2002).

G. Vigarello, 'Le Tour de France', in P. Nora (ed.), *Les lieux de mémoires* (Paris: Gallimard, 1992).

Notes on Contributors

Christophe Campos is a keen cyclist and childhood follower of the Tour de France. Following university postings in Cambridge, Sussex, Oslo and Dublin, he has been Director of the British Institute in Paris (University of London) since 1978, and teaches BA students there about the roots of contemporary French identity. Email: Campos@ext.jussieu.fr

Hugh Dauncey is Senior Lecturer in French Studies at the University of Newcastle. He has taught at university level in Bordeaux, Bath and Paris. His main research interests are in the study of French popular culture, especially television, radio, music and sport. He also works on French public policy in high technology. He co-edited (with G. Hare) *France and the 1998 World Cup* (London: Frank Cass, 1999) and is also the editor (with S. Cannon) of *French Popular Music from Chanson to Techno* (Aldershot: Ashgate, 2003) and *An Introduction to French Popular Culture* (forthcoming 2004). Email: H.D.Dauncey@ncl.ac.uk

Philippe Gaboriau is a CNRS researcher and works at Marseilles in a research group of the Ecole des Hautes Etudes en Sciences Sociales (EHESS), the SHADYC (Sociologie, Histoire, Anthropologie des Dynamiques Culturelles). His various research interests cover the history of sporting practices and the sociology of working-class communities. His major publications include *Le Tour de France et le vélo: histoire sociale d'une épopée contemporaine* (Paris: L'Harmattan, 1995), 'Le Tour de France' in *Encyclopaedia Universalis*, (Paris: Universalia, 1997) and *Les spectacles sportifs: grandeurs et décadences* (forthcoming 2003). Email: gaboriau@ehess.cnrs-mrs.fr

Geoff Hare recently retired from his post of Senior Lecturer in French Studies at the University of Newcastle. He has worked at university level in Paris, Bradford, Leeds and Aberdeen. His main research interests remain in the study of sport and broadcasting in France, especially radio, and in the interaction between television and sport. He edited (with H. Dauncey) *France and the 1998 World Cup* (London: Frank Cass, 1999) and has recently published a book on *Football in France* (Oxford: Berg, 2003). Email: Geoff.Hare@ncl.ac.uk

Dominique Marchetti is a sociologist, working as a CNRS researcher in the Centre for European Sociology (CNRS-EHESS Paris). His work focuses on changes in the organization of French journalism since the 1980s, particularly in terms of its relationship to the legal system, medicine, sport and politics. He is the author (with Denis Ruellan) of *Devenir journalistes. Sociologie de l'entrée sur le marché du travail journalistique* (Paris: Documentation française, 2001) and has published numerous articles in journals such as *Actes de la recherche en sciences sociales* and *Cultures et Conflits*. Email: marchett@msh-paris.fr

John Marks is Reader in French Studies at The Nottingham Trent University. He is the author of *Gilles Deleuze: Vitalism and Multiplicity* (London/Chicago: Pluto Press, 1998) and is co-editor of *French Cultural Debates* (Newark: University of Delaware Press (Monash Romance Studies series), 2001). Email: John.Marks@ntu.ac.uk

Patrick Mignon is Head of the Sociology Department of the Institut national du sport et de l'éducation physique, Paris, and teaches at the University of Paris-IV. A member of the editorial board of the review *Esprit*, he has authored numerous articles on the sociology of football fans in England and France, and the book *La Passion du football* (Paris: Jacob, 1998). Email: Patrick.mignon@insep.fr

Jean-François Polo holds a Doctorate in Political Science and is a temporary lecturer (ATER) at the Rennes Institut of Political Science (IEP), and a member of its Centre for Research into European politics (CRAPE). He has also taught in Jamaica and Turkey. His PhD thesis (L'Harmattan, forthcoming 2003) studied European media policy. He is interested in public policy and European integration and is currently undertaking a survey for CRAPE of the European dimensions of sport in Turkey. Email: Polo@rennes.iep.fr

Eric Reed is an assistant professor of history at Western Kentucky University. He is currently researching the Tour de France, using its history to analyze the commercialization of mass culture in France and as a case study in cultural relations between Paris and provincial towns. Email: eric.reed@wku.edu

Christopher Thompson is an associate professor of history at Ball State University in Indiana. He is the author of articles on the social, cultural and political history of cycling in France and is completing a book on the cultural history of the Tour de France to be published by the University of California Press. Email: cthompso@bsu.edu

Eugen Weber, the celebrated social, political and cultural historian, is the Joan Palevsky Professor of Modern European History at the University of California, Los Angeles. He is the author – amongst many other works – of *Peasants into Frenchmen: the modernization of rural France, 1870–1914* (London: Chatto and Windus, 1977), *France, fin de siècle* (Cambridge, MA and London: Belknap Press of Harvard University Press, 1986), *My France: politics, culture, myth* (Cambridge, MA and London: Belknap Press of Harvard University Press, 1991), and *The hollow years: France in the 1930s* (New York: Norton, 1994). Professor Weber's work in the early 1970s on French sport in the nineteenth century was instrumental in helping to make sport a legitimate object of historical investigation, and he has always taken a special interest in the development of cycling in France and the early Tour de France.

Fabien Wille is a lecturer at the University of Lille 2. His doctorate (1999) was in the field of information and communication, and was entitled *'Le sport un opérateur de changements dans la production médiatique: le modèle du Tour de France'*. Since this thesis on the Tour de France and its effects on the media, he has turned his attention towards issues concerning sports reporting and the public sphere (ethics, expertise, etcetera). He is in charge of the Masters diploma in Sports Engineering of the sports science faculty at Lille University. Email: fwille@univ-lille2.fr

Index